Does Your Body Lie?
Heal the Person, not the Sickness

Luís Martins Simões

Workshops by the author:
  Create a New Life
  School of Spirituality in Matter
  International Healing Workshop

How to reach the author:
  info@luismartinssimoes.com
  lms@ms-leadership.com

Websites:
  www.luismartinssimoes.com
  www.flowsandforms.com

ISBN: 9798648851306

Thank you, Pedro, for a wonderful co-creation

How to consult this book

In a short introduction, the reader will be able to understand the author's purpose for writing this book, as well as some topics that are present in the entire book.

After the introduction, you will find all the symptoms in alphabetical order, just like in a dictionary.

At the end of the book, you will find two indexes: a simple alphabetical index and a category index, with which the reader can look up the symptoms according to their biological system (locomotor system, circulatory system, etc). The category index is not alphabetized.

Whenever you are unable to find the specific name for the symptom you are looking for, look up the affected organ instead.

INTRODUCTION

Esoteric

Esoteric means *coming from within*, as opposed to exoteric, which means *coming from outside*.

It is too bad that today the word esoteric serves as social/professional stance for those who claim to be experts in metaphysics, in plants, in (exotic) teas, etc., under whatever approach. They proclaim themselves esoteric! They claim to be society's non-conformists and portray themselves as such. If possible, they show it by the way they dress, their different look, etc...

They proclaim detachment and announce the discovery of inner journey. This is not the case with everyone but applies to a great majority.

For others, those who cling to some conformism, the word serves as an insult. Often you hear someone say "you are so esoteric!" when they really mean "you are such an idealist!" or "you don't have both feet on the ground!"

So, frequently this leads to two divergent groups, those who are for and those who oppose esotericism.

Neither of the two groups has a clear understanding of the meaning of the word esoteric.

About myself

I have two distinctive professional tracks in my life and they are both deeply esoteric.

On the one hand, I am a consultant and founder of companies in areas related to motivation, attitude, communication and leadership. I believe that all these themes must be treated with an esoteric approach. In other words, all management of companies or any other collective enterprises is esoteric and must be regarded as such. This means that we must look into the company and listen for its signals, be attentive to its reflection on the market and try to understand where there is dysfunction, where our company's health is failing, and identify the internal causes of the community's imbalance.

My position in the enterprise market is rather unique, as I refuse to accept any exoteric reason as the excuse for the malfunction of a company activity, or any other. I am, therefore, an esoteric company consultant and training manager in the true sense of the word.

On the other hand, I conduct research on personal balance, personal development, and I work with the intangible, with the non-concrete, with subtle energy. I teach classes, offer consultations, and I write books. These are all very esoteric activities.

About the book

Those people who understand that they are responsible for what happens to them work from an esoteric perspective. All those who refuse to accept responsibility for what happens in their lives work from an exoteric perspective.

In this case, this book is about the human body. The human body is profoundly esoteric. The majority of people, impelled by our culture diffused through customs, tradition, education and other influences, prefers to look outside the body for germs, for parasites, for all that exists on the planet and on the atmosphere and want to attack us, in order to understand why we have contracted this or that symptom. As if the human body was nature's all time favourite prey! It has never been this way and it will never be this way. The body emits sounds, emits vibrations, emits sensations and emits emotions. All the signs that come from within our body are real instructions for us to live life in a more balanced way.

It does not help us to look for answers outside the body.

Any physical or emotional symptom indicates imbalance. It shows that our mind and beliefs are forcing us to have thoughts which are not healthy for us.

Anyone who desires to live a balanced physical, emotional, and mental life must free oneself from the beliefs inherited from parents, family, clan, society, religion and teachers, and return to the often undervalued process of determining what does and what does not work for him. The body is a superb instrument for that, because it does not lie and tells us all that goes on with our conscience and our way of thinking.

To have self-esteem means to be complete. To quote Ricardo Reis (Fernando Pessoa) "In order to be great, be complete; do not exceed or exclude any part of yourself; give yourself completely to whatever you do; lend yourself utterly to the smallest task you perform…"

When we are not complete, when we are bound by our beliefs, our need for approval from others, and our faulty thoughts, when we attempt to hide a part of ourselves and keep it in the shadows, the body exposes it to the light, literally, in the form of a physical symptom. All the mental obstruction is projected by the body as a symptom. No, the body does not lie.

The goal of this book is to help you understand what your body tries to tell you. So many people look far away (sometimes indefinitely far away) for answers to their lives when the answers are really within themselves. This book helps us to learn about and listen to our body. Therefore, it is an esoteric book about the human body in the true meaning of the word.

As a matter of fact, everything starts with our conscience. Any symptom that the body develops is a wake-up call for us to understand what we must beware of and change both our thinking and our behaviour. This book is a conscience awareness practice.

In this work, the idea of the patient's responsibility is ever-present. Often the term **responsibility** is perceived as a synonym of **guilt**. In fact, the words are not synonyms. Responsibility means *ability to respond*. It is a term that is used in the present tense and thus empowers the person who realizes that he is responsible to change his way of being or acting. Responsibility means that I have a say on the matter.

Guilt, however, attempts to keep people dwelling on the past, where nothing can be changed. To look for culpability and guilty parties intensifies anyone's symptom, whereas assuming responsibility for changing a situation means becoming aware of the responsibility we have for the type of life we want to create.

When you read the description of a symptom and draw the conclusion that the person has a problem with the Father, for instance, be careful not to blame the Father. No! The responsibility to regain a balance rests with the patient. Beware; the responsibility always rests with the person, not the Father, the Mother, or anyone else.

Only when we deal with children does it become essential for parents to alter their behaviour. When there is an adult at stake, the body demands internal action, in other words, responsibility to face up to, deal with, and take action. The other person, the Father for example, may decide to change if he pleases. That is his prerogative.

In our current society, the patient puts himself in the hands of the doctor or the therapist, while refusing any degree of responsibility for what happened to him or what he can do to prevent it from happening again. It is crucial for us, as patients, to understand that the doctor or the therapist can only intervene to help us get out of a bad situation if we become actively involved in the plan of recovery. We may say that the doctor and the therapist have fifty per cent of the responsibility and the other fifty per cent lies with the patient.

This book simply aims to help people become responsible for their lives, to assume responsibility for what happened up to this point, and for what they will change from the moment they realize the extent to which they really created their own unhealthy state.

Patients

In fact there are no illnesses. There are patients. To cure what we call illness and which, in effect, is no more than the physical symptom(s) that the body displays, is to address the effect, not the cause. Nowadays, we frequently hear in everyday talk, the media, on the street, that a person is fighting against this or that disease, that someone won a battle against cancer, that it is necessary to fight to keep alive in face of a disease. After all, we are all declaring war on effects without understanding the underlying causes. The causes are always with the person. The exterior simply catalyzes a process which, in every possible way, is always endemic.

So, rather than attacking the illness, it may be better to embrace the individual, the person, who is solely responsible for the state in which he finds himself. I say responsible, not guilty! This way, rather than fighting, we must learn exactly what thoughts and beliefs that person holds in order to understand how he is hurting himself in his daily existence.

The humble objective of this book is to help cure the patient, not the illness. However, when we find the causes, we must beware of vague causes, sensational and generalized. Certain people and certain works declare that kidney problems are created by fear. Of course they are, but this is very vague. Fear? What fear? Fear not to reach a goal? Fear of himself? Fear of parents? Fear of mother? Fear of spouse? Fear of losing the love of his people? This alone does not help, it is not specific enough. The person spins his wheels and never quite finds the answer. Fear, related to kidneys, is caused by other things, and it is those other things that we need to find. After all, liver problems also have their root in fear.

It is always necessary to find out how patients felt about a specific issue, what they experienced and what they may have done to forget about it. That feeling is present in their everyday lives; it recurs; it is continuous. Furthermore, it is not only present in fears, it is found in other places. There are different people who went through the same things but experienced them differently, some developed symptoms and others did not. It is not the event that causes the problem, but rather how one feels about it. That feeling is unique and, if not verbalized, will cause problems in the body.

About the thinking pattern

All symptoms represent lack of self-love. All symptoms show that we value more what others want us to do than we value what we feel we should do. Who are the others? They are family, friends, society, religion, government and law. One of the more inclusive examples of an enormous cause of physical and psychological symptoms that people feel is related to the use of sexual capacity.

In fact, there are people whose family, friends, society, and religion view sex as an evil which must be repressed and punished, a manifestation of the being in his most deplorable state and his more deplorable animal likeness. It is, however, interesting to point out that in wild animals (I refer to those who are truly wild and free, not pets), the physical and psychological symptoms, when they exist, are resolved in a rapid manner. There are no patients amidst wild animals. There are only the wounded and the dead. In their animal "low standing", they suffer no symptoms. It is food for thought, is it not? In many families, in many clans, instead of supporting their offspring, trying to understand what they feel, and encouraging them to follow their emotions and impulses, parents prefer to control them, police them, and punish them. Brilliant, in fact! Those who should be the greatest advocates for children in this world become, in fact, their policemen, judges, and, jailers.

Everyone needs to live out their emotions.

The word emotion derives from the Latin *ex-movere*, which means to move out. Emotions must be lived out, not necessarily though behaviour, but primarily through verbalization. To verbalize one's feelings is a sure way to avoid physical problems. From an etymological stand, the word means the emotional cry, a cry that comes from within, a profoundly esoteric cry that *ex-moves* (moves out). If for any reason I keep myself from feeling what I feel and, above all, from verbalizing it, the body will need to externalize that emotion in some other way. It will develop a physical symptom. Literally speaking, the body shows the person what he tried to hide and did not verbalize.

The person who does not verbalize what he feels does not verbalize conflict. If a person feels a minor internal conflict and does not verbalize it, he will develop a small physical symptom. If the person feels an internal conflict of great intensity and does not verbalize it, he may develop a cancer or some other serious symptom.

Listen to the body

Listening to the body may consist of listening to the body's cry when we develop a symptom.

It may also consist in listening to the body when the symptom is isolated and only happens once. For example, when I eat cucumber, I do not digest it well. Very well, look no further. Do not eat cucumber. Listen to your body. It is not the time to eat cucumber.

Imagine you drank too much and woke up with a headache. This, by itself, does not constitute a symptom. It is a simple relationship of immediate cause and effect which requires no further analysis. Likewise, imagine that you ate a meal that was spoiled and woke up with horrendous diarrhoea; you are not facing a symptom that requires interpretation. But if you are drinking excessively or constantly eating spoiled food, the symptom becomes of interest because it is no longer a relationship of immediate symptom of cause and effect, but rather an internal body cry that results from an unconscious or hidden tension.

On the polarity of the body's yin/yang

QUESTIONS OF PHYSICAL CONSTITUTION

About incarnation

From the standpoint of physical constitution, we know that the human being is an animal. A particularity of animals is that they are born head first, or from Heaven to Earth. We incarnate from head to toe. It means that we are bound for earth. Plants, on the contrary, grow from Earth to Heaven, "from toe to head". We find a fit, a harmony, between animals and plants in the way animals are born from head to toe and plants grow in the exact opposite direction.

In the dual world of the matter we embody, everything is the sum of two opposites. If it is not so, there is no harmony. Light needs darkness, a male needs a female, and everything is a fit. Evolution can only happen when there are two opposites. This is how we get to the reality of *yin* and *yang* and to the male (Father) and female (Mother) models of human beings.

These two opposites create a polarity which leads to balance and harmony.

Let us now talk about the polarity of the human body.

Human beings receive the strength of Heaven, *yang*, masculine, from the left side, and the strength of the Earth, *yin*, feminine, from the right side. This is the way the human body is built. A person's build is the result of many ingredients which are all related to the purpose of that person's life when it takes form. They are tied to the message he brings to this world where he came to life. And to Karma!

Left-handed and right-handed people

The different stages of animal life on Earth are imprinted on the human brain (collective unconscious) These stages include, obviously, the conflicts of sexual nature, as well as preservation and reproduction of species. In animal life, the highest priority was always the reproduction of species. The species comes first and only then the individual. Territory was always essential to life on earth. Thus, the family in its primitive and brutal stage is imprinted on the brain.

In this duality of earthly life we incarnate, this familiar duality is marked by the duality of man and woman. This duality represents a fit. When there is harmony, there is a fit, and there is a sense of mutual complement. That is the reason why it was necessary to create such duality in family, to differentiate the sexes and guarantee reproduction of species, so that one could take care of the child while the other could take care of protection. This is the reason for the differentiation of sexes in animal life.

In primitive society, men hunted and protected while women tended to children. When there were attackers, men stayed behind and fought while women fled with the children. But who could protect the species to assure their survival if the attackers were stronger than the men in the family? Good question! It was this question that led to yet another dual difference. Not all men went to combat. There was a need for two types of men and two types of women. There were right-handed and left-handed men, as well as right-handed and left-handed women. The same was true for animals, some were right-handed and others left-handed. This way some men went to combat while others fled. Women only went to combat when it was absolutely necessary.

Whenever nature was able to choose, it was always the left-handed who went to combat. The order of departure for combat was as follows: First went the left-handed men, followed by right-handed men, and only then went the women. Left-handed women went next and, on occasions of extreme need, they were followed by right-handed women.

Some humans are born left-handed and others are born left-handed. This characteristic is also connected with the person's physical constitution and his purpose in life, which is not important to discuss, judge, or contest. Simply understand and accept it as a fact. Some of us are born left-handed and others are born right-handed. Period!

About brain polarity

The brain consists of a right hemisphere, which is *yin*, feminine, and a left hemisphere which is *yang*, masculine.

The right brain is creative, soft, sensitive, flexible, submissive, and passive, *yin*; the left brain is powerful, wilful, hard-working, combative, confrontational, commanding, and active, *yang*.

The right side of the body seems to be directed by the left brain hemisphere, while the left side of the body seems to be directed by the right brain hemisphere.

Following this line of thought, and knowing that the right-handed person uses the left side of the body more, we could erroneously deduct that the right-handed person is more *yang* (functions with the left brain hemisphere, more *yang*, and more masculine) and that the left-handed person is more *yin*, or feminine. In fact that is not what was stated above. It does not happen like that at all. The truth is, there is a double crossing in the brain.

The two brain hemispheres, right and left, of the cortex, each **cross** or affect the opposite side of the body but, in a different area of the brain, at the brain marrow, they cross again. There is, therefore, a double crossing.

When it comes to protection, the fuse is at the level of the brain marrow, not that of the cortex. This fuse can be found where there is conflict and it is like a switch. Therefore, right-handed people function from the right hemisphere of the brain marrow (and left hemisphere of the cortex). Left-handed people function at the level of the left hemisphere of the brain marrow (and right side of the cortex).

We can then conclude, from the perspective of his constitution, that the left-handed human is more aggressive than the right-handed human. During pregnancy, left-handed women experienced increased permanency of Heaven's energy, or *yang* energy from the Father. As we seen earlier, it is a matter of physical constitution and karma.

QUESTIONS OF PHYSICAL CONDITION

From a condition standpoint, that is, the way of thinking, feeling, being, dealing with others, and dealing with life and the world, it is not possible to conclusively state that there is a side of the body that is *yang*, masculine, and a side of the body that is *yin*, feminine. Here, under condition, we speak of *yang* behaviours as masculine, and *yin* behaviours as feminine, independently of issues of the person's physical constitution. The *yang* behaviour is hence based on will, force, power, sense of direction, masculinity, determination, warlike attitude, and the possible connection to the masculine way of thinking and acting, the model of man and biological Father. The *yin* behaviour is based on experiencing emotion, sensibility, intuition, femininity, greater passiveness, ability to let go, the feminine way of thinking and acting, the model of woman and of biological Mother. These definitions of *yang* and *yin* are universal, for men and women, left-handed or right- handed.

In this book, I distance myself from any theoretic or dogmatic attempt to define the *yin/yang* polarity of the body based solely on specific sides of the body, because it simply does not exist as such. I do not believe that there is an exclusively *yin* or *yang* side of the body.

About what one reads

Since 1994, in my vast years of experience dealing with the question of polarity of the human body based on the right and left sides, I have heard and read many things. Certain people claim that for right-handed people, the whole right side of the body is *yang* and the left is *yin* and that for left-handed people, the whole left side is *yang* and the right side is *yin*. Others say the exact opposite. They state that for right-handed people, the right side is *yin* and the left side is *yang*, and that for left-handed people the opposite is true. Yet others draw a distinction between an earlier heaven and a later heaven. They believe that all the symptoms that occur during the life of a person (later heaven), if they occur on the right side they are *yin*, and if they occur on the left side they are *yang*. But if the symptoms occur prior to the person's birth or simply during a dream (earlier heaven) then the right side is *yang* and the left side is *yin*. There are still those who defend that the right side and the left side are not necessarily always *yang* or always *yin*. They believe that some organs are simply more *yang* or more *yin*.

Others consider, for instance, that the head (above the shoulders) is more *yang* than the upper body (torso and arms), and that the upper body is more *yang* than the legs.

Others believe that the shape of an organ makes it more *yang* or more *yin*, but its function also makes it more *yang* or *yin*, respectively. Some of these people and a few others also claim that, with regard to polarity, the left-handed person and the right-handed person are opposites, while others claim that they are exactly the same.

What do we settle on? Do we choose a path and follow it? I have already attempted that. At first, I decided to follow the path that claims *yang* on the right side and *yin* on the left side for right-handed people and *yin* on the right side and *yang* on the left side for left-handed people. This worked for a short while. However, with the practical experience of working with people, I noticed that this theory only held true in some cases. So I decided to take the opposite path. For right-handed people, the right side would be *yin* and the left side would be *yang*, and vice-versa for left-handed people. This approach, too, worked for some time until, like before, the practical experience of working with people made me believe that, again, it was only true in some cases.

In any instance, whenever I had a left-handed patient, there was total confusion. And a question remained on my mind. What will I think when a patient with the organs on the opposite side shows up? Because, actually, there are people like that. What seemed clear is that all the theories that stand for a single polarity of the body tend to transform the reading of symptoms into a recipe. And many confuse matters of physical constitution with matters of condition. I believe they do it in order to simplify things or to sell pre-packaged solutions.

My view

The *yin/yang* polarity of physical and emotional symptoms of the body is associated with behaviours and, as a result, exclusively with condition. These behaviours have many causes. Every symptom results from a mental process which does not work despite the person's physical constitution. It is true that people with a stronger constitution are more resistant to certain physical imbalances than those with a weaker constitution. However, physical constitution is not in question when determining the causes for the development of a physical or emotional symptom, except when dealing with fetuses, new-born children, and infants.

The circulatory system

Oxygenated red blood comes out of the left ventricle through the aorta, vigorous and quick blood (yang); a slower blood, rich in knowledge of the body, passes through the veins and arrives through the right auricle to be purified (yin).

And then, the pulmonary arteries, filled with venous blood, leave the right ventricle and carry this blood to the lungs to exchange carbon dioxide for oxygen. The already oxygenated blood is brought back to the heart through the pulmonary veins. This blood is received by the left auricle.

The ventricles are dynamic while the auricles are more passive. Therefore, the ventricles are more masculine (yang) and the auricles are more feminine, (yin). But the right side of the heart deals with venous blood, which is more yin, and the left side of the heart deals with arterial blood, which is more yang.

We are faced with a double duality.

The left side is more yang, but the auricles' side is more yin. Thus, the right auricle displays the yin of yin. The left auricle displays the yin of yang. The right ventricle displays the yang of yin. The left ventricle displays the yang of yang.

The arteries constitute the more yang portion of the circulatory system. They are stronger than veins and are under greater pressure. The vast majority of arteries carry oxygenated blood, except the pulmonary arteries, which carry venous blood from the right ventricle to the lungs.

Artery problems are typical of a more masculine behaviour, very yang, very regimented, very controlling, dominated by Cartesian thought, very radical. Artery problems are more common in the upper part of the body, the more masculine part, namely in the thorax, arms, and head.

The veins make up the yin portion of the circulatory system. They are less strong than arteries and carry slower blood with less pressure. The vast majority of veins carry venous blood, except for pulmonary veins that bring oxygenated blood from the lungs to the left atrium. The heart receives the veins from the liver through the right side, the most passive side of the heart.

Vein problems reflect a not so happy life, a passive life lacking contentment. They are problems which are more characteristic of excessively yin behaviours, of self-denial, of a "there is nothing we can do" attitude. These problems tend to occur in the lower parts of the body, namely in the pelvic area, genitals and legs.

The yin/yang polarity of the circulatory system is as follows: Symptoms in the arteries and symptoms in the torso, arms and head (upper part of the body) reflect excessively yang behaviours, very masculine, very combative. Symptoms in the veins, as well as symptoms in the pelvis and legs, reflect excessively yin behaviours, excessively passive, excessively feminine. It works the same way for left-handed and right-handed people. There is no distinction between left-handed and right-handed people.

The digestive system

Problems in the digestive system are not tied to the body duality of left side, *yin*, and right side, *yang*, and vice-versa, either in right-handed or left-handed people. When it comes to *yin/yang* polarity, there is no single common denominator in the digestive system. Additionally, there is no distinction between left-handed and right-handed people. Each organ is considered as an individual case.

There are only two exceptions: dental caries (teeth enamel) and sinus mucus membranes of the nose and mouth, which are regulated by cerebral hemispheres of the cortex. Thus, here, the right brain, *yin*, affects teeth cavities and mucus on the left side, while the left hemisphere, *yang*, affects teeth cavities and mucus membranes on the right side. In these two cases, a symptom on the right side is *yang* (masculine), and a symptom on the left side is *yin* (feminine), whether the person is left-handed or right-handed.

The locomotor system

In this supportive framework which includes bones, joints, tendons, ligaments, and muscles, it is not always possible to find a common denominator when it comes to the *yin/yang* polarity based strictly on the side of the body where they are located.

The symptoms of the locomotor system are associated with mental inflexibility and undervaluation. Undervaluation and inflexibility are usually connected with communication issues, but they may also be related with the sensation of physical or verbal aggression which leads to different *yin/yang* polarity based on individual cases.

In fact, communication issues are tied to the cerebral hemispheres in the cortex, which have a cross effect in the body, as the right hemisphere controls the left side and the left hemisphere controls the right side. So, in this case, a symptom on the right side of the body reflects excessive *yang* (masculine) behaviour, and a symptom on the left side of the body reflects excessive *yin* (feminine) behaviour. This is the same for left-handed and right-handed people. It is so because the cerebral hemispheres are identical for both left-handed and right-handed people.

Issues related to aggression are not tied to communication. The person reacts to aggression and the tension trigger is connected with the brain marrow. So, in the case of aggression, symptoms in bones, joints, tendons, ligaments, and muscles that happen on the right side show *yin* (feminine) behaviours, while those on the left side show *yang* (masculine) behaviours. This is the same for left-handed and right-handed people. In fact, the effect of the brain marrow on the body is not crossed: the right side of the medulla affects the right side of the body, and the left side of the medulla affects the left side of the body. For these reasons, the diagnostic *yin* and *yang* regarding symptoms in the locomotor system solely based on side polarity must be extremely careful. Nowadays, communication issues are much more common than aggression. It is likely that the symptoms are almost all caused by relationship or communication issues. For this matter, in terms of diagnostic, we may assume that the right side of the locomotor system involves very *yang* behaviours, while the left side involves very *yin* behaviours, but we must allow some flexibility. This applies to left-handed and right-handed people and evaluation must be careful.

The reproductive system

Problems in the reproductive system are only connected with *yin* and *yang* polarity based on the specific side of the body when dealing with organs that come in pairs (ovaries, breasts, fallopian tubes, and testicles) but there is not a constant common denominator. They are treated on an individual case basis. Symptoms in the breasts are linked to right breast/left breast polarity, but without a common denominator. The fallopian tubes are linked to the reproductive system, primary system, which we inherited since the beginning of animal life on Earth. The sensation of aggression that a woman may feel today, and which may show up on a fallopian tube, is connected with the cerebral hemispheres. For that reason, we may assume that symptoms in the right tube are *yang*, and the ones on the left tube are *yin*, but this is not an all-inclusive statement. The gonads (ovaries in women and testicles in men) are linked to the reproductive system, primary system, which we inherited since the beginning of animal life on earth. The polarity of these organs is hard to determine and, actually, that is not necessary. In fact, problems in the gonads are related to the loss of a dear one, and, in most cases, the person is able to readily identify the loss. For the sake of diagnostic, in the rare instance when the person experiences some doubt, try to figure out if the right gonad is *yang* and the left gonad is *yin*. This applies to left-handed and right-handed people.

The breathing system

In the breathing system, the left side/right side *yin* polarity exists for all, left-handed and right-handed people, in organs which are paired such as tonsils, lungs, and bronchi. It does not apply to the pleura or the upper respiratory tract. So, for left-handed and right-handed people, the right side is *yang* (masculine) and the left side is *yin* (feminine). In fact, lungs and bronchi deal with communication issues which are directly linked to the cerebral hemispheres of the cortex that control the opposite sides of the body. Both left-handed and right-handed people have similar cerebral hemispheres located in the same place.

The urinary system

There is a right side/left side polarity in this system but it only applies to the kidneys and ureters and does not work for all symptoms. This polarity is not always noticeable. For matters of diagnostic, we should start by assuming that for all people, left-handed and right-handed alike, the right kidney is *yang*, (masculine) and the left kidney is *yin* (feminine). However, in cases of renal insufficiency (kidney failure), this polarity is not applicable. Thus, one must be careful to assess polarity in this system.

Vision

Many people insist that there is *yin/yang* polarity depending on the side of the face where the eye is located. From the standpoint of the person's physical constitution, it is true that the right eye is *yin* (Mother' side) and the left eye is *yang* (Father' side) for left-handed and right-handed people. However, considering its activity, functioning, and condition, there is not any common denominator to conclusively establish which eye is *yin* and which eye is *yang* based on the specific side. As a matter of fact, we all have a leading eye which is the action eye, the *yang* eye. The other eye is the affective eye, of fear and danger, which is more passive, the *yin* eye. This is the receiving eye.

Hearing

In the case of ears, it is impossible to determine the *yin/yang* polarity in function of their side.

Many people insist that there is a *yin/yang* polarity depending on the side of the head where the ear is located. However, there is no common denominator to know which ear is *yin* and which ear is *yang* based on specific side.

When a child suffers from otitis or loses hearing on the left side, it is not possible to conclude if the child has a problem with the Father or with the Mother. In fact, the child may have his feelings hurt because of something he heard from the Father. In this case it is likely that he will have a problem with the Father. However, he may feel hurt by what he hears about his Father (for example, by what the Mother says about the Father), in which case it is likely that the problem is with the Mother, not the Father.

Solutions

The content of this book is the result of many co-creations.

It is the result of many workshops in which I participated over the last twenty-one years (from 1994 to 2015), workshops dedicated to the relationship between body and mind. I travelled to various countries to participate in workshops on different topics, based on very different philosophical approaches.

It is the result of extensive reading of materials based on different philosophies but all focusing on the same topic.

It is the result of my experience of many appointments with patients, who sought me out in an effort to understand the relationship between their bodies and the tensions they felt.

And lastly, it is based on the personal research I have developed on this topic.

I wrote the book because I consider it a valid reference tool for all: for me, for my patients and potential patients, for doctors and therapists.

I realize that, for the reader, this book represents a proof, an observation, and a step towards awareness of what we can learn from the way our body works.

As for solutions for our lives, ways to distance ourselves from the emotional, mental, and spiritual patterns which bound us and make us unhappy, and ways to rise above our current conditions, those are not found in this book. They are addressed in the workshops I teach and lectures I give frequently on how to create a new life.

If you are interested, you may contact me by email.

Abortion

Abortion represents an interruption of pregnancy. It is customary to establish a difference between what we call an involuntary or spontaneous abortion (a miscarriage or an abortion performed because of life threatening circumstances) and a voluntary abortion (ending an unwanted pregnancy). However, from the point of view of personal energy, they reflect the same thing. The tension on the conscience is the same in both cases. In the voluntary abortion, the person uses her will. In the case of an involuntary abortion, it is the body that manifests itself. However, the conflict and the tension in one's conscience are the same. The same holds true in the case of a still-born. It is a matter of timing. The timing is not convenient. "Not now. Later!" The person is afraid to bring a child to the world. Birth represents the first co-creation (joint creation) involving three consciences. One's incarnation requires the confluence of three wills: the will of the Father, the will of the Mother, and the will of the Baby. For this reason, in any abortion, it is necessary to look at what goes on in the parents' relationship. It is likely that they are experiencing some disagreement. It is also possible that one of them does not want the baby, perhaps neither one does. When this is the case, the parents do not decide to interrupt the pregnancy, it may just happen. The Mother's body shows the tension the Mother feels. The abortion is the manifestation of a great tension in one of the procreators. It should not be punished but, rather, understood.

In families where the mother had spontaneous or voluntary abortions, it is necessary that all descendants know about it. A hidden abortion affects the lives of all family members and, mainly, it affects the lives of any subsequent babies. Abortion may affect the behaviour of pre-existing babies, as well as the lives of any subsequent babies. Many women contract ovaries and/or uterus problems following an abortion or a miscarriage, primarily when they are forced to end the pregnancy against their intimate will to keep the child. This can be imposed by others or by one's own values.

Abortion is a traumatizing experience for women. It is necessary that the woman is able to verbalize all the sensations and emotions she felt.

See *Child delivery*

Abrasions, bruises

See *Skin*

Abscess

An abscess shows us that an inflammation or infection in our life needs to be cut open so that the rotten pus may come out. It shows us that a state of rotten peace must be addressed and confronted. You must see where in the body the abscess occurs and research what that part of your body represents. Indeed, the specific location of an abscess in the mouth, in the arm, in the anus, or in the buttocks, reflects very different tensions in the conscience.

Accidents

The way I move around in life, either on foot or by any type of transportation, alone or with company, represents an extension of my life and of my consciousness. We may analyse what goes on in the mind of a person by examining the house where he/she lives, the car he/she was driving, the person with whom he/she clashed against, the house where the accident took place, etc... All the accidents we have show a tension we feel in our conscience, a conflict. So, every accident is the revelation of a tension a person felt and was unable to verbalize. Often it is a rebellion against poorly exercised authority, but there may be other tensions. It is possible to study the representational meaning of things – a car, a motorcycle, one's family, the room where I sleep, the house where I live, the hot water pan that someone burned himself with – as extensions of one's consciousness. *Feng Shui* provides such an avenue for study.

In any instance, no accident happens without a reason. The question we must ask is: "Why was I there at that time, with that person (those people)? What message do I get from this accident?" In the case of a crash, for instance, ask yourself: "Who does this person remind me of?" It is also important to analyse what part of the body was injured. The specific location of an injury is never random.

When the victim is a child, it is im-portant to understand the relationship he/she has with the parents.

In this case, see *Babies* and *Family*

Acne

Pimples indicate an inflammation of the hair and sebaceous follicles, primarily on the face, shoulders, back and chest.

They are a flare-up, a discharge of tension connected with difficulty in communication.

Teenage acne appears mainly in the face. The face represents a young person's identity. The acne demonstrates the difficulty the young person has in assuming the new identity, mainly when communicating with others. The pimples are the discharge, the physical manifestation of that difficulty. This happens often during adolescence.

Acne appears as a result of sexual repression of the person who reaches puberty, when sexual hormones "wake-up". It is called the hormonal tie-break.

The child feels the desire to seek the opposite pole, love, passion, and a partner.

It just so happens that the skin is precisely the frontier he/she needs to cross to reach the other person, to be able to communicate and be with the other person.

Acne is a vicious circle. "I want to get closer to the other person but my pimples keep me at a distance". This way, the person represses his/her sexuality generating even more pimples.

Adolescent acne happens primarily on the face, for all to see, and sometimes on the back and, in the case of girls, on the chest. Adolescent acne is very localized. By undressing and exposing this new body, showing it and giving it to the sun, the sun can fix the acne quickly. The sun helps the adolescent person. In fact, giving yourself is the best way to get rid of acne.

The act of giving oneself sexually makes acne disappear.

Any flare-up is a sign that something is repressed.

The flare-up shows us something that, until then, was invisible.

The young person who experiences acne considers that what is physically happening to him/her and his/her skin is a bad thing. "This puberty thing makes me so ugly! And precisely when I need to look good the most!"

The adult with acne is a person who is afraid of being caught by surprise and also a person who can not easily communicate with the surrounding environment.

He/she is a person who has difficulty in fully assuming his/her identity.

Acute anterior poliomyelitis (child paralysis)

Like in poliomyelitis, this is an inflammation of the spinal marrow that causes atrophy of the affected muscles.

This is a disease of the spinal marrow and of the locomotor system. It is associated to the feeling of undervaluation and self esteem.

This disease affects children, and, for this reason, it is called child paralysis. The emergence of a new being is linked to the relationship between the parents and with the family, lineage and the clan.

Poliomyelitis indicates that a child is born with a feeling of guilt inside. His body unveils it by destroying the muscle responsible for certain functions. The child arrives into this world already undervaluing himself. The person punishes himself. As if he felt guilty. The event is past already. The baby is born and feels: "Perhaps I should not have been born. What am I doing here? Will there be space for me?"

It is very important to understand that, in this case, we are dealing with a symptom that is linked to the clan and its representatives, the biological parents.

Conception and birth constitute a creation carried out by three people, which will only bear fruit if all three are in agreement (they are the Father, the Mother and the future baby), and jointly create the epiphany that the incarnation of a new being constitutes.

As soon as the baby is born, his memory of lineage becomes non-conscious. In fact, the baby forgets the entire luggage he brought with him, and will need all his living experience and communication skills with the family to slowly understand the thinking pattern of his genealogical tree and also how it thinks and behaves.

Thus, it is crucial that the child is told about his family members, that he becomes fully aware of past events, not just the good and epic ones, but all events! Emotions, wars inside the family, hidden scandals, kept information.

He needs to know about the man figure and about the male model.

Animals, including human beings, are born from Heaven towards Earth. A hiatus occurred somewhere in the come down, maybe already during pregnancy. The Father represents the force of Heaven on Earth. What happened between the Father and the Mother?

See *Partial paralysis, Pregnancy – problems, Babies* and *Family*

Acute articular rheumatism (children)

The cartilage of the joints becomes worn out.

This is to children what evolving chronic polyarthritis is to adults.

The body shows up small childhood conflicts. It happens mostly to children due to daily competition and competitive sports at school, which are almost all extremely harmful for children.

The pre-puberty child is naturally on a hormone standstill, which means that, naturally, no hormone stands out in particular over the others (see *Endocrine system* about the hormonal draw). However, the child is forced to leave this standstill in order to compete.

Sport is good, but competition is not, as it contributes towards the child's undervaluation. Acute articular rheumatism shows that the child was not respected in his deepest energy. This child self inflicts violence, which is not natural at all. For what reason will a child be violent towards himself? It can only be explained by his relationship with his parents, friends or teachers. Even if the schoolteacher imposes a disturbing behaviour on the child, the parents are responsible for their decision to put the child in that school. Why was the child put there? Was it because it was what always happened inside the clan? Was it because the Father wanted this and the Mother wanted that? What is going on with this child's family life?

If this acute articular rheumatism reaches the heart, it can become very serious. If it reaches the kidneys, it shows that the child's system of values has crumbled down. It is only at this stage that the child and parents realise that particular sport was not that appropriate, and that particular school was not that appropriate, or that the most balanced thought for the child was not that of the clan.

When the child realises that his system of beliefs has crumbled, he may feel a cruel and bitter disappointment and develop glomerulonephritis. (protein in urine). In this case, see *Kidneys – renal insufficiency*. Also see *Chronic evolving polyarthritis*

ADD and ADHD

Attention Deficit Disorder and Attention Deficit Hyperactivity Disorder
See *Hyperactivity*

Addiction

All forms of dependence represent an escape. It is an escape which started by being a quest. What actually happens is that the person literally projects the objective of his search on something he found along the way and decided his quest was over. He is pleased with what he has found. He remains trapped in fear and convenience. Anything can cause dependence: alcohol, drugs, sex, tobacco, gambling, food (bulimia, anorexia), but also, and even to a larger extent, money, power, rules, fame, influence, knowledge, entertainment, isolation, asceticism, cult, tradition, ancestral beliefs, religion…

The addicted person is the one who stops halfway through his quest. For this reason, he feels empty. And because he feels empty, he needs to fill the void with external substances which confer him the illusion of being balanced.

Basically, we could say that in all humanity, we are all dependents. The difference between the sick dependent and the healthy consumer lies in the quality of self observation, that is, in the awareness of one self, of one's feelings and path. Dependence is a type of attachment. The non-addict, non-sick consumer is the one who is aware of his attachments and looks for solutions within himself and not on the substance he depends on.

See *Alcoholism, Drugs, Sex – addiction, Tabagism*

Addison's disease

See *Suprarenal glands*

Adenitis

Infection in the lymph nodes.

See *Lymphatic system*

Adenoids

The adenoids (nasopharyngeal tonsils), also called *vegetation* in some languages, swell when the child does not understand the world of adults. The adenoids reflect family tension and arguments. A child who feels he/she is "in the way" or, perhaps, "unwanted" may suffer such symptoms.

Taking out the adenoids does not solve the problems. Often they develop again. In fact the surgical intervention addresses the effect and not the cause.

Adenoma

Adenoma is a benign tumour of glandular origin whose structure somewhat resembles the gland from which it develops.

See *Endocrine system*

Adenopatia

See *Lymphatic system*

Adrenal glands

See *Suprarenal glands*

Aerogastria

This condition develops in the person who wants to control everything and is unable to. It is a person who swallows everything rapidly without distinguishing what is digestive work for the stomach (solid food) and what is respiratory work for the lungs (air).

Contrary to what occurs with aerophasia, in this case the tension does not reach the bowel. It stays in the stomach.

The person with stomach problems does not like confrontation. He/she needs "to be fed baby food".

This person is unable to deal with his anger and/or transform it into aggression, into some open expression. He/she carries his/her stress in his stomach. These repressed emotions that the stomach patient avoids dealing with, are caused by issues related to material things, professional matters, money concerns, and legal and educational questions. Stomach problems are very "down to earth". They have much to do with the roots and essence of the person (work, home, Mother, place where he lives, and money).

This person controls and does not let go. He/she pays too much attention to material things. The stomach swells up.

The burp is a release of air, a release of stomach tension, and it causes relief.

Aerophagia

This condition develops in the person who wants to control everything but is not able to. When the person eats, he/she swallows everything rapidly without distinguishing what is digestive work for the stomach (solid food) and what is respiratory work for the lungs (air). He/she does not chew the food properly and swallows everything in a hurry. He/she is not calm and focused.

This happens when there are material concerns. The person controls and does not let go, pays excessive attention to material things. The stomach swells up. Flatulence is a release of air from the bowel and causes relief. We are in the presence of one tension connected with the stomach and one tension connected with the ascending colon.

The person with stomach problems does not like confrontation. He/she needs "to be fed baby food". This person is unable to deal with his/her anger and/or transform it into aggression, into some open manifestation. He/she carries his stress in his stomach. These repressed emotions that the stomach patient avoids dealing with, are caused by issues related to material things, professional matters, money concerns, and legal and educational questions. Stomach problems are very "down to earth". They have much to do with the roots and essence of the person (work, home, Mother, place where he/she lives, and money).

Flatulence develops in the ascending colon (beginning of the large bowel). The person who has trouble in this area is someone who makes an effort to decide whether to hold or let go. Fermentation takes place in the ascending colon. This is caused by the presence of sugar. The tension of hesitating to hold or let go may cause flatulence and pain. It may be related to the relationship with the Father or with a male model. This man may be a partner, a supervisor, a boyfriend, or even a woman who exhibits masculine behaviour.

See *Bowel – large bowel*

Aging eyes

See *Eyes – presbyopia*

AIDS

Acquired Immunodeficiency Syndrome. Deficiency of immunity. AIDS is associated to a feeling of exclusion and lack of discernment. Immunity is the capacity to distinguish between what is good for me from what is not good for me. This is indispensable to our identity and our species.

When immunity decreases, this means that the body has weakened the person's capacity to say "I Am". The person has ceased to be his own witness.

AIDS is associated to the feeling of exclusion from the group and to lack of self-esteem. It is spread through blood and sexual contact. The identity of human beings lies precisely in the blood and in sexuality (capacity to be with the other person and to give yourself to him), which presupposes that I know who I Am. The person who is on good terms with himself, with his own mind, does not catch AIDS.

People who feel excluded need to understand that their exclusion is not the cause for AIDS. It is the way they feel their exclusion that is the cause. And the reason why people feel their exclusion intensely is more related to their beliefs, theirs thoughts, their mental patterns, than to the actual fact of being excluded. They feel excluded because they are people who need very much to be approved by others. They lack self-esteem. In other words, they

have a problem respecting their identity.

AIDS is not caused by mere sexual contact, nor by the frequency or intensity with which sexual life is experienced.

Its origins lay in sexual addiction. This sexual dependence implies that the sexual addicted person normally has sex with several partners. Having several sexual partners may show a lack of respect for one-self. In fact, in our lives there are people who make us grow, who have a positive effect on us, and there are others from whom we should get away, because they do not make us grow and are not good for us. Going to bed with everybody is a signal there is inability to distinguish what is good for us from what is not. It is a denial of the "I". It denotes massive lack of self-esteem. If I am unable to distinguish what "I" means, I am not able to say what I Am. Therefore, my immunity decreases. The active sexual consumer, non-dependent, chooses his partners and knows how to distinguish those who are good for him from those who are not. He gets selective in his choice of sexual partners.

Some groups, such as some homosexuals in New York, have caught AIDS. They felt excluded from society and also had many sexual partners. Feeling excluded and having many sexual partners may, in fact, both contribute towards AIDS.

The immune system is not an army that is ready to fight off everything that gets near and seems threatening. This idea is something that goes against the natural flowing of the entire Universe. We are not at war with anyone. It is the mind that likes to nurture the idea that life is an ongoing war, that cancer is a war that must be won, that diseases need to be attacked.

Well, life is not a struggle, it is giving in, it is surrender.

What the immune system does is attempt to find a gentle balance between the inner and outer side of the person. It is a type of door that is open to let in microbes that are useful to repair the unbalances and damages of the body and that closes itself again once the job is completed.

There are people who have been excluded from their families and group of friends, in other words, from their clans and who are able to create or find another group, another clan (because they did not need other people's approval) and who are not HIV carriers, and who did not get AIDS. After all, they have never felt excluded.

There are people who have selective sexual relations, although with several partners, and who are actually selective. They are, in fact, aware that there are relationships that are good for them and that there are relationships that are harmful for them, which they should refuse having. These people are not HIV carriers, and did not get AIDS either.

And there are also people who are HIV carriers and still manage to live extremely well for a long time, only because they do not know they are carriers. The posture on the fight against HIV and on the HIV's aggression is a

mental and psychological stance that causes a huge tension in the person who knows to be carrying the virus. The tension is brought about more by the diagnostic than by the actual HIV, which has never bothered the person until that moment.

Therefore, neither sex nor exclusion causes AIDS. What causes it is the feeling of exclusion and sexual dependence.

See *Immune system*, *Family* and *Epidemics*

Albumin

This condition refers to an excess of protein in the urine. It occurs when the kidneys do not function properly and allow non-toxic nutrients to escape, instead of keeping them.

It reflects a lack of discernment of what is good and what is harmful in our lives.

See *Kidneys – renal insufficiency*

Alcoholism

Any form of dependency is an escape. This escape starts off as a search. What happens is the person literally projects the object of his/her search into something he/she finds along the way and considers the search finished. The person settles for what he/she finds. Gets trapped by fear and comfort.

Dependency may be caused by many things: Alcohol, drugs, sex, tobacco, gambling, food (bulimia and anorexia), but also (and in greater percentages) money, power, rules, fame, influence, knowledge, entertainment, asceticism, cultism, ancient beliefs, religion, etc.

The addict is a person who does not complete his/her search. Therefore, because he/she feels empty, attempts to fill that emptiness with external substances that give him/her a false sense of balance.

To some extent, we can say that all humans are dependent. The difference between the addict and the non-addicted consumer lies in the capacity of self-observation and self-awareness, on the ability of acknowledging one's feelings and path in life. Dependency is a form of attachment. The non-addicted consumer is not ill; he is aware of his attachments.

The alcoholic yearns for a world free of conflict.

To achieve that, he avoids conflict, instead of confronting the people with whom he experiences conflict; he gives himself up. He does not resolve his life but gets rid of the momentary frustration, and uses alcohol as a sedative. However, nothing is resolved.

The alcoholic seeks human warmth. What better way to get it than through the use of alcohol, which allows him/her to cross the barriers of inhibition and make quick and easy friends?

The alcoholic literally drowns in alcohol all that opposes his ideal of a harmonious life free of conflict.

It is common for people with kidney problems to like to drink and celebrate. The reason for that is associated with the fact that the person with renal insufficiency has trouble saying *No* to people with whom he associates. He finds it easier to communicate when he is under the influence of alcohol, beer, coffee, or tea, since they are diuretic substances that stimulate the kidneys. Since the kidney is an organ of communication, people feel that their ability to relate to others is improved when they drink.

Tobacco stimulates the lungs, another organ of contact and communication with others.

For this reason, when friends get together, it is customary to drink and smoke to facilitate contact and stimulate the organs associated with contact: the lungs, the bronchi, and the kidneys. Excessive drinking, however, does not address causes; it simply settles symptoms and effects.

Allergies

Any allergy, food allergy, respiratory allergy, or skin allergy, is a defensive reaction of the organism against some external threat. People who suffer from allergies feel victimized, but they are absolutely not the passive type.

And furthermore, in most cases, that external element that the allergic person considers a threat is inoffensive. The allergic person is constantly increasing the possibility of having to deal with potential enemies and so he needs to build a great defensive shield. He is, in fact, a subconsciously aggressive person. A person of repressed aggressiveness (seemingly good-natured), is more likely to have allergies than a person who plays out his aggressiveness.

The allergic person leaves nothing to chance. He fights against everything and everyone and often chooses enemies who have a large symbolic weight. This aggressiveness is caused by his fears.

Most allergies selected by the allergic person are related to nutrition, milk, love, sexuality, libido, fertility, and, also, people. These are all inoffensive elements. Let's take a closer look: Pollen (symbol of fertility and procreation), animal hairs (which are airborne primarily during the mating season), and some foods including milk (which symbolizes the relationship with the biological Mother).

The person who suffers from hay fever is a person who denies his own power. "Whom am I allergic to?" he should ask himself.

Household dust, which suggests dirtiness, filthiness and disgust, is frequently an element of choice (the sense of disgust, curiously, is a fundamental ingredient in the occurrence of skin cancer).

The allergic person manages to allow his aggressiveness to take control without being aware of it. Tyrannically (though subconsciously), he forces all family members to keep away the enemy substances, animals, plants, dust, and certain types of foods. The allergic person needs to confront his own life, fragilities and fears, to stop suffering from allergies.

The allergic person wants to live a sterile life, without aggressions, without microbes, without sexuality, in other words, a lifeless life.

Food allergies (digestive system), skin allergies, and respiratory allergies (lungs, bronchi, asthma, and rhinitis), all respond to a common pattern of allergic person.

The allergic person does not trust. He controls. He has difficulty understanding the laws of co-creation.

Allergies may occur due to memory association. If, for instance, in the past, someone felt an emotional shock of some nature when walking past a cow, it is possible that he feels the same shock every time he sees a cow. If, at that moment, he happened to be eating an orange, it is likely that he will develop an allergy to oranges.

In the old days, the first love encounters often took place secretly in hay stacks. Sometimes a farmer showed up with a pitchfork and a dog. It gave the lovers a big scare. The brain registers that memory of aggression in the hay and associates it with pollen flying, dog hairs, and sex.

See *Immune system*

ALS

See *Amyotrophic Lateral Sclerosis (ALS)*

Alveoli

See *Lungs*

Alzheimer's disease

The Alzheimer's patient refuses to deal with the world as it is. He feels despair and abandonment. He isolates himself and suffers from lack of memory and lack of sense of direction. He regresses to the safe haven of childhood. The Alzheimer's patient is a person with a great need for love and attention.

Prior to becoming an Alzheimer's patient, this person already avoided reality and looking into his inner self. The Alzheimer's patient is someone who, along his life, tried to gain control of others and exercise supremacy over them, primarily those close to him. Alzheimer's patients are people whose families always had trouble dealing with, and who now demand to be completely taken care of. They are hard people who never listened to emotions and always took a rational approach to life; they are very Cartesian and controlling; they want to control everything and everyone.

Their isolation results from their controlling way of thinking, very *yang*, very bossy, very masculine, which wore out the patience of relatives.

They develop Alzheimer's symptoms as a way to keep exercising their control over those around them.

See *Isolation*

Amebiasis

See *Bowel – large bowel – amoebic dysentery*

Amebic dysentery (amebiasis)

See *Bowel – large bowel – amoebic dysentery*

Amenorrhea

Lack of menstrual cycle.

It is described in more detail under *Menstruation*.

Amnesia

Run away from life! "I don't want to face it. I want to get away. There's stuff I don't want to remember. I want to forget that (or those) episode(s) of my life!"

He/she is unable to assume him/herself. There may be problems with the Father, the symbol of manhood, or the male role model. In the case of a married woman, we must analyze the relationship with the husband. In the case of a man, it is important to assess the relationship with the Father or a male role model. Amnesia can be brought on by another symptom, like *Alzheimer's disease* or *senility*, for example. In any case, and despite its causes, it is associated with tension, due to a person's isolation. In order to fully understand amnesia, see *Isolation*.

Amputation

The most common amputations in the human body are the amputation of limbs and extremities of the locomotor system. These include the amputation of arms, forearms, hands, hands fingers, legs, thighs, feet and toes. Since this is the locomotor system, the patient's major tension is a sense of undervaluation. The person who feels undervalued is a person who has a low self-image. It is a person who is easily influenced by the opinion of others. It is a person with a low self-esteem. The amputation is the result of a very traumatic tension that the person experienced and could not verbalize or did not know how to verbalize.

It always consists of a separation process "de facto". As a result of his inflexibility and devaluation, the person was separated from something or someone. It could be the Father, the Mother, the place where he lived, his house, or his home. The amputation may be caused by an illness or an accident. Whatever the cause, the amputation is always associated with a separation and a sense of undervaluation. If you study the part of the body that was amputated, you will understand what tension the person suffered and with whom in particular. If the amputation resulted from an accident, see *Accidents*.

Lepers (fear of separation), for example, were almost always the victims of amputation.

If there is amputation of an organ, see the section on that organ.

Amyotrophic Lateral Sclerosis (ALS)

Amyotrophic Lateral Sclerosis (ALS), also called Lou Gehrig's disease, is a rapidly progressive neurological disease that attacks the nerve cells (*neurons*) responsible for controlling voluntary muscles (muscles of the Locomotor System). It is considered a motor neuron disease that causes gradual degeneration and death of motor neurons.

These motor neurons are nerve cells located in the brain, brain stem, and spinal cord. They control the muscles of the locomotor system. In ALS, both the upper motor neurons and the lower motor neurons degenerate or die, and stop sending messages to muscles. Unable to function, the muscles gradually weaken, waste away (atrophy). Eventually, the ability of the brain to start and control voluntary movement may be lost.

It affects the locomotor system. It is precisely in the locomotor system that we find many contradictions, structural problems, issues related to the ability to stand on your feet.

Problems regarding relationships with the world are located here.

Feelings such as individuality, self-esteem and undervaluation are at stake.

What do I think of myself and what is my role in the world? Where are my assertiveness and my stability? What part of my conscience is in the dark, regarding my relationship with the world? We are talking of conflicts of a personal nature.

Here we are facing a huge feeling of undervaluing. This is the first key-word. The second key-word concerns opposite feelings or opposite ideas.

The person imposes on himself two contradictory orders regarding movement. The person has wishes that contradict each another.

These two contradictory ideas that provoke tension may occur if, for example, the person wished to do something badly, did it and then regretted having done it. I pushed someone off the cliff, she was badly hurt as a result and I felt very guilty about it, unable to forgive myself. In this case, the muscles are affected.

It is paramount to understand what happened between this person and his/her biological Father, or the male model. Was he too demanding? Did the person feel a great pressure to match his/her father's wishes or orders? Did he/she feel undervalued?

See *Multiple sclerosis, Stammering, Myopathy, Paralysis, General paralysis, Child paralysis, Partial paralysis, Parkinson's disease, Poliomyelitis, Nervous tics* and *Stiff neck*

Anaemia

This condition indicates a deficiency of haemoglobin in the blood. There is red blood cell deficiency and, therefore, lack of oxygen in the blood and blood cells. There is a lack of energy and happiness. Everything is reduced to "yes, but…" The person is afraid of life. Nothing goes well. The person is frustrated with family life, perhaps even with the clan, may it be his or the spouse's. "Nothing goes well in my life". Anaemia is a form of neutralization

It is a symptom that is not isolated. It is likely that the patient feels other symptoms besides anaemia. There are situations where the person appears anaemic but, actually, the tension in the conscience does not correspond to anaemia. In this case, it is due to a feeling of undervaluation brought on by the belief that, in the eyes of family members, he is worthless.

See *Bone marrow* and *Leukaemia*

There are also renal insufficiencies which play a part in anaemia. In this case, see *Kidneys – renal insufficiency.*

Anal fistula

See *Bowel – large bowel – anus*

Aneurysm

This is a dilation of the artery wall. It develops where there is a weakness in the wall due to a lesion, a trauma, or a deformity. Sometimes it becomes dilated enough to cause the artery to come in contact with the vein.

Arteries are the *yang* part of the circulatory system. They transport oxygen and nutrients to the cells. Artery problems are characteristic of male behaviour, very *yang*, very warlike, dominated by Cartesian thought and very radical. Artery problems are more common in the upper part of the body, which is more masculine, primarily in the head and thorax.

Artery related problems reflect incapacity to deal with emotions. They reflect an inability to let go and be happy, joyful.

The person who suffers from aneurysms is a very intellectual person who wants to control everything and who does not allow life to flow naturally, a person who wants to show that he is a know-it-all. It is a very *yang* person, with a very masculine way of being, very warlike.

People with artery problems are

people who do not listen to emotions and are driven by rational thought, Cartesian thought.

Vascular accidents that occur in the upper part of the body (head, arms and torso) are more associated with masculine behaviour, very *macho*, very *yang*; problems that occur in the lower part of the body (hips and legs) are associated with problems of self-denial, more passive, more feminine, more *yin*.

Also see *Brain stroke* and *Cerebral aneurysm*

Anger

It is a concentrated energy, a *yang* energy. When I feel angry, I feel I may end up attacking the other person. For this reason, the sympathetic nervous system prepares for this, for the fight, resorting to adrenalin. As a result, energy rises to the neck, shoulders, up the back and the arms and provides a lot of irrigation to the brain. The person loses his senses.

People who have accumulated anger feel chronic tension on their shoulders, necks and arms.

There are three solutions to deal with anger:

1) To annul one-self and pretend everything is ok, and so get stuck in the illusion that the cause has been sorted out.

2) To follow an even more *yang* path, playing a sport like punching boxing bags, play rugby or even hit someone.

3) To follow a *yin* path and cry our heart out, thus becoming completely aware of our feelings.

The first solution does not solve anything and makes the person accumulate anger, something that could cause problems later.

The second solution resolves the effect but not the cause, and makes the person increasingly more depending on that violent activity, which gives him the illusion of emptying his aggressiveness. What the person does not realise is that his aggressiveness is being nurtured, and, for this reason, growing.

The third solution resolves the cause. The person empties his anger batteries through awareness and observation of himself, becoming more genuine and more self mastered. The propensity for anger diminishes.

When anger is of the chronic type and never lived through, the parasympathetic nervous system (the system that regulates the automatic functioning of the majority of internal organs) has little opportunity to come into action, because the sympathetic system (which regulates adrenalin) is extremely active. The parasympathetic is thus unable to regulate the functioning of the body's vital systems that depend on it.

Anger is directly associated to gallbladder problems. Consequently, and by extension, the liver is also involved.

Symptoms may include: headache, pain in the eyes, sciatica, pain in the legs, pain on the shoulders, lack of energy, lack of determination, absence of sexual energy, irritation, impatience and digestive disturbances.

Animal bites

The person feels so much rage inside him that the animal simply shows him that he has been punishing himself, exercising violence on himself. Therefore, the animal punishes him. Animals' instinct never fails. Animals know, through our hormones, what emotion we are experiencing. They co-create with us.

Ankles

The ankle is a joint that allows balance and adaptation to the terrain. Torsions mean that I am not well adapted. Ankles are propitious areas for **torsions** to occur (ligament- related problems) and **tendonitis** (tendon-related problems). A rupture, torsion or tendonitis in the area is provoked by lack of balance in the person's life. As the ankle is a joint, in this case we are referring to inflexibility and undervaluation. The inflexibility is related to inability to adapt to the world where I live, roots, home, work, place where I live, my Mother's beliefs, and it is also inflexibility regarding the decisions I need to make or not to make to maintain harmony and balance within me. The ankle is, therefore, a symbol of our capacity to decide about concrete issues with a full conscience: "The other person does not understand me after all, and the best I can do is leave", or "I cannot dare impose this torsion on my married life".

Thus, ankle-related problems indicate lack of balance at home and/or with the partner, or at work.

In principle, and with regard to polarity, the right ankle is *yang*, masculine, and the left ankle is *yin*, feminine. This applies both to left and right-handed people.

Problems in the *yang* ankle denote inflexibility and also undervaluation [due to the influence of a third person (a man?) or to the person's obsessive beliefs] and denote lack of assertiveness with a man (could even be regarding himself, if the individual is a man), probably with the husband or the Father, or maybe a typically male job, or the boss, at work, or the sports coach. The person does not want to listen to his body. And the body feels he cannot do what is asked of it when it comes to work. However, the person insists and wears out his body. The person does not feel confident but prefers to ignore that feeling. He will not accept himself as he is. He undervalues himself and strains his body. And the symptom occurs.

Problems in the *yin* ankle show inflexibility and also undervaluation [due to the influence of a third person (a woman?) or to the person's obsessive beliefs] and denote lack of assertiveness with a woman (could even be regarding herself, if the individual is a woman), probably with the wife or the Mother, or maybe an issue linked to the home or even the family budget. And the person weakens. The person violates his own sensitivity and does not realise he does not trust himself regarding family or relational issues, but prefers to ignore that feeling. He does not accept himself the way he is, undervalues himself and gets weaker.

The person's mental pattern that accounts for this inflexibility may be explained by the fact that the person is allowing someone to influence him. This rocks his foundations, making him lead a life that is not adequate.

Look at the Father model in the relationship, in case of a man, and to the Mother model in the relationship, in case of a woman.

In ankle-related problems, the first thing we should look at is to the couple, if the person is living a two-person relationship.

Problems affecting the ankle may occur in the ligaments, tendons, and bones or in the skin. In ligaments or tendons, this means the body is showing undervaluation and inflexibility. If it affects the bone, it shows strong undervaluation. In the skin, it indicates communication difficulty or separation.

See also *Gout*

Ankylosing spondylitis

Ankylosing spondylitis is a form of arthritis that primarily affects the spine, although other joints can become involved. It causes inflammation of the spinal vertebrae that can lead to severe, chronic pain and discomfort.

In more advanced cases this inflammation can lead to ankylosis -- new bone formation in the spine -- causing sections of the spine to fuse in a fixed, immobile position.

As it can also cause inflammation, pain, and stiffness in other areas of the body such as the shoulders, hips, ribs, heels, and small joints of the hands and feet. Sometimes the eyes can become involved (known as iritis or uveitis), and -- rarely -- the lungs and heart can be affected.

The hallmark feature of ankylosing spondylitis is the involvement of the sacroiliac vertebrae during the progression of the disease. The sacroiliac vertebrae are located at the base of the spine, where the spine joins the pelvis.

The spinal cord is part of the central nervous system. Any symptom here denotes difficulty to act and to get close to other people. What is going on with the Father symbol, or even with the male symbol? What is going on with the sense of humbleness? Which path is my own? Where shall I go? Because it is an inflammation, the person's body is showing him he is boiling. The person is unaware he is boiling and that his structural foundations are unstable. Since it affects the bones in general, it means the person's deepest beliefs have been affected.

The skeleton and the bones represent our inner structure. The bone holds the conscience of the self. The bone structure is where the deep undervaluation of the being is kept. The bone structure indicates firmness and accomplishment. Specific and intense undervaluation shows up in the bones.

Please examine each part of the body that is affected individually.

See *Vertebrae*

Anorexia

This reflects the desire to stay thin that affects primarily girls when they reach puberty and adolescence. They refuse to eat. This may occur later in life as well.

This symptom also occurs in boys who refuse to live their homosexuality and also in very effeminate boys.

There are different ways to get there. There are those people who categorically refuse to eat. There are others who refuse to eat during daytime and in the presence of others, but who, at night, raid the fridge and kitchen cupboards, eat immensely, but then, they make themselves throw up all they ate earlier (often called anorexic-bulimic). Others, yet, use laxatives non-stop to defecate and empty themselves out through the bowels.

Either way, the goal is to stay thin.

Many of these people also have problems with their menstrual cycle and, in some cases, do not have one at all. They isolate themselves. In fact, unlike obesity, which is often a way to call the attention of others, the conflict in the anorexic mind works just the opposite way: "I need to disappear. Don't look at me!" And the person isolates herself in order not to be seen. It is a death wish. The joy of living is gone. It is also a reflection of the frustrated desire for power and strength.

The anorexic person does not deal well with sexuality and hides herself in an ideal of purity and spirituality. She has a real problem with her femininity and does not accept well her new body at puberty.

It is fundamental to analyse what went on in that person's relationship with her biologic Mother, what she may have heard about sex, sexual impulses, and the evils of sex. Anorexia happens primarily in puberty when the sexual hormones start to go wild, with the hormonal tie break.

The Mother may have been absent, or a Mother who did not display affection.

Perhaps the Mother or the Father would have preferred a son instead of this daughter. In any instance, the anorexic person has a serious problem dealing with her incarnation. She does not want to be nourished.

Therefore, the person's tension has to do not only with the biological Mother, but also with Mother Earth where she was incarnated, i.e.,with the planet. It is important to understand what happened with her delivery.

The anorexic person hates the vital function of the earth. She wants to be a spirit.

In nature, this phenomenon does not exist. It is the fruit of an absolutely abnormal human mental creation.

Anorgasmia

This is the absence of orgasm.
See *Frigidity* and *Impotence*

Anus

See *Bowel – large bowel – anus*

Anxiety

This is the so called mental anguish, in which the person pays more attention to preoccupation (pre-occupation) or, in other words, in which the person thinks about the future anticipating what has not yet happened. The person worries about what has not yet happened and, because it is in the future, it means it does not depend on the person. This tends to create several problems. They may be stomach problems, namely aerophagy, aerogastria, and others. It can be hypermetropia or far-sightedness or bulimia. In conclusion, the person becomes totally drained from anticipating future events, yet unknown, and wants to control what he can not control and detach himself from reality. He must let go, allow life to flow, and enjoy the present.

See *Panic*

Apathy

Apathy indicates a weakening of the Self. There is resistance to feelings and emotions; self-denial; self-neutralization. This is a form of seclusion.

See *Isolation*

Aphasia

This condition is a deterioration of oral and written language caused by a neurological dysfunction of the brain. This symptom results from an excessively Cartesian approach to life, an approach too distant from our emotional side; it results from fears of being unable to control everything and everyone, and problems dealing with a sense of humbleness.

It is a total loss of the ability to communicate.

It is a form of isolation.

It is essential to pay attention to the relationship of this person with his/her biological Father, with his/her male model, and with masculinity.

See *Isolation*

Aphonia

The fear is so great that it is best to stay silent and avoid calling the attention of the "predator", the person who may cause us harm. The vocal cords are located in the larynx. For this condition, see *Larynx (larynx, aphonia, hoarseness)*

Aphtas

See *Mouth sores (thrush)*

Apnea

This means that breathing stops during rest.

The person with apnea needs to relax. He must not be so intellectual and busy. He must take better care of himself.

When this symptom happens in new-born babies, and primarily while sleeping, there is a risk of sudden death. In this case, the apnea indicates that the baby does not fit well in the parents' relationship. The child has a nonconscious wish to disincarnate. If this happens, parents must assume the responsibility.

See *Babies*

For information on stopping to breathe during sleep, see also *Snoring*

Aponeuroses

These are the muscle sacs, the organs' protectors that defend them from attacks and foster defence. They protect from physical or verbal attacks. They protect the person. Period! It is just a quick reaction. There is no time to think. The person does not consider which side to use to defend himself. It is an impulsive reaction to an attack from a dear or a close one. So, despite the fact that we are discussing the locomotor system, there is no left side/right side polarity in aponeuroses. In cases when the muscles get caught, however, we can consider polarity.

Problems in aponeuroses indicate that the person felt attacked or that something caused him disgust. Disgust can be material or a feeling regarding a person or something the person did. "He disgusts me!" It is usually about someone close to the person. It can also be a teacher, or a boss.

There is no common denominator in *yin/yang* polarity or any distinction between left-handed and right-handed people.

Appendix

The appendix is a lymphoid ganglion. It is in the same family as the tonsils. Like the tonsils, it functions as a sentinel because, unlike the small bowel, which is free of bacteria, the large bowel has bacteria. The appendix allows the blockage of bacteria that move up the larger bowel, to keep them from entering in the ileum, which is the last part of the small bowel.

Appendicitis is a conflict of anger and upsetness the person kept to himself. This conflict of anger and upsetness takes place at the junction of two things. There is a violation of something intimate. And it is not clean! "What filth! It's not right!" This junction of two things can be over many events. It can be over a sexual relationship that a person feels guilty about. It is always associated with someone close.

So, in appendicitis, the appendix is unable to stop the flow of bacteria from the large bowel to the small bowel. The appendix swells. Appendicitis is a form of self-inflicted violence. It requires urgent care because it may develop into peritonitis. In that case, see *Peritonitis*

Appetite

See *Bulimia* and *Anorexia*

Arm (shoulder to elbow)

The arm is located in the area between the shoulder, which is responsible for rhythm changes in our actions, and the elbow, which decides the radical changes in direction we make in our lives with regard our route and goals.

At the outset, our right arm is *yang* (male) and the left is *yin* (female). This applies to both right and left-handed people. However, we must not forget that we are dealing with the more *yang*, more male side of the body and that polarity in the locomotor system is not always obvious. Problems in the arm reveal the presence of tensions and difficulties at the time of acting.

Problems affecting the *yang* arm denote undervaluing and inflexibility [due to the influence of a third person (a man?) or due to own beliefs]. The individual wants to go further than what is reasonable. He will insist, be stubborn, a fighter, somehow aggressive. His objectives blind him, as he is not paying attention to the eventual changes he may need to undergo in his own personal route and goals. He will not, therefore, attain what he wanted, and will feel undervalued as a result.

Problems in the *yin* arm represent undervaluing and inflexibility [due to the influence of a third person (a woman?) or due to own beliefs]. The person's sensitivity is hurt in the process of attaining his goal. Here, too, the individual is not paying special attention to eventual changes he may need to do in his own personal route and objectives. As a result, he feels undervalued.

Humerus fractures represent a shock at the level of deep beliefs, with regard difficulty in acting, and, at the same time, a tremendous relief of the tension the person was experiencing. People with accumulated anger have chronic tensions in their shoulders, neck and arms. Problems affecting the muscle of the arm indicate undervaluing and inflexibility. If they occur in the bone, it shows strong undervaluing, and if

it affects the skin, it denotes a feeling of separation or communication difficulties. Depending on the type of lesion, it is advisable to see *Bone fracture*, *Muscles* or *Skin*. In the concrete case of amputation, see *Amputation*. In case of paralysis, see *Paralysis* and *Partial paralysis*.

Arms (as upper limbs)

The arms ensure mobility, flexibility, the activity of pursuing objectives and attaining them.

They allow us to go to (someone, somewhere), touch, catch, hold, push, embrace, clasp, asphyxiate or close.

They are action vectors in the sense of dominance, power and strength and, above all, choice.

They allow us to go from theory to practice. They are the extension of the shoulders, which are part of the *yang* waist, male waist, symbolized by the Father.

This is the place where the body expresses itself regarding what his objectives really are and what it does in order to achieve them.

Symptoms in the arms reflect undervaluing tensions in our will to act upon the external or the inner world.

The sense of accomplishment flows from the shoulder to the hand (from the least concrete to the more concrete).

At the outset, our right arm is *yang* (male) and the left is *yin* (female). This applies to both right and left-handed people. However, we must not forget that we are dealing with the more *yang*, more male side of the body and that polarity in the locomotor system is not always obvious. Problems in the arm reveal the presence of tensions and difficulties at the time of acting.

Problems affecting the *yang* arm denote undervaluing and inflexibility [due to the influence of a third person (a man?) or due to own beliefs]. The individual wants to go further than what is reasonable. He will insist, be stubborn, a fighter, somehow aggressive. His objectives blind him. He will not, therefore, attain what he wanted, and will feel undervalued as a result.

Problems in the *yin* arm represent undervaluing and inflexibility [due to the influence of a third person (a woman?) or due to own beliefs]. The person's sensitivity is hurt in the process of attaining his goal. As a result, he feels undervalued

The connection to what we want to reach in order to attain our goals lies in the arms.

Arm problems may occur at the level of the muscles, bones or skin. Depending on the type of lesion, it is advisable to see *Shoulder, Arm (shoulder to elbow), Elbow, Wrist, Hand* and *Fingers*. In the concrete case of amputation, see *Amputation*. In case of paralysis, see *Paralysis* and *Partial paralysis*.

Arrhythmias

See *Heart – arrhythmias*

Arterial tension

See *Blood pressure – high* or *Blood pressure – low*

Arteries

See *Circulatory system – arterial system*

Arteriosclerosis

Arteriosclerosis is a general term for the hardening of the arteries and, according to medical records, the primary cause of death in the western world. Atherosclerosis is a type of arteriosclerosis that affects medium and large calibre arteries, such as the coronary, carotids, and the arteries of the iliac and femur. It is characterized by the deposit of fat, calcium and other elements on the artery walls, which reduces their width and diminishes the flow of blood to tissues. This may lead to blockage (thrombosis), ischemia, and gangrene.

It seems to happen predominantly to men between the ages of 50 and 70. It also seems that people with high cholesterol levels and high blood pressure are prone to arteriosclerosis. The arteries are the *yang* portion of the circulatory system. The vast majority of them (except the pulmonary arteries) carry oxygen and nutrients to cells.

Artery problems are typical of a more masculine behaviour, very *yang,* very regimented, very controlling, dominated by Cartesian thought, very radical.

Artery problems are more common in the upper part of the body, which is the more masculine part, namely the thorax, arms and head, but they may also occur in the legs.

Artery problems reveal an inability to deal with emotions. They show incapacity to do what is necessary to let go and be happy. This manifests itself in the relationship with socially close people. The person refuses to see what is good for him. Artery problems denote resistance, tension and much control. The person's emotional process is exhausting. The person lost the joy of living. He is a very controlled person, very much driven by a deeply rooted limited vision that is very harmful to him. We mentioned earlier that the person with high cholesterol levels is prone to arteriosclerosis. In fact, cholesterol is a fat, and fat exists to protect the body. But to protect what is necessary. High cholesterol level shows that the person is protecting himself from the family and the clan lineage. It shows that the person is trying to protect himself from the inside out.

It happens, for instance, when the person is trying to protect himself from the spouse, parents or her husband. The person, however, acts in the worst possible way and hurts himself. The person feels that the clan is hurting him and instead of creating a suitable life for himself, he limits the free circulation of his life, thus slowly blocking the channels of happiness (blood vessels). The person is afraid to accept happiness. He feels guilt and does not allow his life to flow.

We stated before that people with high blood pressure are prone to arteriosclerosis. In fact, blood reflects the being, the identity. The walls of the blood vessels are the limits, the boundaries within which our incarnation as human beings must develop.

It is natural to want to test those boundaries, those limits of resistance of the blood vessels.

Contrary from the person with low blood pressure, the person with high blood pressure is ready for action, determined to act and, therefore, the blood circulation accelerates and so does the blood pressure. Nevertheless, the person with high blood pressure never materializes the action because he never ends up confronting the person who bothers him, and so there is no discharge of energy, it remains stored. The person with high blood pressure cannot engage in the process of being frontal and direct with others. He is afraid of conflict and does not realize that becoming frontal is something that must happen as soon as possible, in a simple and easy way, by expressing what he thinks and feels.

It is common for the person with high blood pressure to convince himself that next time he will be able to act. This keeps the organism ready for action, keeps it from relaxing, and the person develops chronic high blood pressure and never really engages in frontal confrontation.

The person with high blood pressure always stays on the edge of conflict, always troubled by conflict, but he never reaches any solution.

Of course, if things are not cleared up, one day the person will say what he has to say; he will do it in an angry, cowardly and exaggerated way, thus creating even more conflict, when things could have been resolved in a calm manner. The person whines, complains, shows rage, and ends up blowing his top off, seldom with the right person and often with the wrong person.

This lack of frontal attitude gives rise to a major internal conflict. The person remains on the defence, always prepared for a conflict that probably he will never carry out.

These are people with long lasting unresolved emotional problems and who have great difficulty living life with happiness.

Arthritis

This is the inflammation of a joint due to a strong feeling of personal undervaluation.

See *Joints*

Arthrosis

The bones of a joint are kept in the right place by ligaments and tendons which allow only normal movement. The muscles also determine the maintenance of joint stability. Joints are enclosed in fibrous capsules filled with a thin layer (joint cap mucus) that continuously produces liquid, called synovial fluid, which acts as the cartilage's lubricant and nutrient. In healthy joints, the tops of the bones are covered by a "layer" of off-white elastic matter called cartilage (the one at the knee is called **meniscus**). The cartilage allows the smooth movement of the bones

and acts as a cushion that absorbs the shock of bone movement and weight. Arthrosis results from the progressive wear and tear of the joint tissue, and in particular the cartilage, which leads to increasing pain, deformity, and difficulty of movement. The onset of hip arthritis starts with the deterioration of the cartilage, which loses its elasticity and becomes less effective. In the absence of part, or all, of this "cushioning" effect of the cartilage, the bones rub one another and cause friction, inflammation, pain, and difficulty in moving. In very advanced stages of this condition, pieces of cartilage and bone may get loose and lodge themselves in the joint, seriously limiting or blocking movement altogether. The hips, knees, shoulders, feet, and fingers are the most frequently affected by this condition.

We saw earlier that the articular cartilage is located at the centre of the joints where the bones come together. In the knee, for instance, the femur and the tibia meet. This cartilage is the meniscus.

Here we are at the movement level. If the movement is not adequate, we develop a joint problem. Undervaluation of movement is reflected on the joints. It can be reflected in a movement in sports or in any movement, in any action of our lives which indicates change of direction or flexibility. The movements of life are reflected in the body, and the injuries of the body are reflected on life.

We are in the presence of movement quality. A person may undervalue himself through movement.

Sports and manual occupations are excellent examples of this. Consider the surgeon, the dentist, the pianist, and the secretary.

Joint problems indicate conflicts of movement undervaluation. "I didn't do the right move. I'm not worth a thing!"

In the case of rheumatism, for example, the person says, "I'm no longer as good at this (movement)…"

When the person develops arthrosis, it shows that the bone is healing, regaining strength, following undervaluation. The undervaluation has been repaired. The tension was resolved, perhaps not its causes, but at least the effects.

Study the joint where you experience problems.

Asphyxiation

This is a problem in the breathing system.

Breathing links us, thanks to its duality, to the supernatural, to the universe, to the source of creation, to the metaphysical world. Breathing allows us to be linked to life. Consequently, breathing prevents the isolation of human beings.

Breathing is, therefore, both contact and relationship. This contact with what comes from the outside is made through the pulmonary alveoli.

Contact we make with others through the skin is a voluntary act. We either want to touch or not. But contact through breathing is no longer a voluntary act. It just occurs, and that is it.

Two key-words reflect the duality which characterises the respiratory system: freedom and constraint.

The one who asphyxiates is the one who has decided to get totally free from the constraints that we experience in life. In the case of babies, there is a nonconscious desire to disincarnate.

See *Babies*

Asthenia

Asthenia means intense lack of energy. It is provoked by the absence of references and loss of the feeling of being part of the herd, of the group, of the clan. It occurs at the level of the subconscious, both individually and collectively.

In order to better describe what a person suffering from asthenia goes through, we shall take an example from the animal world.

Contrary to what happens with wolves, where each individual wolf in the pack is not essential (one wolf leaving the group does not impact on the pack), in the case of sheep, and, more precisely, a sheep herd, any reduction in the number of heads originates a situation of danger. Sheep depend on the group, reason for which they bet on it. The herd cannot attack nor run away, only gather together. Predators do not attack a herd. What they see when looking at the herd is a huge sheep. The sheep led astray is the one which becomes the prey.

For the lost sheep, the only valid direction is the course which will take it back to the herd. For this reason, the lost sheep does not know which way it should run to, because it does not know where the herd is, and so it stays still. It stays very still, so not to give itself away to the wolves. The lost sheep has to focus on itself, and for this reason, its body has to generate a mechanism that calms it down. What the body does then is to act over the suprarenal glands, calming them down and literally draining them. The sheep becomes exhausted as a result. It becomes worn out, and then lies down, still. When we see a sheep looking like this, it means it is lost. It is trying not to move any further away from the herd. It waits for it to show up, and, when it happens, then its suprarenal glands come back into force and the sheep runs fast to the herd, to be part of it and feel safe again. An animal under stress is a very active animal.

The lost sheep has to focus on itself, and for this reason its body has to generate a mechanism that calms it down.

When the sheep parted from the group, there are natural mechanisms through which the herd sends signals, from brain to brain. Since the lost sheep is very calm and in asthenia, it is very apt to capture this type of signalling from the herd and start moving in its direction. If it was not in asthenia, it would not be able to detect the radar signals sent by the herd. The same happens with elephants. They turn around in rotation and translation movements. It is all very fast.

The person suffering from asthenia is alone, and has to stop. For this reason, the brain produces fatigue. The person who feels very tired is a person who is lost. He would like to find his former group, family, herd, clan, or to find a new one. The person suffering from asthenia needs to stop his mental turmoil; he is leading a very fast and logical life, a very *yang*, very masculine, very controlled life. The more one fights off fatigue, the more it makes itself felt. One needs to accept and not move.

It is necessary to thank fatigue and to adopt a *zen* attitude, in other words, to let intuition win over. And to keep an ear out for the signal that will take him back to a clan, a herd.

We all derive from a clan. It is difficult to uproot the values of that clan. The clan always calls back the person who moved away from it. And it is very powerful. One may change clans. Anytime one is between clans, a crisis presents itself in his life. If the person manages to set up another clan, then balance returns. Independence is not lived in isolation. Independence means that one is able to choose his herd, his group.

The safety that comes when a person reencounters a group regenerates him. The suprarenal glands fill up again and the person recovers his vitality.

The individual person matters to the species, and for this reason the species has a programme for the individual.

Human beings are gregarious. The person who shows up with new ideas is the outcast, the black sheep. The clan fears its safety is in jeopardy.

For this reason, it is advisable to always respect the herd, not destroy it.

47

Advancement is achieved by beginning a new herd, not by destroying the old one.

Usually, we act fully in accordance with the clan, or totally opposed to the clan, but always with the clan as a reference, which is not good for the individual person. A person should act in accordance with his balance.

The combination of brains in a herd leads to a collective brain, with its own identity.

The same applies to politics, to society and to the system in general.

For the person suffering from fibromyalgia, please see *Fibromyalgia (chronic fatigue syndrome)*.

Also see *Family*

Asthma – bronchial asthma

It consists of a straightening of the bronchi and bronchioles which can be provoked by muscular spasm, inflammation of the respiratory routes or by the congestion and secretion of mucosa. One feels suffocating.

This is a person who tries to receive a lot but who has difficulty giving back. The asthmatic person poisons himself with carbon anhydride, because he cannot breathe out. This symptom is typical of children who are too spoiled or are prevented from crying.

In babies and children, asthma indicates they do not wish to be here. It reflects a desire to depart from life, in the case of babies, and an indication that they do not wish to be here, they would rather be there, in the case of young children.

However, it also happens a lot in adults.

Asthma comes from the Greek and it means "chest constriction". In Latin, the closest root seems to be *angustus*, the root of the word anguish. This Latin root is also present in words such as amygdale (tonsils) and angina. And tightness and constraint are linked to anguish and fear.

Asthma is often linked to allergies, for example, hay fever. The keywords for asthma are fear and unwillingness to accept.

The person suffering from asthma also has a wish to dominate, although, when confronted with this fact, he always denies it.

The asthmatic person feels as if he is always about to burst out, but he cannot externalize yelling and insults. For this reason, he cough and expectorates.

The adult asthmatic normally is a very cerebral, mentally oriented person. He tends to blame his own sexuality and to bring his sexual impulses up to the chest region (he confuses love with sex). Therefore, instead of leaving mucosa stimulation down there, at the level of the sexual organs, he brings it, literally, to the mouth. In a way, that rather makes sense, given the clear similarity between the mouth, which expresses love, and the genital organs, which express sex.

The person suffering from asthma is thirsty of love. He longs for love, above all else. But he looks for it in other people.

Asthma and skin eruptions are related to issues of contact and relationship.

The asthmatic person shows some resistance in his contact with the world.

Astigmatism

See *Eyes*

Auricles

Communicating auricles.

Left auricle, right auricle communication.

See *Heart – communication between auriculae*

Authority

Authority, whose etymological root means "the one who enables growth", is always represented by a third party. He or she, who, to us, represents authority, is the one (male or female) with whom we feel we are growing. The one who makes us grow is the one who shows us the route, the rhythm, the path which we should take. He or she is the one who gives us a sense of direction, of communication and humbleness. The person who is on good terms with authority is disciplined, that is to say, he considers himself to be the disciple of that particular person. He feels he is growing with that person. For this reason, he gives himself and lives a humble life. That person does not follow the master out of a sense of obligation towards him, nor obedience, but due to discipline, that is, as a result of a personal choice.

In our society, authority is centred on human beings. On the god, on the biological Father, on the male figure.

Authority should not be mistaken with power. Power demands obedience, not discipline.

The concept of authority is directly linked to that of humbleness.

The person who feels growing with another person will follow him in humbleness. The one who stops feeling he is growing with the other person, instead of criticizing or destroying him, only has to separate himself from him, in humbleness. And he needs to respect the fact that, if he no longer grows with that other person, maybe others are still growing with him, and for this reason he should not destroy him, simply separate from him.

The same goes for the person who is no longer accepted as an authority by his disciples. He should accept that fact with humbleness and not attempt to persecute or destroy the former disciple, rather allow him to take a different path, in humbleness.

Whenever a person does not respect other people as an authority, he develops an arrogant behaviour and resorts to power. Consequently, he is weakening his own authority.

People with mental disorders, isolation problems or even with movement impairments have problems at the level of authority and humbleness.

They are people with a blockage in the Crown Chakra, the purple chakra. For this reason, in each of these cases, it is necessary to look out for what is happening with the male model, with the biological Father, with the idea of family and of clan.

See *Family*

Autoimmune diseases

See *Immune system*

Autonomic nervous system

See *Nervous system*

The autonomic nervous system is a part of the Nervous system.

Babies

Babies, people, are born out of a parental project (conscious and unconscious) as a result of fecundation. A baby incarnates a human being, and his birth gives a purpose to the parents' project.

The new-born child, like the baby who is still in his Mother's womb, is totally linked to his parents, his makers, particularly to the Mother. The physical and psychological symptoms that foetuses, new-born babies and infants experience, until they are about six, seven years old, are fruit of the relationship they have with their parents. During this period, these human beings feel everything that happens to their parents, through their intuition. Consequently, they transform the tension they experience in the relationship each of the parents has with the baby into a physical symptom. They also do it regarding the relationship each of the parents has with each other. And the same applies to the relationship each of the parents has with him or herself, in the way each parent assumes his or her own emotions, tensions, conflicts and self-esteem.

Babies do not speak a language parents can understand. For this reason, they express themselves through physical symptoms.

Thus, in the face of any symptom experienced by a child of any of these ages (fetus, new-born and up to six or seven years old), it is necessary to understand what is going on, or happened to the parents before the child's symptom manifested itself. Babies' illnesses are a produce of what was going on in their parents' heads at the time of conception or throughout pregnancy.

If the Mother kept thinking about burns, then the baby may keep on burning himself.

For instance, if the parents only wanted a sexual relation without love, that is to say, if the child was conceived at a separation moment, the child is likely to suffer from eczema (skin problems).

A baby who is prone to **ear infections** is a baby who was hit by what he heard from his parents. A baby who goes **deaf** is a baby who protected himself from what he heard from his parents, thus generating deafness.

There are new-born and young babies who suffer from ear infections, young children who have myopia (nearsightedness), new-borns with a heart or liver condition, etc. In any symptom shown by children up to six or seven years old, one should always look out for the organ that was touched and the relationship between the parents.

The word bear (the animal) in latin comes from *urs*, which in turn comes from *Uranus*, which means light. The bear is thus the symbol of light. This is the reason children are given teddy bears when they go to bed, so that they can go to sleep with a symbol of light.

Throughout pregnancy, the baby is connected to the mother's emotions for nine months. It is very important to respect the woman's gestation period and to stop thinking that it must be a very active and *yang* period.

See also *Child delivery*

For prepubertal children, see also *Endocrine system.*

Bacillary dysentery

See *Bowel – large bowel – bacillary dysentery*

Back

Spine, shoulder blade and vertebrae problems, as well as muscular and skin conditions, may occur on the back.

See *Spine, Muscles, Shoulder blade* and *Vertebrae*

Pimples on the skin indicate the presence of an inflammation of the hair and sebaceous follicles, particularly on shoulders, face, back and chest.

They are an eruption and expelling of tension related to communication difficulties.

Pimples on the back indicate major communication problems at home, with the family, with parents and most probably with the partner.

Pimples on the back occur as a result of repression of a person's sexuality and/or emotions. It is likely that the person's emotions, sexual desire, sexual drive or even sexual fantasies need to be externalized, told to someone very close, but the person does not allow himself to do so. The person does not feel strong enough, with sufficient dorsal spine do be able to do it. The skin is precisely the border that needs to be crossed over to get near the other person, to be able to communicate and be with the other person. What does not come out through communication, gets out through the body, through the skin.

Back pain

A back pain can take its origin in a Vertebrae problem, in a Lumbago or a Sciatica. Please see *Vertebrae – cervical vertebrae, Vertebrae – discs, Vertebrae – dorsal vertebrae, Vertebrae – lumbar vertebrae, Vertebrae – sacral vertebrae, Vertebrae – terminal vertebrae – coccyx, Lumbago* and/or *Sciatic nerve pain*

Bad breath

Bad breath indicates problems of gastric nature, difficult digestion. Difficult digestion is a symptom that the person deals poorly with the emotions he feels. He can not digest what other people did or continue doing to him on a daily basis. On the other hand, the fact that he has bad breath forces him to keep his distance to avoid an unpleasant situation for him and others. The tensions of bad breath are associated with the person's partner who, after all, is the most affected by that condition and from whom the individual must keep a physical distance. It is possible that this partner who is affected by the bad breath is the main relational cause of the person's incapacity to digest his emotions. Bad breath may also result from dental caries. Caries result from enamel problems in the teeth. The person who suffers from enamel problems is someone who feels he does not have the right to bite. This person's bone is harder than enamel. The jawbone is stronger than the tooth.

"I don't have a strong enough bite!" This situation causes caries. Tooth problems have to do with a single psychological problem: not being able to bite. To bite constitutes a decision, both in literal and figurative senses. It is possible that it is still the same partner – affected by the bad breath – who is the relational cause of the person's inability to make decisions.

Balance – lack of balance

People who display a clear lack of balance (and we are not talking about older people or people with motor problems) are people who have difficulty maintaining a sense of discernment. They are people who are not attentive to what should be good for them. They are people who are obstinate about their ideas, which, by the way, do not serve them well. They are people affected by a lack of balance of their roots. It is in the roots that we find the biological Mother, the way of thinking and acting of the family or the clan, and home. People with kidney problems are also people with noticeable balance problems, which is common, since the kidneys, with their filtering function, are directly connected with discernment.

Baldness

See *Hair*

Bechterew's disease

The spine is too stiff and takes the shape of bamboo. It denotes a non-conscious huge ego and a tremendous lack of flexibility that the person does not acknowledge. With time, the spine solidifies from top down and the head leans forward. The sinuosity (the S) disappears or gets inverted. This is the body showing the person what the person never wanted to see. When the S becomes inverted, this is the body showing the person that he is living in the opposite way he should.

See *Spine*

Bells's paralysis

This is a paralysis or weakness of the facial muscles on one side only. The face reflects our identity to others, to society. A person's whose muscles go weak is someone who felt undervalued in his identity as part of a relationship with someone. The person feels embarrassment (feels undervalued) about part of his identity. He feels that part of him is ugly, but will not say it to anyone. The body assumes the responsibility to show it to everybody

Also see *Paralysis* for other types of paralysis.

Berger's disease

See *Kidneys – renal insufficiency*

Bile

See *Gallbladder*

Bilirubin

See *Liver – jaundice*

Bipolarity

Mood swings. Swinging between intense crying and bursts of joy. A person may sometimes appear to be very happy but he is often unbalanced, because he is searching for answers in his life outside himself, externally, in society, in his friends, but not inside himself. It reveals that the interior and the external beings are not aligned.

This person is hardly predictable, because he lives in an alternating way.

This will normally be a person who has lived for a long time with a Father and a Mother who did not get along, or with male and female models who were not compatible. In other words, he lived amidst incompatible *yang* and *yin* behaviours.

The type of male and Father models this person had needs to be understood, particularly regarding the relationship he had with close relatives. These relatives are normally very cerebral, very stubborn and show a need to control everything and be right about everything.

The cause behind this process is always connected with the relationship with the man (Father, Grandfather), in other words, the male model that he had in his family and who was very dominating and determining.

Bipolar people are normally individuals who, as a result of being very mentally oriented and wanting to explain and control everything, lack affection and care, and who cry out the need to feel loved and held. This type of person will cry out of self pity, more than as a result of letting himself go or out of detachment.

In any case, bipolarity symptoms do not come alone. They are always corroborated by other body symptoms.

This can be the case of people who are bipolar and suffer from psoriasis. If you see *Psoriasis*, you will note that the tension in the person's conscience is also linked to alternating patterns.

Birth

See *Child delivery*

Bladder

The urinary system gets rid of residual waters (the large bowel disposes of organic matter). The bladder stores the liquids that have been rejected by the kidneys.

The subterranean waters of the body are deeply connected to ancestral memories. Fecundity (fertility) and toxins (urine-waters) are part of the same structure, although they belong to distinct systems. The urinary system shows the fears and resistances to eventual changes. We all know that certain situations of discomfort such as fears, stress, tension, make us urinate, in other words, relieve the bladder. In fact, the urge to pee serves as an excuse to move away from a situation in which we felt uncomfortable.

When one is afraid, he feels that the other person may attack. For this reason, the sympathetic nervous system gets ready to run away. Here, as opposed to the energy caused by anger, which moves up to the scapular waist, the energy that comes from fear goes down to the lower limbs. Legs get ready to start running! The fact that one may need to run for a long time may make one empty the sacs of urine and faeces one carries in order to run faster. This is the reason why the person who is afraid may suffer from urinary incontinence or bowel incontinence. Accounts of people who pee down their legs out of fear are very usual.

If escaping is not possible, then energy gets trapped in the middle of the back, putting weight on the anus and on the urethra, as well as on the eyes.

The bladder is the ultimate warehouse of toxins. Kidneys and bladder eliminate toxins out of the body.

Deep fear, that is, fear associated to a feeling of danger, of extremely serious consequences, is directly linked to the kidneys. The bladder is linked to social relationship conflicts, to external communication, as well as to territorial conflicts and socialization.

In fact, human beings, when settling somewhere, have always started by building fences, thus marking their territory: "It is mine!" It is part of their roots. This is how we mark our territory. Animals, well before us, started demarcating their territory, not with fences, but with urine. And this concept of marking the territory with urine still prevails amongst us.

Therefore, when someone is unable to mark his territory, he shows symptoms associated to the bladder. He may have **enuresis**, urinate a lot during the day, his urine may have a strong smell, he may urinate during the night, or he may have **cystitis** (urinary infection).

The role of urine is to mark the territory. It has to do with the marking of the person's vital space.

Generally speaking, the bladder's capacity is smaller in women, because of the space occupied by the uterus, which stands right above the bladder.

Since primordial times that females look after the nests more, while the males deal more with the externals borders. Thus, women feel they have bladder problems when they are unable to organize their vital space. When everything is a mess. And males feel they have bladder problems when they cannot limit the external borders of their territories, and when they feel threatened in their own space. Each may, as a result of the tension they are experiencing, develop an ulcer (a hole) in the mucosa of the bladder. This additional space inside the bladder indicates that the body is responding to that person's need to have more space, in order to hold more urine which, in turn, will enable him to better mark his territory, with increased intensity. The body develops the space that will allow an increased flow of urine.

Once this tension, whether it affects women or men, has gone, urinary infections develop, such as cystitis, burning pee, enuresis and urethritis (urethra infection).

If a person feels under a lot of tension and for some reason does not verbalize it, then cancer of the bladder may occur.

Cystitis occur more in girls and enuresis in boys.

People suffering from bronchial cancer often have bladder conditions (territorial conflicts in both cases).

See *Cystitis* and *Enuresis*

Blepharitis

See *Eyes - blepharitis*

Blindness

See *Eyes – blindness*

Blood

The blood contains a person's identity. The blood shows we belong to a lineage, a clan, and it simultaneously shows the unique and complete character of the person's own identity. Identity also appears in sexuality (capacity of being, of giving oneself to other person). This presupposes that, as we all have blood, we all know who we are. Blood is, therefore, identity, virility and our belonging to blood lineage.

The heart is the engine of blood, which rules the emotional side of our lives. The bone marrow is the place, in our body, where maturation of red blood cells, white blood cells, and platelets occurs. The cells and the platelets are directly associated to blood, that is, with the person's identity. And this identity is in continuous evolution. It is in permanent movement. One may change the way he is!

These cells and platelets change every one hundred and twenty days.

Therefore, what is at stake is the person's capacity of understanding what is good for him, and also regarding what is good for him in his relationship with things, people in general, with family members, with the people from the clan and with the latter's thinking pattern, so that the person realises what is good for him and what does not work for him.

What the body is showing here is the person's capacity to be himself without seeking the approval of others.

This is where our self-esteem lives, right here in the blood.

See *Heart* and *Circulatory system*

Blood pressure

See *Blood pressure – high* and *Blood pressure – low*

Blood pressure – high

Blood reflects the identity, the being. The walls of the blood vessels are the frontiers within which our incarnation into human beings must develop.

It is natural for us to want to test the limits of these frontiers, the limits of resistance of blood vessels.

Contrary to the person who suffers

from hypotension, a person who suffers from hypertension prepares himself for action and is determined to take action. Accordingly, blood circulation accelerates and pressure increases, but this person never really confronts the person he has trouble with and, consequently, there is no discharge of energy, it remains stored. The person who suffers from hypertension is not able to reach a confrontation.

He is afraid of confrontation and does not realize that the confrontation must happen as soon as possible, in a simple and easy way, by expressing what he thinks and feels.

It is common for the person with high blood pressure to convince himself that next time he will be able to act. This keeps the organism ready for action, keeps it from relaxing, and the person develops chronic high blood pressure and never really engages in confrontation.

The person with high blood pressure stays on the edge of conflict, is always troubled by conflict, but never reaches any solution.

Of course, if things are not cleared up, one day the person will say what he has to say, but he will do it in an a angry, cowardly, and exaggerated way, creating even more conflict when things could have been resolved in a calm manner. The person whines, complains, shows rage, and ends up blowing his top off, seldom with the right person and often with the wrong people.

This lack of confrontation gives rise to a great internal conflict. The person remains on the defense, always prepared for a conflict that likely he will never carry out.

They are people with long lasting, unresolved emotional problems.

The person with *Arteriosclerosis* also suffers from high blood pressure.

Blood pressure – low

Blood reflects the identity, the being. The walls of the blood vessels are the frontiers within which our incarnation into human beings takes place. It is natural for us to want to test the limits of these frontiers, the resistance of the blood vessels. The person with low blood pressure never tests these frontiers, never takes it to the limit. He greatly resists who he is and steers away from conflict. So, blood, too, holds back and often causes the patient to pass out. The person renounces his personal power, resigns from his responsibilities, and runs away. He shows lack of enthusiasm and courage. The individual is defeated in face of any challenge. This symptom is common among people who suffered from lack of love as children. They have a defeated attitude. "What good does it do, anyway?" The person who suffers from hypotension has an overly feminine behaviour, is excessively passive. He cancels himself out.

See *Fainting* and *Circulatory system*.

Body hair

Hair, body fine hair and nails are skin excretions produced by a protein called keratin. All of these excretions have a protective role. Nails, body hair and hair are annexes of the skin.

They may work as antennae, means of seduction, protection or have a sexual/social nature. They reflect health condition, fidelity to the clan, strength.

Body hair is a more male attribute.

Body hair is created by the force of Heaven (*yang*). Hair is created by the force of Earth (*yin*). The latter is a more female attribute.

See *Hair* and *Nails*

Body lateralization

See *Introduction page 11* about brain polarity.

Boils

The person is mad, burning with rage. "It's not fair!" The person needs to express his anger, to look for a confrontation, but ultimately cannot do it. This infection he feels in his body is a reflection of the tension he feels in life. The boil must be cut open to let out the pus. The person settled for a condition of rotten peace which must be dealt with. Check where in the body the boil is located.

Bone

Bones represent our deepest beliefs. It is the carcass, the structure that supports all of the tissues of the body. The skeleton and the bones represent our inner structure.

The bone holds the conscience of the self.

The bone structure is where the deep undervaluation of the being is kept. "My action was not appropriate."

The person who wishes to be incinerated upon dying only because he believes that he is worth nothing and that there is no point in taking up space and bothering others, may be doing so, out of pure undervaluation. This is when the bones may become affected.

A man who has been cheated on and feels deep undervaluation will end up with problems in his bones. This does not happen to women who have been cheated. A woman will feel tension in one of her feminine organs (breast, for example). For a very masculine and *macho* man, the fact that he feels deceived represents a total crumbling of his foundations and of his beliefs. For this reason, his bones are affected.

The bone structure indicates firmness and accomplishment. Specific and intense undervaluation shows up in the bones.

A broken bone, upon calcification, will not fracture again in the same place. It has become stronger.

To **fracture** a bone means the release of a great deal of energy. When the fracture occurs, stress levels are reduced. Then the bone is immobilized with plaster and the person calms down, gets free and smiles.

When a bone is fractured, this in fact means that the body is asking the person to break off with a belief from the past and to change himself. Fractures normally result from dynamic activities, which can be physical or mental. This happens to excessively active people. The body says: "Stop, take a different route." The person who fractures a bone is a person who has become too rigid and inflexible regarding an activity he was carrying out.

When referring to bones, it is important to distinguish three levels: the actual bone, the bone marrow and the periosteum (the membrane that covers the bone).

For instance, when fracturing a bone, the pain we feel is in the periosteum, the membrane covering the bone. This is where the bone connects with the conscience, through pain. This is where contact is made. This is where separation of the action occurs, between what I did wrong and what I simply failed to do.

This part of the bone, the membrane, is more dynamic than the skin covering our bodies. A pain in the bones calls for immobility. I must stop and rethink my actions. A non-stopping pain leads to inactivity.

Pain is ninety per cent periosteal and so, it may be worked on from a psychic perspective. Ten per cent of pain is, nevertheless, truly physical, which makes it much more difficult to deal with and means that pain killers need to be used.

Bones are part of the locomotor system. The right side of the body is *yang*, masculine, and the left side is *yin*, feminine. This applies both to left and right-handed people, but this polarity is not constant. Therefore, it must be examined carefully.

You should examine each part of the body individually.

See *Bone marrow*

Bone fracture

See *Bone*

Bone marrow

When referring to bones, there are three levels: The bone itself, the bone marrow and the periosteum (the membrane that lines the outer surface of bones). Bone marrow, particularly in long bones such as the sternum and the hip, is where the maturation of red blood cells, white blood cells, and platelets occurs. The cells and the platelets are directly associated with blood, that is, with the person's identity. And this identity is in continuous evolution (maturation). It is in permanent movement. One may change the way he is!

These cells and the platelets change every one hundred and twenty days.

Therefore, what is at stake is our belonging to a lineage of ancestors and our identity as unique beings.

Bone marrow related problems denote maximum undervaluation conflict. The marrow represents one's deepest beliefs regarding himself. It denotes the way a person looks after himself and finds support. The way the person deals with his strongest beliefs. It is where the capacity the person has to say no to his clan and family beliefs lies, because those beliefs are bad for him. Problems in this area reflect profound lack of self-esteem.

Myeloma (a tumour, almost always malignant, which develops at the expense of the bone marrow), **multiple myeloma** (the inner conflict, here, is very close to the leukaemia one) and **leukaemia** (blood cancer) are forms of cancer that have their origins in bone marrow.

These are typical of a person who allows himself to be vampirized by the family way of thinking and who believes that his family finds him worthless; A person who undervalues himself. He wants to be looked after as if he was a baby. However, he should not be spoiled, otherwise he will never take responsibility for his actions. This person should be helped so that he can feel valued. If we look after him as if he was a baby, we will be proving him right and reinforcing the undervaluation feeling he has about himself.

See *Leukaemia*

Bone structure

See *Bone*

Bowel – large bowel

This is the sixth and final segment of the digestive canal. It belongs to the metal element of the five elements of eastern philosophy. It is divided into ascending colon, transverse colon, descending colon, sigmoid, upper rectum, lower rectum and anus.

The large bowel is the realm of the underworld, of the unconscious, where the fermentation and death of food takes place, and waste is 'buried', expelled. Problems in the large bowel show the body exposing the person's underworld.

By defecating, the person is marking his identity, not his territory (when the person urinates he marks his territory). Most symptoms of the large bowel are pointed out in the rubrics:

Bowel – large bowel, Bowel – large bowel – amoebic dysentery, Bowel – large bowel – anus, Bowel – large bowel – ascending colon, Bowel – large bowel – bacillary dysentery, Bowel – large bowel – colic, Bowel – large bowel – colon, Bowel – large bowel – Crohn's disease, Bowel – large bowel – descending colon, Bowel – large bowel – descending colon – sigmoid, Bowel – large bowel – lower rectum (incontinence), Bowel – large bowel – transverse colon, Bowel – large bowel – ulcerative colitis and *Bowel – large bowel – upper rectum.*

Also see *Aerophagia, Tapeworm, Worms* and *Threadworms*

Bowel – large bowel – amoebic dysentery

See *Bowel – large bowel – ulcerative colitis*

The condition of the **amoebic dysentery** is characteristic of mind tensions similar to those associated with ulcerative colitis.

Bowel – large bowel – anus

The anus is the point of elimination. It is the end of the discarding territory. Anus problems are always related to conflicts with people close to us. Symptoms in the anus are related to feminine tensions, that is, with feminine behaviours, passive behaviours; they are associated with women and fears.

An **abscess** in the anus shows much rage regarding something the person does not want to release, let go of. An abscess shows that an inflammation or infection in our lives must be cut open so that the rotten pus may get out. It indicates that a situation of rotten peace must be confronted but the person is too passive to do it. **Pain** in the anus indicates guilt and conscious or unconscious desire to be punished. "I deserve this, I was not good enough."

A **fistula** in the anus shows incomplete discharge of waste. I hang on to the garbage, to the rubbish of the past.

Anus prurience (itch) shows regret, guilt about the past.

Haemorrhoids consist in pain and bleeding of the anus when the person defecates. Defecating is painful. In fact the person is afraid to release. In the case of haemorrhoids, there is a swelling of the veins in the exact point of discharge. Varicose veins develop in the area of the anus due to excessive contraction, which shows insecurity in releasing. A varicose is a vein swelling. Varicose veins result from excessive blood accumulation in the veins, blood that should have returned to the heart but did not.

The person has difficulty in letting go. **Haemorrhages** show fear of the future, due to lack of self-esteem and happiness. The person is so afraid of what may happen that can only let go with pain, shedding her happiness, shedding blood.

People who suffer from haemorrhoids are usually stressed with deadlines for material projects. They dwell on the consequences. The tension may be related to the material relationship this person has with the spouse (husband or wife). It may have to do with the potential death of a cycle (the end of a relationship with the spouse) or someone's death.

See *Bowel – large bowel – colon*

Bowel – large bowel – ascending colon

This is where fermentation takes place. The person who experiences problems in this area has difficulty deciding whether to keep or let go. Fermentation happens because of the presence of sugar. When a person doubts his ability to decide whether to hold on to or to release, he may develop **flatulence** and pain. The person with problems in the ascending colon may be an individual with problems in his relationship with his Father or male role model. It may involve a partner, a supervisor, a boyfriend, or any model of masculine behaviour.

The anus and other parts of the colon show feminine tensions, while the ascending colon exposes more masculine tensions.

Cancer of the colon, like all cancers, is associated with a great tension that the person experienced and did not verbalize, kept well hidden. This tension is associated with unhappiness at home, a feeling that the person was the victim of some dirty and infamous deed.

Tensions associated with the ascending colon are clearly masculine, *yang*, and connected with the biological Father, the male model, and masculine behaviour.

This person must assume his or her *yang* side. He or she needs to make a decision, to be more assertive, to use his or her masculine behavior.

Try to find out who was responsible for the infamous deed, dirty behaviour, or fraud.

See *Bowel – large bowel – colon*

Bowel – large bowel – bacillary dysentery

See *Bowel – large bowel – ulcerative colitis*

The condition of the **bacillary dysentery** is characteristic of mind tensions similar to those associated with ulcerative colitis.

Bowel – large bowel – colic

We are less conscious of tensions associated with bowel problems than of tensions associated with the stomach. Many times they express themselves as spasms. **Spasms and colic**: "Either I control or I release." These tensions that a person feels in the intestine are associated with his roots, and in particular with the home, spouse (husband or wife), work, and the female role model (the biological Mother).

See *Bowel – large bowel – colon*

Bowel – large bowel – colon

In the large bowel, the digestive process is already over. This is the rubbish bin. The colon keeps the organism from getting clogged up and intoxicated with the stuff it does not need. Therefore, it contributes to the respiratory process (complements the Lungs).

In the colon, the body extracts and recuperates water from the food it did not digest and is going to expel. This is where the garbage collects, though some intake still takes place. Here, just like in the small bowel, the question of what must be kept and what must be thrown away persists.

In nature, to defecate is considered as a gift of excrement, a fertilizer for the earth. Excrement and money are associated in many ways. For example, in many European countries, there is a belief that to step on excrement brings luck and money.

The small bowel is associated with the process of discrimination to allow proper absorption. The large bowel is associated with the underworld, the unconscious, the realm of the dead. It is in the large bowel that decomposition takes place. It symbolizes the nocturnal side of the body.

Constipation (lazy bowels) shows that the person does not want to give, to offer. The person hangs on to what he has. It is characteristic of people who are frugal, skimpy, with money. It reflects the desire to hold on to material possessions. People who suffer from constipation are very egocentric.

Colon **cancer**, like all cancers, is

associated with a great tension that the person experienced and did not verbalize, a tension that was kept well hidden. This tension is associated with unhappiness at home, a feeling that the person was the victim of some dirty and infamous deed.

Cancer of the colon is more prevalent in the ascending colon, in the sigmoid, and in the upper and lower rectum.

Colon tensions are almost always feminine tensions, except those that occur in the ascending colon, which are usually masculine, and those in the lower rectum, which are connected with tensions in the relationship between male and female.

See *Bowel – large bowel, Bowel – large bowel – amoebic dysentery, Bowel – large bowel – anus, Bowel – large bowel – ascending colon, Bowel – large bowel – bacillary dysentery, Bowel – large bowel – colic, Bowel – large bowel – colon, Bowel – large bowel – Crohn's disease, Bowel – large bowel – descending colon, Bowel – large bowel – descending colon – sigmoid, Bowel – large bowel – lower rectum (incontinence), Bowel – large bowel – transverse colon, Bowel – large bowel – ulcerative colitis* and *Bowel – large bowel – upper rectum*

Also see *Aerophagia, Tapeworm, Worms* and *Threadworms*

Bowel – large bowel – Crohn's disease

This chronic inflammation affects primarily the bowel but may affect any part of digestive canal.

It is an inflammation of the colon. It may also affect the ileum, the final segment of the small intestine. The most common symptoms include abdominal pain, diarrhoea, weight loss, fever, painful spasms, blood loss, and anal fistulas. There may also be skin and joint problems.

Though the symptoms are similar to those of ulcerative colitis, Crohn's disease affects all layers of the intestinal wall, while ulcerative colitis affects only the innermost layer.

In several European countries they use expressions that illustrate tensions on the mind related to Crohn's disease: "the guy who rolls on somebody else's faeces", "ass licker." These expressions point out the thinking pattern of a person who wants to gain approval from others. This is a person who sacrifices his own life to serve someone else. He is a hypocrite, an 'ass licker", a "brown-noser".

Among other symptoms, the person with Crohn's disease loses blood and mucous. Blood and mucous are basic substances of life, vital substances.

The body shows that the person renounces his identity, his life, for fear of being alone. This person needs someone else, needs company, even at the cost of loosing his own identity. This may happen due to issues with the spouse (husband or wife) (or someone at home) or an employer.

The person gives his life to another and bleeds and sweats from the anus. The individual may suffer from skin and joint problems. Skin problems show fear of separation, which, again, shows that the person is, in fact, afraid to be alone. Problems with the joints are associated with inflexibility of thinking and undervaluation issues. This also supports the theory that the person cancels himself out, gives his life to another, and totally loses his value. He does it at the mercy of great inflexibility regarding thinking patterns which he adopted but do not work for him. However, he insists on keeping these patterns, either because he is deeply attached to family and past beliefs, or because some member of the clan or family does not allow him to change the way he thinks. A person with Crohn's disease suffers from a great lack of discernment and sensibility.

See *Bowel – large bowel – colon*

Bowel – large bowel – descending colon

In this area we may look for problems in the relationship with the Mother, not the Father; the descending colon is associated with the female role model, feminine behaviour, and more *yin* behaviour.

Here we find legacy and things that must be released, the attachment to matters related to roots. (Money, family objects, home)

Cancer of the colon, like all cancers, is associated with a great tension that the person experienced and did not verbalize, kept well hidden. This tension is associated with unhappiness at home, a feeling that the person was the victim of some dirty and infamous deed.

Most cases of cancer of the descending colon take place in the sigmoid and the rectum.

The person should adopt a more *yin* behaviour but, instead, he does not want to let go of what has caused the tension he is undergoing. The person is too *yang*, to competitive, too masculine.

See *Bowel – large bowel, Bowel – large bowel – amoebic dysentery, Bowel – large bowel – anus, Bowel – large bowel – ascending colon, Bowel – large bowel – bacillary dysentery, Bowel – large bowel – colic, Bowel – large bowel – colon, Bowel – large bowel – Crohn's disease, Bowel – large bowel – descending colon – sigmoid, Bowel – large bowel – lower rectum (incontinence), Bowel – large bowel – transverse colon, Bowel – large bowel – ulcerative colitis* and *Bowel – large bowel – upper rectum*

Bowel – large bowel – descending colon – sigmoid

The sigmoid is the area of the descending colon (before the rectum) where faeces accumulate prior to being released. It is located at the end of the left colon or descending colon, followed by the rectum and the anus. In carnivores, it is short. In herbivores, it is long. Humans who have a short sigmoid are more carnivorous. Humans with a long sigmoid are more vegetarian. A carnivorous human (one with a short sigmoid) must not become vegetarian. Colon **cancer**, like all cancers, is associated with a great tension that the

63

person experienced and did not verbalize, kept well hidden. This tension is associated with unhappiness at home, a feeling that the person was the victim of some dirty and infamous deed. Any inflammation of the sigmoid relates to the Mother. Cancer of the descending colon is more frequent in the sigmoid and the rectum. The person should adopt a more *yin* behaviour but, instead, he does not want to let go of what has caused the tension he is undergoing. The person is too *yang,* too competitive, too masculine.

Diverticulosis are pouches (pockets) that appear in several places in the large bowel. It happens more frequently in the muscular fibres of the large intestine walls. Some faeces can be stuck in there, as well as bacteria in some cases. Many people have asymptomatic diverticulosis. In fact, they don't even know they have it.

Sometimes, these pouches inflame or infect, and this causes diverticulitis. Most commonly, diverticulitis happens in the descending colon, and mainly in the sigmoid.

Here, what one is asked to do is to let go. So here we find things that must be released. As seen above, this person should adopt a more *yin* behaviour but, instead, he does not want to let go of what has caused the tension he is undergoing.

Diverticulosis happens in the muscle of the colon. And muscles have to do with undervaluation, poor self-esteem. It is because of poor self-esteem that this person becomes too masculine. He may be defining himself for

what he has (and holds on to it – although he should naturally let go) instead of defining himself for what he is.

See *Bowel – large bowel – descending colon*

See *Bowel – large bowel – colon*

Bowel – large bowel – lower rectum (incontinence)

Our conscience perceives this part of the rectum differently from the upper rectum. It has to do with the role of the sphincter. The sphincter is a frontier. Conflicts in this area are experienced in a feminine manner, due to a specific characteristic.

It is important to understand that the tension is *yin*, feminine, due to a lack of boundary setting on the part of the Father. In other words, if the Father was too lenient, the person does not know his limits, becomes excessively passive, excessively feminine, and may suffer from **incontinence**. If the person suffers a great tension and does not verbalize it, it may develop **cancer**. Here, in this part of the body, conflicts are experienced in a feminine manner. The person releases, releases, and releases. He never ceases to release and can do nothing to stop the outflow. The person is tremendously *yin*, tremendously passive. Bowel incontinence shows a constant revelation of the person's underworld, of his subconscious, of his hidden side, his hidden emotions, and his true identity. The person with incontinence cannot position himself from an identity standpoint.

When a woman (or a very *yin*, very

feminine man) does not know her limits, her sphincter ceases to work effectively. It is a reaction grounded on our collective subconscious. In fact, in pre-historic times, men imposed the limits on women.

In older people, incontinence happens due to senility, due to loss of control of the masculine side, of the *yang* side. Incontinence also happens to some homosexual men and some women, due to their preference for anal sex. It is not because they practice anal sex, but rather because they are very submissive, too *yin*, too passive. They are people who overdevelop their feminine side at the expense of their masculine side.

Incontinence may also happen, in isolated episodes, due to a great fear.

When a person feels fear, he feels that someone may attack him. As a result, the sympathetic nervous system prepares to escape. Here, contrary to the energy of rage, which rises up to the scapular waist, the energy of fear goes down the lower limbs. The legs prepare to run and the anticipation that the person may have to run for a good while may give him the urgency to empty out the sacs of urine and faeces to run faster. This is why, sometimes, a scared person may experience urinary or bowel incontinence.

See *Bowel – large bowel – colon*

Bowel – large bowel – transverse colon

This is a bridge between the ascending colon and the descending colon.

See *Bowel – large bowel – colon*

Bowel – large bowel – ulcerative colitis

An ulcerative colitis happens when there is an acute or chronic inflammation of the large bowel. In several European countries they use expressions that illustrate tensions related to Ulcerative Colitis: "a guy who rolls on somebody else's faeces", "Ass licker." These expressions show the thinking pattern of a person who wants to gain approval from others. This is a person who sacrifices his own life to serve someone else. He is an hypocrite, ass licker, a brown-noser.

The person with an ulcerative colitis has pain, diarrhoea, and loses blood and mucous. Blood and mucous are basic substances of life, vital substances.

The body shows that the person renounces his identity, his life, for fear of being alone. The person needs someone else, needs company, even at the cost of loosing his own identity. It may happen due to issues with the spouse (husband or wife) (or someone at home) or an employer.

The person gives his life to another and bleeds and sweats from the anus.

See *Bowel – large bowel – colon*

Bowel – large bowel – upper rectum

The upper rectum is located after the sigmoid. It is connected with decision-making. "Shall I defecate or not? Do I let go or not?" This is the area for terminal decisions. We are at the end of the intestine. This is an area for problems with grave consequences or problems involving deadlines.

Problems at the junction of the sigmoid and the rectum show that the person understood that he must let go of something, that he must truly make a decision. The person hesitates, however, because he is not sure of what he must let go. That is when **cancer** of the rectum happens, when the person feels great tension and does not share it, does not verbalize it. The cancer shows that the person experiences a great tension dealing with indecision and attachment. Tension, in this case, is due to the lack of strength to decide.

See *Bowel – large bowel – colon*

Bowel – small bowel – Crohn's disease

This chronic inflammation affects primarily the bowel but may affect any part of the digestive canal.

It is an inflammation of the ileum, the final segment of the small bowel. It may also affect the colon. The most common symptoms include abdominal pain, diarrhoea, weight loss, fever, painful spasms, blood loss, and anal fistulas. There may also be skin and joint problems.

Though the symptoms are similar to those of **ulcerative colitis**, Crohn's disease affects all layers of the intestinal wall, while ulcerative colitis affects only the innermost layer.

In several European countries, they use expressions that articulate tensions on the mind related to Crohn's disease: "the guy who rolls on somebody else's faeces", "Ass licker." These expressions illustrate the thinking pattern of a person who wants to gain approval from others. This is a person who sacrifices his own life to serve someone else. He is an hypocrite, ass licker, a brownnoser.

Among other symptoms, the person with Crohn's disease loses blood and mucous. Blood and mucous are basic substances of life, vital substances.

The body shows that the person renounces his identity, his life, for fear of being alone. This person needs someone else, needs company, even at the cost of loosing his own identity. This may happen due to issues with the spouse (husband or wife) (or someone at home) or an employer.

The person gives his life to another and bleeds and sweats from the anus. The individual may also suffer from skin and joint problems. Skin problems show fear of separation, which, again, shows that the person is, in fact, afraid to be alone. Problems with the joints are associated with inflexibility of thinking and undervaluation issues. This also supports the theory that the person cancels himself out, gives his life to another, and totally loses his value. He does it at the mercy of great inflexibility regarding thinking patterns that he adopted but do not work for him. However, he insists on keeping these patterns, either because he is deeply attached to family and past beliefs, or because some member of the clan or family does not allow him to change the way he thinks. A person with Crohn's disease suffers from major lack of discernment and sensibility.

See diarrhoea and cancer in *Bowel – small bowel (diarrhoea and cancer)* and the duodenum problems in *Bowel – small bowel – duodenum*

Bowel – small bowel – duodenum

The word duodenum means "twelve fingers of length" which does not offer much light regarding the function of the duodenum, but rather regarding its size.

The duodenum is part of the digestive tube. It is the first segment of the small bowel. The duodenum is strongly attached. It receives vessels from the pancreas and the liver. It is here that they start the selection, the overseeing. The duodenum is attached to the lumbar dorsum spine. This is the point where the spine does its inflexion. So, the duodenum represents rhythm.

"Am I in good rhythm? If all goes too fast, I may not digest properly." We saw that small bowel (diarrhoea and cancer) problems are related to fear and discernment. Here, additionally, we have an issue of rhythm.

A **gastroduodenal ulcer** has to do with a person's relationship with others. These others are people who are close family members, friends, and people from work. They include the spouse, people who live in the home, co-workers, and the female role model (biological Mother).

The person is unable to digest. The outside world is too large and compact for the person to take in. The individual fails to find his identity in his small world.

The image we choose to illustrate the person with duodenum problems is that of a person with a water hose in his mouth: "I cannot deal with so many emotions." The individual constantly moves things around in order to understand what goes on. It is important to take a look at his intimate and professional development, but most of all at his home life.

A baby born with **hypertrophic pyloric stenosis**, a condition characterized by a closed pylorus (the pylorus is a valve which regulates the passage of semi-digested food from the stomach to the duodenum), is a baby born without suitable rhythm for the family that he is to join. The child cannot adapt and refuses to accept love, the nourishment of life. This is a child who felt a lack of love during his time in the mother's womb. It is a person with a tendency to have liver problems, since the liver is associated with tensions that result from a sensation of lack of nourishment, lack of love.

See a possible ileum problem in *Bowel – small bowel – Crohn's disease* and see diarrhoea and cancer in *Bowel – small bowel (diarrhoea and cancer)*

Bowel – small bowel (diarrhoea and cancer)

The small bowel belongs to the fire element of the five elements of eastern philosophy. It makes up the fifth, and next to last, segment of the digestive tube. It is divided into duodenum, jejunum, and ileum.

The small bowel gets some help in its digestive functions from secretions of the liver (bile) and of the pancreas as an exocrine gland which are injected into the duodenum. The large bowel (colon) absorbs primarily liquids.

Digestion proper takes place in the small bowel. The small bowel separates the ingredients and assimilates nutrients. The bowel analyzes, discerns, and separates just like the rest of the elimination system (sweat glands, kidneys, and intestines). The small bowel, in its assimilation function, stands for nutrition, the relationship with the Earth, with the biological Mother, which symbolizes Earth. In the small bowel we find problems related to home, family, money, family budget, and work. (All root problems.)

People who suffer from **cancer** of the small bowel are people who do not like to look forward and confront their problems. They are afraid to look. Since the person is afraid, he does not look and looses his capacity to discern. Therefore, he cannot digest because, if he does not look, he is forced to absorb everything, without discrimination, and that is impossible. Yes, it is impossible to absorb everything without discrimination. So, these people release without digesting, without even looking. "I don't want to see that." And they come to the conclusion: "I can not digest everything, so I prefer not to look." It is a vicious circle.

People who suffer from cancer are individuals who are unable to verbal-ize their fears and their inability to discern. Subsequently, they are usually opinionated people who always have something to say. They are not humble; they are bony people, dry, and somewhat bitter. They are in constant denial.

In the bowel we find disorders of assimilation and discernment associated with fear. **Diarrhoea** (I'm shit scared) is caused by anguish and fear. One may die from hunger if he does not digest. Diarrhoea causes the person to lose much fluid and may result in dehydration, a sign of inflexibility. The person has many fears and needs some flexibility in his life. So, he must drink plenty of water.

When the body develops diarrhoea, it is telling us: "don't hold on to the consequences, don't fear what may happen. Don't hold on, do not get attached." The body does not lie. The body forces the person to release. The student who must understand all that he learned but is not able to differentiate what he must remember from what he does not have to, does not assimilate. Therefore, he has a violent bout of diarrhoea.

We are less conscious of tensions related to bowel problems than we are of tensions related to the stomach. Many times they express themselves as spasms. **Spasm and colic**: "Either I control or I release." People who never have an opinion, or a critical opinion, people we refer to as having no backbone, people with no character, are also prone to intestinal problems. In their case, the cause is more likely found in the pancreas (in its digestive function) than in the small bowel.

All tensions that a person feels in the small bowel are associated with his roots, and in particular with the home, spouse, work, and the female role model (the biological mother).

See a possible ileum problem in *Bowel – small bowel – Crohn's disease* and the duodenum problems in *Bowel – small bowel – duodenum*

Brain

Human beings have two centres: the brain and the heart. Reason, rationality, mind, are in the brain, whereas emotion and feeling reside in the heart. The mind alters emotions. Emotions alter the heart. The brain and its way of thinking affect the person's experience of emotions and, consequently, the heart.

The brain stores the various stages animal life has undergone on earth. The sexual, preservation and perpetuity conflicts of the species are obviously contained in these stages. In the animal world, the perpetuity of the species has always been the most important factor. The species come first, only then the individual. And territory has always played an essential role in life on Earth.

The family, in its raw and original stage, is imprinted on the brain. In this world of earth life matter into which we have incarnated, duality is always present, marked by day and night, *yin* and *yang*, **man** and **woman**, large and small... This duality means there is an insert. Whenever there is harmony,

there is something that fits, a complementarity. This is why in animal life on Earth it became necessary to create duality in the family, so as to ensure the perpetuity of the species and thus differentiate the genders, to allow one to look after the children and the other to guarantee protection. This is the reason for the difference between the genders in biology. In primitive societies, male behaviour had the purpose of protecting and hunting, and female behaviour had the purpose of looking after the children.

Whenever there were attackers, men fought them off and women fled with the children.

But, if the attackers were stronger than the men in the family, who could protect the species and guarantee its survival? Good question. This is when another distinction, equally dual, was created. Not all of the men fought. It was necessary to have two types of men and two types of women.

There were **right-hand** and **left-hand** sided men and right-hand and left-hand sided women. The same happened with animals. Some were left-hand sided and others were right-hand sided.

Therefore, part of the men went fighting, while the other part fled. Part of the women went fighting, the other part had to flee.

Women only fought when necessary. Whenever nature could decide, it was only left-handed people who fought. The order for fighting was as follows: first, the left-handed men, then, the right-handed men, and only then could women participate, first, the left-handed and, then, the right-handed.

Male behaviour (*yang* behaviour) is one of fighting and female behaviour (*yin* behaviour) is one of fleeing, although, from an anatomical perspective, either men or women can do both.

Fleeing has the purpose of protecting the species. It is **not** cowardness; it is the protection of the species, although nowadays men who run away are called chicken. And, in biology, the preservation of the species is the most important thing, as we have seen earlier.

In the animal world, fleeing is as noble as fighting. We are now referring to working at the level of the *yin* (female) and *yang* (male) behaviours.

In the brain cortex hemispheres, there is a right side that is female and a left side that is masculine. The **right side of the brain** is creative, soft, sensitive, flexible, submissive and passive, *yin*; **the left brain** is powerful, wilful, hard-working, combative, confrontational, commanding and active, *yang*.

It is commonly stated that the right side of the body is commanded by the left side of the brain, and that the left side of the body is led by the right side of the brain.

According to this reasoning, one could deduct that right-handed humans would be more *yang* (functioning with the left brain hemisphere, more *yang*, and more masculine), and left-handed humans would be more *yin* (using the more *yin*, female, right side of the brain), and this would re-sult in left-handed people fleeing and right-handed people fighting. However, that is not what was stated above. It does not happen like that at all. This is due to the fact that there is a double crossing in the brain.

The two brain hemispheres, right and left, of the cortex, each cross and affect the opposite side of the body but, in a different area of the brain, at the medulla, they cross again. There is, therefore, a double crossing. When it comes to protection, the fuse is at the level of the medulla, not that of the cortex. This fuse can be found where there is conflict and it acts like a switch. Therefore, and from a perspective of **constitution**, right-handed people function from the right hemisphere of the medulla (and left hemisphere of the cortex). Left-handed people function at the level of the left hemisphere of the medulla (and right side of the cortex).

From a **condition** standpoint and not one of constitution, the brain polarity and a person's behaviour depends on whether we are in a situation of aggression/protection (medulla) or in a situation of communication (cortex).

In other words, in case of aggression and protection of the species, left-handed people are always the first to attack, because of their constitution. However, in a communication stage, left-handed people may be less aggressive.

We can conclude that, from a constitution perspective, left-handed people are more aggressive than right-handed people, male or female. But from a condition standpoint, that is, way of living, thinking, being, left-handed people are not necessarily more aggressive than right-handed people.

Let us imagine that in nature, amidst a community, a snake suddenly shows up. The issue now is one of aggression and protection.

Therefore, the women are the first to run away, followed by right-handed men. Left-handed men will attack. In the absence of left-handed men, the attack will be led by right-handed men, while the women will flee. If there is only one man and if he is right-handed, he may choose to run away or fight. The right-handed woman, nevertheless, will always flee.

During pregnancy, left-handed women experienced increased permanency of Heaven's energy, or *yang* energy from the Father. As we have seen earlier, it is a matter of physical constitution.

See *Brain – left-handed men, Brain – left-handed women, Brain – right-handed men, Brain – right-handed women, Brain – brain disorders, Brain – tumour, Brain – blocked brain* and *Brain – double brain*

Brain – blocked brain

A blocked brain in both hemispheres means total dysfunction; Loss of meaning. A person in this condition needs to exit life. Normally, he will find two ways. The spiritual elevation illusion path of the badly lived spirituality, experienced in separation, in the sense of sect, in the loss of the concept of au-

thority, in giving up being in charge of one self, in the judgement of others, in the need to find his identity in a separatist group which will be his consolation and comfort and which, on many occasions, will lead to the death of the person and to the collective death of the separatist group. The need for isolation has just found a perfect solution. And, as a result, the person dies.

Or alternatively, the person will find the fastest way of getting under through **suicide**. It is a short cut. It is the fastest route to the final destiny. It is radical isolation.

In any of the cases, the sense of awareness should be sufficient to restore balance and unblock the brains. One needs to accept the tears. The person must become aware of what he felt, of what provoked this blockage. A big emotion has been repressed.

Brain – brain disorders

The symptoms we have in the brain, which will be dealt with separately, result from an excessively Cartesian life, too remote from our sensitive side, and from fears regarding our ability to control everything and everybody, from a lack of humility. They are a consequence of the repetition of a too masculine and Cartesian pattern that exists in the family.

Brain – double brain

There are people who separate their brains. Each half brain will provide an answer. The person acknowledges both realities but cannot split up, create divisions, decide. These are people with a double brain.

This could happen to children from divorced parents, who have two homes, two beds, two bedrooms. Or where there are two ethnic groups, two religions, two cultures.

These people need solutions for almost everything. They may be in constant doubt. For this reason, they will need two solutions: a car and a motorbike, for instance. Or they always need the opinion of two people. It is important to explain to people who have a double brain that this is not a problem, only a way of living. And this is all right. This is their way of finding balance. This form of living must be accepted.

The person with a double brain can never be a leader. He is too versatile, and he may make two contradictory decisions. Double brain people are indecisive. Yet, watch out, because there are indecisive people who do not have a double brain.

Brain – left-handed men

As a result of their constitution, left-handed men use much more the left brain than the right brain, and they can be quite hard, strong, with masculine attitudes and aggressive.

For them, work is a matter of survival, much more than for right-handed men.

When facing problems at work, they are confrontative and, if possible, they will fight. They are warriors. Fights at work are relatively acceptable to them.

They are dominating men and expect women to be passive.

Let us imagine that a man like this finds out that his wife has deceived him. In this case, he will feel a great urge to have her back or to find another woman. He will thus attempt to strengthen his right brain, his softer side. If he fails to achieve this, he will then need to hold on to his left brain as hard as he can, thus blocking his right brain and, in the process, increasingly losing the sensitivity of his feminine side. He will become so violent that he will end up turning that aggressiveness on to himself, in various ways.

Left-handed men are naturally more aggressive, because it is part of their constitution. However, that tendency to block out their right side of the brain is not natural. It is not part of what he was meant to do when he incarnated. If he incarnated as a left-handed man, this is because amidst his family, clan, society where he lives, he has a purpose he is not allowed to question, only accept it and live as truthfully and genuinely as possible. That tendency to block out one of the sides of the brain, in this case the right side, must be observed and acknowledged, because it encloses a mental pattern that has its origins in the models of female and male the person has become accustomed to and which are not good for him, or which he may want to confront violently, despite that action bringing him no benefit.

In these cases, priority should be given to look at the model of woman he had, particularly that of the biological Mother. The model of woman comes from the female pattern he has become used to, or which he wants to resist, when living with his biological Mother, Grandmother, Great Grandmother, aunts, etc. How did this left-handed man feel the contact with the women of his Mother's lineage, even with his Mother? Were they very masculine women? How did he feel amongst them?

Then, one should also look at the model of biological Father he had. The model of man also comes from the pattern he has become used to, or which he wants to resist, when living with his biological Father, Grandfather, Great Grandfather, uncles, or even the absence of a man model.

Brain – left-handed women

As a result of their constitution, left-handed women use much more the left brain than the right brain. They are very masculine and quite *yang* women.

If a woman of this type has a problem at work, she will be aggressive and confrontational; she will meet conflict in the eyes. For her, work is a fighting arena which she will not turn her back to. However, if, for example, she is fired, she may then block out her left brain in order to allow the right side to develop, and thus be able to carry out more feminine tasks, such as looking after her family. The problem is, if her performance is soft and little motivated to carry out feminine tasks, or, if, for instance, her husband deceives her

or leaves her, this will give her a natural excuse to weaken her right brain further and develop more the left side, which will impel her to commit further to work, becoming more *yang* than men, more *macho* than males. This is a door leading to a lesbian behaviour. Just one, there are more.

Left-handed women are normally more aggressive. It is part of their biological nature.

However, this tendency by left-handed women to block out their right brain is not natural.

It is not part of what a woman of this type was meant to do when she incarnated. If she incarnated as a left-handed woman, this is because amidst her family, clan, society where she lives, she has a purpose she is not allowed to question, only accept and live as truthfully and genuinely as possible. This tendency to block out one of the sides of the brain, in this case the right side, must be observed and acknowledged, because it encloses a mental pattern which has its origins in the models of female and male she has become accustomed to and which are not good for her, or to which she may want to confront violently, despite that reaction bringing her no benefit.

In this case, the person must give priority to examining her relationship with the biological Mother. The absence of the Mother or a lineage of warrior women may be at the root of this blockage. The female model comes from the female pattern she has become accustomed to or which she wants to resist, when living with her biological

Mother, Grandmother, aunts, etc.

Then she should look at the model of biological Father she had. Was he a man who annulled her mother? The male model also comes from the male pattern she has become accustomed to or which she wants to resist, when living with her biological Father, Grandfather, Great Grandfather, uncles, etc.

Brain – right-handed men

As a result of their constitution, right-handed men use much more the right brain than the left brain. They are quite sensitive, soft men, with a somehow feminine behaviour (yet not homosexual) if they let their real essence come to the fore.

Problems at work affect this type of man much more than left-handed men, but he will not be outspoken about them, because he finds comfort in the family relationships, in the relationship with his children, wife, and hobbies.

Yet, this man may not deal well with work fights or typically male wars, and this will lead him to block out his left brain. In this case, he will be highly prone to homosexuality. He will have a very feminine behaviour that is not an emotional natural impulse, but just a brain blockage, out of defence. He will become as feminine as a woman.

This is a door to male homosexuality. Yet, there are other doors.

Right-handed men are naturally, given their constitution, more feminine. However, this tendency by right-handed men to block out their left brain is not natural.

It is not part of what this type of man was meant to do when he incarnated. If he incarnated as a right-handed man, this is because amidst his family, clan, society where he lives, he has a purpose he is not allowed to question, but accept and live as truthfully and genuinely as possible. This tendency to block out one of the sides of the brain, in this case the left side, must be observed and acknowledged, because it encloses a mental pattern that has its origins in the models of female and male the person has become accustomed to and which are not good for him, or to which he may want to confront violently, despite that reaction bringing him no benefit.

In this case, the person must give priority to examining how he felt in his childhood with regard to the model of biological Father, who must have been very *macho*, demanding, and even cruel. Or his Father may have been totally absent. Or maybe this was the man model that he perceived to be that of the clan and which he became accustomed to, or which he wants to resist, when living with his biological Father, Grandfather, Great Grandfather, uncles, etc. Where is thus the man model of this person?

Then he should look at the model of the biological Mother he had. The female model comes from the female pattern he has become accustomed to or which he wants to resist, when living with his biological Mother, Grandmother, aunts, etc.

Brain – right-handed women

As a result of their constitution, right-handed women use much more the right brain than the left brain. They are quite intuitive and feminine.

When faced with a problem at work, this will not affect them that much, because their priority, as a result of their femininity, lies in the family. That is what really matters to them. When confronted by others, this does not matter that much. They run away from confrontation, not out of cowardness, but because their priority is comfort and the safety of their children.

Let us imagine that a woman of these characteristics discovers that her husband is cheating on her. In this situation, she may block out the right brain and develop as much as possible the left side, and then start working like crazy.

She will become aggressive to defend her children.

Right-handed women are naturally more feminine. Therefore, the tendency that right-handed women have of blocking out the right brain only to function with the left is not a natural tendency. It is not part of what this type of woman was meant to do when she incarnated. If a woman incarnated as a right-handed woman, this is because amidst her family, clan, society where she lives, she has a purpose she is not allowed to question, only accept and live as truthfully and genuinely as possible. This tendency to block out one of the sides of the brain, in this case the right side, must be observed and acknowledged, because it encloses a mental pattern which has its origins in the models of female and male she has become accustomed to and which are not good for her, or to which she may want to confront violently, despite that reaction bringing her no benefit.

It is important to examine first the model of biological Father she had, and how she felt about it. Was he a man who allowed himself to be asphyxiated by her Mother? The male model also comes from the male pattern she has become accustomed to or which she wants to resist, when living with her biological Father, Grandfather, Great Grandfather, uncles, etc.

Then one needs to look at the Biological mother model. The female model comes from the female pattern she has become accustomed to or which she wants to resist, when living with her biological Mother, Grandmother, aunts, etc., or even in the absence of a pattern of woman.

Brain – tumour

A tumour in the brain shows the person affected that he has a serious problem with the meaning of authority.

Authority, whose etymological root means "the one who enables growth", is always represented by a third party. He or she, who, to us, represents authority, is the one (male or female) with whom we feel we are growing. The one who makes us grow is the one who shows us the route, the rhythm, the path which we should take. He or she is the one who gives us a sense of direction, of communication and humbleness. The person who is on good terms with authority is disciplined, that is to say, he considers himself to be the disciple of that particular person. He feels he is growing with that person. For this reason, he gives himself and lives a humble life.

In our male-centred society, authority is focused on the man. On god, the father, the male figure. The person affected by a brain tumour is someone who has problems with his biological Father or with his model of father. A person suffering from brain cancer is a person with problems in his relationship with men. If the affected person is a woman, it is necessary to look at once at what is happening in her relation with her husband or living partner. The man with whom a woman lives is normally a copy of her Father. In fact, this woman would like the husband to be different. And he is not. Besides looking at what is happening with the relationship with the husband, one should find out what is going on with her relationship with the biological Father. There is a common pattern in the relationship this person has with men in general.

If the person with brain cancer is a man, look at the men in the family, the Father, the Grandfather, the Great Grandfather. Particularly at the Great Grandfather.

If the person with brain cancer is a young man or woman, look at his/her relationship with his/her Father and/or the history of the men in the clan.

As we have seen earlier, the sense of authority and direction lies in the brain. Let us imagine that a married man decides to leave home, because he no longer feels he is growing with his wife. At that very moment, the son gets brain tumour. The Father feels sorry, the family exerts a great deal of pressure and the Father changes his mind. In other words, he changes his path and does not leave home. It is likely that his son will end up dying from cancer. This is because the Father also has a problem with his sense of direction. He violated himself in his sense of direction, by changing his mind and stopping doing what made sense to him, and not leaving home.

The Father's initial intension was to leave home. This was an indication he was being genuine and acting upon his feelings. However, instead of doing it, he let illusion take over, believing that, if he stayed, he would help his son. On the contrary, instead of giving him an example of assertiveness and authority, instead of teaching him how to affirm himself, to be an authority, the Father simply gives him the opposite example. The Father annuls himself for the son. So, the son never gets to realize what he should be doing to live better with authority. For this reason, he will continue to feel the same tension, with the illusion that the problem is sorted out, and he creates cancer in his brain.

See *Authority*

Brain embolism

See *Brain stroke*

Brain paralysis

The person who suffers from brain paralysis thinks in such a way that there is little room to let things flow. He likes to control everything around him. He even attempts to control the people who have to look after him. He is ruthless with others and with himself too. The person has created a prison for himself, through his extremely rigid life.

For this reason, this person feels isolated. Since he does not like to be isolated, he feels he needs to bring the family together in a demonstration of collective love. Then he develops brain paralysis. This is an extremely violent process. It can only be orchestrated by someone who has always been very mentally oriented, and always centered on himself. If the paralysis happens to an adult woman, it is necessary to examine her relationship with her husband or with the man (men) in her life. If it strikes an adult man, it is necessary to ask which male model representation he wanted to impose on his children but failed. When brain paralysis occurs at birth, then one needs to look out what is happening between the Baby and the Father, and between the Father and the Mother. What is going on with the way men in the clan behave? Animals, including human beings, are born from Heaven to Earth. In this particular case, there was a lapse during the descent. It probably happened during pregnancy. The Father represents the power of heaven on Earth. What happened between the Father and the Mother?

See *Pregnancy – problems* and *Babies*

The person who suffers from paralysis is isolated from the world.

See *Isolation*

Also see *Paralysis* for other types of paralysis.

Brain stroke

A cerebral aneurysm demonstrates blood circulation problems in the brain. It happens to the person who is very intellectual, who wants to control everything and does not allow life to flow, the person who he a knows-it-all. This is a very *yang* person, with a very masculine stance, a true warrior. It is advisable to learn about this person's views on authority, to understand this person's relationship with the father's role, with the model of masculinity and the model of manhood. The person who suffers from a cerebral aneurysm has not acted very intellectually recently only. No, his Cartesian side, tough in nature, has been in existence for a long time. It is important to know how this person relates to his biological Father or to his male role model.

People who suffer from aneurysms are people who do not listen to emotions and are prone to rationalizing everything, a Cartesian attitude.

This type of problems occurs much more frequently in intellectual people than in people with manual occupations who have a more practical approach to things. They keep it simple.

Vascular accidents which take place in the upper part of the body (head, arms, and torso) are linked to very masculine behaviours, very *macho* attitudes, very *yang*. Vascular accidents in the lower part of the body (hips and legs) are linked to self-denial behaviours, more passive, more feminine, more *yin*.

Cerebral aneurysms, **brain embolism**, they are all considered as brain strokes.

The heart, the engine of the circulatory system and the brain are intimately connected. If you would like to look into this topic further, see *Circulatory system*, see *Heart* and see *Aneurysm*.

Brain tumour

See *Brain – tumour*

Brain tumor is a condition of the brain.

Breastfeeding

The mother's milk is a great immunization factor in babies. The child who is not breastfed is deprived of maternal contact with the mother. The child is deprived of the milk and of the sense of protection that comes from being held on the Mother's lap. This child will have a tendency to develop lactose intolerance.

When the child is not breastfed, it reveals that the Mother does not wish to feed him, to protect him, or to take care of him personally.

This decision may reflect the Mother's conscientious will due to discomfort, time constraints, or any other reasons. It may also be because the Mother does not produce milk. However, mothers who do not produce milk are those to whom the body simply shows (by not creating milk) that they have little desire to feed the child.

Breast **mastitis** is an inflammation of the mammal glands caused by the concentration of milk and is more common during post partum, mainly following the first gestation. The mastitis may occur in one or two breasts at the same time and the symptoms include pain, swelling, redness, and increased temperature of the breasts. It shows that breastfeeding is not an easy process for the Mother of the new-born child. It is natural and desirable that all children be breastfed by their mothers. It is through breastfeeding by the Mother that the child experiences with greater harmony the passage from the world of unity, from where he came, into the world of duality he entered, upon earthly incarnation. The child spent nine months sheltered in the Mother's womb, completely fed and loved in a totally darkened environment, sheltered from outside interventions. The child was literally part of the Mother. Delivery is a violent moment of descent into the world of duality for the Mother and for the child, although it was desired by both. It is a moment of difficult adaptation for the child. To be deprived from the physical contact of regular breastfeeding with the Mother is a violent event for the child. When this happens, the passage between the two worlds is done without transition, without gradual adaptation. Besides, as stated above, the mother's milk is a great source of immunization and, in this case, the child is deprived of it.

In some cases, the child does not tolerate the mother's milk. **Intolerance** of mother's milk must be considered in the same manner we consider intolerance of cow's milk. The intolerance of cow's milk is much more common. The child who is lactose intolerant is a child who, whenever in the presence of milk, is reminded that his Mother left him and, at that moment, develops a skin problem. Skin problems always indicate separation. And, after all, that is what happened. The child felt the separation from the Mother. The lactose intolerance is no more than a reminder of the separation from the Mother.

In the whole animal world, milk symbolizes the Mother and the relation with the Mother.

Let us now consider the opposite case, the case of the adolescent or teenager who drinks milk every chance he gets. This also shows a problem with the biological Mother but, in this case, it shows the inability to cut the umbilical cord. This is the child who continues to need his mother. In the case of females, they will have a difficult time assuming the role of mothers if they bear children, since they still consider themselves simply as daughters.

In the case of men, they will have the tendency to select women who resemble their Mothers. They anticipate problems with their spouses whom they will treat as if they were their mothers, and not their wives.

Breasts

Any breast-related problem denotes a woman who has a problem living with her femininity. This happens for several reasons. Either because she forgets she is a woman and believes that she is just a Mother, or because she leads an excessively regimented, controlled, very *yang* life.

The following five situations are common to symptoms in the breasts. Each has its own particularity, but they are all linked to the femininity that the woman refuses to live.

To solve breast cancer effects only, without dealing with the causes (through surgery, for instance) leads, later in life, to the reappearance of those causes, through other symptoms in another feminine part of the woman.

See *Breasts – cancer in the milk ducts*, *Breasts – carcinoma (nipple cancer)*, *Breasts – mastitis*, *Breasts – melanoma (skin cancer)* and *Breasts – neurofibromatosis*

Also see *Cancer*

Breasts – cancer in the milk ducts

This type of cancer is related to tensions regarding separation from the husband or from a family member, and to tensions of lack of communication inside the home, either between the couple or between the couple and a son or daughter.

Keywords: separation, communication and home.

The person is anxious to embrace the person who is distant from the home, and to hold her tight against her breasts, but she cannot do it because the other person distanced himself. It may just be a temporary geographical separation, from the husband, son or daughter. It may be that the son or daughter is studying away from home, or that the husband has been professionally posted abroad. It may also be a permanent separation.

This cancer appears in the milk ducts. Cancer attacks the inner walls of the ducts. The ducts expand and produce more milk. The flow is immense. Milk is much more nutritious when the person has this breast cancer.

In this particular case, the inner dialogue in the person's conscience could be: "The kid is only here for the weekend, I have to feed him(either figuratively or physically) abundantly." Or, "my husband is only here for the weekend, I need to feed him (either figuratively or physically) abundantly".

The breast's polarity, in this case, is determined by the cerebral hemispheres of the cortex. So, for both left and right-handed women, the right breast is *yang* (masculine) and the left breast is *yin* (feminine).

The right breast, *yang*, masculine, is affected when the problem is with the husband, the man. This applies both to left and right-handed women.

If the tension is associated to a son or daughter, the conflict will take place in the left breast. Problems with a son or daughter affect the *yin* breast, both for left and right-handed women. One could ask why children affect the *yin* breast. The answer is simple. For these women who get breast cancer, sons and daughters will, in their minds, always be children, delicate, tender, *yin*, whether they are sons or daughters. This explains why the *yin* breast, which is the breast of sensibility, is affected if the situation is related to children. Even when they become adults, this woman will continue to treat them as if they were very young, pre-adolescent children.

If only a small conflict in the conscience occurs, the woman will only get eczema, but, if the conflict is big, she will develop a tumour in the ducts. She only gets the tumour because she is unable to verbalize her feelings.

Please see *Breasts – carcinoma (nipple cancer), Breasts – mastitis, Breasts – melanoma (skin cancer)* and *Breasts – neurofibromatosis*

Also see *Cancer*

Breasts – carcinoma (nipple cancer)

Breasts nourish and protect ("to give the child her breast")

Mothers who protect adult sons or daughters, hen mothers, the so-called priority mothers, correspond to the pattern of women with nipple breast problems. They use their mother side more than their woman side. The nipple represents everything the woman believes to be a priority. The person thinks she is indispensable to the other members of the family, particularly to the children and husband.

In her understanding, if she is absent (we are not talking about the feeling of being separated because the other person went away, but about her feeling that she cannot be present – she is the one who is absent), the other person will not be able to manage. She is the one who feeds him. She is the one who knows. This is an absolutely ghastly feeling. And it is also a very masculine, very *yang* attitude. She deals with her husband and children as if they were mentally retarded.

The Mother who feels abandoned by the son (the son lives because he is tired of having the hen on top of him) also falls into this pattern. She sees it as a break. This tension in the conscience may be felt regarding virtual sons. For example, this is the case of someone the person in question looks after as if he was a son, although he is not.

It may also happen to the woman who was not loved, not protected, not embraced by her own biological Mother, or even not breastfed by her.

Here, in the nipple, polarity is different. Here we have a difference between left and right hand-sided people: the problem associated to excessive protection of children or husband always shows up in the *yin* breast, feminine, delicate, this is, in the left breast of the right-handed woman and in the right breast of the left-handed woman. It happens in the left breast, in right-handed women, because they use the right arm when giving their breast to the child, when breastfeeding. And vice-versa, for left-handed women.

Animals may also develop breast cancer. However, in animals, the situation is temporary and disappears naturally when they get pregnant again.

In humans, it gets more complicated due to the person's own beliefs and thoughts.

When somebody who may symbolize aggression against the person's nest intervenes, the lesion is on the *yang* breast, not on the *yin*. It can be a tension with the husband, for example, but not in his role of the protected one, but rather in his role as the aggressor. This affects the right breast of the left-handed woman, and the left breast of the right-handed woman. Effectively, the *yang* breast, masculine, is associated to the man. This is because, regarding protection, this is the breast which is closest to the hand that one gives the child when it becomes necessary to hold it to protect him or her.

The nest's aggressors can be, for example, the Father who leaves home to be with another woman, or the Father who cheats on the Mother. In this situation, we are referring to the woman who feels she was betrayed, cheated on, deceived. And someone very close (almost always the husband) did this to her.

If the cause for aggression was the mother-in-law who wanted to separate everything about the couple, the *yang* breast will equally be the one that is affected. Even if the aggressor is a woman. The aggressor, man or woman, is always perceived as a *yang* force, masculine, warrior, aggressive.

The breast is an exclusively feminine organ.

The nipple is masculine and feminine, although the male nipple, from a hormonal perspective, is not prepared to produce milk. Although it rarely happens, there are men who get nipple cancer. The reasons for it are the same as in women. The only difference is that, in this case, we are dealing with a man who has completely blocked his masculine brain, who has feminised himself to such an extent that he developed the same symptoms as a woman regarding his own children or, more likely, regarding those he considers to be his virtual children in life. If he is homosexual, it may be a tension he has developed regarding his boyfriend.

Please see *Breasts – cancer in the milk ducts, Breasts – mastitis, Breasts – melanoma (skin cancer)* and *Breasts – neurofibromatosis*

Also see *Cancer*

Breasts – mastitis

Mastitis is an inflammation of the glands of the breast, caused by accumulation of milk. It happens more frequently after childbirth, mostly after the first pregnancy. Mastitis may affect one or the two breasts, causing them to become red, hardened, painful and hot.

Please see *Breasts – cancer in the milk ducts, Breasts – carcinoma (nipple cancer), Breasts – melanoma (skin cancer)* and *Breasts – neurofibromatosis*

Also see *Cancer*

Breasts – melanoma (skin cancer)

In this case, tension is associated to filth, disgust, to an aggression perpetrated against the person's identity. Like the case of a woman who was raped or grabbed. "They have soiled me, stained me, I have been damaged, raped! It was filthy!" In this case, it is not possible to find out, in terms of right or left side, which breast was affected. The symptom occurred in one of the breasts. Besides, looking for which is *yin* and which is *yang* is not even interesting, because the person will immediately identify who was responsible for her tension.

Please see *Breasts – cancer in the milk ducts, Breasts – carcinoma (nipple cancer), Breasts – mastitis,* and *Breasts – neurofibromatosis*

Also see *Cancer*

Breasts – neurofibromatosis

This indicates a problem at the nervous extremities. The tension here is associated to a desire to be no longer touched, or even to a wish for physical separation, even if of temporary nature, due to lack of capacity to communicate. In the active stage of the person's tension, these are jelly like lumps or spots that form in the breasts, and later become hard lumps.

The lumps prevent the person from feeling contact. In fact, caressing becomes painful. The woman has succeeded to push the husband away from touching her breasts. It may also be that the woman wants to move away from the doctors who touch her breasts or who perform radiotherapy treatment on her. In short, this means driving contact away.

In this case, it is usually a woman

who rejects her feminine side and only wishes to use her breast to breastfeed her children. She is a woman who finds sexual intercourse disgusting and who does not understand that breasts can be object of female sexual pleasure. She refuses to feed her feminine Self. She is a woman who is too masculine, maybe not so much in the way she looks, but in the extremely regimented and regulated way of thinking.

Neuro comes from nerves, *fibro* comes from fibre and *matosis* means processed substances. The breast contains many nervous extremities.

Nervous extremities give the mother the sensitivity to know the child is being properly fed and that the milk is flowing. The hardening of the nervous extremities denotes great difficulty in communicating. If it affects the right breast, the communication difficulty is with a man, and if it affects the left breast, the communication difficulty is with a woman. This applies to both left and right-handed women. These nodes, cysts, fibroses, which are benign, disappear when the woman gets pregnant. Her conflict is solved. The cause is not solved, but its effect is. These women who rescind their femininity will have other manifestations in other parts of their bodies. For instance, they may have early menopause. In this case, see *Menopause.*

Please see *Breasts – cancer in the milk ducts, Breasts – carcinoma (nipple cancer), Breasts – mastitis* and *Breasts – melanoma (skin cancer)*

Also see *Cancer*

Breathing system

The breathing, or respiratory system is made up of the upper respiratory airways (nose, nasal cavities, and pharynx) and the lower respiratory airways (trachea, bronchi, and lungs).

Respiration exemplifies the highest profile of duality. If we only inhale, we die. If we only exhale, we die. We need both. The act of inhaling is a contraction and the act of exhaling is an expansion. The act of breathing holds the polarity of welcoming (receiving) or the refusal to receive (I will not take in what is not good for me); as well as the polarity of giving or not giving.

In Latin *spirare* (root of the word respiratory) means to 'breathe'. In Latin *spiritus* means 'spirit'. The Latin roots of 'breath' and 'spirit' are close. The word 'inhale' also comes from the same root. In Greek *psyke* means 'soul' as well as 'puff' or 'blow'. In Hindustani the word *atman* is very close to the German word for 'breathe', *atmen*. The same root is found in the word that describes the one who reached perfection, *mahatma*. Hindus use the word *prana* to describe the act of breathing as the carrier of vital force. In the Bible, God blows on a clay figure and brings it to life.

Also in Greek, *pneum* means wind, spirit.

The act of breathing, through its duality, connects us with the supernatural, the universe, the fountain of creation, and the metaphysical. Breathing allows us the union with life. Breathing keeps human beings from isolation.

Consequently, breathing represents contact and relationship. This contact with the outside is carried out through the alveoli.

The contact we have with another person through the skin is voluntary. Either I want to touch or not. The contact through breathing, however, is not. It just happens, period!

Asthma or bronchial asthma and skin flare-ups are related since they are both associated with contact and relationships. The first occurs in the respiratory system and the latter on the skin.

The first blow gives life, the last releases it.

The first blow detaches us from the Mother. We become individual entities.

Here we use two keywords to describe the breathing system's own duality: freedom and grasp.

In the breathing system, there is right side, *yang*, and left side, *yin*, and polarity in organs which are paired such as tonsils, lungs, bronchi and bronchioles. They are communication issues associated with cerebral hemispheres. The polarity does not apply to the pleura.

So, for all humans, right-handed and left-handed, the right side is *yang* (masculine) and the left side is *yin* (feminine).

Problems on the *yang* side show that the person felt victimized by a man and on the *yin* side, victimized by a woman.

Bright's disease

See *Kidneys – renal insufficiency*

Bronchi

Bronchial problems are less serious than lung problems. As opposed to what happens with lung problems, these are problems of a more intimate relational nature, more familiar and related to people who are close to us. This includes also people with whom we have been for a long time, such as colleagues.

Bronchitis and **bronchiolitis** result from an inflamed family environment, characterised by arguments and shouting. Sometimes, they reveal the feelings of those who do not want to yell but who experience an inner screaming feeling.

In French the expression used is "On s'engueule", which means "we yell at each other". However, the word *gueule* means muzzle. The muzzle is the area comprising the nose down to the beginning of the chest, and it includes the throat and jaws. This is the area affected by bronchitis. Bronchial problems remind us of territorial conflicts animals have, a territory which is linked to sex and females, but which, in humans, is more associated to issues pertaining to the home, work and family. In this particular case affecting the bronchi, tensions are more linked to the home territory, although some work issues are also covered: "Let me breathe!"

A yell ("un coup de gueule") is a rush of air that comes from the bronchi.

In the presence of a bronchial problem, the question that must be posed is: "Do I have sufficient respect for myself in order to be able to defend my own territory?"

Territory conflicts represent a male conflict in animals and also in human beings.

When bronchitis and mucose infection occur, this is after the yelling and the psychological tension took place.

If the person realizes that the tension is over, he will understand that the conflict has gone and, consequently, that bronchitis will disappear fast.

Bronchi are commanded by the cerebral hemispheres, as they deal with communication issues. For this reason, the right bronchus is *yang* (male) and the left is *yin* (female), both in the case of right and left-handed people. Thus, a lesion in the *yin* bronchus shows yelling (or desire for a yelling session) with a woman, and. in the *yang*, indicates yelling (or desire for a yelling session) with a man.

The smoker who takes in the smoke stimulates the bronchi. It is his way of saying "I am marking my territory". It is a male attitude.

A woman who smokes is marking her territory. Woman smokers are more aggressive.

People with bladder problems often have bronchial problems. In fact, in both cases, we are in the presence of territorial conflicts.

See *Tabagism*

Bronchopneumonia

Inflammation of the bronchi.
See *Bronchi*

Bruises (ecchymoses)

This is a coagulation in the blood provoked by trauma. When a person bruises very easily, this is because he has a weakness in the so-called conjunctive tissue. It denotes inner lack of elasticity and some degree of mental inflexibility: Too much control and inability to let things flow. Examine each of the places where the bruising took place.

See *Haematomas*

Bulimia

It is one of the causes of obesity.

If the hunger to live is not sated with the experiences lived, it will get transferred to the body as hunger for food. Bulimia is an attribute of people who have the illusion they can fill the emptiness in their lives with food. These are people who lack love.

People suffering from bulimia live love at the level of the body. Feeding themselves is a way of giving themselves love. Those who suffer from bulimia live under a lot of anxiety. They need to store up reserves.

When these people are women, they will put on weight, mostly around their female parts and the legs. In the case of men, they will put on weight mostly around their shoulders (male waist) and their bellies. However, this rule does not apply to everyone.

Men suffering from bulimia fear losing their vigour and their territory. They are afraid of losing their resources. This could be from a sexual viewpoint. Those suffering from bulimia, be them women or men, are people who feel strongly attached to their Mothers. They intend to solve everything by eating food. And, accordingly, the biological Mother is the first feeding symbol in our lives.

People suffering from bulimia feel a strong inertia to start their lives again. It is possible for a man to start suffering from bulimia after losing his mother, to whom he was deeply attached.

See *Obesity*

Bunions

Bunions result from an inflammation and enlargement of the inner portion of the joint at the base of the big toe. It causes the joint to project outwards and the big toe to turn towards the smaller toes. Sometimes there is also bone dilation.

This symptom is much more frequent in women than in men.

The part of the toe where the bunion occurs corresponds to the liver meridian. In fact, the liver meridian pushes the spleen meridian out.

Bunions can be very painful. There are two keywords here: **discernment** and **fear of scarcity**. This scarcity may be of money, of food or of love.

The first thing to check here is the relationship with the biological Father, the husband/boyfriend, or the male model. People with bunions may be megalomaniacs and have a great desire for expansion, to the point of losing any sense of discernment of what they truly need.

This extends to what they eat and drink, and of course to their relationships (fear of scarcity in love). Since the beginning of time that megalomania is a masculine characteristic. The great territorial conquests, conquests of power, and love conquests, were perpetrated by men.

The person with bunions has an overly masculine behaviour, excessively *yang*, lacking discernment, and with a great fear of not having enough.

Bunions happen more frequently to women. But to women with a very masculine behaviour.

Burns

The person feels burnt inside. What the external agent that burns the person is doing is to show the person what he is like inside. It is interesting to see in which part of the body the burning occurred. In any case, we are in the presence of a strong feeling of aggression that the person experienced regarding someone. The person has a major communication problem with someone close. If the burn is on the leg, this indicates tension at home, with the biological Mother or the female model. If it happens in the upper part of the body, it indicates tension with the biological Father, with the male model, with a boss and with the goals to be attained.

A mother who, at the time of conception or during pregnancy, kept thinking she would get burnt, and lived with that fear without verbalizing it, may have led the baby, upon birth, to make that tension clear and ending up being the one who got burnt.

In this case, see *Family*.

Burping

See *Aerogastria*

Bursitis

Bursitis is the inflammation of a bursa, which, in turn, is a fluid-filled sac, lined with synovial membranes, placed near the joints and whose purpose is to avoid friction between the tendon and the bone, the tendon and the muscle, or even to protect the bone protuberances.

Bursitis is the inflammation of a fluid-filled sac. It indicates impotence and passivity, as well as a great deal of undervaluing.

See *Bunions* and *Joints*

Buttocks

The buttocks are the posterior part of the human body. In many languages they are called the "posterior", and, sometimes, they are called the cheeks of the bum. The French call them *fesse*, which, etymologically, means "crack". The buttocks are located in the person's feminine waist. People with wider buttocks are more feminine. In fact, nowadays, the masculinization of women has implied that they have increasingly thinner, more masculine buttocks.

Buttocks are a symbol of femininity, of giving, but also a sexual symbol.

Buttock related problems denote tensions in accepting the person's feminine side, or sexual problems. Cellulite on the buttocks reveals a tight protection of anything that is sexually related.

If you have problems in the bone that can be felt in the buttocks, it means you have problems in your iliac bone.

See *Vertebrae – sacral vertebrae*

Buzzing noise

See *Tinnitus*

Cancer

A cancer cell is not an agent that attacks the body from the outside. It is a cell that, at a particular moment and for a particular reason, decides to alter its job at the service of a particular organ. This cell has ceased to identify itself with the community where it fulfilled its role. It is a cell which starts pursuing its own objectives, with intense determination, and it is a lot more productive than other cells. A breast with cancer produces more milk.

And what was the reason why the cell decided to change its role? This is the crucial question that needs to be asked. The reason is that life in the organism where it performed its task is no longer adequate.

Fighting a cancer cell only makes it stronger. Let us recall what we said at the beginning of this book: Everything starts at conscience level. In other words, the person has created cancer through his own way of thinking and living.

We need to understand what message the cancer cell is telling us about our lives. We need to understand what we need to change in our lives. Cancer allows us to unravel our mental addiction, the causes of our suffering.

There is no space for cancer when the person respects himself just as he is, in his essence, fundamental nature, when the person does not exaggerate or annul anything in him.

Cancer is the product of deep tension in a person's life, which, for some reason, he decided to hide and repress.

It is important to find out in which part of the body cancer occurs, and understand what that part of the body is trying to show us (see each organ separately). In any case, the less a person verbalizes his emotional tensions, the more his body will show him those very tensions in the form of a symptom, and, in the case of intense repressed tension, in the form of cancer. It is important to persuade the cancer patient to realize and understand what is going on in his conscience. To be at a hospital ward where all the patients are experiencing the same type of tension, for instance the same type of cancer, allows us to realize, by talking to those people, that all of them share a common tension in their consciences. There is a clear common denominator in those patients.

When there are other cancer areas subsequent to the so called initial cancer, this means that a succession of conflicts, tensions, took place in the person's conscience, provoked by the tension caused by the original cancer (the trigger). It is these other often cascading conflicts that give origin to problems and symptoms in different parts of the body.

Here is an example of cascading tensions in the conscience:

Starting point occurrence, tension trigger: a woman underwent breast cancer surgery and had her breast removed. The cascade could start at this point, which, in this case, is just an example. This woman, due to the fact that she feels less attractive, fears her husband may leave her. Accordingly, she starts thinking she has already lost a loved one. However, she will not voice it. She keeps it silent. The tension she feels in her conscience triggers ovary cancer (if this was a man, it would be in the testicles). The loss of her husband could lead, on the other hand, to the loss of her sexual partner, and this would frustrate her very much. Here, it would be her cervical canal of uterus that would be on the spot (if in a man, it would be the prostrate) and she would end up with cervical canal cancer.

This person could also feel undervalued as she may think she was no longer able to do the things she did before. For instance, that she would not be able to keep the house clean anymore. In this case, the muscles would be affected and develop cancer.

Or she might be afraid of dying and here it would be her lung that would be at stake, and she would develop lung cancer. And, in this last case, she would worry about the loss her death would mean to her children, and then she would develop liver cancer.

If the husband indeed left her, she may think this was due to the fact that she was now less attractive and feel it was grossly unfair. "Blimey, God does not exist!" If this was the case, she might develop cancer in her pancreas. She might even develop another type of tension provoked by the worry of ending up apart from everything she loves. In this case, eczema or any other type of skin disease would develop.

This is just an example. The order in which it was presented is not important. These are potential conflict risks.

All one has to do is to ascertain if these conflicts that originate other cancers are present or not.

Let us look at another example:

A woman was dumped by her boyfriend. She feels the loss of a loved one. It affects her ovaries. If she felt it meant the loss of a potential father of her children, then her cervical canal of uterus would be affected. Or she may feel the nest is falling apart and, in this case, her breasts would be affected. Or she may feel undervalued: "I am not worth anything. I am dirty." In this case, the problem would show up in her blood. She may feel abandoned, and here she would put on weight. Or she may feel that the problem was stuck in her throat and here the tonsils would develop problems (angina). Or she may feel that she was the victim of a "bastard" action, although that feeling frightens her and she tries to avoid

it. Then she develops hyperglycaemia (diabetes). Or she feels she would like to run away from this awful truth, and then develops hypoglycaemia.

In short, it is very important to speak to the person and find out what were the cascading events and tensions she experienced and which affected her. This is because everything starts in our conscience.

In fact, if we accept that everything starts in our conscience, we will realize that we are responsible for everything that happens to us.

Responsibility, not guilt!

Extreme stress triggers off other stresses.

An intense tension may come up again when the new conflict has nothing to do with it, after all. For instance, a man who suffered from liver problems for a long time but who has sorted it out and been cured, one day experiences an undervaluing conflict (which is linked to bones and muscles) and develops a problem in his bones. This is not at all related to the liver. But this person may have liver problems again. We need to understand that what is linked to the undervaluing conflict is not the liver, realize that the manifestations in the liver are of a secondary nature and that the problems affecting the liver are not serious, since there is no loss association conflict. What happened was that the body memory brought back the recollection of the liver conflict. What is healed will remain healed. If the symptom in the liver recurs, this is because the liver was not properly cured in the first place.

Candidiasis (thrush)

This is a fungal infection (mycosis) caused by a fungus called Candida which affects the mouth and vaginal mucous membranes.

Fungal infections are of a parasitic type. The word parasite is essential, in this context. If the person lets herself be affected by parasites, this is because she is not centred, does not show firmness to the people who live around her, and it means that there is someone in her life who is a parasite and lives off her. The person is clinging to the past and to her beliefs, and this is the reason why she cannot stand up to this person who is sucking her out like a vampire with the degree of assertiveness she ought to have.

The fact that it develops both in the mouth and in the vagina is deeply meaningful. Actually, both the mouth and the vagina are places which symbolize giving one self and reception regarding the other person.

Caries

See *Teeth – caries*

Cataracts

See *Eyes – cataracts*

Cellulite

In the first place, obesity has nothing to do with cellulite. Obesity is characterized by excessive fat in many parts of the body (see *Obesity*).

Cellulite (or adiposity) is characterized by excessive subcutaneous fatty cells located in specific parts of the body.

It is a layer which forms over the dermis, provoked by an infiltration of fat. It has little to do with obesity, because obesity does not occur at the level of the dermis, and here, we are dealing with the dermis. Cellulite denotes a tight protection of everything that is related to sex (since it is on the legs and buttocks that most cellulite appears), or, if not on this part of the body, it means a tight protection of other part of the body (in this case, check that part of the body).

The tensions that provoke symptoms in the dermis are associated to feelings based on protection and aggression in their most primary meaning. They are typical of people who feel their territory invaded, feel injured in the most basic meaning of the word and who feel deep tension regarding uncleanness. This could be physical uncleanness or something disgusting that someone may have done to that person. It could be of a sexual nature, or some filthy swindle, etc.

The person who has cellulite should investigate what is going on in her life to understand why she needs to protect herself so much from sex, which is the most common situation, or from something that has disgusted her, or still does, or from a scam, a filthy swindle.

Central nervous system

See *Nervous system*

The central nervous system is a part of the Nervous system.

Cephaleas

See *Headache*

Cerebral aneurysm

A cerebral aneurysm demonstrates blood circulation problems in the brain. It happens to the person who is very intellectual, who wants to control everything and does not allow life to flow, the person who he a knows-it-all. This is a very *yang* person, with a very masculine stance, a true warrior. It is advisable to learn about this person's views on authority, to understand this person's relationship with the father's role, with the model of masculinity and the model of manhood. The person who suffers from a cerebral aneurysm has not acted very intellectually recently only. No, his Cartesian side, tough in nature, has been in existence for a long time. It is important to know how this person relates to his biological Father or to his male role model.

People who suffer from aneurysms are people who do not listen to emotions and are prone to rationalizing everything, a Cartesian attitude.

This type of problems occurs much more frequently in intellectual people than in people with manual occupations who have a more practical approach to things. They keep it simple.

Vascular accidents which take place in the upper part of the body (head, arms, and torso) are linked to very masculine behaviours, very *macho* attitudes, very *yang*. Vascular accidents in the lower part of the body (hips and legs) are linked to self-denial behaviours, more passive, more feminine, more *yin*.

The heart, the engine of the circulatory system and the brain are intimately connected.

If you would like to look into this topic further, see *Circulatory system*, see *Heart* and see *Aneurysm*.

Cerebral haemorrhage

See *Brain stroke*

Cervical

See *Vertebrae – cervical vertebrae*

Cervical canal of the uterus

See *Cervix (neck of the womb – cervical canal of the uterus)*

Cervix (neck of the womb – cervical canal of the uterus)

The neck of the womb is examined separately from the womb (uterus), because the tensions associated with the cervix are very distinct from those affecting the womb.

The neck of the womb is the passage from the vagina to the body of the womb. The word neck means passageway, corridor, narrow path. It is in the narrow path the man's penis gland rests when there is copulation.

It is important to remember that territorial issues, amongst animals, are related to reproduction. For them, the survival of the species stands above the existence of the individual.

Thus, the territory is linked to the species, to reproduction and to off-spring.

Conflicts of a sexual nature and undervaluing are included in the concept of territory. The animal that contributes towards the continuity of the species feels useful. His sense of usefulness is, in fact, indispensable. He feels fulfilled.

This animal ancestral feeling means that we, humans, feel territorial conflicts and sense of usefulness in the neck of the womb, in the case of women, and in the prostate, in the case of men.

It is in the cervix that women feel sexually and virtually fulfilled.

When a woman experiences problems in the cervix, the body is telling her that she feels sexual frustration or frustration in her life. It means she does not feel fulfilled. The loss of sexual partner, be it an actual loss of partner or frustration in the sexual act, may mean that the woman feels she is no longer useful. In fact, the woman feels territoriality in the sexual act. Without a partner, she no longer has a territory. She does not feel useful any longer. The non-verbalized feeling of lack of usefulness projects itself, literally, in the woman's neck of the womb. This is an ancestral feeling coming from the collective unconscious, from the experience of animals on Earth. However, this is a dependence related tension.

If this absence of partner tension

that the woman feels is very big, and if she fails to verbalize it, or even be aware of it, she may develop cervical **cancer**.

Here, the strictly sexual dependence may also be associated to sexual frustration. Either because the woman may always want more and her partner does not correspond to her wishes, or because the partner may always want more, which leaves her feeling like a sexual object.

After menopause, there is never a risk of cervical cancer.

When the grandfather lost all of his lands, for example, and never verbalized his frustration, his granddaughter may experience territorial conflicts or cervix problems, as well as feelings of sexual frustration (see *Family*). The granddaughter somatises the feelings the grandfather never verbalized.

When the problem is in the **junction of the neck of the womb with the body of the womb**, the tension here is different and reveals the division the person feels between being a woman and being a Mother.

This is because this area, whether the neck or the junction, is part of the genital system. It is the area of the body waters, of the influence of deep rooted beliefs, of the collective unconscious brought by the family, by the pattern of the woman of the clan, by the loose existence, guilty or not, of sex.

Charcot's disease

See *Amyotrophic Lateral Sclerosis (ALS)*

Chest angina

See *Heart – angina*

Chickenpox

This refers to communication problems and occurs more frequently in children. Chickenpox involves high fever, high blood pressure and spots that, after being scratched, will leave scars. It occurs more often to children and it denotes weariness and tension/irritation with the outside.

Eruptions indicate that something has been repressed. Eruption uncovers something that had until then remained invisible.

As in all children's diseases, eruptions bring out something new in the child, and they contribute to the significant advancement in the child's development.

The more virulent the eruption is, the quicker the child will develop.

All skin-related problems denote aggression. Being born into this world, and growing up, are not easy processes for children, because of the very strong identification of society and of the families with the ego, religious beliefs, ancient beliefs of the clan and the unstoppable absurd need to obey rules that go against nature.

The child is beginning to develop his own defenses against society.

Catching chickenpox makes the child immune to it forever.

The child goes through a mourning process of non-verbal communication (he leaves the magic world – enters the ego).

The child capitulates to the verbal reality of words.

When this occurs earlier, it is likely that a separation between his parents may have taken place.

In this case, see *Babies*

Chilblains

Chilblains are caused by exposure to cold and affect primarily the body parts that are more exposed to air and humidity: hands, feet, nose, and ears. Less frequently, they may also appear on the elbows, knees, and legs.

People who suffer from chilblains have abnormal reactions to cold and experience difficulty in maintaining the body temperature in exposed parts of the body. This is due to changes at the level of small surface blood vessels which contract and expand excessively thus keeping the blood from circulating freely and warming up the skin. Blood represents our identity and our joy of living. The circulatory system is directly associated with the experience of emotions. People with chilblains are people who control their emotions and do not free themselves or take advantage of the joys of life.

Child delivery

We are going to talk about natural birth and complications at birth.

The living process swings between two verbs, two actions: accept and set free.

It is precisely at our own birth that we start talking about life in its literal sense.

A delayed birth must be provoked by caesarean section, in the majority of cases. A child not born in a natural way, in other words, when it became necessary to resort to a caesarean section, or an epidural, or an underwater birth, is a child likely to have reduced immunity.

In fact, passing through his Mother's vagina, something that deeply contracts the baby requires a degree of effort, a *yanging* action and a fortification that will make the baby stronger and, consequently, have higher immunity.

Animals are born Heaven to Earth, from head to toes. Animals are brought down to Earth thanks to the power of Heaven. Vegetables grow from Earth to Heaven. Vegetables are taken upwards to Heaven thanks to the power of Earth.

The Heaven-Earth way of animals indicates the presence of an incarnation, and the wish to come down to Earth. This is the goal of animals.

The baby is in the dark for nine months and, after that, he is born into duality, where he will find night and day, light and darkness, *yin* and *yang*. He descends from unity (Heaven) to duality (Earth).

Birth is the first co-creation (joint creation) between three consciences. For a being to incarnate, the confluence of three wishes is required: The wish of the Father, of the Mother and of the Baby. Birth is a manifestation of fluidity in nature. It is something that should be uncomplicated. In any type of **unnatural birth**, be it through **cae-sarean**, **epidural** or **underwater**, **suction** or even **forceps**, the energy that impels birth had a hiatus somewhere in the middle. Something went wrong. It went wrong between the parents, or between the parents and each other's families. It is likely that they are going through some quarrel. Or maybe one of them, or even both, felt that something was rigid and not working in their life together. The Mother's body reflects the tension she is experiencing.

A **caesarean** section is a surgical birth delivery. And surgery is always a form of aggression. The Mother needs to be cut open to give birth and deliver the child. The coming down does not happen through the vagina. This child delivery brings no physical pain, but the psychic pain is very much there. Recovering from surgery is not an immediate process. It can be said that caesarean births constitute a form of aggression to the Mother. The body shows the person that giving birth is not a natural phenomenon. It shows her that the person is hesitant on how to welcome this new being in her home.

Epidural is a form of pain denial during child delivery. It is also an escape from natural birth. The Mother who requests an epidural is refusing to suffer and to give herself for the sake of her baby. Birth should imply pain. In fact, both feel pain; Both the Mother and the Baby. Few people think about the baby. For the baby, birth is a traumatic experience that implies the passage from a life in a golden shelter to a life of duality, where he is expected to create his own space and for which he needs to be quite strong, quite *yang*. We have seen earlier that births such as caesarean sections, epidural and underwater omit the Mother's vaginal compression and the subsequent *yanging* effort on the child's part. The Mother who requests an epidural is not aware of the epiphany that is to come. She believes she is the only one who suffers and gives in. But she is not the only one.

Child deliveries with the aid of **forceps** or through **suction** mean that the baby does not wish to come out. He does not wish to land in the middle of confusion. It denotes some kind of regret, on the child's part, about being born. Once more, one should look at the relationship between the parents. The duality the child is bound to (his new home) is not in a state of harmony. "Let me stay in my shelter…"

When the birth is **delayed**, this means the Mother felt a need to keep the baby and not let him go or not let the breaking the umbilical cord. The Mother does not want to accept the death of a cycle, pregnancy. These mothers may experience the same difficulty in letting go of their children when they leave home as adults and decide to live their own lives. It is hard for these mothers to let their children fly away.

When the birth is **premature**, it is necessary to distinguish between two situations:

The first is when the baby is in perfect health and does not require special care, other than what is normal in a birth. In these cases, the tension in the conscience of the Mother or of the Baby is not exactly relevant.

The second situation is when the baby is premature and his life may be at risk, unless he is assisted and given exceptional care. In this case, it means the Mother had to urgently get rid of the baby. What is the tension and the urgency (which has nothing to do with the delivery) that the Mother is experiencing to make her feel the need to hurry the delivery so that she can take care of that urgent matter? This Mother is disturbed about something that already exists in this world and is afraid of keeping the baby inside her any longer. Why?

If the baby is born **feet first**, not head, as would be natural, this indicates that the baby is quite *yin*. His build is less strong. It also shows that in the home he is going to, the Mother plays the Father role, and that the home is in a state of confusion and has little harmony.

If the baby has the **umbilical cord around his neck**, this means the baby tried to hang himself upon birth. It is the same tension that occurs in abortion. But here, it is felt at birth delivery. The baby runs the risk of being stillborn. "If this is what I need to put up with, I may as well hang up now. These parents of mine need to realize that this is not the plan that was initially programmed for me!"

When the baby is **stillborn**, the tension is the same as the one that occurs in abortion. The child refused to enter the home (see *Abortion*).

When the baby has the **umbilical cord around his feet**, the risk of death is not imminent. Smaller complications may, nevertheless, occur. This baby brings tension with him, and is apprehensive regarding the possibility for movement he will have in his life. "Will I be able to fit in freely?" Are the Mother's movements sufficiently free with that Father?

It is important that these babies, who had difficult or less natural deliveries, may be allowed to talk about their difficult or less natural births when they are older. It will be very useful to them. It is also important that they understand why their births were not very natural. It is paramount to ask questions about what was the psychological state of the family at the time, particularly regarding the parents' relationship.

Asking about their own births is equally very important for mothers who are about to give birth. "What happened to my Mother when she was ready to give birth? How was I born? What complications were there? What did I hear people say?"

Child paralysis

See *Acute anterior poliomyelitis (child paralysis)*

Acute anterior poliomyelitis is the common child paralysis.

Chin

See *Jaws*

Cholera

The cholera follows an earthquake, a natural catastrophe and it also occurs after a civil war, when brothers kill their brothers.

Everything shakes, everything burns, everything explodes, and then that is it.

"It is filthy! Really difficult to swallow up!". Then cholera strikes. The person empties himself out, from above and below. And he must drink 20 to 30 litres of water per day. He needs to be purified, cleansed by water.

Cholera epidemics are only declared 48 hours after the event is over, and people are contaminated through water.

The psychological conflict associated to cholera is the sensation of having lost everything at once.

When the process is an individual one, then the person will have gastroenteritis.

If it is a collective one, then cholera strikes.

See *Epidemics*

Cholesterol – high cholesterol levels

Cholesterol is a fat, and fat exists to protect people; But only to protect up to a point and in a balanced way.

Cholesterol, in balanced doses, is necessary, as it allows the person to regulate his identity and to live his life in a unique and proper way, with self-esteem. High cholesterol levels indicate that the person is protecting himself from the family and from the strand of the clan. It reveals the person is attempting to protect himself from within.

This happens, for example, when the person feels he needs to protect himself from his wife, or from his parents, or from her husband, in the case of a woman. However, the person will act in the worse possible way and will end up hurting himself. The person feels the clan has hurt him and, instead of creating a genuine life for himself, hampers the free circulation of life within him, increasingly obstructing the happiness channels (blood vessels). The person is afraid of accepting happiness and of living it. And because he feels guilty, he does not allow his life to flow.

See *Blood*

Cholesterol – low cholesterol levels

When the person has low cholesterol levels, it means that person is cancelling himself in the family and he becomes passive and powerless to such degree that doesn't even think of protecting himself, only escaping (from himself obviously).

Chronic epicondylitis

Chronic epicondylitis is an inflammation of the elbow tendons which forces the person to keep his hand closed.

It is caused by an inflammation of the small bone protuberances in the elbow, called epicondyles, and it causes pain.

The tendon is very un-expandable.

It fixes the bone to the muscle. When tendon problems occur, we are talking about a feeling of undervaluing in a certain gesture.

It is the undervaluing of the action, in the present. "He is better than me." "I cannot beat him." "I am not powerful enough." "I cannot get there." This may occur when practicing a sport or merely while crossing a street, or even while cooking or reading. It is the gesture that could also have been the gesture of confronting the other person, of going against the other, perhaps with a raised fist.

In other words, this occurs to the individual who believes he has little value compared to the other person, or to the individual who believes he is worth little because he was unable to express something to the other person, or even to the individual who has little value because he could not affirm himself regarding the goals he wished to attain.

In the case of chronic epicondylitis, in which the hand closes to a fist due to inflammation in the tendons, the person is revealing that he repressed his aggressiveness and felt undervalued for not being able to express his aggressiveness. The image of the closed fist speaks for itself (I should have punched him!" – here is the gesture). In fact, the person did not find it appropriate to explode at the right moment. The person let himself be undervalued regarding the rigidity of norms, values, regulations that he imposed or imposes on himself. And, on top of it all, this inflammation is painful. It is a form of self-violence. It is the result of tremendous control.

See *Anger*

Chronic evolving polyarthritis

It happens only to adult women. It is also called **chronic polyarticular rheumatism or rheumatoid polyarthritis**.

This occurs frequently to adults. It is associated to undervaluation. This is for adults what acute articular rheumatism is for children. This affects adults who center their lives around the question: "Am I skillful or not? Am I competent or not?"

The joints have grown old but these adults behave like children.

It only affects women.

"I would like to keep my juvenile side. I would like my gesture to be spontaneous. I must be perfect first time."

This condition is often tied to thyroid problems.

Chronic polyarticular rheumatism

See *Chronic evolving polyarthritis*

Circulatory system

It performs the functions of feeding the body, transporting nutrients through the blood, and blood purification.

It represents the delivery of life and the joy of living. It is made up of heart, arterial system, and venal system. It represents the number 8, just like the diagram of the earlier and later heavens in Chinese philosophy.

Circulation problems indicate a lack of joy to live, a lack of love for a certain part of my life, or lack of self-love. They show problems of identity and self-esteem. Blood is also the symbol of belonging to a family, a lineage, or even a clan. The lifestyle and thinking pattern of the clan is extremely important.

Blood is the centre of our emotions. Emotional problems show up in this system.

The diagnosis of problems in the circulatory system is not associated with left side, *yang* and right side, *yin*, polarity. Neither is it associated with the distinction between left-handed and right handed people. No, here side is not a determining factor.

The *yin/yang* polarity of the circulatory system is as follows: Symptoms in the arteries and symptoms in the torso, arms and head (upper part of the body) reflect excessively *yang* behaviours, very masculine, very combative. Symptoms in the veins as well as symptoms in the pelvis and legs reflect excessively *yin* behaviours, excessively passive, excessively feminine. It works the same way for left-handed and right-handed people. There is no distinction between left-handed and right-handed people.

Circulatory system – arterial system

Arteries are the more *yang* part of circulation. They transport oxygen and nutrients to the cells, except for pulmonary arteries, which carry venous blood from the right ventricle to the lungs to evacuate carbon dioxide and replace it with oxygen.

Artery problems are typical of a

more masculine behaviour, very *yang*, very regimented, very controlling, dominated by Cartesian thought, very radical.

Artery problems are more common in the upper part of the body, the more masculine part, namely in the thorax, arms, and head. Artery problems reveal an inability to deal with emotions. They show incapacity to do what is necessary to let go and be happy. **Hardening of the arteries** reflects our personal hardening. **Arthritis** shows rage, inflammation. **Thrombosis** shows control and the inability to let life flow.

Circulatory system – venal system

The veins make up the *yin* portion of the circulatory system. They carry used blood to the liver and kidneys to be filtered, except for pulmonary veins that carry oxygenated blood from the lungs to the left atrium.

Vein problems reflect a not so happy life, a passive life lacking contentment.

They are problems more characteristic of excessively *yin* behaviours, of self-denial, of a "there is nothing we can do" attitude. These problems tend to occur in the lower parts of the body, namely in the pelvic area, genitals, and legs. **Phlebitis**, **varicose veins**, **haemorrhoids** and **deep venal thrombosis** take place in the veins. It is a way of expressing that we are tired of the life we lead, that we are enraged but passive, excessively *yin*.

Clavicle (collar bone)

Clavicle comes from the word *clave*, which means key, and the suffix *icle*, which means small. This, in turn, means that clavicle is the small key.

The clavicle is part of the shoulder, the core joint of the upper limbs, thus forming part of the scapular waist, which is the masculine waist in each of us, the *yang* axis, the masculine axis, the axis of willpower, symbolised by the Father.

Collar bone fractures represent a shock at the level of deep beliefs when it comes to taking action, and, at the same time, an enormous relief of the tension the person was experiencing. They normally occur at a dynamic moment. It is the result of the major undervaluing the person experienced in his ability to deal with a professional issue, or with a money related issue, with a very well defined objective, in other words, with a typically *yang*, masculine issue.

Due to the fact that the clavicle is the small key, clavicle associated problems indicate that the person affected is having difficulty discovering the key to a question. It is a *déclic*.

Any problem in the clavicle is related to bones. And the person's undervaluing shows up in the bone. Therefore, a person suffering from collar bone related problems is having a problem in his relationship with someone, and is failing to assert himself, given the fact he has been unable to find out exactly what he should do.

This person cannot live his life in

a straightforward, fluid way, and he tends to provoke war and consider the other person the guilty one.

Therefore, the body, through the fracture, forces the person to discover in that relationship the key to his life. This person is thus forced by his body to drop his warier attitude and realize that he is also responsible for the problem and that he should take his life forward independently from the other person.

It is important to see which of the clavicles is affected, because the right side is *yang*, masculine, and the left side is *yin*, feminine, both for right and left-handed people. This *yang* right side and *yin* left side polarity is not always obvious. Therefore, it must be approached with caution. The affected *yang* side denotes relationship and lack of firmness in dealing with problems in the case of a man, and the affected *yin* side indicates relationship and lack of firmness in dealing with problems in the case of a woman.

Claw feet

See *Feet – pes cavus (hollow claw foot)*

Cleanliness – cleanliness freaks

These are people who have a vital need to be self-sufficient. They are proud people who refuse other people's assistance, who feel sick about several things, namely about sex, about what they see in other people, or about what they hear from other people. These people are more prone to skin cancer.

Coccyx

It is formed by small vertebrae joined together, in varied number but usually four. They are at the end of the sacrum vertebrae. They are the "little tail" of human beings; The tail that no longer exists. Coccyx related problems are directly linked to the person's *yin* axis, the feminine axis, the axis of femininity, symbolized by the Mother.

Here we are referring to bones on the back, and the bones are part of the locomotor system. The common denominator here, as in other vertebrae, is undervaluing. The person feels undervalued and loses his self-esteem.

Coccyx related problems represent fear of imposed homosexuality, fear of imposed excessive feminine behaviour or even compulsory submission (in the animal world, this is the case of the non-dominating wolf with his tail lowered, denoting submission).

It is important to understand what is going on in this person's relationship with his partner, with his model of Mother or his model of woman. If the person with a coccyx problem is a man, this is undoubtedly a relationship problem with the person he lives with and which creates in him the huge tension he is feeling. If the person with a coccyx problem is a woman, she needs to understand why she is so scared of her husband or of the man, and look out for the pattern of woman in her clan.

Colds

They are directly linked to the

breathing system, that is to say, to the relationship with the outside. It is important to ascertain if the person felt hit by something, or, above all, by someone. Colds reveal little sorrows and some degree of mental disorder. It is likely that there is a problem with someone living close to the affected person; Parents, husband, wife, girlfriend or boyfriend, teacher. Try to find out, in the first place, what is going on with the partner and/or at home.

Coli bacillus

It denotes the presence of bacterium in the organism which manifests itself through urinary infection. This bacterium is normally located in the large bowel, not in the urinary system. The person is confused. Something is not working at all at home. The person is on fire. His relationship with someone at home, someone close, is infesting him.

There may be several problems in the urinary system and each has its own symptom. They are all related to the way of life, the influence of family and religious beliefs, lineage, ancestors, deep social beliefs, the clan, society, as well as with the person's own birth, the relationship with the parents, and between the parents. This applies both to children and adults.

Colic

See *Bowel – large bowel – colic*

Collar bone

See *Clavicle (collar bone)*

Colon

See *Bowel – large bowel – colon*

Colour blindness (Daltonism)

See *Eyes – Daltonism – colour-blindness*

Coma

People who are in a coma, such as those who faint, suffer from amnesia or from Alzheimer, are individuals who flee because they fear something intensely. "Get me out of here!"

Basically, this is a person who enters isolation. It is a person on a deathbed, but who has not taken the last step to get completely free from all the ties. It is also a person whose brain frequency has decreased and remains at a level between zero and four brain cycles per second, which means that, from an intuitive perspective, he is awake. He has perception of what goes on around him through his intuition, although he is unable to communicate with relatives around him. It is paramount to speak to these people, telling them the truth on how we feel and not lie to them, something which most people do (lovingly, yet erroneously). The person who is in a coma perceives everything that is going on. He understands the living. But the living do not understand him. At this point, the living have to make a serious attempt to focus and understand what that person may be saying to them regarding his condition, his feelings, the ties holding him to that indefinite limbo situation. He does not depart and he does not return. He is as if stuck in the passage. He is awaiting the light, but above all, he waits for light to illuminate the living too. The person needs that the living keep talking to him, to let him know that they understood what he wanted to tell them. This is a moment of truth for the living and the person in a coma. It may last a long time, particularly in families that do not disclose their emotions, their sensibility, and shut down authenticity in their relationships and the truth in their hearts.

Conjunctivitis

See *Eyes – conjunctivitis*

Conn's disease

See *Suprarenal glands*

Constipation

Constipation results from unwillingness to give, to offer oneself and to let go. It denotes attachment. The person holds on to what he has. It could be to a person.

A money-grubber behaviour (niggardly, stingy, avaricious behaviour) will show itself in the person's large bowel.

This occurs a lot to people who are very close to their money. It indicates they are attached to material things.

These are people who pay too much importance to themselves.

The large bowel is connected to the subworld, the unconscious, and to the kingdom of the dead. It is in the large bowel that putrefaction actually takes place. It symbolizes the nocturnal side of the body.

Constipation may be a way for the body to show the person that he is afraid to let his unconscious come to light. It denotes an attempt to carry on hiding and to repress information on some beliefs.

Convergent strabismus

See *Eyes – convergent strabismus*

Convulsions

Convulsions occur when the central nervous system, whose engine is in the brain, short-circuits. This will lead to a continuous activation of all the muscles in the body, including the respiratory ones.

This symptom stems from an excessively Cartesian life, too remote from the sensitive side, and from fears regarding the capacity to control everything and everybody, and from problems with the meaning of humbleness.

Coronaries

Problems in the coronaries denote a fighting attitude, little sensitivity to emotions, and a very much *yang*, mentally oriented and egotistic stance.

See *Arteriosclerosis, Thrombosis, Circulatory system – arterial system* and

Heart

Coronary thrombosis

It is thrombosis in a coronary artery.
Please see *Thrombosis, Circulatory system – arterial system* and *Heart – heart attack*

Cough

This is the expulsion, through expiration, of something that is blocking breathing.

Dry coughs indicate that the person is feeling a strong irritation and reaction. It also shows that the person is not able to externalize the problem. He is unable of verbalizing.

Wet coughs indicate that the aggressor agent is beginning to get out. It is a good sign. Something started to be sorted out inside the person.

See *Breathing system*

Coxarthrosis

See *Hips*
The hip arthrosis is often called coxarthrosis. It occurs following undervaluing.

Cramps

Muscular problems indicate, without doubt, that the body wishes to stop. They represent an inner cry towards no-action, at least not on those terms.

Muscles reveal what happens before, during and after the action.

The **"before the action"** is charac-terized by everything related to projects to come, whatever they may be. Doubts and fears.

The **"after the action"** is related to regrets regarding the action that was taken.

The **"during the action"** concerns what the person is thinking about, either in a conscious or unconscious form, at the time the action is taking place.

In every case, muscle related problems denote a feeling of undervaluing, and they show that the individual lets himself be undervalued because he leads a life that does not flow naturally. It does not flow naturally because the person pays too much attention to what other people tell him (and/or demand from him), which means he will end up being influenced by thoughts that do not work well for him.

A cramp is an involuntary contraction. It is like a ball. The muscle goes through major contractions, as if it was at the strongest point of the action. It may occur during and after the action. But it may also take place when it is at rest, before the action. In this case, the person is resting and his Cartesian thought may throw his strongest fears and doubts on his face. "You must do it no matter what! Can you do it?"

Cramps may also occur during the action, as we have seen, namely when the person believes that he is not running fast enough and, for this reason, feels undervalued. The mental thought, the ego, impels him to run faster, and it is obvious that the person will end up with cramps during the action. The person let himself be influenced, started thinking with his ego and not with his intuition. He stopped respecting his body.

The person who has cramps is the one who demands from himself a lot of effectiveness in his actions. He has the behaviour of a predator. When the body has cramps, it is showing us that we are raising the stress levels, revealing that, once more, we are paying no notice to our intuition and are attempting to resolve everything rationally, resorting to very *yang*, masculine and controlling thoughts.

Why does this person need to show increased performance? What makes him feel undervalued if he does not succeed in attaining the desired performance? What makes him harm a part of his body? What is happening to this person's life balance? The reason is that, in fact, all the problems affecting the locomotor system, and, in particular, the muscles, have their root in the person's undervaluation. If he plays a sport in order to prove something, but in fact he does not like that particular sport, then he is acting like a predator, instead of accepting that he does not like it, and be more *yin*, less masculine, less *yang*. More focused. As it is, he is accepting himself more in the role of prey.

For this type of people, who, after all, are acting like predators due to their egos, pretending to be who they effectively are not, stop eating meat to avoid having cramps is very effective. In fact, To a prey who wishes to be a predator, if instead of meat we feed him vegetables, his body will thank us for it.

Cramps may also be abdominal. And the procedure is the same. The muscles on the right side of the body (not the muscles of the internal organs) are, in principle, *yang* (masculine) and those on the left side are *yin* (feminine) both in right and left-hand sided people. However, we must remember that we are talking about the locomotor system, and that the *yin/yang* polarity regarding the sides of the body in this system is not obvious. Cramp on a *yang* side muscle indicates lack of strength, which the person wishes to ignore due to an excessively masculine behaviour warrior like, and/or which is likely due to influences of a man's thought. On the *yin* side, it means lack of strength of the person's sensible side, which is equally ignored by the person due to the likely influence of a woman's behaviour.

Cramps occur often when playing a sport, but that exercise may simply be a way of showing the undervaluation that was already taking place on the person's mind.

Cranial trauma

See *Skull*

Cranium

See *Skull*

Crohn's disease

See *Bowel – small bowel – Crohn's disease* and *Bowel – large bowel – Crohn's disease*

Cubit bone

Bone located in the inner part of the forearm. A fracture of this bone indicates a strong feeling of undervaluing.

See *Forearm*

Cushing's disease

See *Suprarenal glands*

Cystitis

Since immemorial times, human beings, when arriving somewhere, start by fencing off the area, thus marking their territory. "It's mine!" This is deeply rooted in us, and this is how we mark off our territory. Before us, animals started by marking their territory, not with a fence but with urine. This idea of marking territory through urine is still within us.

Therefore, when a person cannot mark his territory, he has urine related symptoms.

Cystitis in children indicates that one of the parents has been unable to mark his or her territory. The child feels alone, abandoned. He does not feel able to defend his territory. Parents do not understand this and the child thinks: "What happens if our territory is attacked? Who will defend it? I am on fire! Please get your act together, mark the territory!"

Children from both genders may have cystitis. In adults, cystitis is more frequent in girls.

Cystitis and urinary infections cause a burning pain, which enables the person to understand that letting the waters of his body flow causes pain and hurts him. Cystitis is a typical girls' infection.

The woman will have problems in her bladder (urinary infection, cystitis) when she cannot manage to organize her vital space. When everything is a huge mess. The man will have bladder problems (enuresis, infection) when he fails to ring off the external borders of his territory and feels threatened in his own space.

Generally speaking, cystitis associated tensions are related to the relationship with the partner or lover. The person tends to blame others rather than accepting responsibility for his own balance.

Cysts

Check in which organ the cyst appears. Cysts are benign tumours.

Daltonism (colour blindness)

See *Eyes – Daltonism – colour-blindness*

Dandruff

See *Hair*

Dark rings under the eyes

Permanent dark rings under the eyes indicate tiredness in the kidneys. They may also be the product of a heavy night out. In this case, they do not represent a symptom, merely a direct cause-effect relationship.

Frequent dark rings in the inner corner of the eye, near the nose, denote intense activity of the suprarenal glands.

See *Kidneys* and *Suprarenal glands*

Deafness

See *Ears*
Deafness is a condition of ears.

Dementia

See *Isolation*

Dependence

See *Addiction*

Depression

The word depression comes from the Latin *deprimo*, meaning to subdue and to repress. Depression is guilt. It manifests itself through a wide range of symptoms, such as tiredness (asthenia), insomnia, constipation (see *bowel – large bowel – colon*), headache, palpitations, backache, alterations in the menstrual cycle, lack of muscular tonicity. (You may look up these topics separately).

Guilt, which is the same as saying a violence turned inwards, has its causes in something that took place outside the person, with someone or something (normally, with people who are very close). And because the person cannot solve nor even face up to this conflict he has with the outside, he blames that need for aggressiveness he feels towards others and turns it inwards. Depression is a subtle way of suicide. At the same time he is depressed, the person manages to shun and get out of his responsibilities and not act, merely vegetating.

The depressed person is confronted to renunciation, loneliness, isolation, old age (if we are dealing with an old person) and even death (the death of a close person may provoke this type of depressive attitude in people), but he will always do it in a repressed form.

Depression is, after all, a fabulous sign from the body. It clearly shows the person that he does not know (or does not want to) how to face life and, above all, the living people. And also, that he does not want to confront death either. This leaves him in a limbo that is difficult to describe and within which many people take refuge.

A girl who loses her boyfriend and blames it on her self may develop a feeling of undervaluing and guilt. She turns inwards. She becomes depressed. Depression is the result of the combination of undervaluing and guilt. Of course we are not referring to depression associated to disease, but to depression in itself.

The person who is suffering from depression may have problems in the pineal gland. He will be a person with serious disturbances at the level of direction, the path he should take in his life, as well as at the level of humbleness and authority. This person has a major problem in the relationship he has with his biological Father or with his man model, or with the boyfriend, husband or boss. He is a very mentally oriented person, extremely rational, who wants to solve everything by himself, who thinks he knows all the answers and believes he should be in charge.

He leaves no room for intuition.

The ultimate form of depression is pride. This happens when the person is extremely proud of what he has done or does, and not of whom he is. The person who can only define himself by what he did or does and not by whom he is, is undergoing a huge undervaluing process, without realizing it. This is because the person, in fact, does not value anything about who he is. Only what he does or did. In this case, the relatives may have to take the burden of carrying the weight of the undervaluing of the person who is undervaluing himself. Why? Because they feel guilty for not being able to help the person or because they feel they are accomplices in the process, which creates in them a huge feeling of guilt. This means that they will also become depressed, not just the undervalued person.

Depressed people are false kind people.

The state of depression is, in short, a condition of chronic sadness. In other words, it becomes an ongoing process because the patient finds this state of sadness advantageous. These are the advantages that it is necessary to uncover (It is very necessary to discover this side pleasure they find in being depressed) in the patient suffering from depression: it may be the pleasure of having someone looking after him, or the pleasure of preventing the other person from going about his life in or-der to be tied to him.

See *Authority* and *Pineal gland*

Dermis

See *Skin*

Diabetes

See *Pancreas – endocrine gland (diabetes)*

Diarrhoea

The person lets things go without digesting. It denotes fear, rejection, and escape. The person refuses to look and loses discernment. The tension is connected to people who are close. See all the details in *Bowel – small bowel (diarrhoea and cancer)*.

Difficult digestions

See *Stomach*

Digestive system

The digestive system is made up of six segments: mouth, pharynx, oesophagus, stomach, small bowel (duodenum, jejunum, and ileum) and large bowel (ascending colon, transversal colon, descending colon, sigmoid colon, rectum and anus).

This system, along with the breathing system and the reproductive system, deals with the more primitive functions of life. These needs are primary. To get the food, eat it, absorb what is good and throw away the rest. These are all essential needs to the body.

This is associated with total and absolute needs. It is about the geographic location where we live, about food in the strict sense of the word, which is represented by the biological Mother; it is also about food in a symbolic sense, associated with the roots of the person, affection, mainly about childhood affection, the objects of our desire that we would like to acquire, such as a house, a car, and, therefore, also work, money, an inheritance…

Here there are vital exchanges with the outside world. In the digestive system, we are connected to the fatality of starting over. There is desire, necessity, and fulfilment of desire.

This is what connects us with the fact of being incarnated.

It is the law of cycles. That is why there are relapses in conflicts, in tensions. Relapses in primary needs are more difficult, harder. Here we ruminate, we do not think. It is hard to leave the track we have been on. There is need for help. In this case, to help someone, it is necessary to suggest a very practical approach to solutions. Often it is no use talking about spirituality to people with these symptoms. They have trouble understanding. It is necessary to quickly direct them to topics that address **how to do**, give them practical directions.

There is no great precision in the digestive system. People are trapped in a present cycle. The tensions we find in the digestive system are tied to fears of doing without (fear of lacking) and conflicts of identification of emotional needs and primary needs. In the digestive system, there are two extremes: People who resolve things instantly and people who never resolve them.

In fact, from a biological perspective, to resolve things immediately is easy, because the digestive system reacts quickly because it is the most superficial of all the systems. And healing takes place from outside the body inwards.

As a system, it is the most *yin* of them all. The nervous system, on the contrary, is the slowest to react, because it is the deepest. As a system, it is the most *yang* of them all.

Problems affecting the digestive system are not connected with the *yin* left-hand side and the *yang* right-hand side polarity, or vice-versa, either in left-hand sided or right-hand sided people. There is no common denominator regarding the *yin/yang* polarity. And no distinction between left-hand sided or right-hand sided people.

There are only two exceptions: dental caries (teeth enamel) and sinus mucus membranes of the nose and mouth, in which the right side is *yang* (masculine) and the left side is *yin* (feminine), for everybody, left-hand sided and right-hand sided people. Problems in the *yang* side reveal lack of determination and absence of assertiveness due to difficulty in the relationship with a man. Problems in the *yin* side also demonstrate lack of determination and absence of assertiveness due to difficulty in the relationship with a woman.

Discal hernia

A discal hernia takes place on the intervertebral discs. The discs are the moving part of the column and play a corrective role. The discal hernia may be intermittent or permanent. Check the exact disk where the hernia is present to understand the type of tension that causes the symptom the person feels. Anyway, we may say that the person's structure was severely shaken up by some event in his life and that he lost all mobility in the spine.

See *Vertebrae and Spine*

Disease

Diseases, as such, do not exist. Sick people exist, that is, people who are unbalanced. What is more difficult to sort out is not the disease, but people.

Everything starts in my conscience. Everything that happens to me was produced by me. It is my duty to see where I am creating unbalances which end up manifesting themselves through my emotions and my physical body.

Disease is not more than the manifestation, in the body, of what I have been producing with the way I live and think.

To be ill is to be distant from oneself. To be ill means that the person is creating a distance between his deep nature and the type of life that, for some reason, he is leading. Cure is not more than an alignment process in my conscience. When the patient is balanced, the alleged disease disappears.

A symptom is a sign that attracts our attention, our interest and above all our energy, and which prevents the routine course of our life.

Divergent strabismus

See *Eyes – divergent strabismus*

Diverticulosis

Diverticulosis are pouches (pockets) that appear in several places in the large bowel. It happens more frequently in the muscular fibres of the large intestine walls. Some faeces can be stuck in there, as well as bacteria in some cases. Many people have asymptomatic diverticulosis. In fact, they don't even know they have it.

Sometimes, these pouches inflame or infect and this causes diverticulitis.

Most commonly, diverticulitis happens in the descending colon, and mainly in the sigmoid.

This part of the intestine has to do with a feminine, *yin* condition. Actually, here, what one is asked to do is let go. So here we find things that must be released. The person should adopt a more *yin* behaviour but, instead, he does not want to let go of what has caused the tension he is undergoing. The person is too *yang*, too competitive, too masculine."

Diverticulosis happens in the muscle of the colon. And muscles have to do with undervaluation, poor self esteem.

It is because of poor self esteem that this person becomes too masculine. He may be defining himself for what he has (and holds on to it – although he should naturally let go) instead of defining himself for what he is.

See *Bowel – large bowel – descending colon*

Dizziness

Dizziness is similar to vertigo, the difference being that it occurs when the person is standing on the ground, and not in a high place.

This means that the person has lost some of his roots. The person feels insecure about his life, his roots. In other words, he feels insecurity regarding everything in his home, work, the place where he lives or the biological Mother. People with kidney problems tend to lose their balance more easily and are prone to dizziness. This actually makes sense, because these people have strong relational problems with the people they live with.

Dorsal

See *Vertebrae – dorsal vertebrae*

Dreams

There are several types of dreams. Dreams related to what we did during the day; dreams about active conflicts; dreams about a stage in the healing of a tension and of the cure of a symptom; dreams or insights of something that has taken place, is taking place or will take place. There are also the dreams we have when we are awake, the creative visualizations.

Drugs

All forms of dependence represent an escape. It is an escape which started by being a quest. What actually happens is that the person literally projects the objective of his search on something he found along the way and decided his quest is over. He is pleased with what he has found. He remains trapped in fear and convenience. Anything can cause dependence: alcohol, drugs, sex, tobacco, gambling, food (bulimia, anorexia), but also, and even to a larger extent, money, power, rules, fame, influence, knowledge, entertainment, isolation, asceticism, cult, tradition, ancestral beliefs, religion…

The addicted person is the one who stops halfway through his quest. For this reason, he feels empty. And because he feels empty, he needs to fill the void with external substances which confer him the illusion of being balanced.

Basically, we could say that in all humanity, we are all dependents. The difference between the sick dependent and the healthy consumer lies in the quality of self observation, that is, in the awareness of one self, of one's feelings and path. Dependence is a type of attachment. The non-addicted, non-sick consumer is the one who is aware of his attachments and does not attempt to fill up with exogenous substances, preferring to look inwards, to himself and his unbalances.

Drug consumption is always a manifestation of a quest for love. The person's life is void of meaning. The person is extremely deprived.

Drugs are a catalyst of a search process which stopped halfway. In fact, the drug addict wants concrete results fast. He has a problem with the notion of time and the notion of now. He finds it difficult to live the present. It is true that not living the present moment causes anguish to anyone. The drug addict puts an end to that anguish very rapidly, by jumping to a different level and creating the illusion he achieved the result he was craving to achieve.

With these people, it is important to ask them about their relationship (present or past) with the Father, or with the symbol of man, the masculine model they know; And, also, about their relationship with the Mother, if the leading role at home was played by the Mother and not the Father.

All drugs consumed as a form of addiction are like walking canes.

Hashish soothes the person and confers him the desired effect of serenity almost immediately. "Cool!" The effect has been solved, but not the cause.

Cocaine is a stimulant, such as the well known medical drugs that contain **amphetamines**, only with worse consequences. It has the opposite effect of hashish. It increases performance artificially and may contribute to a faster attainment of material successes (again, here we have the quenched desire for a speedy result). Given that one arrives to the goal faster, anxiety diminishes. However, the problem with the inability to live the present moment remains. For this reason, consumption continues.

As for **heroine**, it enables one to push aside, or even put behind, the problems of the world. It provokes alienation and, here again, with immediate results. It may even be on a permanent basis (and always rapidly), through death. **Hallucinogenic** drugs, such as **mushrooms**, **mescaline**, **LSD**, **acids**, what some call **psychedelic drugs**, have a different purpose. They allow consumers to carry out transcending experiences at conscience level.

This way, they quickly change the world they live in, and access higher levels of conscience. The desire for fast results is solved . But when they land after the trip, they do not like the world they see at all, and they wish to get high again. Accordingly, consumption persists.

The well known **ecstasy** is a mixture of a stimulant and a hallucinogenic drug.

But it is very possible to reach transcendence through other means. The only snag is that the addict is in too big hurry. And drugs satiate his hurry. The result is immediate.

Whichever type of stupefacient one consumes chronically, that is, as an addiction, what the person always looks for is to fill the void inside him. This emptiness comes from two things which are interrelated: difficulty to live the present and difficulty to be patient.

For this reason, the drug addict finds it unbearable to live in a world that does not fulfil him, that is upside down and that needs to be changed rapidly.

Dry skin in the face

Dry skin in the face, particularly around the mouth and nose areas, reveals dehydration of the epidermis in that part of the face and a light tension which is related to communication difficulties and self-esteem. In his personal or social relationship with others, the person shows a need to please.

See *Skin – epidermis*

Duchenne's disease

See *Myopathy*

Duodenum

See *Bowel – small bowel – duodenum*

Dyslexia

See *Eyes – dyslexia*

Dysmenorrhoea

Dysmenorrhoea is difficult and painful menstruation. It is a condition that affects women who are very rigorous and demanding of others and with themselves. These are women who find it difficult to be feminine and to live their femininity. You can find out more in *Menstruation*.

Dyspepsia

See *Heartburn*

Ears

Here, we will start talking about the **outer ears** (the shape and the constitu-tion of the ear). They are indicators of the whole body and also of the size of kidneys.

The bigger the outer ears, the stronger the kidneys will be, from the perspective of their structure, and the stronger the person's physical build. The bigger and stronger the ears are, the better the person's build will be.

Outer ears are shaped like an inverted foetus. In fact, ear acupuncture is informed by the principle that the ear represents the entirety of the body.

The lower part of the outer ear thus represents the upper part of the body. To have a fallen, loose and long lobe is very good. It is a sign of a good build. The upper part of the outer ear represents the internal organs. A malformed outer ear may indicate a kidney problem. If the malformation is in the right outer ear, then the condition will affect the right kidney. This denotes propensity, it is not compulsory. A lesion in the lower part of the outer ear may denote tensions in the upper part of the body (on the head) and a lesion in the upper part of the outer ear may indicate strong emotional tensions.

Now, let's talk about the **inner ear** and the **sense of hearing** and listening.

In nature, the senses of smell, touch, taste, sight and hearing are vital for animals. Hearing is extremely developed in preys, to enable animals to escape aggression.

Otitis normally takes place in the Eustachian tube. However, the Eustachian tube is also part of the digestive system. It goes from the ear to the mouth. It is the mediator between the sound I hear and the piece (physical food or virtual, affectionate food) that I need to get hold of. In other words, it is the liaison between what I hear and how I eat. The person's tension is "I do not digest what I hear". Normally, this refers to what one hears from the parents, about the parents or about one parent. Otitis and **earache** happen mostly to young children, at an age when they have to align, to obey. This is also the age when children hear things they dislike, and that upset them, from their parents or from adults. The child who is hurt by what he hears will express that pain by developing otitis.

It is advisable to find out what is happening between the parents, what others are saying about the parents, what parents say to each other, what parents are saying about the child, if they yell etc.

The capacity to **listen** is the body's manifestation of humbleness, of wisdom, of discipline.

Adults with hearing problems are people who protect themselves from what they hear. **Deaf** people, or **hard of hearing**, are people who do not hear because they do not want to hear what displeases them, and so that they do not feel attacked anymore. This is because, in actual terms, they do feel attacked by those who do not agree with them. They are egocentric people. It is very difficult to explain this to a deaf person, precisely because the person will not want to listen.

Deafness develops more often in elderly people who are very mentally oriented and stubborn, who just want to do what they have on their minds and end up being a nuisance to everybody around them. In Western society, so-called civilized, they tend to become intolerant and inflexible. Old age merely reveals all the problems the person has failed to solve in his life. The body of the deaf person is telling him "look inside, listen to what comes from within, and don't be thick-headed..." If the person looks inside himself, he will be better equipped to listen to others. As a matter of fact, the person who looks inside himself focuses more and is able to communicate with his intuition. Through communicating with his intuition, he will be more able to hear the signs that surround him. And, in fact, what others tell us are always signs to us.

Some babies are born deaf. In this case, it is paramount to look at the relationship between the parents during pregnancy or even at the time of birth. A child who is born deaf into this world is a child who comes already blocked in what comes to communicating with others. See *Babies, Pregnancy – problems* and *Child delivery*.

If one of the parents dies when the child was very young, it is also important to see what the child heard about his father after his death.

The child who cannot run away from his verbal aggressors needs to turn off his ears. It is not possible to determine before hand the *yin/yang* polarity of any symptom in terms of right or left side.

Many people insist on the existence of a *yin/yang* polarity in terms of which side of the face the ear is placed. However, there is no common denominator to allow us to know which is the *yin*, feminine ear, and which is the *yang*, masculine ear, depending on which side the problem occurs.

When a child has otitis in the left ear, or when he goes deaf in the left ear, it is not possible to establish if the child has a problem with the Father or with the Mother.

Because, in fact, the child may feel hurt by what he hears **from** the Father (what the Father tells him), in which case it is likely that he has a problem with the Father, or maybe he feels hurt by what he hears **about** the Father (for instance, by what the Mother tells him about the Father), and here it is likely that the problem he has is related to the Mother and not to the Father.

Eczema

The body reveals a separation that was actually experienced. I was separated. And I did not like it at all.

When the person is undergoing the tension of separation, the skin becomes dry and rough, scaled, and the hands become coarse and cold. The body basically creates a hole on the skin, to enable the individual to get close to the other person again. That is to say, by creating the hole, the body physically reduces the distance that separates it from the other person.

When the psychological conflict of separation vanishes (contact has been resumed), the body starts producing a raised mass, as if to increase the area of contact of the skin. This is the healing. "I do not want separation ever again!"

Eczema occurs not just when physical separation takes place. It may simply be caused by the feeling of separation.

If eczema covers the totality of the body, it means the person feels separated from everything and from the entire world. If it covers just a few areas of the body, those are normally places of usual contact.

If, during pregnancy, the parents were separated (it may be that they only came together to have the sexual relation that gave origin to the baby), the baby has registered everything. At birth, the baby will be covered by eczema.

Amniotic fluid gives babies the air they need to breathe. Their survival depends on the help of the Mother. The Mother's contact with the baby is indispensable; otherwise he will die, because it is this contact, this tenderness and this love that represents the baby's safety, his survival. To cuddle the baby is very important.

The skin reacts very rapidly. Much more rapidly than, say, the liver.

Be careful, because to be abandoned has nothing to do with separation. It is not the same conflict. It is not the same tension. Abandon leads to obesity.

In the case of abandon, the identity of the person who is abandoned remains unaltered, but that of the person who abandons disappears. Only one person here takes the initiative.

When separation occurs, two identities become separated. The initiative is taken by two people.

Two geographically separated girl friends may develop eczema.

Elbow

The elbow represents the capacity for radical change in direction in what we do in our lives regarding our own path, our goals. It represents a professional change or one that concerns our objectives.

The elbow is the knee of the arm, only more flexible on all sides except backwards. Here, flexibility is measured in what concerns the will for action.

Once more, in this case, given that it is a joint, the key words are inflexibility and undervaluing.

Normally, elbow related problems occur in the tendon or bone. In both cases we shall talk of undervaluing. When the tendon is affected, this is called **tendonitis**. In the world of tennis, it is given a well-known name: **tennis elbow**. Tendons are rather un-expandable. They help to keep bones tied on to the muscles. This is where the bone starts to be muscle, and where the muscle starts to be bone. Two different realities come together here. We talk of undervaluing of the gesture at the exact time it starts. This is where the image becomes still. It is the undervaluing of the action, in the present. Tendonitis reveals that the person feels some tension regarding the action he has to carry out or has just completed. "He is better than me", or "I cannot beat him."

This lesion may occur when practicing a sport or when pursuing an objective. In any case, it has to do with the person's life and his goals.

The right elbow is *yang*, masculine, and the left elbow is *yin*, feminine. This applies both to left and right-handed people, despite the fact that this polarity is not obvious and must be handled with care, as we are dealing with the locomotor system.

Problems affecting the *yang* elbow denote undervaluing and inflexibility [due to the influence of a third party (a man?) or to the individual's obsessive beliefs]. The person wants to reach further than what is reasonable. The capacity for radical change in direction is in the elbow. Inflexibility, insistence and stubbornness, the warrior behaviour contradict the role of the elbow, and then problems arise. Objectives make people go blind. With this type of beliefs, the individual will fall rapidly in a stage of undervaluing, because of the highly demanding pattern of thought with himself. And he will feel undervalued because he did not achieve what he wanted.

The question that needs to be posed is: Why do I let myself undervalue for this? Am I flexible in the way I think and live? Which man is influencing me (or has influenced me)?"

Problems in the *yin* elbow reveal undervaluing and inflexibility [due to the influence of a third party (a woman?) or to the individual's obsessive beliefs]. The person's sensitivity is hurt in his path to reach his goal. Objectives blind the person and violate his sensitivity.

The capacity for radical change in direction lies in the elbow. Inflexibility, susceptibility and the victim's behaviour contradict the role of the elbow, and problems arise. With this type of beliefs, the individual reaches the stage of feeling undervalued very rapidly, because of the highly demanding pattern of thought with himself. And he will feel undervalued because he did not achieve what he wanted. The question that needs to be posed is: Why do I let my self undervalue for this? Am I flexible in the way I think and live? Which woman is influencing me (or has influenced me)?"

See also *Arms (as upper limbs)* and *Chronic epicondylitis*

Elderly people

An issue that often raises questions regarding symptoms in elderly people is that they have symptoms associated with tensions with the biologic Father or Mother. Since they no longer have parents, how can they feel tension regarding them?

When we mention parents in relation to elderly people, we refer primarily to the models of masculinity or femininity. These models can be found in their beliefs, their way of thinking and, if they are married, it is possible to find answers to the tensions of the elderly in their husband or wife. In any event, these tensions may also be old tensions that people have carried around for a long time, since the time when they still had parents.

Emotional shock

When an unexpected emotional shock occurs, the person's energy takes refuge inside the body. The person becomes cushioned, insensible to external stimuli and may become depressed. Blood pressure drops, the nervous centres become lethargic and sensitivity is taken away from the body. The person is sort of preparing for a huge physical or psychological pain.

Emphysema

Emphysema is characterised by a loss of elasticity in the pulmonary tissue, which makes the tissues too distended and leads to the destruction of the structures supporting the alveoli, and to the destruction of the capillary vessels that feed the alveoli. This is an obstructive form of pulmonary disease.

The person has difficulty breathing and may start hypoventilating. Symptoms include loss of air intake and expanded chest. It also means distended lungs.

The person fears the death of one cycle and the beginning of another. He sees the end of the cycle like a small death. And he fears it. He is afraid of welcoming the new life. He does not believe he is worth living. The person needs a lot of air. The type of life he is living is asphyxiating him, and, for this reason, he requires more air. The person is leading a sad, joyless life. This often happens to people who were forced to change their lives, for example, because they retired.

Enamel

See *Teeth – caries*

Encephalitis

Inflammation of the encephalon, of the brain and of the spinal marrow, followed by cognition deficiency and convulsions.

Encephalitis and Encephalomyelitis indicate the person's fear of not being sufficiently efficient from a brain perspective. The Father (or whoever plays that role) is excessively demanding. He is merciless towards mistakes. Encephalitis reveals that the person felt attacked, harassed, not physically but intellectually, by someone who is very close; If not by the Father, by someone who plays that role. It could even be by the Mother.

Encephalomyelitis

See *Encephalitis*

Endocrine system

This system is formed by the pineal gland (epiphysis), the pituitary gland (hypophysis), the thyroid, the thymus, the pancreas, the suprarenal glands (adrenal glands) and the gonads.

Prostate (which is not an endocrine gland), thyroid and pituitary/hypophysis are the places where benign tumours in the glandular tissues (adenomas or fibromas) develop.

See each of these glands separately.

Animals, through the hormonal process, know how to develop behaviours that place them in the so-called **hormonal draw**. When the person is in a state of hormonal draw, the pituitary/hypophysis, the thyroid, the adrenal/suprarenal glands and the gonads are all at the same level. They are at a state of hormonal draw. When this happens, no hormone is stronger or more prominent than others.

When the animal is in a state of hormonal draw, it is unable to mark the territory.

The same happens with human beings. A pre-adolescent child is unable to mark his territory. He is in hormonal draw. The person has his own dynamics, but does not act in any way in particular. Everything is suspended.

We shall look at the case of a child, an old person, a patient, an adult and a pregnant woman.

A pre-adolescent **child** is in a state of hormonal standstill. This child is not prepared to mark his own territory.

If the child is not in a state of hormonal draw, he will not be able to learn. Nowadays, children are not allowed to be in a state of hormonal standstill. They are required to behave like adults, and/or to compete all the time with other children at school. Society, families and the school encourage this behaviour. As it is, nowadays children reach puberty around the age of eleven or twelve, sometimes even ten, although the age of puberty has always been thirteen or even fourteen years of age. The person that does not get in a stage of hormonal draw is always saying "I know, I know" and then always does thoughtless things. He becomes arrogant and stops respecting authority while growing up.

As for the **old person**, it is quite advantageous for him to be in a state of hormonal draw, otherwise he will start bothering his family, who will end up finding a way of neutralizing him, such as packing him off to an old people's home. The old patriarch and the old matriarch refuse to enter the state of hormonal standstill. However, they would be a lot wiser, which is in fact their role, if they were in a state of hormonal draw.

The chief of the primitive tribe takes advice with the old people, the elder, although he is responsible for the ultimate decision. Old people in a state of hormonal standstill symbolize wisdom. Old people who do not know how to be in a state of hormonal draw end up feeling isolation and, as a result, end up feeling many symptoms related to isolation.

In what concerns the **patient**, he also needs to be in a state of hormonal draw to allow care to be made on him.

All patients need to be in a state of hormonal draw if they are to be cured. They need to give themselves in.

Things are quite different with **adults**. The adult person must not be in a state of hormonal standstill, because he needs to take care of other people. The adult person is the one who guarantees that the species will survive. However, the adult person must allow himself to be in a state of hormonal draw, particularly if he is feeling tired or sick. The adult person must accept to be looked after every now and then.

He must go on holiday, rest, and allow others to look after him.

The **pregnant woman** is not in a state of hormonal standstill either. She is alert, so that she can protect the territory. While she remains pregnant, she will never be in a state of hormonal draw. Unless she was already depressed before she got pregnant. As it is, pregnant women freeze their symptoms while pregnant, as long as they do not feel tensions regarding the pregnancy or birth.

Love is the engine of the hormonal draw. It is quite normal in the animal world, and the same should happen in the world of humans. But it is not, and, more and more, it is increasingly less. Love has given way to fighting, to war and to an excessively *yang* behaviour.

In the animal world, the wolf society is a paradigm of hormonal standstill. It could never work without this hormonal draw. Wolves fight so that one will become the head. One of the wolves, the dominant one, gets into a flamboyant state (hirsute) to reveal the smell of its hormones. He is the alpha wolf. The other wolves remain in a state of hormonal standstill, in order to hide the smell of their hormones and to get impregnated with the smell of the dominant wolf. Nevertheless, to find out about their own hierarchy, who is number two, three, four, etc., they hide their own smell increasingly from number two to number four. It is important to realise that, although they are in a state of hormonal draw, they are not depressed.

The alpha wolf will reproduce itself, whereas the other wolves will not. In the clan of the wolves, everything depends on the lineage of the dominant male.

One of the doors into homosexuality is to be in a state of hormonal standstill. This, in fact, is the only way out for the dominated wolves. Dominated wolves are all homosexual.

As soon as the dominant wolf dies, wolf number two leaves the state of hormonal draw at once.

There is also a female wolf that dominates the other female wolves. The alpha female.

As long as it remains the dominant female wolf, it will be the only one who procreates. If any of the other female wolves has offspring, the dominant female will kill it at once.

This is the law that rules in the wolf clan. Everything is organized around a dominant brain. The behaviour of the female wolf that is in a state of hormonal drawing is a bit like that of families in which one of the female members is childless and looks after her nephews and nieces extremely well. She becomes a full time aunt.

The hormonal standstill is a very good thing if it happens at the right time.

The engine of the hormonal draw is love, without any doubt.

Enuresis

Enuresis means the person urinates a lot, mostly during the night. Enuresis is connected with marking territory.

We all know that certain uncomfortable situations, such as fear, stress and pressure make us pee, that is, to empty our bladder. In fact, the urgency to pee is often an excuse to get out of a situation in which we felt uncomfortable.

Enuresis is precisely a way to release pressure, which can also be considered an internal crying.

Enuresis denotes the total loss of references. The child pees to draw his parents' attention. And he gets comfort in his own smell. This is a desperate marking of territory. One of the parents is absent, or simply cannot mark his territory. Most probably, it will be the Father. The child feels Fatherless. This father gives in to the ideas and strength, possibly very masculine, of the Mother. And the child feels the absence of the Father. The Father does not affirm himself. This happens to couples where, due to some belief, the Father is convinced that his own withdrawal is more important for the couple to function. The Father is too soft. However, children make it noticeable immediately through the symptoms they develop. "What will happen if our territory is attacked? Who will defend it? Mark up the territory! I depend on you! Look, if you do not mark out the territory, I will do it! I am here! I exist!" And then he pees.

Enuresis (mostly during the night) happens mostly to young boys. A good trick is to give the child a cloth smelling of his Father when going to bed. The child will feel safer.

See *Bladder* and *Cystitis*

Epidemics

Here, we are talking at the level of the collective unconscious.

Epidemics, outbreaks, are the result of the collective conscience of the herd. Outbreaks are very archaic things from immemorial times that have the function of separating the wheat from the shaft. In nature, epidemics are useful for the survival of the species. They are a "divine" tool that separates the wheat from the shaft. The shaft is appropriate for recycling and the wheat can be stored and eaten.

Cholera, plague, always had the purpose of separating humankind. Of course the human beings of today cannot find a moral reason in this.

In the collective unconscious, some carry the seed of the wheat (and they will remain and continue) and the others are the shaft (and they will be recycled). Of course the human mind does not find this ethical. But it is dual, hence, natural, although not acceptable by the majority of people. (This notion is very much linked to the planetary co-creation which is one of the subjects in my workshops).

Any form of outbreak is a biological separation. The herd is the object of epidemics, not the individual. It is the collective brain that is gripped by collective disease.

One should note that, nowadays, there are many holocausts on the planet. They are signs we are entering a new era, a new collective way of thinking. Some call it the Age of the Aquarius. It may be called anything. We are right at the core of an epidemic. The human collective conscience needs to change dramatically. And new and old phenomena come up and become re-current: Wars, risk of pandemics, the chronic sadness of populations all over the world and the invasions by certain types of animals, in their millions, plagues that decimate whole portions of some countries.

See *Plague, Lung plague, Cholera* and *AIDS*

Epidermis

See *Skin*

Epidural

See *Child delivery*

Epilepsy

Epilepsy is like a disconnection between the autonomous nervous system and the central nervous system.

The person needs to elevate himself and dive into his deep inner self. This person's lifestyle is very far from the one he desires. The person feels as if he is being persecuted, yet refuses to move an inch away from the person he has a conflict with. Life is a struggle. The person exercises violence against himself because he does not move away from where he is. If it is a child, it means the child does not allow himself to have bad thoughts about his father. If it is a married woman, bad thoughts about her husband. It is true that a child seldom moves away from his father. He does not have much choice.

Grown-ups, however, do have choices, but many refuse to move away because of beliefs that keep them from living free. In any case, we must closely watch that person's relationship with a male, with the male role model, and with the biologic Father.

When epilepsy surfaces in a child, it is most important to understand what goes on between the child and the father, step father, or the man in charge of raising the child. It is there that we find the cause of the problem.

Epiphysis

See *Pineal gland*

Erection – erectile dysfunction

See *Impotence*

Eustachian Tube

See *Ears*
Eustachian Tube is a part of the inner Ear.

Eye infection

See eye infections in *Eyes – conjunctivitis* and *Eyes – glaucoma*

Eye spots

See *Eyes – eye spots*

Eyes

Many people insist on the existence of a *yin/yang* polarity that depends on the side of the face the eye is. From the perspective of a person's build (constitution), it is true that the right eye is *yin* (the Mother's side) and the left eye is *yang* (the Father's side). This applies to everybody, left and right-handed people. However, from the viewpoint of the activity, functioning and condition the eye performs, there is no common denominator that allow us to know if a symptom in the eye is related to the *yang* or the *yin* side.

However, we all have a directing eye that takes action, and that is the *yang* eye, masculine. The other eye is the eye of affection, it fears danger, is more passive, *yin* and feminine. This is the receiving eye.

Trying to find out which is our directing eye (the *yang* eye), whether it is the right or the left eye, and which presents more symptoms, could be an interesting exercise. When referring to the eyes, we do not talk of problems with the Father or the Mother, rather of masculine and feminine behaviours.

See *Eyes – astigmatism, Eyes – blindness, Eyes – cataracts, Eyes – conjunctivitis, Eyes – convergent strabismus, Eyes – Daltonism – colour-blindness, Eyes – divergent strabismus, Eyes – dry eye, Eyes – dyslexia, Eyes – eye spots, Eyes – farsightedness, Eyes – glaucoma, Eyes – nearsightedness, Eyes – nystagmus, Eyes – opacity in the middle of the eye, Eyes – presbyopia, Eyes – retinal detachment, Eyes – retinitis pigmentosa, Eyes – stains in the eyes, Eyes – strabismus* and *Eyes – sty*

Eyes – astigmatism

This is due to a defect in the curvature of the cornea. The person deforms reality but says nothing about it to the people around him. He keeps this to himself. He does not accept reality as it is.

The person lives in a world that he himself created. By developing astigmatism, he discovers the best method to deform what he does not wish to see.

Eyes - blepharitis

Blepharitis is the inflammation of the eyelids. It's a common cause of sore, red eyelids and crusty eyelashes. Eyelid inflammation is very common and can affect people of all ages.

Blepharitis and dry eyes often occur at the same time, causing confusion whether dry eye causes blepharitis or blepharitis causes dry eye. See *Eyes – dry eye.*

Blepharitis usually is associated with an overgrowth of bacteria that live along the margins of the eyelids and at the base of the eyelashes. Over time, these bacteria multiply and create a structure called a biofilm.

Blepharitis does not affect vision, but it causes rash and discomfort.

The purpose of eyelashes is to protect the eye from light, from dust and from other pollutants in the environment.

The person with blepharitis is very upset and incapable of using his eyelashes in a natural way. The person cannot protect himself from what he saw.

See *Eyes*

Eyes – blindness

Blindness is the ultimate, extremely traumatizing, indication that a very mentally oriented, rational person has refused to look at reality other than the one he created for himself. For this reason, the body makes him look inwards. This could be, for instance, via a glaucoma (see *Eyes – glaucoma*) or a cataract (see *Eyes – cataracts*), even via an accident (see *Accidents*), It is very difficult to explain this type of tension to a person who has turned blind. Blindness from birth is associated to the relationship between the parents. It is not as traumatic as blindness that develops through life, because the person has never experienced the sense of vision. The child who was born blind is a child who came to work on his other senses, particularly intuition.

Blindness can occur following an immense spiritual elevation, whereby the person totally renounces his body and, consequently, his vision, given that intuition is his compass in life.

Eyes – cataracts

Cataracts cloud the crystalline lens of the eye and blur vision. Seeing things clearly becomes difficult. And what we can see with some clarity looks sharp, blunt, and aggressive.

The person draws a curtain so that he does not see what upsets him. The person falls under the illusion he is keeping danger at bay. This, however, is dangerous, as it can lead to blindness (see *Eyes – blindness*).

There is loss of elasticity of the

crystalline lens. It happens to elderly people. As their presbyopia (see *Eyes – presbyopia*) develops, they start to take things at a distance. But now they feel powerless in the face of death. This could be physical death or death of a cycle in their lives. For this reason, they draw the curtain, and cataracts develop.

This is a fatal outcome. I do understand, but I do not wish to see. The person may feel: "My children no longer want to be with me", or "I cannot stand being with my husband/wife any longer".

The person draws a curtain to reality; he puts a veil over himself. He does not deform things, but resigns himself to them. These are normally perspicacious people on their way to reaching wisdom, but who cannot sublimate the feeling of danger. They believe they cannot fail.

Cataract surgery removes the crystalline lens but this does not resolve the tension, only the effect. Therefore, the conflict will probably extend to another part of the body.

Eyes – conjunctivitis

Conjunctivitis only eases off when we close our eyes. The eyes are hurt, inflamed. This is the body showing us the presence of a conflict that is hurting us and to which we close our eyes, in other words, which we do not want to face. This tension is the result of something the person saw that disgusted him, looked unclean to him. It is necessary to clean up. It is necessary to wash off what one saw.

The person has difficulty accepting and loosening up, finds it difficult to focus. The sun represents authority. People who develop conjunctivitis when exposed to the sun denote problems with authority (see *Authority*).

The wind represents communication and people who develop conjunctivitis have difficulty communicating when exposed to the wind.

There is also allergic conjunctivitis. This condition is provoked by an allergy. If this is the case, see *Allergies*

Eyes – convergent strabismus

It happens to people who have to keep something strictly under control. The person is extremely self-controlled and tries to avoid that something happens to him.

"I am keeping an eye on you!" "I must not let Mother go away". Or, "I cannot let Father go away".

This often starts even before the parents divorce. I am keeping an eye on the two of you!!!

This is the problem that invigilators have. It denotes stiffness, extremely localised danger. The problem has not taken place yet.

See *Eyes – divergent strabismus* and *Eyes – strabismus*

Eyes – Daltonism – colour-blindness

This is blindness regarding life's diversity and colour. It affects people who tend to see grey in everything, who show indifference but who in fact try to get rid of all differences. They are grey people.

It normally occurs to the eldest son and only happens to men. In our society, human beings pass on their name, their blood. The eldest son has always represented blood and lineage. He is the eldest.

However, colour-blindness is not something that happens necessarily only to the eldest son.

The person who does not want to see blood may not be able to recognise the colour red. He confuses red with other colours.

The person who has problems regarding his own lineage, with his clan's blood, may have problems with the colour red.

It also happens with other colours, but it normally happens with red.

In the case of nobility, this may occur with blue (*blue blood*).

Eyes – divergent strabismus

One of the parents has gone. It has happened. To see my two parents, I need to look in two different, opposing ways.

Some animals have eyes on the sides. Preys have a 360-degree all round vision. Predators have eyes at the front. The person with divergent strabismus is the prey. He is someone who fears being attacked for what he is. I am a potential victim. I feel as if I am a prey.

"Following this separation, what is going to become of me"?

See *Eyes – convergent strabismus* and

Eyes – strabismus

Eyes – dry eye

This occurs when a person is undergoing a very *yang*, masculine stage. "A man does not cry". This means a person who has hardened his life as far as feelings and emotions are concerned. This person can be venomous. He would rather die than forgive. It denotes refusal to see things with love. The person is very angry.

Eyes – dyslexia

This happens when the Father and the Mother do not get along, when there is confusion between the person's masculine and feminine sides. The person has taken up, silently, the tension he felt regarding his parents squabbling. The body takes it on itself to show that tension.

Eyes – eye spots

This means arterial pressure in the eye.

The person needs to be vigilant regarding some stressing matter.

This is not the same as stains in the eyes.

Should you need, see *Eyes – stains in the eyes*. It is not the same as glaucoma, although glaucoma is also characterized by high ocular pressure.

See *Glaucoma*

Eyes – farsightedness

In fact, depending on the mother

tongue, some people use the expression far-sightedness, others hypermetropia or hyperopia.

The person who has farsightedness sees very well at distance and sees not well at short distances. Farsightedness is the opposite of nearsightedness (see *Eyes – nearsightedness* (myopia)). In the case of farsightedness, danger is far away. It is in the future.

Sentinels, for example, may develop farsightedness. They look out for danger that is at a distance.

A farsighted person's neck is bent to the front, as opposed to the myopic person, whose neck muscles are contracted, very stiff. His head falls down as if it was a small hump. The hypermetropic person needs to be calm in order to see correctly. The person whom wishes to see well at a distance needs to remain calm.

The farsighted person is constantly worrying about the possibility of having to change. A change is always possible. He is constantly on guard, like the sentinel. The nearsighted person, on the contrary, does not have the time to react when danger strikes. The farsighted person is able to see danger from far. The farsighted person has too much future in his life. He lives anxiously.

The farsighted person lives in constant apprehension, anxiously, because he fears being caught. For this reason, he is said to have too much future in his life. He does not like surprises at all. He is always on guard, so that he knows how to deal with them.

As for the nearsighted person, he has too much past in his life. He lives in fear.

The nearsighted person is afraid. He has been caught before. This must not happen again. This is why he is said to have too much past in his life.

The farsighted person is watchful, so that he knows where (future) danger may come from. He is anxious.

For the nearsighted person, danger is immediate. The present is dangerous. He lives in constant fear.

Farsightedness should not be mistaken with presbyopia (see *Eyes – presbyopia* (tired eyes)). The presbyopic person needs to distance himself and do an overview of his life.

In my experience, many people have managed to cure nearsightedness. These are mostly young people. Getting rid of farsightedness is much more complex.

Eyes – glaucoma

Glaucoma is always known as the green cataract, to distinguish it from the common cataract, also called grey cataract. This is caused by hypertension in the eye. The internal ocular pressure increases.

Eyes turn red. The destruction of the eye has begun. This is an ophthalmologic urgency and a painful symptom.

The eye acts as a magnifying lens. The person focuses, concentrating the rays of light. In this particular case, the person experiences a progressive contraction of his field of vision until he reaches a tubular vision, losing his vision of the whole. He can only see the area he is focusing on. Glaucoma denotes the person's obsessive fear of not being able to attain the (that!) goal on time.

The person projects the solution over himself with great intensity, in a situation he perceives as excessively dangerous. He ends up seeking refuge in his lack of sight.

This is a creepy attitude, since no objective can be so important to make it necessary to go blind on its account. What is more dangerous then? Not to attain the goal or to go blind?

The person who is prone to developing glaucoma feels great insecurity and stubbornness with matter-related things. He is a person who needs to take his foot off the accelerator and go over his life. His priorities are completely reversed. The person is caught in a vicious circle of extremely *yang*, fighting behaviour. This *yang* behaviour is due to the major insecurity the person is feeling.

Eyes – nearsightedness

In fact, some people call the nearsightedness myopia. The nearsightedness occurs when a person cannot see well at a distance and sees well at short distances. To see well at short distance is what is important for the person. One needs close distance not to fail, to be able to see coming dangers distinctly. This condition normally starts during adolescence (teenage) or even earlier.

Nearsighted people see the world more than they listen to it. Essential things in life come to them through eyesight. Nearsighted people cannot see well at a distance because they can only be available for what comes close to them. The ocular globe therefore gets distorted.

The person who turns nearsighted will suffer from this condition because he feels that, in the past, he was little attentive, little vigilant. He was slapped but failed to see the hand coming close. The slapping was far too close coming when he realised what was happening. Too late!

This is a person who turned a corner and was struck by an unexpected danger, very close and full of movement (here, nearsightedness was caused by a dynamic action). Some children become nearsighted when they are around six years of age, when they learn how to read. This is not because they strain their eyes. It is mostly related to the behaviour shown by the people who taught them how to read, which they find dangerous.

Basically, the six-year-old nearsighted child is afraid of people around him.

The nearsighted person brings things close to himself. "Danger is getting close to me!"

The crystalline of nearsighted people is always under strain. The nearsighted person is constantly strained about something. He must be under a dynamic situation. This is not something spontaneous. He is always ready for something dynamic.

He is afraid of everything. When feeling confident, he may take his glasses off.

The nearsighted person needs to be reassured. He can see what is close very well, but he hates what comes from afar and does not want to pay any attention to it, for the time being.

Thus, nearsightedness denotes major subjectivity and lack of self-knowledge. What is it that I do not want to see?

Basically, the nearsighted person does not want to see himself, he does not want to see inwards. The more the person fails to see who he really is, the bigger the problem will be.

Young people, normally, only see immediate things, and they lack farsightedness and an overview of things. Nearsightedness starts at an early age. The person refuses to see himself as a whole. He then becomes vulnerable, short-tempered or defensive, not wishing to be surprised by anything that might surprise him. Nearsightedness forces the youth to look closer to his own involvement. One of his parents, for example.

The fact that a nearsighted person needs to wear glasses from an early age means he gets used to them, thinking he can see everything very well. This is not true, however, just an illusion. Contact lenses are even worse, because they become invisible. Lenses and glasses put down the call from the body.

Nearsightedness may also have been programmed (in a non-conscious way) by the parents. Even when it starts at around six or seven years of age. The earlier it manifests itself, the more related it is to the parents' programme

(See *Family* and *Babies*).

The nearsighted person is an intellectual. He needs a lot of information because he is always on guard.

His neck muscles are always very stiff. The nape (back of the neck) is where the muscles that control eyesight are located. The nape is the *yang* part of the neck. nearsighted people have a very *yang* behaviour to make up for their intense fear. And they do not know how to relax.

The nearsighted person has too much past in his life. He lives in fear. The nearsighted person is afraid (he has been caught before. This must not happen again) and, for this reason, he is said to have too much past in his life.

The farsighted person is the opposite, he lives in constant apprehension, anxiously (I may be caught) and, for this reason, he is said to have too much future in his life. He is always on guard so that he is able to know where danger comes from. He is anxious. He does not even want to allow himself to be caught. As for the nearsighted person, he has already been caught. For him, danger is immediate. The present is dangerous. He is very much afraid of the near future.

Nearsightedness surgery is successful and eradicates the effects of nearsightedness. However, if the person does not sort out the tensions in his conscience, Nearsightedness will come back very quickly. In my experience, many people have managed to cure Nearsightedness. These are mostly young people. Getting rid of farsightedness is much more complex.

Eyes – nystagmus

This is constant movement of the pupils.

The body is showing the person's inability to assert himself: "I want, but, after all, I do not want." "I have the right, but then, I do not have." This is a nervous system-related problem. This denotes the person's inability to make decisions. This symptom does not come on its own. It is worth asking about this person's dental condition, for example. Nystagmus indicates tension brought about by two opposing ideas that pervade the person, and his inability to decide on any.

Eyes – opacity in the middle of the eye

On the one hand, the eyes have rods (small sticks) that specialize in seeing in the dark and light. They are located in the side part of the eye. In the animal world, preys have eyes on the side.

On the other hand, eyes have cones, placed in the middle of the eye and they account for very precise vision. Predators have this type of eyesight.

Human beings' mental problem, in today's society, is that they are taught not to be squashed and, therefore, to become predators. Society has decided that a person needs to be successful at any cost, otherwise he will be crushed.

People who follow this society's programme can only see what is right in front of their eyes (cones). And they have poor sight at dusk (the rods do not work).

The person is afraid of the dark. He only wishes to live in brightness, in the light.

The person suffering from opacities in the middle of the eye and who can only resort to lateral vision is a person to whom the body is saying: "You have been too *yang*, too much of a predator. Stop being so *yang*."

Eyes – presbyopia

It is also called tired or aging eyes.

The person suffering from presbyopia needs to stretch his arms to see well. So things close up, he needs to move objects away from him.

He measures up the distance, moves away. He overviews. He feels closer to death.

Everything is ok, but what have I done with my life?

This condition normally starts at the beginning of the second part of the person's life. It represents the quest for purpose. "I only have X years left. And I still have so much to do. Ah, if only I could push the deadline further away…"

Old people should be wiser and have an overall view of things. It is a shame that many can only see well at a distance when presbyopia prevents them from seeing properly close up. What the body shows the person suffering from presbyopia is that he still has a long way ahead. That he can see very well in the distance. In order to force the person to do this, the body has reduced his capacity to look things up closely, its capacity to see the details.

In our western society, old people do

not cultivate wisdom but rather regret being old and not having lived enough. Nostalgia… "Ah, if only we could go back a few years!"

It is actually common that the majority of old people are unable to remember recent events, while having a vivid recollection of the past.

Farsightedness should not be mistaken with presbyopia.

The person suffering from presbyopia needs to take a distance and to have an overview of life.

The person suffering from Farsightedness lives in constant fear and anxiety: " I may be caught!"

Eyes – retinal detachment

Something too horrible to be seen has happened. I do not want to see. It means a major shock.

The person attempts to get rid of the vision he had and this is when retinal detachment occurs. The body shows what the person attempted to hide.

The person remains deeply perturbed by what he saw, fails to get rid of the vision and lives it up silently.

If you tell someone with healthy eyes about some horrible thing that until then the person had not been aware of, then the person may end up with a detached retina.

This condition happens more often to old people.

The detachment will continue if the person continues to see horrible things, either by keeping in touch with the people who did what he saw or even by watching horrible things on TV, things

the person cannot stand but does not tell anyone about it. In this case, retinal detachment persists. The tension persists.

Extremely myopic (see *Eyes – nearsightedness*) people tend to have retinal detachment. Horrible sights have an immediate and strong effect upon them. These people are more prone to retinal detachment.

Seeing horrible things provokes sight destructuring. Laser is a coherent, structuring light, and for this reason, retinal detachment is cured with laser.

Eyes – retinitis pigmentosa

This means intense pigmentation of the eye, leading to defective dark adaptation. This is conjunctivitis times 10. Melanin has the purpose of protecting. Just like skin moles. It does protect, but it should not protect more than is necessary and it should not leave a person in the darkness.

When we referred to conjunctivitis (see *Eyes – conjunctivitis*), we said that it only eases off when we close our eyes. The eyes are hurt, inflamed. This is the body showing us the presence of a conflict that is hurting us and to which we close our eyes, in other words, which we do not want to face. This tension is the result of something the person saw that disgusted him, looked unclean to him. In this case, instead of washing it off, the person covers it with pigmentation.

When the person needs to protect himself, this indicates that he saw something filthy, something that disgusted him.

This is a filth-related conflict, which is located in the vision.

The person would like to turn his retina opaque to prevent himself from becoming dirty. The person becomes progressively blind.

Eyes – stains in the eyes

These are opacities inside the eye, differing in size, in the form of grey or white stains.

These stains or shadows are people from the person's past who are gone (either dead or people he has not seen again), and whose disappearance the person has not yet come to terms with.

This is not merely sorrow. It is true suffering.

The symptom is not the same as in spots in the eyes.

Should you need, see *Eyes – eye spots.*

Eyes – strabismus

In order to see an object in its full dimension, we need two images. However, if the visual axes of the eyes are not aligned, the eyes will turn inwards (convergent strabismus) or outwards (divergent strabismus), because two non-coincident images are formed in each of the eyes' retinas. Therefore, the brain chooses to show only one. And it will show us the image projected by the eye with the correct axis.

Everything becomes flat, even, without depth. The person starts having a distorted and unilateral vision.

The crossed-eye person is someone who has decided to see life from just one perspective, be it the paternal or the maternal.

See *Eyes – convergent strabismus* and *Eyes – divergent strabismus*

Eyes – sty

The person needs to throw away something he has seen and has not liked. He is angry with someone. Normally, it is with his partner.

The ring (symbol of union, of the partner) heals the sty.

"A part of myself is missing". The ring may give the sensation of giving back the part of oneself that the person feels he has lost.

Face

Conditions of the face always have to do with tension connected to aestetics and also to the impossibility of covering up. Everyone can see what goes on with someone's face. However, this tension is connected with other tensions, depending on the symptoms the person may have.

See *Acne, Pimples, Lupus – discoid lupus erythematosus, Lupus – systemic lupus erythematosus, Bells's paralysis, Sinusitis* and *Nervous tics*

Fainting

"Let me out of here! I cannot deal with this problem. I am scared! Let me out of here! I do not want to have to face up to this. I would rather disappear, I would rather die." Fainting symbolizes a type of momentary death.

The person is unaware his is annulling himself. This is typical of people whose homes are undergoing difficult moments, lack of understanding or lies. However, it is equally typical of people who have abandoned their lives, who annul themselves because they are linked to powerful beliefs that do not work for them. They can be beliefs of a religious type, or related to the family, clan, good manners etc.

Fallopian Tube

The egg leaves the ovary and is brought down to the womb (uterus) via the fallopian tube. Infection in a fallopian tube may lead to obstruction. This is a blockage of the person's femininity in her genital function. This is not necessarily linked to sex or sexual intercourse, it is mostly associated to tension, conflict or even major aggression that the person is experiencing in her relationship with someone. This person feels attacked and the aggression she feels, almost always in verbal form, in the form of communication, may come from a man or a woman. Nevertheless, it is more likely that it comes from a man, or from a very masculine, warrior, *yang* woman. In other words, from someone who symbolizes a male, the masculine model. Infected fallopian tubes may lead to small loss of blood.

Blockage or infection in one fallopian tube may not necessarily prevent child conception. It is possible to conceive a baby when only one tube is operational.

There is no concrete reason to state which of the tubes is *yin*, feminine, or *yang*, masculine. When carrying out a diagnostic, it is advisable to consider the right tube to be *yang* and the left tube to be *yin*. This applies both to left and right-handed women. However, this is not a certainty.

Family

The parental project (conscious or unconscious) results in a baby, a person. A being is incarnated. This birth is what gives meaning to the parents' project. Likewise, when these parents were born, they gave meaning to the grandparents' project. Let us not forget that upon birth, the child already knows what parents and family he joins. He brings with him a deep knowledge of the type of ancestors and clan thought processes that this family possesses. In his soul, the child carries the knowledge of genealogic lineage, the wisdom of the clan. The group of brains of a herd creates a collective brain with an identity of its own, the clan brain.

Conception and birth are a creation which involves three people and which only gives fruit if all are in agreement (that is, the Father, the Mother, and the future baby) and jointly create that epiphany which results in the incarnation of a new being.

As soon as the child is born, the memory of lineage he brought with him becomes unconscious. In fact, he forgets all the baggage he brought along and will need to experience living with his family to slowly start to understand the thinking patterns and way of being and feeling of his family. So, it is important that the child hears references to family members, that he learns about past events, though not only the great and epic ones. He must learn about all: emotions, family conflicts, hushed scandals, and all the hidden information.

One of the great problems of the present is that many people are confronted with a family pattern that hides the past, and mainly the emotions of the past, which forces the body to reveal it as a symptom as the person lives. In fact, as stated in the introduction, the body does not lie and always reveals what is hidden. Hidden family problems may resurface two generations later, in the grandchildren, both physically and psychologically, always under the appearance of a symptom.

In agricultural society, grudges, shame, and feelings of culpability pass from generation to generation and appear as symptoms.

In religion, tradition, patriotism and in all other forms of "ism", the dogma is passed on from generation to generation through a common way of thinking and a common approach to life.

For instance, a grandfather who lost all his land may cause a granddaughter to have territorial conflicts, thus giving rise to cervical canal of uterus or heart problems.

There are women who, for generations and generations, personify a model of the suffering woman, lied to, beaten up, guilt ridden; And that

is why all generations of women recurrently experience the same or similar symptoms in organs that represent femininity, such as breasts, ovaries, fallopian tubes, uterus, cervix, or cervical canal of uterus, and vagina.

Families affected by liver problems have a functioning pattern that is well grounded in group behaviour. Consequently, all members suffer from liver issues.

Families where cancer prevails are families where information is hidden, instead of being available to all members of the clan, as non-verbalization of intensive feelings may cause cancer. Child illnesses are the result of what parents had in mind during pregnancy, at the exact moment of conception or at birth.

If parents simply wanted a sexual relation without love (getting laid) and a child is born as a result, it is possible that this child will suffer from eczema (skin problem) since the child results from separation in love. Let us not forget that during pregnancy, for nine months, the child is connected to the Mother's emotions, her way of life, and the way the parents relate to each other influences the child.

On account of this, because of this influence family and lineage have on a person, it is always important to consider the herd, the clan, and not destroy it. It is by creating a new herd, a new group, and not by criticizing the original one, that we move forward. To move away from the clan, to reject it and seek isolation, is to deny the origin of the joint creation, to negate the reason why one is born into a specific family, and to miss the meaning of the message that a family has on a person. To move away from the clan and settle for an opposite life style does not resolve any problems.

Some people are born into families that have little or nothing to do with what they will accomplish in this life and that is the message they must understand. However, we are born into a family and must learn to love it, to accept it, to understand what beliefs we must forget, without violence, to follow our path, often in solitude but not in isolation. You may not like the way of life of your family members and choose to move away. That is fine. But do not kill the clan, do not destroy it, do not do it harm, and simply accept it. Move away from the members but let them live as they wish and go about living the life you want.

If the person is a male, the great-grandfather (fourth generation, Father's grandfather) corresponds to a person's mission in life.

Many people tend to live exactly as the clan dictates or to do the direct opposite. Neither of these approaches is good as both run away from the self and fail to listen to the body. Breaking the connection with ancestors creates separation for you and for the other descendants of those same ancestors.

In his life, from the moment of birth, the child lives an unconscious project that will, one day, give rise to a tension and a physical symptom. And that health problem is always correct because it corresponds to something

the child created (albeit unconsciously). Symptoms are actually grounded on the way of thinking and living.

To overcome the symptom and find the way back to health, the person must gain awareness of his project and learn what does and does not work for him and what does and does not work in the way he relates to his family and clan.

A person who wants to be cured but has no project will die, anyway. It is necessary to change the project (which is the goal) so that the cure (which is not the goal in itself) will take place. It is necessary to take charge of your life. Someone with renal insufficiency must go from a subconscious to a conscious project. He must quit living the archetypes of parents and clan, separate from the clan's beliefs. If he does not do it, he will not be able to maintain the kidney he received in a transplant, for example. The kidneys belong to the waters of the body, the deepest and most ingrained part of the clan's collective brain.

We may act at four different levels to find a person's balance: the memories of ancestors; nine months of pregnancy; birth; and the life of the person.

If I cure myself, all other members of the family who descend from the same old great-grandfather will be cured as well. This is not a goal but simply a positive consequence.

When you cure yourself, you also cure the descendants, transversal family members, and ancestors (through a collective unconscious: planet, race, tribe, clan, and family).

The Bible says: "You will be damned until the 77th generation. One of you will know and you will be blessed until the 7th generation."

We should all complete a family tree using what we know, what we can find from other members, and what we remember. Then we must add all the illnesses, divorces, and accidents. We must also add the occupations and professions of each member, when available. Each one of us will interpret his genealogy in his own way. The individual is important to the species and that is why the species has a project for the individual. The clan is very powerful and always calls back the person who moved away.

The human being is gregarious. The one who has new ideas is always the black sheep of the family. The clan feels threatened by the black sheep and tries to control it, keep it in line. That is common.

It is very important to accept ancestors and the family. To accept does not mean to live with them. You may change clan. When you are between two clans, life becomes a crisis.

Independence is not lived in isolation. Independence means to be able to choose your herd, to choose your group; The security of finding a group again, whether a new group or the old one, devolves energy to the individual. The person finds a new positive way of being again and may find a new project, leaving behind the archetypes of his parents and family. If I take that step, however, I cannot go on having my laundry done at my mother's or having lunch at my parents', because that is not independence.

Fat

Fat is vital to any body. But, sometimes, some people have too much fat in there bodies. It shows a clear conflict in their lives. But a person who has cellulite, for instance, feels a different tension from the one who has obesity. Please see *Cellulite*, *Obesity* and *Lipoma*.

Fatigue

See *Asthenia*

Fear

Fear, as opposed to anger (see *Anger*), makes one think the other person may attack us. Accordingly, the sympathetic nervous system prepares itself to run away. In this case, contrary to what occurs with the energy brought about by anger, which moves up to the scapular waist (shoulders and neck), the energy brought about by fear goes down to the lower limbs. Legs get ready to run away! The fact that the person may have to run a lot may lead him to empty his sacs of urine and faeces in order to run faster. This is the reason why fear may lead to urinary or bowel incontinence. If escaping is not an option, energy will become trapped halfway down the back, putting weight on the anus and on the urethra, and often on the eyes too.

Deep fear, which is fear connected to a sensation of danger, which has extremely severe consequences, is directly linked to the kidneys.

Problems in the bladder are caused by stress. Kidneys problems are provoked by obsessive fear.

If fear is repressed, it may lead to rage and anger, or even panic.

Feet

Feet represent our contact with Mother Earth. For this reason, in many cultures, people go barefoot in order to feel the Earth's energy, and to feel gravity and counter gravity. Feet must be dynamic. They show our awareness of being on Earth, of having incarnated. They allow us to walk on and to endure. They are the place for dialogue between levitation and gravitation. The feet are where the world of our stances and affirmation of our attitudes is located. Feet represent our life criteria and the fulfilment of ideals.

Children who are born with **malformations** in their feet are children who find it difficult to incarnate and to have contact with earth. See *Child delivery*, in this particular case. People who have **cold feet** are people who experience difficulty in carrying things out. It denotes fear of not doing things correctly root-wise (home, work, money, connection to the area or place where one lives, to the biological Mother). Life does not reach those parts of the body.

There is no certainty if one foot is *yang* (masculine) and the other is *yin* (feminine). Nevertheless, it can be said, *a priori*, that in most cases the right foot is *yang*, masculine and the left foot is *yin*, feminine. This applies both to right and left-handed people. In any case, problems in the feet always indicate that the role of the biological Mother in the person's life is weak. This could be due to the fact that the Mother cancels herself off in the presence of the Father, or because the Mother did not feed the person properly, or did not allow him to have a good rooting. It is advisable to look at the history of women in the clan.

Problems in the feet can take place in the Bones, Joints or Skin. Bone-related problems show strong undervaluation. If they occur in the joints, it is a sign of lack of mental flexibility and undervaluation. If it affects the skin, it shows separation-related tensions or difficulty communicating with someone.

If a person has sweaty feet and, accordingly, his feet smell strongly, see *Perspiration*.

See *Feet – pes cavus (hollow claw foot)*, *Feet – flatfeet* and *Feet – athlete's foot*

Also see *Toes*. See also, if appropriate, *Amputation*.

Feet – athlete's foot

This is a fungal infection in feet.

The person has stagnated over beliefs that do not work out. His past controls his everyday life. He is stuck to the past. Accordingly, he catches fungi and develops moss. Fungal infections are caused by parasites. The word *'parasite'* is essential in this context. If the person allows parasites to affect him, it means that the he is not centred, that he can not be firm with other people; someone around him is a parasite trying to take advantage of him, whether at home, work or amongst his friends. It could also be his Mother. The person is stuck in the past and in old beliefs, so he cannot deal as firmly and effectively as he should. He feels frustrated because he feels this person will not accept him if he changes his attitude towards him.

See *Feet, Feet – pes cavus (hollow claw foot)* and *Feet – flatfeet*

Also see *Toes*. See also, if appropriate, *Amputation*.

Feet – flatfeet

This happens when there is absence of curvature in the foot's arch. All children have flatfeet until the age of three or four. After that, the fat that filled the arch of the foot goes away. By just walking, the fibres of the feet's arch become stronger, and feet cease to be flat. The person who has flatfeet is someone who has a desire to remain a child, because he is afraid of not being able to root himself down on his own. The body demonstrates the wish to root. This person depends on his biological Mother.

See *Feet, Feet – pes cavus (hollow claw foot)* and *Feet – athlete's foot*

Also see *Toes*. See also, if appropriate, *Amputation*.

Feet – pes cavus (hollow claw foot)

This is the opposite symptom of flat-foot. The curvature of the foot's arch is higher than normal, due to muscular hypertrophy. The tension that is felt is the same as in flatfeet. This is a question of incarnation. In this case, the person moves away from the earth, and the muscle is the issue. Muscles represent the ability to move in life, they represent flexibility and activity, dynamics and, above all, undervaluation.

Muscle-related problems unveil resistance to new experiences. In this case, they show the presence of a contradiction, doubts regarding the fact of having incarnated on Earth. It is necessary to look at the home where the person incarnated.

See *Feet, Feet – flatfeet* and *Feet – athlete's foot*

Also see *Toes*. See also, if appropriate, *Amputation*.

Femoral head

The femoral head is one of the bones of the hip joints. The other one is the iliac bone. This is the bone we use when we push the cupboard or the fridge. This bone fractures, often, in old people who feel under pressure by their children and, for this reason, undervalued. The individual's strong sense of undervaluing is centred on the bone.

Problems associated with femoral head decalcification, fractures of the femoral head or of the femur indicate a major feeling of undervaluing and that the person's foundations have been completely shaken.

Femoral head problems are particular to very determined people, but also to people who are obsessed with the same everyday beliefs. They expose inflexibility and undervaluing.

In the animal world, there is one example of lesion of the femoral head. It occurs with male musk oxen in Canada (they have pre-historical origins) at the mating season, when they fight for leadership of the herd. Lower head crashes are extremely violent, and their legs have to withstand a tremendous weight in order to keep on pushing as hard as possible. The losing male feels strongly undervalued, and he ends up with a major decalcification of the femoral head. With time, the male will slowly recover from the lesion. A stronger and more resistant bone callosity is formed, which will allow him to dispute the leadership with a rival the following year. This repetitive, animal, instinctive and determined process is very *yang*, very masculine.

Femoral head or femur lesion means a serious blow for any person. In this case, the body requires that the person breaks with a belief from the past and that he changes. The body asks for flexibility. The fracture is normally the result of a dynamic activity. It happens to hyperactive people. The body says: "Stop, go a different way". However, it is also a characteristic of older people, who, as we have seen earlier, feel undervalued.

Femur or femoral head problems literally require that people reflect on the way they are leading their lives. To act like the ox and to show too much determination and stubbornness with the same everlasting beliefs is not an act of intelligence. A person who fractures a bone is a person who has become too stiff and inflexible regarding what was going on, and did not manage to get what he wanted, thus feeling very undervalued.

Should the problem affect the hip joint, see *Hips*.

Femur

The femur, which is located in the thigh, is the largest bone in the human body. Bone structure represents a person's deepest beliefs. Bone decalcification problems and fractures of the femur head or of the femur show a great sense of undervaluation of the person whose foundations were severely shaken up.

In the animal kingdom, there is a great example of damage to the femur head. It is the case of the brutal front impact of the Canadian musk oxen, during the mating season, when they fight for leadership of the pack. The impact, with lowered heads, is very violent and the leg strength to remain standing and pushing with great force is astounding. The male that loses this struggle always feels great undervaluation and is left with decalcification of the femur head.

With time, this lesion heals and a callus of stronger bone forms. This allows him to challenge a rival for leadership in the following season. .

This repetitive process, animalistic, instinctive, and very determined, is very *yang*, very masculine, and very warlike.

To break a bone means to release a lot of energy, but breaking a femur is a serious shake-up for anyone.

The body asks, violently, that we break with a belief from the past and make a change. The fracture is usually the result of some dynamic activity, either physical or mental. It happens to physically and mentally hyperactive people. The body yells "stop! Follow a different path."

This also happens to old people who feel undervalued. Problems with the femur or femur head exist so that people draw conclusions.

To act like the ox and show excessive determination and strong will with the same old beliefs is not an act of intelligence. The person who fractures a bone is a person who has become too inflexible in what he thinks.

Problems in the femur show undervaluation due to inflexibility in the way a person thinks about his life, his foundation, his roots, his deep beliefs, work, home, family, and money.

The locomotor system is not very clear on the certainties of the *yin/yang* polarity regarding the sides of the body. It is important to presume that the right femur is *yang*, masculine, and the left femur is *yin*, feminine, for both right-handed and left-handed people.

So, problems with the *yang* femur show obstinacy with the way of thinking and living, mainly with work and professional projects, as well as the influence of a male way of thinking (possibly the Father or the male model in the home or couple). Problems in the *yin* femur show obstinacy in the way of thinking and living mainly associated with the home, family, or money in the home budget, as well as the influence of the way of thinking and being of a woman (the Mother or the female model in the home or couple).

Fever

Fever is beneficial because it is the way the body lets you know that it is burning. Our obsession to lower the fever has serious risks as it keeps us from understanding what our conscience is crying out about through this symptom. To lower fever artificially is to have the illusion of lowering conflicts in our conscience.

We may consider giving an aspirin, but not without first talking to the person about what makes him burn in life. It is likely that tensions are related to home or work life.

See also *Infections* and *Flu*

Fibromyalgia (chronic fatigue syndrome)

Although Fibromyalgia and Myalgic Encephalomyelitis (Chronic fatigue syndrome in both cases) may not be the same technically, they indicate the same type of inner conflict the person has felt. This is why we will treat them together in this article.

The person experiences aches and pains all over the body, extreme fatigue, and sleep disturbances. The person also has problems in the muscles, skin, and colon, and shows difficulty concentrating.

The great fatigue (asthenia) is due to the lack of references and the loss of the herd, the group. It happens at the subconscious level of individual and collective minds. We will use an example from the animal kingdom to better illustrate the process that someone with asthenia goes through.

Contrary to what happens with wolves, where each individual wolf, when part of a pack, is not essential (one wolf leaving the group does not impact on the pack), in the case of sheep, and, more precisely, a sheep herd, any reduction in the number of heads originates a situation of danger. Sheep depend on the group, reason for which they bet on it. The herd cannot attack nor run away, only gather together. Predators do not attack a herd. What they see when looking at the herd is a huge sheep. The sheep led astray is the one which becomes the prey.

For the lost sheep, the only valid direction is the course which will take it back to the herd. For this reason, the lost sheep does not know which way it should run to, because it does not know where the herd is, and so it stays still. It stays very still, so not to give itself away to the wolves. The lost sheep has to focus on itself, and for this reason, its body has to generate a mechanism that calms it down. What the body does then is to act over the suprarenal glands, calming them down and literally draining them. The sheep becomes exhausted as a result. It becomes worn out, and then lies down, still. When we see a sheep looking like this, it means it is lost. It is trying not to move any further away from the herd. It waits for it to show up, and, when it happens, then its suprarenal glands come back into force and the sheep runs fast to the herd, to be part of it and feel safe again. An animal under stress is a very active animal.

When the sheep parted from the group, there are natural mechanisms through which the herd sends signals, from brain to brain. Since the lost sheep is very calm and in asthenia, it is very apt to capture this type of signaling from the herd and start moving in its direction. If it was not in asthenia, it would not be able to detect the radar signals sent by the herd. The same happens with elephants. They turn around in rotation and translation movements. It is all very fast.

The person suffering from asthenia is alone, and has to stop. For this reason, the brain produces fatigue. The person who feels very tired is a person who is lost. He would like to find his former group, family, herd, clan, or to find a new one. The person suffering from asthenia needs to stop his mental turmoil; he is leading a very fast and logical life, a very *yang*, very masculine, very controlled life. The more one fights off fatigue, the more it makes itself felt. One needs to accept and not move.

We have just discussed the fatigue that characterizes Fibromyalgia and Myalgic Encephalomyelitis.

A great feeling of undervaluation creates muscles problems; a feeling of separation creates skin problems.

Colon problems are associated with infamy, filthy things that a person noticed in the behaviour of someone close to him, either in the family group (more likely) or in the work group.

Mental problems are caused by excessive *yang* behaviour, by excessive control, by the great need to fight and show that you are right. See *Isolation*.

Fibromyalgia and *Myalgic Encephalomyelitis* symptoms force the person to stop, primarily mentally, to let go of the controlling *yang* behaviour and to experience a behaviour of surrender, a more *yin* behaviour, gentler, more feminine. This is not the time for a person to feel self-pity or look for blame on others. This is a time for the individual to focus, change his way of thinking, and probably change his way of living.

A person must be thankful and adopt a *zen* posture, that is, to follow his intuition. He must listen for the sonar that will lead him to a herd, a group. We all come from a clan. It is difficult to get free from the values of that clan. Generally speaking, we act with the clan or in total opposition to the clan, but always because of the clan. The clan always calls back the person who got away. The clan is very powerful.

It is possible to change groups. Every time that one is between two groups, life becomes a crisis. If a person is able to create another group, then he regains balance. You do not live independence in isolation. Independence means having the ability to choose your herd, your group.

The safety of finding a clan reener-gizes the person. The suprarenal glands fill up again and the person regains his energy.

The individual is important to the species and that is why the species has a project for the individual. The human being is gregarious. The one who brings new ideas is always the black sheep of the family. The clan feels its security challenged and tries to straighten up the black sheep. For that reason, it is important to always respect the clan, rather than to destroy it. It is by creating a new herd, and not by criticizing the old one, that we move forward.

The assembly of brains of a herd creates a collective brain with its own identity. It is the same for politicians, for society, and for the system in general.

Fibula

See *Legs (knee to foot)*

A fracture in the fibula indicates strong undervaluation.

Finger and toe calluses

Here we shall not talk about calluses provoked by using the hands or feet in any manual activity. We will refer to a natural tendency to form calluses, which happens mostly in the toes.

Toes are the accessories which allow the foot to stand and maintain its balance. A person without toes experiences more difficulty walking, and has a lot more trouble running when it is necessary to run away.

Toes are thus the feet's details, the

final look of our positions.

Therefore, calluses reveal a hardening of the skin's dead layers. They are related to communication difficulties, which are due to the person's stiff thoughts, as he clings stubbornly to past suffering, since he has rigid ideas and concepts. This is a very *yang*, very Cartesian person, in the way he thinks.

Fingers

Fingers have multiple purposes. To get hold of (grab); communicate (write, signal, call for attention, prevent, call for silence, point to people and things, accuse); to express emotions (to hold, cuddle); to pay a musical instrument, scratch....

Fingers are real tools. We could sum it up and say that fingers are meant to handle delicate things and to maintain what we have managed to obtain.

However, fingers without hands are not useful, and hands without fingers are not, either. For this reason, they should be examined together.

Problems affecting hands and fingers expose people who believe they are not worthy of what they receive, of what they get. It also depicts indelicate people.

There is not always a common denominator regarding the *yin/yang* polarity of fingers when it comes to the locomotor system (bones and muscles). However, it is good to assume that, both for left and right-handed people, fingers on the right hand are *yang* (masculine) and those on the left are *yin* (feminine).

See *Fingers – joints (arthrosis), Fingers – bones and muscles* and *Fingers – warts*

Fingers – bones and muscles

Lesions in the bone or muscle on a *yang* finger, masculine, denote undervaluing regarding the fragility of the communication between a person and a close male individual, or who plays a man's role (could be a woman boss). Lesions in the *yin* finger, feminine, denotes undervaluing regarding the fragility of the communication between a person and a close female individual, or who plays a woman's role. When amputations occur, this is because an actual separation has taken place, provoked by huge undervaluing. If it affects a *yang* finger, the tension was with a man, and if it occurs on a *yin* finger, it was with a woman.

Problems affecting the bone of the **thumb**, which is the finger with which we indicate our state of mind, joy, sadness and defeat, indicate undervaluing, because the person felt unprotected in the presence of a third party. If it takes place in the *yang* thumb, the tension is with a man, and in the *yin* thumb, with a woman.

See *Fingers* for *yin/yang* polarity.

Problems affecting the bone of the **forefinger**, which is the finger we use to point out, denote undervaluing because the person was unable to keep something that linked him to someone at home and felt infamy, disgust about the person with whom he had the problem with. If it takes place at the *yang* forefinger, the tension is with a man, and in the *yin* forefinger, with a woman.

Problems affecting the bone of the **middle finger**, which is the finger we use to show our rage, our repudiation, imitating a penis, denote undervaluing because the person was unable to keep something and felt angry. If it happens in the *yang* middle finger, the tension is with a man, and, if in the *yin* middle finger, with a woman.

Problems affecting the bone of the **ring finger**, which is the finger of union, where we use our wedding ring, denote undervaluing because the person was unable to keep something related to the partner, or to a boyfriend/girlfriend, someone he was intimate with. If it happens in the *yang* ring finger, the tension is with a man, and in the *yin* ring finger, with a woman.

Problems affecting the bone of the **little finger**, which is the finger we use to scratch our ears, but which represents mostly the posh side (this is the finger where seal rings are used) and also appearance and superficiality, denote undervaluing because the person was unable to keep his vanity or superficial image. If it happens in the *yang* little finger, the tension is with a man and in the *yin* little finger, with a woman.

Fingers – joints (arthrosis)

Joints confer mobility to people.

Problems in the joints denote major undervaluing in the identity of the gesture (it happens a lot when playing sports – the individual did not like his gesture performance) and/or inflexibility. The key words for all joint related problems are, therefore, inflexibility and undervaluing.

Stiffness, inflammation, tearing, distensions, sprains, tendonitis or ligament ruptures in the joints of the fingers denote the person's lack of sensitivity regarding what he thinks, and his mental pattern. And, of course, an inflamed joint impedes movement. It makes one stop.

Undervaluing may be felt through rage, anger, and wrath. When it strikes the fingers, it indicates that the person felt undervalued for not being able to keep what he had managed to obtain.

Problems in the **thumb** joint, which is the finger with which we indicate our state of mind, joy, sadness and defeat, indicate undervaluing and inflexibility, because the person felt unprotected in the presence of a third party and was unable to keep up his happy and winning spirits. If it takes place in the *yang* thumb, the tension is with a man, and in the *yin* thumb, with a woman. See fingers for *yin/yang* polarity.

Problems in the **forefinger** joint, which is the finger we use to point out, denote undervaluing and inflexibility because the person was unable to keep something that linked him to someone at home and felt infamy, disgust, about the person with whom he had the problem. If it takes place in the *yang* forefinger, the tension is with a man, and in the *yin* forefinger, with a woman.

Problems in the **middle finger** joint,

which is the finger we use to show our rage, our repudiation, imitating a penis, denote undervaluing and inflexibility, because the person was unable to keep something and felt angry towards the person he had the problem with. If it happens in the *yang* middle finger, the tension is with a man, and in the *yin* middle finger, with a woman.

Problems in the **ring finger** joint, which is the finger of union, where we use our wedding ring, denote undervaluing and inflexibility because the person was unable to keep something related to the partner, or to a boyfriend/girlfriend, someone he was intimate with. If it happens in the *yang* ring finger, the tension is with a man, and in the *yin* ring finger, with a woman.

Problems in the **little finger** joint, which is the finger we use to scratch our ears, but which represents mostly the posh side (this is the finger where seal rings are used) and also appearance and superficiality, denote undervaluing and inflexibility because the person was unable to keep his vanity or superficial image. If it happens in the *yang* little finger, the tension is with a man, and in the *yin* little finger, with a woman.

Fingers – warts

Warts are rough parts of the skin confined to a small area.

This is a symptom of frustration and undervaluing. It is related to the skin and the nervous system.

The person feels undervaluing and frustration because he has a need to please others as well as himself. Therefore, he is a person who is always comparing himself to others and who becomes very competitive. This individual has poor self-esteem and he allows himself to be influenced by issues related to image.

A wart may take years to show up.

Let us look at one example.

At school, the teacher is critical of a child's writing. And the child concludes that his fingers are writing words badly. "I realize that my fingers do not write correctly." And the child develops warts in his fingers. The child will seek perfection, in order to escape the likely bad grade he will receive and which he fears may undervalue him. This is a non-conscious phenomenon. It is important that the child is talked to and encouraged to verbalize his undervaluing, namely through communication with the individual involved. This person should be helped because he is not aware of his undervaluing tension, nor of his inability to communicate and will probably say he has never felt anything.

Flatulence

Fermentation takes place in the ascending colon (beginning of the large bowel). The person who suffers from problems in this area tries to decide whether to keep stuff in or let it out. Fermentation is caused by sugar in the body. When the person experiences doubts about his capacity to decide whether to keep stuff in or let it out, he may suffer from flatulence and pain.

Flatulence is the release of tension and air from the bowel and it causes relief. It may be associated with tension with the Father or with a male role model: perhaps a partner, supervisor, or boyfriend. In short, it involves tension with a model of masculine behaviour.

See *Aerophagia*

Flu

The body reacts by expelling the excess of toxins, fatigue, and tension. It is more common in the autumn and onset of spring. It also means that the person has more trouble protecting himself from the outer world. In other words, the person is not focused. He feels strong inner tensions that weaken him and make him more susceptible to adverse climatic conditions. Flu is associated with psychological tensions at home and in the workplace.

Fever is beneficial because it is the way the body lets you know that it is burning. Our obsession to lower the fever has severe risks as it keep us from understanding what our conscience is desperately telling through this symptom. To lower the fever artificially is to have the illusion of lowering conflicts in our conscience.

We may consider giving an aspirin, but not without first talking to the person about what makes him burn in life. It is likely that tensions are related to home or work life.

Food poisoning

Food poisoning is usually an isolated incident but it does not happen by accident. Food poisoning shows a great lack of dietary balance on the part of the person, and, consequently, a great imbalance at the level of his roots, his position in the world, and the people he associates with, and why.

Sometimes food poisoning happens to a group of people, which shows that they feel similar tensions in their minds, though individual reasons may differ.

Besides, there is always someone in the group who is not affected. Why? Because he does not feel the same tensions in his mind, does not feel the same as the others. So, he escapes the poisoning. Food poisoning, in fact, is not an accident but rather the result of a co-creation. It is important to ask yourself: "Who tried to poison me? Who bought the snacks that made me so sick? Who chose this restaurant? How did I feel prior to joining them for dinner? Did I go against my will? Why was I there, in that place, on that day, with those people?"

It is common for a person with food poisoning to suffer from gastroenteritis, which shows a tension associated with the emotion of losing everything at one time. This '*everything*' is subjective. '*Everything*' may be an exaggeration, but that is how the person perceives what he experienced. In reality, it may be a relationship, a dear person, or money, and the person feels that it is not worth living like this. It is a sensation of momentary collapse, but a very intense one.

The person who suffers from gastroenteritis has problems in the stomach and the intestines. Food is compulsively expelled through the mouth by vomiting and through the anus as diarrhoea. The body shows the person the sensation of losing everything and gets rid of everything through its openings.

The stomach is associated with the digestion of emotions, namely in what concerns roots (home, money, work, place where we live, close friends and relative, and biological mother).

The small bowel is associated with discernment. The person expels without telling what is good from what is bad. In the small bowel, like in the stomach, tensions are related to roots, close relatives and friends.

Forearm

The forearm is located between the elbow, the joint that controls radical changes in direction in our lives regarding our path and our goals, and the wrist, which is the most flexible joint in the human body and allows transmission of action to the hand, which, therefore, allows fine-tuning of movements before a decision takes place.

The sense of confirmation extends from the shoulder to the hand (from the least concrete to the more concrete). Accordingly, the forearm represents the capacity to start doing something that was already accepted (something that started at the elbow). It represents, for instance, the difficulty to choose the means to act. When the person fails to find the means to act in the most practical way, he feels undervalued. His self esteem is at stake. Perhaps the person was influenced by a third party or perhaps he simply has a poor image of himself. In general, the right forearm is *yang* (masculine) and the left forearm is *yin* (feminine). This applies to left-handed and right-handed people. We must remember, however, that we are in the most *yang* part of the human body and that locomotor system polarity is not always obvious.

Problems in the *yang* forearm reflect undervaluation or inflexibility due to the presence of a third party (a man?) or the person's obsessive beliefs. The person does not want to listen to his body. The body feels inept to perform some predominantly masculine task related to work or a job. The person feels that he can not get closer to his goal but insists, causing damage to the forearm. The person does not feel confident, but prefers to ignore it and strains the body.

Problems in the *yin* forearm reflect undervaluation or inflexibility due to the presence of a third party (a woman?) or the person's obsessive beliefs. The person violates his sensibility and does not realize that he lacks confidence in himself regarding some emotional issue; he shows lack of respect for himself.

Any problem in the forearm muscles indicates inflexibility and undervaluation; a problem in the bone shows strong undervaluation; and a problem in the skin indicates separation anxiety or difficulty in communication.

See *Arms (as upper limbs)*

In case of an amputation, see *Amputation*. In case of paralysis, see *Paralysis* and *Partial paralysis*.

Friedreich's disease

The so called Friedreich ataxia is characterized by difficulty in coordinating movements, associated to other neurological signs (loss of reflexes, reduced deep sensibility), *pes cavus* (claw feet), scoliosis, myocardiopathy and, sometimes, diabetes. It would take too long to explain the meaning of all of these symptoms. They are explained in detailed form in *Myopathy*, *Feet – pes cavus (hollow claw foot)*, *Pancreas – endocrine gland (diabetes)*, *Scoliosis*.

This condition, although rare, occurs more frequently in children and adolescents. It is directly and intensely connected to the relationship between that person's parents and also between the individual in question and his Father and the individual and his Mother. The incarnation on Earth project was violated, adulterated, in short, to be born was a deceit. However, the individual is not aware of all the tensions that run through his conscience.

Frigidity

A person who suffers from frigidity is a person who is afraid of losing control. It is a calculating and intellectual individual. This person does not want to lose self-control and lend himself to pleasure. Frigidity is characteristic of someone who lives a very structured life and is centered on his ego.

In our society, emotions are often punished. This is particularly true for emotions associated with sexuality, emotions that are all but forbidden in certain segments of our society. Religion and controlling families with overly structured routines try to convince their members that sex is only for procreation.

The frigid person is someone who does not know how to experience his body. He is very analytical and controlling. This is a person who probably suffers from other physical symptoms because the sexual impulse and emotions associated with it are great stress releasers, but the frigid individual does not take advantage of them. He is tense and does not allow himself to enjoy those moments. The fact that he does not allow himself to experience emotions in full may lead to several blockages and other symptoms.

Fungal infections

See *Fungi*

Fungi

The person is stagnant with beliefs that do not work. His past controls his day to day life. The individual clings to the past and "gathers moss", develops fungi. Fungi infections are parasite infections. The word '*parasite*' is essential in this context. If the person allows parasites to affect him, it means that the he is not centered, that he can not be firm with other people; someone around him is a parasite trying to take advantage of him. The person is stuck in the past and past beliefs, and so he can not deal as firmly and effectively as he should with the one who is sucking his energy and acting like a vampire.

Gallbladder

The gallbladder belongs to the tree element (wood) of the five eastern elements. It works directly with the liver.

It gets bile from the liver, stores it and concentrates it, and then it sends it to the duodenum. The bile ensures a better digestion, mostly of fats. The gallbladder is a little sac very irrigated by nerves.

Therefore, the gallbladder is an aid to digestion. It is a form of psychological aid. The tension the person feels is anger, rage, something that left a bitter taste in the mouth.

Problems in the gallbladder indicate trouble dealing with feelings and, particularly, clarifying them." What is my place? Am I being granted recognition for what I do?" The person goes through fits of anger but will not express his feelings. For this reason, he does not get rid of his bile and, instead, he stores it.

The person who suffers from gallbladder problems is someone who feels invaded by someone close and is unable to express his feelings.

When I feel anger or aggressiveness, I feel I may attack the other person. For this reason, the sympathetic nervous system gets ready for it, gets ready to fight and resorts to adrenalin. The energy rises up to the neck, shoulders, back and arms and it irrigates the brain quite substantially. The person loses his mind. People who store anger have chronic tension on their shoulders, neck and arms.

There are three solutions to deal with anger:

1) To annul oneself and pretend everything is ok, stuck in the illusion that the cause has been sorted out.

2) To follow a very *yang* path, playing a sport like punching boxing bags, play rugby or even hit someone.

3) To follow a *yin* path and cry our hearts out, thus becoming completely aware of our feelings.

The first solution does not solve anything and makes the person accumulate anger, something that could cause problems later.

The second solution resolves the effect but not the cause, and makes the person increasingly more dependent on that violent activity, which gives him the illusion of emptying his aggressiveness. What the person does not realise is that his aggressiveness is being nurtured, and, for this reason, growing.

The third solution resolves the cause. The person empties his anger batteries through awareness and observation of himself, becoming more genuine and assertive. The propensity for anger diminishes.

When anger is of the chronic type and never lived through, the parasympathetic nervous system (the system that regulates the automatic functioning of the majority of internal organs) has little opportunity to come into action, because the sympathetic system (which regulates adrenalin) is extremely active. The parasympathetic is thus unable to regulate the functioning of the body's vital systems that depend on it.

Anger is directly associated to gallbladder problems. Consequently, and by extension, the liver is also involved.

Symptoms may include: headache, pain in the eyes, sciatica, pain in the legs, pain on the shoulders, lack of energy, lack of determination, absence of sexual energy, irritation, impatience and digestive disturbances.

See *Gallbladder – gallbladder stones* and *Gallbladder – hepatitis*

Gallbladder – gallbladder stones

Gallbladder stones are more characteristic of a quarrelling and angry feeling, but, nevertheless, they go hand in hand with a *yin* behaviour, feminine, excessively passive and impotent. Basically, the person feels impotent and furious.

Gallbladder stones are aggressiveness in a petrified form. It happens a lot to mothers with families, as many of these women feel their families as a structure that stops them from letting their aggressiveness go wild, but that will not do anything to change it. They merely suffer and live off their petrifying anger. Bile symbolises aggressiveness. Gallbladder stones thus symbolise aggressiveness whose causes have not been sorted out.

Kidney stones are more in line with a *yang*, masculine and controlling behaviour. Bile symbolizes aggressiveness.

Gallbladder stones thus symbolize unresolved causes for aggressiveness.

See *Gallbladder* and *Gallbladder – hepatitis*

Gallbladder – hepatitis

Hepatitis indicates a joint problem involving the liver and the gallbladder. The bile ducts start in the liver. Hepatitis denotes a feeling of discernment and need associated to huge anger and resentment. Resentment and rage are associated to the gallbladder and not to the liver (see *Gallbladder*).

Hepatitis A is food-related. Rage and resentment play no role here. This is a shortage of food, a nutritional conflict (feeling of lacking). It could relate to actual lack of food or virtual undernourishment (under affection).

It could be, for instance, because the person did not receive his alimony.

The infection is done through the collective subconscious. This is the brain of the herd working on. It is quite commonly found in children who have a very demanding Father or Mother who are unable of truly loving them.

This tension is frequently associated to the biological Father or to a Mother with a very masculine behaviour.

Hepatitis B is a conflict of anger that originates in a feeling of lacking. For instance, it could happen when the person is disinherited or excluded from the group, from the clan, and feels angry. Or, for instance, when the person loses his parents, or when the young person who is kicked out of the house by his parents feels anger and resentment. The fear of lacking, the lack of discernment and a certain share of megalomania come together here. The person was expecting a lot more than what he ended up receiving. And, accordingly, he feels enraged.

Hepatitis C is a conflict of resentment associated to the sensation of lacking and to the unknown. It happened in the dark. Some information has been hidden. This may be because the person left home and misses the children (the feeling of lacking the children's love can be quite effective, it does not have to be just material, as we will see in *Liver*), and is afraid of the unknown (this is a situation the person never thought she would go through). "I do not know how to live like this. What will happen to the kids? I do not handle what I do not know well!" Sometimes, to make things even worse, something unclear has happened.

Another example is provided by the person who was born to an unknown father. Hepatitis C is common amongst drug-addicts. In fact, drug-addicts do not live in the real world; they live in the unknown, in another dimension. Drugs provide them with that different, unknown dimension (see *Drugs*). They catch Hepatitis C out of anger and because they are unable to access (feeling of lacking) that other dark, occult, unknown world in a different dimension, without having to resort to drugs.

Hepatitis C can also be caught when a young drug-addict is kicked out of the family. The fact he was kicked out, or marginalized by the clan, may force the person to face a totally unknown situation. This does not have to happen just to drug-addicts. It may happen to anyone.

In the case of Hepatitis C, it is important to find the male model that the person has met: Father, husband, men of the clan. Here lies the root of the problem.

See *Gallbladder – gallbladder stones* and *Gallbladder*

Gallstones

See *Gallbladder – gallbladder stones*

Gangrene

Skin gangrene involves the death of tissue usually due to a decrease in blood supply to the affected area followed by a bacterial invasion. Gangrene is the result of a bacterial infection. Serious lesions (for instance, a crushed leg) may block the access of blood and oxygen to the damaged area and create conditions for the development of bacteria. Infection progresses within hours or days of the lesion. Gangrene may also develop as the result of a surgical wound, particularly when the amount of blood that reaches the affected area is limited. This is particularly dangerous for people with poor circulation.

In conclusion, we may say that gangrene develops when a tissue dies due to lack of blood irrigation and becomes exposed to complications of infectious nature. Self-esteem and self-respect are associated with blood. In this case, blood ceases to irrigate the area of the lesion. What is at stake here is one's capacity to understand what is good for him and his ability to be who he really is without need for approval from others. It is often necessary to amputate the area affected by gangrene.

It is useful to consider what part of the body was affected and how. If amputation is necessary, see *Amputation*.

Gas

See *Aerophagia*

Gastroduodenal ulcer

A gastroduodenal ulcer has stomach issues and also duodenum (first part of the small bowel) issues.

Please see *Stomach* and *Bowel – small bowel – duodenum*

Gastroenteritis

A person suffering from gastroenteritis felt a tension associated with the emotion of losing everything at one time. This *'everything'* is subjective. *'Everything'* may be an exaggeration, but that is how the person perceives what he experienced. In reality, it may be a relationship, a dear person, or money, and the person feels that it is not worth living like this. It is a sensation of momentary collapse, but a very intense one.

When the process is individual, we have a person suffering from gastroenteritis. When the process is collective, we are confronted with an epidemic of cholera, which presents the same symptoms but with much greater intensity. Here, with cholera, we are not talking about a subjective feeling, no, here, it is very objective, since it usually follows great cataclysms.

The person who suffers from gastroenteritis has problems in the stomach and in the bowels. Food is compulsively expelled through the mouth by vomiting and through the anus as diarrhoea. The body shows the person the sensation of losing everything and so gets rid of everything through its openings.

The stomach is associated with the digestion of emotions, namely in what concerns roots (home, money, work, place where we live, close friends and relatives, and biological Mother).

The small bowel is associated with discernment. The person expels without telling what is good from what is bad. In the small bowel, like in the stomach, tensions are related to roots, close relatives and friends.

Gastroenteritis may result from food poisoning, which is usually an isolated incident but which does not happen by accident. Food poisoning shows a great lack of dietary balance on the part of the person, and, consequently, a great imbalance at the level of his roots, his position in the world, and the people he associates with and why.

Sometimes food poisoning happens to a group of people, which shows that they feel similar tensions in their minds, though individual reasons may differ.

Besides, there is always someone in the group who is not affected. Why? Because he does not feel the same tensions in his mind, does not feel the same as the others. So, he escapes the poisoning. Food poisoning, in fact, is not an accident but rather the result of a joint creation. It is important to ask yourself: "Who tried to poison me? Who bought the snacks that made me so sick? Who chose this restaurant? How did I feel prior to joining them for dinner? Did I go against my will? Why was I there, in that place, on that day, with those people?

General paralysis

Technically speaking, this is a meningoencephalic problem (affecting the meninges and the brain).

This causes neurological and psychic disturbances. It is normally progressive.

Meninges are a set of membranes covering the brain and the spinal marrow.

This is where tensions with the immediate surroundings, with close ones, are located. This is mostly with the Father figure, or the male model. Communication with the outside does not work. The person does not understand, and is not understood. It denotes major isolation.

General paralysis shows to the person that he must stop, that he cannot go on like this. This is a massive self-inflicted violence. It reflects the person's enormous difficulty understanding the meaning of authority (see *Authority*).

General paralysis is the result of an excessively Cartesian life, too remote from its sensitive side and denotes fears regarding the ability to control

everything and everybody. This is the product of a very *yang*, warrior and masculine behaviour. This results from problems related to humbleness. The person convinces himself that his ideas are correct; he becomes very stubborn about it and is unaware of the major consequences that this type of thinking will bring. However, he is a person who feels sad and alone. Contradictions in his life were simply too strong for him. And the body put a stop on his locomotor system.

This results from the repetition of an excessively masculine and Cartesian thinking pattern running in the family. This results from the feeling the person felt from all of those who did not agree with his ideas and thinking.

See *Authority*

Also see *Paralysis* for other types of paralysis.

Glands

Glands are groups of cells that separate certain blood substances and use them to produce other substances (secretions).

There are two types of glands: **endocrine glands** which secrete internally into the blood (secretions are injected into the blood); and **exocrine glands**, of external secretion (which secrete substances that are not injected into the blood).

Examples of exocrine glands include: sweat glands, salivary glands, lachrymal glands, and pancreas (in its digestive capacity), to name a few.

Secretions from endocrine glands

are called hormones and they affect the metabolism of human beings.

They are chemical agents that affect the functioning of the organs of the body.

See the affected gland.

Glandular fever

See *Mononucleosis*

Glans (head of the penis)

See *Penis*

Glaucoma

See *Eyes – glaucoma*

Glomerulus – glomerulonephritis

See *Kidneys*

Goitre

See *Thyroid*

Gonads

Gonads are the endocrine glands of the genitals (testicles in men and ovaries in women). Testicles produce sperm and the ovaries produce eggs. The hormones produced by these glands control sexual characteristics such as hair growth, breast development, etc. Both men and women have male and female hormones but in different proportions. Problems in the gonads indicate a true sense of loss of a dear one. It may be a boyfriend or girlfriend, a son, etc. **Cancer** of the testicles and ovaries makes these glands overly productive, as if the body wanted to show the person's desire to procreate, to create a new loved being. Cancer in these areas of the body shows the person's incapacity to verbalize what he feels relatively to the loss he experienced.

See *Testicles* and *Ovaries*

Gonorrhoea

Gonorrhoea is a bacterial infection. It is an inflammation of the urinary and genital canals that causes a purulent discharge and pain. It is contagious through sexual contact.

"I was bad! I must be punished!" The person must steer away from any sexual contact. It shows some violence and, above all, guilt, including guilt directed at others. It may happen to the person who feels a great responsibility to fulfil a sexual role with a sexually demanding partner and, consequently, feels a great sense of culpability regarding the partner's demands.

It may also happen to the person who fooled around (had sex outside the relationship) and feels guilty relatively to the person who led him astray. It may also occur when the person totally rejects his partner at a subconscious level and the body brings it to a conscious level in the form of a symptom.

Gonorrhoea is contagious through sexual contact. This shows that the person with gonorrhoea must stay away from sexual contact for some time. "It's enough! Stop for some time!"

Gout

Gout is created by the build up of uric acid and is characterized by joint problems in the ankles. When gout occurs, there is a tendency for uric acid to accumulate in the joints and fingers. It is an almost exclusively male problem. This symptom results from a great accumulation of uric acid in the blood. It is caused by faulty kidney functioning, but also by swelling of the lymph nodes, or by a great increase in the production of white and red blood cells. The person has too much acid, is very bitter. This is an individual who has a tendency to blame others and avoid being introspective. He is inflexible in his beliefs. The person has an overly masculine attitude and needs to look inside himself and understand that others are not to blame.

In the case of kidney problems, see *Kidneys – renal insufficiency.*

Growth (growth disorders)

Growth disorders are very much associated to the endocrine system. There are three glands that participate in the balanced growing up process of individuals: the pituitary gland, the thyroid and the thymus.

If a child believes it is not worth growing, his body will expose this tension from a physical standpoint. And the child will not grow. And why will the child believe that it is not worth growing up? There could be several reasons, but they all point to the child's parents and to the masculine and feminine models he had: "If adult life is what I can see is happening with my parents, then I want to remain little..."

The **thymus** plays a very important role until the child reaches adolescence. It is involved in growth and metabolism, as well as in the child's immune system. Human beings' memory is located in the thymus, and this memory is deep rooted in the experiences the child had in life and with his parents (mostly with his parents), as well as with the man and woman models he has met in life. The child concludes:" If adults are the way they are, then I do not want to grow up." The conflict is both silent and deep. This is what the child comes up with to gain immunity from adult life.

The **thyroid** is an essentially feminine gland. It regulates the body's metabolism, growth, weight, all of the body's harmony. And it denotes the person's capacity to express and make himself understood. The thyroid is where the body finds the calculating stance that taught it when to say something or when it is better to remain silent.

A child, who does not feel allowed to express himself, or who has realized that no one makes any effort to understand him, can give up on himself. Hence, he gives up accelerating his metabolism and puts breaks on it. The child stops manifesting himself and expressing his emotional crying. And growth does not take place. The tension the body is revealing is: "I cannot create my own space in the world of adults. There is no point growing up. I do not wish to become like them."

When this tension occurs during pregnancy, the child will be born showing smallness, nanism symptoms.

The **pituitary/hypophysis gland** is the conductor of the orchestra of glands. It has multiple functions. It also plays a role in the growth system. Not so much in what concerns smallness, much more when it concerns gigantism.

One of the hormones the pituitary produces is the growth hormone, which influences the person's growth and maturing factors.

At the level of the pituitary, the tension lies in the misalignment between the inner being (the person's interior voice, his intuition) and the outer world (his everyday life and what the person pretends he is).

The person may end up being a lot taller than his family, with very long extremities. The tension here is: "I am not tall enough to...", so he will grow very tall (we are talking here of tall people who come from much smaller families).

When a child believes he needs to grow very tall to be valid, his body will raise him up to the top.

This normally comes from the parents; Once more, from the parents' example. And most probably from the Father, or male model in the family, who wanted to go further, higher. So, the child grew up to get the reward.

Guilt

This is an emotion which does not exist in the animal world. It is an emotion invented by human beings and a controlling tool which causes huge unbalances, normally in what concerns self-esteem.

Gums

Gums are the support of teeth. They allow teeth to cut, that is, to make decisions.

The gums represent the basis of our vitality, our firmness, our security, and our self-confidence.

People who bleed from the gums are people whose confidence is shaken in face of adverse circumstances, even relatively minor ones. They are people who keep themselves from making any decisions, people who are loosing their character. When this goes on continuously, the gums recede and cease to properly support the teeth. This keeps people from biting, cutting, tearing, and making decisions.

Haematomas

A haematoma is an accumulation of clotted blood due to trauma. People who bruise very easily do so as a result of a weakness in conjunctive tissue. It indicates some mental obstinacy and lack of internal flexibility.

See the part of the body where bruising took place.

Haemophilia

This is a symptom that affects primarily men. The blood does not clot. It shows that the person has trouble assuming his own identity. It indicates dependency. It shows inability to be assertive, be your own person. The sense of belonging to a clan or family is associated with blood. If a family puts too much importance on its lineage, on its name and titles of nobility, the child may not feel confident trying to live up to the family's expectations and becomes haemophilic.

What goes on between this child and his Father? Why is the young man cancelling himself out? What went on with the males in this family? What pattern do we find? Is this a lineage that must be followed even if the young person is not predisposed to do it?

Haemorrhages – capillary or vascular

All blood loss represents an adversity and a lack of self-respect. A capillary haemorrhage shows an excessively demanding attitude with yourself and others. In any case, it indicates an unconscious lack of happiness. Haemorrhages may happen in many parts of the body, like in the brain, for instance. They occur when blood vessels burst. Capillary weaknesses indicate poor self-esteem in social occasions and when dealing with others. Vascular weakness must be interpreted in function of the part of the body where it takes place. If it happens in the brain, we have an extremely intellectual person, very Cartesian. If it happens in the reproductive organs, we are in the presence of a woman who cancels herself out as a woman. If it happens in the arteries and/or the upper part of the

body, it results from an excessively *yang* behaviour, excessively controlling, excessively warlike, masculine, Cartesian, and mind oriented.

If it happens in the veins and/or lower parts of the body, it results from an excessively *yin* behaviour, excessively passive, excessively self-denying, feminine, helpless, as well as Cartesian and mind oriented.

Haemorrhoids

See *Bowel – large bowel – anus*

Hair

Hair, body hair and nails are annexes of the skin and a form of skin excretion. All of these excretions have the role of protecting and communicating. But they also serve as antennae, means of seduction, reflection of health, example of loyalty to the clan, symbol of strength and they even have a sexual and social purpose, particularly when going in the direction of the other, in the way of communicating.

For all, men and women, the hair is the thread of our souls and it represents our ideas, thoughts, even personality.

Women's hair denotes their relationship with Mother-Earth. Men's hair represents their relationship with Heaven. Short hair is more *yang*, more masculine, and long hair is more *yin*, more feminine. For instance, men who shave their hair (like in Buddhism), do it in order to be closer to the Father of Heaven. Men who wear long hair have a good relationship with their inner mother, that is to say, with their feminine side.

There is a link between men's hair and the way testosterone is used.

In animals, hair is an attribute of strength, might (for instance, the lion's mane) and of loyalty to the clan.

Animals prefer to be beautiful rather than ugly. This makes them more effective.

Male lions have their manes so that they can protect females, which do not possess them, and which are less good looking and thus let themselves be protected.

Warriors of ancient times had long hair, in many cultures (Samson). It represented power on Earth.

For women, hair represents the right they have conferred to themselves of being beautiful.

It is more natural for men to lose their hair, but women may also lose their hair as a result of losing their antennae, their intuitive capacity. They can no longer contact the collective unconscious of the planet.

In all cultures, women-priests, priestesses have long hair.

The root of the hair lies at the dermis of the scalp. Dermis related problems are linked to feelings of being hit, to feelings of being invaded in one's territory and feelings of disgust towards someone or something. Hair also depends a lot on the management of emotions through communication.

Hair is related to fears and the subsequent stimulation of the suprarenal glands, which provoke its loss. **Baldness**, or hair loss, indicates the fear of loosing something in our lives. The suprarenal glands of the bald person are likely to be very active. This person has the feeling of being constantly struck and he is not able to communicate effectively.

Hair loss or baldness may indicate excessive male hormones and difficulty to communicate assertively. It shows mostly on men, but also on women whose behaviour is more *yang*. A proof of this is that nowadays women who have a professional activity and who become more *yang*, more masculine, also increasingly suffer from hair loss. Women are becoming more masculine. One of the characteristics of masculinity is to try to control everything, and not trust the flow of life.

Patchy hair loss is a small size bald area in a particular place. The tension experienced is the same as the one the person feels with baldness.

Dandruff indicates that the individual is experiencing a feeling of separation or communication difficulties, and that his ideas are not compatible with those of his partner, or someone close.

Dry hair is synonym of dry person. **Oily** hair denotes a slippery person, who does not want to be caught, and for this reason, runs away.

Hand

Hands, together with fingers, have a variety of functions: to hold something (grab – the ability to keep what was gained); to communicate (greet, write, signal, call for attention, warn with a gentle touch, call for silence, point out to people and things, accuse, show understanding); express emotions (hold, caress, give and receive cuddles); play an instrument (gentleness); scratch; dig.

Hands are real tools. One could sum it up and say that hands, together with fingers, are made to perform delicate things, to communicate and hold on to what we managed to achieve.

Nevertheless, fingers without hands are not useful, and hands without fingers neither. For this reason, it is advisable to examine them as a whole.

Problems on hands and fingers denote people who believe they do not deserve what they receive, what they achieve. It exposes undervaluation.

The right hand is *yang* (masculine) and the left hand is *yin* (feminine), in almost all cases, both for left and right-handed people. Problems in the *yang* hand indicate problems with a man, with someone who has a very masculine behaviour, rather invasive, hard, warrior like. They also denote excessive warrior behaviour on the person's part, but always with an undervaluation feeling.

Where did this person get his role model? He was surely a very much warrior type of person. Problems in the *yin* hand indicate problems with a woman, with someone who touches our sensitivity and even with someone who is too passive, but always with a feeling of undervaluation. It also reveals that the person's behaviour is too passive. Why? Could it be thanks to the influence of someone?

Amputation of the hand shows that the person believes he does not deserve to receive or keep something for himself.

People who have **cold hands** are people who are afraid of not acting correctly. They have blood circulation problems in their hands. Life does not reach that part of the body.

For the person with very **sweaty hands**, see *Perspiration*.

A **wart** is a hardening on a particular spot of the body. This is a symptom of frustration and a feeling of undervaluation. It is associated to the skin and to the nervous system.

The person feels undervalued and frustrated because he has a need to please others and also the need to please the image he has of himself. For this reason, he is a person who compares himself to others and who becomes very competitive. This person lacks self-esteem and allows himself to be influenced by others in issues related to his image.

Warts may take years to come up.

Let us look at some examples.

At school, the teacher criticises a pupil's writing. The child concludes that his fingers write badly. "I am aware that my fingers cannot write properly." Consequently, the child develops a wart on his fingers. The child is looking for perfection to keep others satisfied and to run away from the negative assessment from other people that he fears will undervalue him. This is a non-conscious phenomenon. It is important to talk to the child and make him verbalize his undervaluation, namely by talking to the person involved. It is important that the person is helped, as he is not aware of his undervaluation tension, not of his inability to communicate, and he will probably say that he did not feel anything important.

When warts show up on the back of the hand, the person believes he is not sufficiently good at what he does. His undervaluation is perceptible to all. Everybody can see a wart on the back of his hand. The body reveals his frustration through his guilt and belief in ugliness (severe undervaluation).

When warts show up on the palm of the hand, this happens only to those who work with their hands, either manual workers or those involved with sport-related activities requiring work with the hands. It indicates a slight undervaluation.

In the cases of **chronic epicondylitis**, which causes the hand to close in the form of a fist due to inflammation of the tendons, the person indicates he has contained his aggressiveness and felt undervalued for not being able to express it. The image of the closed fist speaks for itself. In fact, the person did not think it was appropriate to explode at the right moment. The person allowed himself to be undervalued regarding the rigidity of rules, values, regulations that he imposed on himself. And on top of it all, this inflammation is painful. It is a form of self-inflicted violence. It is the product of immense control. It is true that, although the cause lies in the tendons of the elbow, the effects are felt in the hand.

Hard scar

This is a psychological wound which has not completely healed. There is something left to forgive. Look out where in the body the wound took place and try to understand which tension that side of the body is associated to. This will help you know who you have not been able to forgive yet.

Hay Fever

See *Allergies*

Headache

The pain we feel in our head indicates that the way we live and think is not working for us, that the goals we pursue are not good for us and that we must put an end to obsession, insistence and fanaticism, and ask ourselves what it is we need to change in our lives.

The person who feels **pain in the frontal part of the head**, is annoyed. It often happens that the person feels fine and when he gets to work starts feeling this huge pain in the frontal part of the head, or gets home and feels the same. This means that the person is unable to be himself in those places and amidst those people. He is merely playing a role and has a false behaviour. The person is very annoyed. In short, headaches represent the misalignment between the balance of our inner life and our everyday life. **Headaches in the temples and even in the eyes** are often associated to incapacity to express one's feelings (anger?) to someone and also incapacity to deal with certain situations. **Aches on the top of the head**, extending over the occipital zone, denote difficulty to understand something that has already happened or is taking place. Pain on top of the head is associated to the so-called violet chakra, or crown chakra, and is connected with desires, fears or intuitions. The person is feeling things he does not understand or which upset him. It is likely that something will happen soon in his closest surroundings. When the person finds out what it is, the headache disappears. We are not referring to headaches provoked by brain tumour. There are many headaches that vanish when people vomit or even have an orgasm. These are called migraines.

See *Migraine*

Hearing

See *Ears*

Heart

Heartbeat is sinusoidal. Doctors call it sinus rhythm, which is the rhythm that begins at the sinus node. Anyway, the heartbeat draws a curve with a wave shape.

The heart is commanded by the autonomous nervous system. In other words, it is autonomous. The heart regulates itself according to the body needs. However, it does follow the respiratory frequency. And the respiratory frequency is commanded by our will, by our mind. This is the reason why when a relaxing period takes place, when the respiratory frequency changes and calms down, the heartbeat also suffers alterations.

The heart is closely associated to the emotional side. It reacts to emotions and feelings. It is not ruled by will or by the intellect. Any emotion or feeling, be it fear, joy or passion, makes the heartbeat faster; To the extent that we can almost feel it beating in our throats.

Human beings thus have two centres: the brain and the heart. Reasoning, rationalisation, thoughts, lay within the brain, whereas emotion and feelings are part of the realm of the heart. Emotions and feelings alter the heart. Anything related to passion and emotion in a relationship takes place in the heart. It is the organ of love, of ephemeral passions. "He broke my heart! It is as if she pulled my heart out. My heart is pounding."

But when the person controls his natural emotions (in other words, when he allows the mental process, the brain, to intervene in the dominion of emotions), such as fears, joys, passions, sadness, envy… this is when problems arise. The mind starts to control those natural emotions and feelings, thanks to beliefs or any other type of rules that the person imposes on himself, either in a conscious or unconscious manner. In effect, when the Cartesian mental process intervenes, it deregulates the heart (as well as other organs).

The person who suffers from a heart condition is a person who does not accept nor live his emotions and feelings. Especially grief. It is a very *yang* person, with a very masculine behaviour. This person is a fighter. Long term problems that the person has not faced up to, lack of joy, a belief in the need of effort and stress, constitute good ingredients for the emergence of heart related problems. When horror to emotions becomes chronic, then we need to resort to pace-makers or any other sort of artificial devices in order to ensure a balanced rhythm. Heart related problems indicate a huge quest for power. They denote a giant ego. Only a hardened, tense, constricted and made of stone heart can be broken and explode.

Arrythmias show a loss of rhythm. Heart angina and heart attack show territory conflicts. Communication between auriculae show even different conflicts.

The function of the autonomous nervous system and the function of the heart complement each other and live naturally in harmony. Our mental intervention only spoils the process. Besides, we only feel our heart beat when it changes for no reason, in other words, when the mind stops respecting the body and starts to control us. The cardiac patient is a very mentally oriented person, very controlled. And given the fact that he is a very controlled person, he needs to do regular medical check-ups to test out the condition and pace of his heart. He has entered a controlling vicious circle. He is a person who finds it difficult to love and/or to feel and live up his emotions. The heart is the core part of the body. When referring to ourselves, we touch our body with our hand, in the area where the

heart resides. The person who suffers from a heart condition is someone who does not know how to centre himself.

The autonomous nervous system is divided in two systems, the Orto sympathetic system (also called Sympathetic) and the Parasympathetic system. The Parasympathetic system regulates the effective function of internal organs. The Orto sympathetic system is used for attack and defence. It segregates hormones like cortisol and adrenalin.

The vagal nerve of the Parasympathetic system calms and slows down the heart, and the Orto sympathetic system accelerates and contracts the heart. It is the lack of balance between both that is responsible for many heart diseases. The worse the infection of the myocardia, the lower the level of the Parasympathetic system is.

The lack of activity of the Parasympathetic system comes from a very *yang*, competitive and warrior behaviour. He who has a normal functioning of the Parasympathetic system, when exposed to an Orto sympathetic shock, does not create a cardiac disease. The condition is a very inactive Parasympathetic system. In most people with heart diseases, the Orto sympathetic system takes over the Parasympathetic system.

The Parasympathetic system can be activated through spiritual work, through a more *yin* (more zen) life style, through the contact with nature, love and sex relationships, the contact with animals and the exposure to sun and moon. A stable and safe economic situation also helps.

The heart is formed by two sides, one on the left and the other on the right. It is dual. On the other hand, its beat is bitonal, which means the heart expresses our life in a dual world, in the world of matter. The right side of the heart is the feminine side, *yin,* and the left side of the heart is masculine, *yang.* This applies to everyone, both left and right-handed people! The auricula and the ventricle are on the left side, and the same happens with the right side.

The slow, venous blood (yin), rich in the knowledge of the body, brought by the veins, arrives to the heart through the right auricle, to purify. When it reaches the right atrium, this blood accumulates, and then the tricuspid valve opens so that the blood goes to the right ventricle in a vertical direction. When blood enters the right ventricle, it accumulates, acquires a spiral movement and only later does the pulmonary valve open.

At this point, the blood acquires a horizontal movement and goes to the lungs to purify itself. In the lungs, through the capillaries, the blood acquires normal movement, no longer spiraling, passes through all the lungs and goes horizontally to the left atrium. This blood, already oxygenated (yang), is brought to the left atrium by the pulmonary veins. Here, in the left atrium, it accumulates and only then does the mitral valve open to let the blood flow to the left ventricle. Here, in the left ventricle, the blood again takes a spiraling vertical motion and accumulates, waiting for the aortic valve to open and let it be carried to the ends of the body.

Thus, the function of the heart is to form spirals and to accumulate the blood before opening the floodgates.

The ventricles are more dynamic, and, inside of them, the blood has vertical and spiral movements. The auricles are more passive. Therefore, the ventricles are more masculine (yang) and the auricles are more feminine (yin). We then have a dual duality. The left side is more *yang.* But the auricular side is more *yin.* Thus, the right auricle shows the *yin* of the *yin;* the left auricle shows the *yin* of the *yang;* the right ventricle shows the *yang* of the *yin;* and the left ventricle shows the *yang* of the *yang.*

See *Heart – angina, Heart – arrhythmias, Heart – communication between auriculae,* and *Heart – heart attack*

Heart – angina

Territory, in our current life, is represented by roots: house, car, family, the financial management of the family, the environment where the person feels well (his friends club) and, of course, home, parents, children, place of work, colleagues, employees, money. The person who overruns someone else's territory, unsolicited, is a person who is watching out the other's territory. He is a trespasser.

From a physical perspective, angina is clearly a constraint of the heart, due to a territorial conflict. That person needs to set himself loose. He must leave himself alone. He needs to relax.

Oxygenation is insufficient. Normally, it is known as coronary insufficiency. It can be violent. The person forgets about himself and focuses excessively on territorial conflicts, on duty, on business, on responsibilities, on divorce fights…

Depending on the violence of the territorial conflict, the person may suffer from arrhythmia, angina, a stroke or even a fatal heart attack. This will depend on how the person has felt the psychological conflict caused by the intrusion in his territory or loss of that very same territory.

Heart – arrhythmias

The word arrhythmia is used to describe many symptoms related to the abnormal heartbeat.

Arrhythmias usually show changes in heart rhythm, loss of harmony, loss of inner order. If we lose the pace, it is possibly because we are living the rhythm of someone else.

People who are very confrontative, even when it is not necessary, who do not allow themselves to live their *yin* side, their inner side, their inner peace, their sensitivity, their feminine side or their emotions are potential candidates for arrhythmia.

This person is *yang* and does not surrender to life.

In fact, the heart problems in general belong to very *yang,* very willful people, who think it all depends on them and that they are in charge. They are always facing. They have a very masculine behaviour. They do not know how to surrender at the right time.

There are several types of arrhythmias.

There are those that are characterized by regular beats with low frequencies (less than 50 beats per minute). They are called sinus bradycardia.

There are those that are characterized by regular beats with high frequencies (over 100 beats per minute). They are called sinus tachycardias.

"Sinus" means that the rhythm is regular, though high or low. And because they are beating regularly, they are considered benign arrhythmias.

And then, there are the arrhythmias characterized by irregular beats. In these cases, beats can be between 50 and 100 beats per minute, which shows beats with normal frequencies, but what really matters here is that they are irregular.

There are mainly three types of irregularly beating arrhythmias:

Extrasystoles, atrial fibrillation and ventricular fibrillation.

I will not talk much about extrasystoles, which are characterized by early beats that occur earlier in the heart cycle. They are very common in the population and, for the most part, are benign. The most frequent symptom is called "palpitations". In these cases, doctors usually see no need for medication or other intervention. These are punctual moments when the person was very *yang* for some reason. Rest and calming resolve these arrhythmias.

Let us then talk about the most severe arrhythmias, such as atrial fibrillation and ventricular fibrillation.

The heart has two auricles and two ventricles. The auricles are more *yin* and the ventricles are more *yang*. On the other hand, the left side of the heart is more *yang* and the right side more *yin*. Thus, the right auricle is the *yin* of the *yin;* the right ventricle is the *yang* of the *yin;* the left auricle is the *yin* of the *yang* and the left ventricle is the *yang* of the *yang*.

Atrial fibrillation occurs in the left atrium, the *yin* of *yang*.

Pulmonary veins are the only veins of post-fetal life that carry oxygenated blood, unlike all other veins that carry venous blood. Pulmonary veins carry oxygenated blood from the lungs to the left atrium.

Fibrillation is triggered by an uncoordinated response given by the left atrium to various rapid impulses that occur in the pulmonary veins or in the atrial tissue itself. They are called ectopic impulses (the word "ectopic" means "produced outside its natural place"). These are impulses that happen outside their natural place and at unnatural moments. There may even be a kind of explosion of these ectopic impulses located in the pulmonary veins that give rise to the fact that, when blood reaches the vein-auricular junction curvature, these ectopic impulses fragment and give rise to two rotating vortices in opposite directions.

And this is where the key lies, in these two rotating vortices in opposite directions.

The person with atrial fibrillation feels a double conflict. She wants to follow two opposite directions. She starts a conflict, but she does not really want to start that conflict. And it is this duplicity of wanting and not wanting to go into conflict that gives rise to opposite signals in opposite directions, leading to the two rotating vortices in opposite directions. And atrial fibrillation arises.

It usually begins with very punctual situations where the person has short episodes of atrial fibrillation, which disappear while the person rests. Over time, the person not changing anything in his way of dealing with others has more frequent episodes and may eventually have to resort to cardioversions to reset the sinus rhythm. If the person remains in the same vibration, he may end-up with permanent atrial fibrillation, the cardioversions no longer taking effect.

This is a phenomenon that is triggered in conflicts with strangers, rather than with close people. The person with atrial fibrillation feels assaulted by a stranger.

Atrial fibrillation shows that this person, in the *yang* moments of his life, cannot stay *yin*. In a moment of tension, in a *yang* situation, this individual adopts a *yang* behaviour when, in fact, he wanted to stay *yin*. Atrial fibrillation happens in the left auricula, with oxygenated blood. Oxygenated blood is part of the circulatory system. And the problems with oxygenated blood have to do with some very masculine, very *yang* and very controlled behaviours.

We are talking about an individual who is angry with someone (a stranger, normally), yet never ends up hitting or

163

beating that someone.

Should this individual who is angry with someone hit or beat the other person, he would not have atrial fibrillation. There would be no double conflict.

The person with atrial fibrillation is violent emotionally but not physically.

While atrial fibrillation is quite common in today's society, ventricular fibrillation is much more dangerous and is much rarer.

So, let's talk about **ventricular fibrillation**.

The exact technical term is sustained ventricular tachycardia, that may or may not trigger ventricular fibrillation. It originates in the ventricle and no longer in the auricle. Ventricular tachycardia is characterized by rapid ventricular beating that can culminate in ventricular fibrillation, which may lead to cardiac arrest or sudden death.

Ventricular fibrillation causes uncoordinated tremor of the ventricle with useless contractions. It gives rise to immediate syncope and death within minutes.

Rather than contracting and relaxing alternatively, as is normal, the ventricles make rapid, weak contractions (flickering) produced by multiple electrical impulses originating from various points in the ventricle, which are thus unable to promote normal blood circulation.

Science is unclear as to the causes of ventricular fibrillation. It has long been thought to have originated in the left ventricle, but it has been suspected for about twenty years to have originated

in the right ventricle.

In any case, it occurs in the most *yang* part of the heart, the ventricles. These ventricles suffer a lot of flutter in moments in which they should be relaxed. Many of these ventricle contractions are in fact useless.

It is important to remember that, in a normally functioning heart, before the blood in the right atrium passes to the right ventricle, the latter is relaxed. And it is relaxed until completely filled with the blood it receives from the right auricle. Only then does it become more active. (By the way, the same happens with the left ventricle. It is relaxed until it is completely filled with the blood it receives from the left auricle. And only then does it become more active).

In ventricular fibrillation, the command for heartbeat, which usually begins at the right atrium sinus node, begins at various points in the right ventricle.

Here, unlike atrial fibrillation, ventricular fibrillation happens with venous blood, which is the blood the right ventricle deals with. And we know venous blood is part of the *yin* part of the circulatory system. And problems with venous blood show an unhappy, passive life that lets joy pass away. They are more typical of too-*yin*, too-passive, too-feminine, self-defeating, "nothing to do" behaviours.

Ventricular fibrillation shows that this person is frequently in a state of extemporaneous (at the wrong times) arousal (yang). This individual has poor judgment about the timing of relational decisions. This person lacks discernment regarding relationships. He is buzzing with his love relationships. He lives great passions and great sorrows. It's an individual who is very dependent on the love of others. And this dependency can be deadly. Here, unlike atrial fibrillation, which occurs with strangers, here we are in close love and friendship relations. These friendship relations may include groups of followers or fans who like this person very much. He can't stay balanced in love. Love relations can kill him.

See *Heart*

Heart – communication between auriculae

During pregnancy, the subdivision of the heart between left and right side does not occur, because the baby lives in total unity with the Mother. It only occurs when the baby breathes for the first time after birth, which is when he is parted from the biological Mother and the dividing wall of the heart is closed forever.

If the symptom shown by the child is the communication between the two auriculae of the heart, which is not supposed to happen, then one should find out what happened at the time of the birth/delivery, during pregnancy or at the conception stage, and, at this point, look at the relationship between the Father and the Mother (see *Babies*). It is likely that the father annulled himself in the war between his wife (the baby's Mother) and his mother (the baby's grandmother and the wife's mother in

law), opting not to intervene.

If the occurrence of communication between the two auriculae occurs in an adult, it is likely that it happens to a woman. Then it becomes necessary to ascertain what is going on (surely some sort of tension) between two women. Possibly, the situation between the mother in law and the woman should be looked at. In fact, the symptom of communication between auriculae is a typically feminine, *yin* symptom.

Heart – heart attack

Territory, in our current life, is represented by roots: house, car, family, the financial management of the family, the environment where the person feels well (his friends club) and, of course, home, parents, children, place of work, colleagues, employees, money. The person who overruns someone else's territory, unsolicited, is a person who is watching out the other's territory. He is a trespasser.

Territory is essential to life on Earth. Conflicts of a sexual nature and undervaluing in animal life are part of it. Heart attacks, in animals, are linked to the defence of the territory.

The process has always been the same. Initially I marked the territory, then I took someone in there and now, in third place, there is someone who covets my territory.

Heart attacks stem from a territorial conflict.

The example of deer in the animal world is very interesting.

Deer are typically territorial animals. In 90% of the cases, in the society of gazelles, deer, stags and reindeers, the old male die of heart attack and, in 10% of the cases, they die of depression. Gazelles expel all those who are not members of their clan. A gazelle has its females and offspring and does not want anyone else in there. Nothing new about this, many animals do the same.

Once a year its territory is endangered. It happens just before the mating season, in autumn. It lasts three weeks.

Young males have three weeks to win or lose the fight against the old deer. And they fight for dominance of the clan.

They confront each other; Again, nothing new here.

And let us give an example:

The old deer exerts a pressure of one thousand kilos, and the younger deer applies a weight of eight hundred kilos. The old deer wins the combat and remains in control. He keeps its territory. The young male loses but does not suffer any consequence either.

They both remain healthy.

The following year, the old deer exerts his one thousand kilo power and the younger male, by now stronger and older, opposes an identical one thousand kilo pressure. Here, in the face of matching physical powers, the old deer has a lot to lose, while the young one has nothing to lose. At this point, the older deer makes one last effort and exerts increased power, and goes up to one thousand one hundred kilos. The aorta artery and the coronaries swell

tremendously (*yang* side, warrior, masculine side of the heart operating full blast). The old deer wins the fight. It keeps its territory. The young deer only loses the battle and does not win anything. They both remain healthy.

The following year, the old deer is weaker and exerts a pressure of eight hundred kilos and the young deer opposes the same one thousand kilo power. The old deer makes one last effort, making the coronaries and the aorta swell up to nine hundred kilos. But this is not enough, and loses. The young deer expels it from the territory. The young deer remains healthy, becomes the master of the clan and starts mating and procreating to maintain the species.

However, the older deer who lost the combat, who is undergoing an emotion of major frustration, feeling undervalued because it lost its territory, suffers a heart attack when the coronary arteries, which swelled a lot during the fight, begin to get back to normal following the huge cardiac effort. This characteristic is typical of all types of deer.

Ninety per cent of male deer die of heart attack when they lose their territory. When they do not lose it, the coronaries get back to normal with no damage done. The ten per cent that do not die feel undervalued and end up dying of depression. They enter into an hormonal draw again (see *Endocrine system* about the hormonal draw).

A heart attack always takes place following a territorial conflict. It can be some months afterwards. According to the psychological tension the person experienced, he may develop arrhythmia, angina, a stroke or even a fatal heart attack. This will depend on how the person experienced the psychological conflict of intrusion in his territory, or loss of his territory without verbalizing it effectively.

A heart attack is, above all, a cerebral disease. In this stage of the attack, there are huge oedemas. This is the brain expressing itself at the level of the masculine temporal lobes (masculine temples). The person experiences cerebral oedemas, which cause headache, nausea and photosensitivity. Heart attack pain is cerebral. It is the brain that feels the pain. One does not die of heart failure, but of cerebral oedema. People do not die of coronary failure, but from a massive cerebral oedema.

Heart attack is not a symptom that occurs during stress. It always takes place when the stress period is solved. The attack is a consequence of stress; it only comes after stress, not before. It is a huge hangover.

Heart attacks strike people who are very territorial, very *yang*, very much warriors, very controlling, very masculine.

To finish up, it is important to remember that territorial issues in animals are associated to reproduction. Animals defend their territory because, for them, the preservation of the species stands above the individual. Therefore, the territory is linked to the species, reproduction and offspring. This ancestral animal feeling means that nowadays we, humans, feel territorial

conflicts in the neck of the womb/cervical canal of the uterus, in the case of women, and in the prostate, in the case of men.

Heart attacks occur more often at midday.

Heart attack

See *Heart – heart attack*

Heartburn

One of the functions of the stomach is to produce corrosive acids which attack the food, thus processing it. In the communication sense of the word, the stomach has the purpose of digesting one's emotions.

When the emotional conflict is very active, the stomach requires increased amounts of gastric fluid in order to digest better. The person keeps on ruminating, going over and over again what has been done to him. On this occasion, the emotional tension makes him think: "Bastard, I can't digest!"

The patient with a stomach condition does not like frontal communication. He is unable to deal with his anger and/or to transform it into aggression, that is to say, to change it into an acknowledged emotion, observed or even demonstrated (emotion comes from *ex-movere*, which means to move outwards). For this reason, he has to digest his bad temper, his anger, that is to say, to literally swallow up his bile. Then, he will feel the stomach acids under the form of heartburn, because the stomach, having had to digest all the emotion which did not *ex-move*, needs to produce more gastric fluid.

Heels

Feet represent contact with Mother-Earth. For this reason, in many cultures, people go about barefoot in order to feel the energy of the Earth, gravity and counter-gravity. Feet must be dynamic, as they reveal our awareness of being on Earth, of having incarnated. They allow us to walk on, in order to be able to progress and resist. Feet are the place where the dialogue between levitation and gravitation takes place. They are the world of our stances and of the affirmation of our attitudes. They represent our life's criteria and the accomplishment of ideals. The heel is the basis of our steps. It is the beginning of the foot's movement.

Heel problems indicate the person has difficulty moving, stepping on and imprinting energy in what concerns his roots: home, work, money and connection to the Earth or to the place where he lives and biological Mother. "Don't let me go!"

In principle, the right foot reveals the *yang* (masculine) side, and the left foot reveals the *yin* (female) side, both in right and left-handed people. However, we must remember that we are talking about the locomotor system, and that the *yin/yang* polarity regarding the sides of the body in this system is not obvious. Problems in the *yang* heel indicate that the person does not trust his *yang* side, that is, his male model, and problems in the *yin* heel indicate

that the person does not trust his *yin* side, that is, his female model, and that, for this reason, he felt afraid of doing things correctly at the level of the roots. They also reveal undervaluation regarding the family, the couple or work. In any case, feet problems always mean that the role of the biological Mother in the person's life is weak. This may be due to the fact that the Mother annuls herself in the presence of the Father, or because the Mother did not allow the person to be properly fed and/or rooted. It is advisable to check the history of the women in the clan.

Hematuria

It is the presence of blood in the urine. All blood loss (with the exception of menstruation) represents a lack of self-respect. It may also indicate an excessively demanding attitude with yourself and others. In either case, it represents an unconscious lack of happiness. It is probably due to a malfunction of the kidneys.

See *Kidneys – renal insufficiency*

Henoch-Schonlein Purpura disease

Henoch-Schonlein Purpura (HSP) is a disease involving inflammation of small blood vessels. It most commonly occurs in children. The inflammation causes blood vessels in the skin, intestines, kidneys, and joints to start leaking. The main symptom is a rash with numerous small bruises, which have a raised appearance, over the legs or buttocks. Most cases occur in children between the ages of 2 and 11. It is more common in boys than girls. Adults with HSP are more likely to have more severe disease compared to children.

It is important to underline that HSP, especially in children, is not a very serious symptom.

Here we are in the circulatory system, which performs the functions of feeding the body, transporting nutrients through the blood, and blood purification. It represents the delivery of life and the joy of living.

HSP indicates a lack of joy to live, a lack of love for a certain part of my life, or lack of self-love. It shows problems of identity and self-esteem. The blood is also the symbol of belonging to a family, a lineage, or even a clan. The lifestyle and thinking pattern of the clan is extremely important. What is the life style of my clan that I dislike so much?

The diagnosis of problems in the circulatory system is not associated with *yang* and *yin* polarity. Neither is it associated with the distinction between left-handed and right-handed people. In this symptom, side is not a determining factor. Organs such as the kidneys and bowels may be affected.

In this case, please examine individually each part of the body that has been affected.

Hepatitis

See *Liver – hepatitis*

Hernia

Hernias may be of many different types: inguinal (groin), umbilical, epigastric (stomach area), incisional (following surgery), femoral (hip/thigh), and hiatal (oesophagus), just to mention a few.

The most commonly referred to is the hernia that consists of a bulge or exposure of an internal organ of the body due to the weakening of the muscle cavity or aponeuroses (aponeuroses are the envelopes that cover the muscles) that surround it. The exposure of that organ may happen through a natural cavity or one that results from an accident and it may happen in several different areas of the body.

The organ shifts from its usual place. It shows that the person is undervaluing and abusing himself. He is trying to solve problems that he does not want to face, resorting to dubious creativity, seeking solutions which do not work, doing everything possible to avoid the people and circumstances he must face. The questions he must face vary according to the type and location of the hernia. See the organs affected by the hernias in question.

The discal hernia has nothing to do with this type of hernia. See *Discal hernia*

Herpes

Herpes can be of oral or genital type. Genital herpes may occur in the vagina or the penis. Herpes are associated with nervous issues and the skin. It happens in mucous skin areas, in the junction between the skin and the mucous area, commonly in the lips of the mouth and labia of the vagina, and the glans penis. These are the areas where contact is usually done with more gentleness. It indicates tension relatively to communication with the partner, whether husband or wife, boyfriend or girlfriend.

Herpes is cultural. In a culture where contact is not expressed through kisses, there are no cases of oral herpes. The mucous represents my intimate self. I seek the kiss for myself. The mucous area (mainly the vagina) is the place where the woman momentarily lets her guard down and surrenders completely.

Herpes may be painful.

It is the illness of tender touch. It is typical of couples where both parties madly love each other but fight constantly. The person desperately wants to feel the touch, has a real 'live wire'. However, when communication fails and the person spends too much time fighting, the body takes charge of exposing that conflict through herpes. Herpes is painful and ultimately makes kissing (in the mouth) or having sex impossible. Herpes shows that the physical relationship with the partner is difficult.

People with tendency to develop herpes are people who have trouble being alone and feeling love for themselves. They are addicted to love. Herpes shows self-inflicted violence in the relationship. If the person recurs to self-inflicted violence in the relationship, it is because he feels guilty about something. Yet in fact guilt does not exist. It is a total fabrication of a person's mind.

Hips

The hip is the main articulation of the lower limbs. It connects the iliac bone of the pelvis with the upper femur. It is the *yin* axis, the feminine axis, axis of femininity, symbolized by the mother. This is where a person's verticality starts. It is where you go from being tetrapod to being biped. It shows the relationship with autonomy, the capacity for internal and external mobility. "I accept to make a personal project for life." From old times, we read that the hip is the place of struggle between Jacob and the Angel. A person with large hips is a more feminine person, a person with more feminine hormones. Today, with the higher degree of masculinity in women, women have much narrower hips.

Hip problems show lack of flexibility, when the person's (man or a woman) deepest beliefs regarding his or her roots are shaken. This lack of flexibility must be understood in the sense that the person believes that the other people are wrong, that it is the others fault.

Hip problems also reflect undervaluation.

The keywords in this articulation are inflexibility and undervaluation. A hip problem may result from a movement while playing a sport, i.e., from the undervaluation that a person feels in the lack of agility for that movement. It may happen during a tough sport or any other. It can happen during a rugby match, while dancing or walking. It may also be in a figurative sense, in a simple and routine movement at work or at home when the person felt undervalued.

The person with hip problems must ask himself why he feels so undervalued. He must also ask whose influence he felt to the point of developing such an inflexible attitude.

Generally speaking, the right hip is *yang* (masculine) and the left hip is *yin* (feminine). This is true for both left-handed and right-handed people. Let us not forget, however, that this is the more feminine part of the body and that polarity in the locomotor system is not always obvious. Problems in the *yang* hip reflect inflexibility and undervaluation due to the influence of a third party (a man, perhaps) or obsessive beliefs on the part of the patient. The person does not want to listen to his body. And the body feels incapable of doing what he is asked. He feels inept to perform some predominantly masculine task related to work or a job. And the person demands of it with persistence. This situation causes wear in the hip area. The person does not feel confident but prefers to ignore that feeling and strains the body. Here lie the tensions of the roots relative to the relationship with a professional project or even with a man, the Father and/or the Authority.

Problems in the *yin* hip reflect inflexibility and undervaluation due to the influence of a third party (a woman, perhaps) or obsessive beliefs on the

part of the patient. The person violates his sensibility and does not understand that he does not feel confidence in himself regarding a problem with the house, home, or money and the family budget.

Here lie the tensions of the roots relative to the relationship with the house, home, Mother, emotional life and dangers, fear and money.

When a person suffers from **hip arthrosis**, this condition follows a devaluation of the person regarding any action, following an inflammation of the articulation (what is known as **arthritis**). The body is healing following undervaluation. The tension is gone.

The bones in the joints are held in proper position by ligaments and tendons that allow only normal movements. In healthy joints, all the bones are covered by a layer of off-white matter called cartilage. The cartilage allows the smooth movement of the bones and acts as a cushion that absorbs the shock of bone movement and weight.

Arthrosis results from the progressive wear and tear of the joint tissue, particularly of the cartilage, that leads to increasing pain, deformity, and difficulty of movements. The onset of hip arthrosis starts with the deterioration of the cartilage which loses its elasticity and becomes less effective. In the absence of part, or all, of this cushioning effect of the cartilage, the bones rub one another and cause friction, inflammation, pain, and difficulty in moving. In very advanced stages of this condition, pieces of cartilage and bone may get loose and lodge themselves in the joint, seriously limiting or blocking movement altogether.

The hips, knees, shoulders, feet and fingers are the body parts most frequently affected by this condition.

As we saw, the cartilage is located in the centre of the joints, where the bones come together. The hip is where the iliac and the upper femur meet. The muscles are also crucial in the maintenance of joint stability. The joint is enclosed in a fibre capsule (synovia) with a thin layer that produces a small amount of fluid (synovial fluid) which acts as cartilage lubricant and nutrient. When strain on a joint is coupled with a leakage of fluid, the problem is more severe.

The bone marrow is very important at the hip level because it is primarily in the large bones, and in the sternum, that the maturation of red cells, white cells, and platelets takes place.

Hives

Hives forms part of the symptoms associated to communication issues. The person feels apart from his family. He tries to be part of a group, community or even of the home (mostly the home), but when he is there, that irritates him a lot. In this case, hives (urticaria) symptoms extend to communication problems, as far as roots are concerned. The main problem here could be, in the first place, the atmosphere at home, namely the attitude of one of the parents, or the attitude from someone from school or work.

The person finds it difficult to be part of that community, due to the way it acts and, mostly, due to the actions of one of its members. Hives always comes with rash (pruritus).

See *Rash*

Hoarseness

See *Larynx (larynx, aphonia, hoarseness)*

Hoarseness is a condition of the larynx.

Hodgkin's disease

See *Lymphatic system*

Humerus

The humerus is a bone in the arm that runs from the shoulder to the elbow. A fractured humerus shows strong undervaluation. "I am not much good at this."

See *Arm (shoulder to elbow)*

Hump

Humps denote a problem similar to very stiff spines. It is non accepted humbleness which is forced on the body.

See *Spine*

Hydrocephaly

The term Hydrocephaly comes from the Greek and means "water in the head". In reality, it is not water but cerebrospinal fluid (CSF), a clear liquid which is constantly produced in the cavities (or ventricles) of the brain.

It passes from one ventricle to another (there are four in total) through narrow canals and then circulates on the surface of the brain. A small portion descends through the spinal medulla and is absorbed into the blood system. This absorption is carried out by specialized veins inside the cranium that have a surface similar to that of a strainer. Though much slower than blood, cerebrospinal fluid undergoes constant production, circulation, and re-absorption. Hydrocephaly is almost exclusively the result of a blockage of CSF circulation or re-absorption. In this situation, where CSF is constantly produced but unable to circulate, it builds up and causes an increase in pressure inside the brain that may result in damage to brain tissue.

Hydrocephaly must be considered as a cerebral vascular accident caused by the tension that a person feels.

See *Brain stroke*

Hyperactivity

Hyperactivity is not a symptom but it is fashionable to talk about this condition. There are plenty of movies, books, and lectures on this topic. Why? In fact, over the last few years we have witnessed the birth of an increasing number of children with somewhat different characteristics. They differ primarily in the way they react to the social environment in the developed world. This is verified by many technicians and specialists in human interaction, and child interaction in particular. This type of children always existed but now it seems to be much more prevalent and will continue to grow in numbers. These children are more open, and more idealistic. They are not absorbed in society.

Since they are different, society tends to label them as 'children with problems'.

But in fact, they are simply not adapted.

Children who are not adapted are not ill. In the Anglo Saxon countries, they use the terms ADD (Attention Deficit Disorder), which means that they cannot focus their attention and ADHD (Attention Deficit Hyperactivity Disorder) when they are also hyperactive.

In fact they may be inattentive, disobedient, contradictory, difficult, idealistic, and dysfunctional …

But what are, really, the characteristics of these children? These children are much more likely to be childish, in the sense of daydreaming, fantasizing, being idealistic. The child labelled ADD does not, in fact, suffer from attention disorder but rather from a heightened sense of attention that is not limited to the four walls around him. His attention goes beyond the room, disappears from the room and explores the surrounding space. This child is paying attention to everything, captures thousands of details, and is not focused on the teacher. His attention is based on his intuition and is, literally, connected to the environment. He is like a butterfly! He does not focus on any object for too long because, in a matter of seconds, he captures much more than the "normal" child does in a thirty minute span. This child does not focus his attention in a restricted way. Rather, he allows his attention to wander but when something catches his interest, then, he can focus. The basic difference between the ADD child and the ADHD child is that the hyperactive child must let his body follow whatever gets his attention. It is not enough to look or sense, it is necessary to go to it. He moves constantly as if he were three or five years old.

For instance, Flaubert, the great French writer, did not learn how to write until he was thirteen years old. The great creative thinkers were, in their majority, bad students in school. They were too open.

These more open children experience great frustrations with the way their families act, the same regarding school and society in general.

Each child must be accepted the way he is. However, society seeks to change him rather than to accept him as he is.

These children hate answering rote questions, assessment questions. They only enjoy answering questions for which no answer has already been given. For example, they will say: "I won't answer this question because it is not a true question. The teacher already gave the answer in class." It is as if they feel like they are being assessed: "Are you testing me? What business is it of yours? That's my deal."

These children must be surrounded by adults who understand that they follow their intuition and that the realm of the ego does not make sense

to them; they are true geniuses with many talents.

These children despise obedience. They prefer discipline, which is very different from obedience. They despise theoretic values devised by an adult abstract society. They need to have behaviour references. These children need to feel that they are partakers in the decisions made by adults. They must feel involved in the process and be able to propose ideas. They must be consulted with real questions, not false and manipulative questions or orders. Adults should praise, emphasize, and play up these children's talents instead of punishing them for the fragility they feel when they come in contact with order and obedience. If the adult understands what it means to work with intuition, he has much better contact with these children who, after all, came to help humanity change.

Hyperglycaemia

See *Pancreas – endocrine gland (hyperglycaemia)*

Hyperopia (far-sightedness)

See *Eyes – farsightedness*

Hypertension

See *Blood pressure – high*

Hyperthyroidism

See *Thyroid*

Hyperventilation

This refers to an excessive volume of air in the alveoli. There is lung distension.

The person fears the end of a cycle and the beginning of another. The person senses the end of a cycle as a small death and fears it. He does not consider himself worthy of living and is afraid to welcome the new life. The person needs air. He feels asphyxiated in the life he leads and asks for more air. This person leads a sad life, without great joys. It happens when a person was forced to change his lifestyle completely. Retirement is a good example of this.

Hypoglycaemia

See *Pancreas – endocrine gland (hypoglycaemia)*

Hypophysis

See *Pituitary gland*

Hypotension

See *Blood pressure – low*

Hypothyroidism

See *Thyroid*

Iliac bone

The iliac is the bone we feel when we sit on our buttocks over a hard surface. It is located under/behind each buttock and forms part of the pelvis. It is an hip bone.

It is usually referred to as the sacroiliac, which is the area covering the sacrum and the iliac bones.

See *Vertebrae – sacral vertebrae*

Immune system

Immunity is the capacity the human being has to evolve in harmony, in his ability to adapt to the environment, while evolving. Sometimes it means the person's capacity to live amongst "beasts" without becoming one and keep on evolving in harmony.

When we incarnate, we come from a world of unity and incarnate into a world of duality, where all matter needs an opposite to be total, integral. The body is a demonstration of the duality of matter.

Although people should always remember they are part of a whole, in the dual reality each person must be able to interpret what is harmful and what his good for him.

Immunity has the purpose of enabling the person to know what he should refuse and what to let in, in order to carry on in his evolution path.

What I must refuse should not be considered as an aggression to me, no. It is just the energy of someone who has a way of being that is not suitable for my own evolution in harmony. That is why I must keep him or her away from me.

Failure to acknowledge the duality that exists in our lives means death. It is to refuse incarnation.

People who keep hugging others all the time have no idea of what immunity is. They hug everyone because they believe in what they call unconditional love.

But unconditional love is not to like unconditionally. To love is to accept, not to like. It is true that acceptance favours union, and that rejection favours separation. But, <u>not to like</u>, does not mean <u>to reject</u>. That is the mistake that many people make. Not liking is not to create separation, it is to acknowledge duality. Not liking something or someone is perfectly normal. This is the reason duality exists. To allow me to choose whom I want to be around with. To like everyone is not accepting oneself. Not liking someone does not mean rejection. But failing to accept a person as he is, that is to reject him. It is raising a barrier.

To accept is to lower defences. It is an act of love, even if I do not like the other person. To accept is to acknowledge that, at the origin, we are all one. Rejection consolidates the separated ego. Acceptance consolidates the whole. For this reason, human beings these days find it easier to reject than to accept, because their goal is to nurture their egos. And egos need to feel their boundaries. Every time the ego rejects someone, it is able to feel its boundaries. Human beings confuse the emotion of liking with the feeling of acceptance and love.

Unconditional love does not just mean unconditional acceptance of others, but also accepting myself unconditionally. This means not hugging or even getting closer to a person I do not like. The fact that I accept that per-son does not imply I have to embrace him. I need to understand that there are people in this world who are not part of my evolution.

Maybe they are part of the neighbour's evolution. When the people we do not like cross our path, they do it so that we can say <u>No</u> to them, gently and lovingly. We become immune by not allowing ourselves to be influenced by what is not good for us. It is not by killing everything around us that may eventually attack us, no. Life is not a struggle. It is giving oneself with discernment.

People with self-immunity symptoms, allergies or intolerances, are people who feel attacked, in most of the cases, by harmless things. The role of the immune system is not to carry out an inexorable war. That idea makes no sense.

People who suffer from **allergies**, for instance, are people who defend themselves from many things that are, in their majority, harmless. The allergic person is constantly increasing his idea of a potential enemy and builds a large defensive body armour around him. The allergic person has an aggressive behaviour, but is unaware of it. In other words, a docile person who represses his aggressiveness is as prone to allergies as an aggressive person.

Leucopoenia is a lowering in the number of leucocytes (white blood cells) and, accordingly, a drop in the person's immunity. This person does not know how to defend himself nor to say <u>No</u>.

In the case of **leukaemia**, **discoid**

lupus erythematosus and **systemic lupus erythematosus**, the tensions people experience are also related to the immune system, but in another way.

Thymus related conditions are also related to the immune system.

Immunity

See *Immune system*

Impotence

Sexual energy creates life. It is the vital energy of the human body. Impotence is the incapacity of the male to consummate the sexual act due to the inability to have an erection. The erection results from the hardening of the penis caused by blood pressure on the veins. This, in turn, results from the pressure of the muscles that surround those veins. Blood circulation represents the distribution of life and/or happiness around the body.

Circulation problems expose a lack of joy in living, a lack of love for one aspect or another of my life and even a lack of self-love.

Impotence shows the man's inability to live out his masculinity in a sexual relation. The erection and sexual act that follows give the man an incidence of pleasure. His pleasure and hers!

Impotence illustrates the lack of vitality of the man in question, his lack of self-esteem and happiness. The keywords regarding impotence are 'lack of self-esteem' and 'a problem with the masculine side'.

For that reason, impotence may have several causes.

We may be in the presence of a man who has assumed himself as a woman, who fully developed his feminine side and has adopted a submissive role in any relationship. This is the case with some homosexuals.

Impotence may also happen to a man who feels a great responsibility to fulfil a demanding sexual role and fears that he will not be able to live up to his partner's expectations. In this case, he may develop tensions associated with guilt.

It may happen to a man who cheated on a partner, regrets it, and feels guilty.

It may also occur when a man totally resists his partner but is not aware of it. The body, through the symptom of impotence, makes the man aware of his feeling.

Finally, in rare instances, it may take place when a person experiences such a spiritual awakening that the body no longer interests him. This is the case of the person who renounces sex, not as a free or imposed decision, but simply because it happened as a result of his spiritual experience.

See also *Priapism*

Incontinence

A person who suffers from incontinence is someone who lost control of himself. Things get away from him. The person has trouble structuring his internal management.

Incontinence may be of urinary or

bowel nature. Urinary incontinence is associated with the functioning of the bladder, whether it is caused by malfunction of the bladder or by the central nervous system. In the latter case, it happens mainly as a result of senility. Urinary incontinence is a form of permanent enuresis. It is a desperate marking of the territory. Urinary incontinence denotes a complete loss of references. The person urinates to call the attention of relatives and finds comfort in his own odour. It is a desperate marking of the territory. It is the person's way of saying: "Count me in, too! I am here and I mark my territory. Look!"

This person returned to tender childhood. The tensions he feels result from lack of discernment and the need to mark his territory. It happens frequently with older people.

Bowel incontinence is associated with the anal sphincter, in the lower rectum. The sphincter is a boundary. Here, conflicts are experienced in a feminine manner. The person releases, releases, and releases. He never ceases to release and can do nothing to stop the outflow. The person is tremendously *yin*, tremendously passive.

Bowel incontinence shows a constant revelation of the person's underworld, of his subconscious, of his hidden side, his hidden emotions, and his true identity.

Here, in this part of the bowel, it is the Father's function that establishes the boundary. If the Father was too lenient, the person does not know his limits and may suffer from incontinence. In other words, if the Father had an overly feminine attitude the person did not have a model for recognition of limits, a model for stopping.

The person with incontinence cannot position himself from an identity standpoint.

When a woman (or a very *yin*, very feminine man) does not know her limits, her sphincter ceases to work effectively. It is a reaction grounded in our collective subconscious. In fact, in pre-historic times, men imposed the limits on women.

In older people, bowel incontinence happens due to a loss of control of the masculine side, of the *yang* side. Incontinence also happens to some homosexual men and some women due to their predilection for anal sex. It is not because they practice anal sex, but rather because they are very submissive, too *yin*, too passive. They are people who overdevelop their feminine side at the expense of their masculine side.

Incontinence may also happen in isolated episodes due to a great fear.

When a person feels fear, he feels that someone may attack him. So, the sympathetic nervous system prepares to escape. Here, contrary to the energy of rage, which rises up to the scapular waist, the energy of fear goes down the lower limbs. The legs prepare to run and the anticipation that the person may have to run for a good while may give him the urgency to empty out the sacs of urine and faeces to run faster. This is why, sometimes, a scared person experiences urinary or bowel incontinence.

Indigestion

See *Stomach*

Infections

This is one of most common symptoms ever.

In terminology, we recognize infection by the suffix *itis*: colitis, phlebitis, conjunctivitis, hepatitis, encephalitis…etc.

An infection is the result of contact of bacteria, viruses, or toxins with our body. Often it involves fever, swelling, and pain.

There is inflammation, a condition whose name comes from the Latin *flama*, which means fire. We are burning.

The infection does not depend so much on the infectious agents that are always around, as it does on the condition of the body to receive them or not, and to coexist with them.

To live in a sterile environment is not a solution. It is important to understand what goes on in the person's mind so that he feels attacked by agents, who after all, only attack certain people. Why this person?

The person who prefers to ignore conflicts at the conscious level runs the risk of having to face them in the form of physical symptoms. The body does not lie. The place where the infection takes place will give him an indication of where the conflict lies in his conscience. Speculating over our conflicts never keeps them from materializing in our bodies as symptoms, some more serious than others. It is necessary to verbalize them, to deal with them.

See also *Allergies*

Infertility

The body does not lie. Basically, a man or a woman who is infertile finds unconscious comfort in that. For a variety of reasons, most of them of material nature or related to the relationship, they do not want to conceive a child. The body makes a point to expose that hidden tension.

Often, one of the parties who was in a relationship where he was infertile, moves on to a new relationship and becomes fertile.

Material reasons (money reasons), or any other, may be associated with the moment of procreation, which may seem ill timed to one or both parties. There are also issues related to the negative connotation of sexual relations, over copulation, which allow certain people to have *in vitro* babies, but not to conceive through sexual intercourse. In other words, the person was only sterile when attempting to procreate naturally.

The person who is infertile seldom accepts the fact that he is so of his own will. This is not a conscious decision; it actually originated in his mind. In the case of a woman, it may be associated with the female pattern of the clan she comes from. In some families, the female thinking pattern goes from generation to generation and it is normal (they say) to have some infertile women. It makes no sense; it is simply a mental pattern.

Some women are infertile though

they have a menstrual cycle. However, there are women who are infertile and do not even experience menstruation. In this case, see *Menstruation*.

Inflammation

See *Infections*

Influenza (flu)

See *Flu*

Inner bites

They may take place in the walls of the mouth or in the tongue.

The mouth is the door to acceptance, to welcoming food, either solid food or affection and emotional food. The person who bites himself on the inside is someone who is not satisfied. He is biting the wrong place. He makes decisions at the wrong point in his life. He is not happy with what he is offered in life and he does not like what he has been doing either. Tongue biting indicates that the persons is violent on himself and stops himself from enjoying the tastes of life.

Normally, this is a one-off episode.

Insanity

This is the condition of running from the family, from reality, and seeking isolation. It is a violent separation from life. It is a true form of isolation.

See *Isolation*

Insect bites

When a person is regularly bitten by insects, his body is showing that the person is tough on himself, and that he feels he needs to punish himself, and that he probably feels guilty regarding small things. Being bitten by a swarm of mosquitoes is not the issue here. When this happens, everybody is bitten.

See *Malaria*

Insomnia

When we are asleep, life is as real as when we are awake. While we are asleep, we return to the source, to our essence, to the "I", our soul, our spirit, our inner self. Call it what you will. In fact, while we sleep, while we dream, we are connected to our intuition. In our sleep, whether we accept it or not, there are movies which are as real as our lives. Here, sincerity expels the lies and the person is confronted with his truth, his honesty, and his essence.

The lack of desire to face certain conflicts in our lives is betrayed by nocturnal restlessness. Suddenly we have answers, insights, which do not fit in with our daily life. Our ego wakes us up, does not allow us to get back to sleep, for fear that we may face the truth. The ego does not want to stop thinking.

During the day, the majority of people stimulate their ego, its masculine side, and its left cerebral hemisphere, which is Cartesian, logical, and intellectual. In an effort to live consciously, they think about what is well and ignore what is not. At night, we see the flip side of the coin: people have access to the unconscious, the irrational, feelings, intuition, and death. We recognize what we turned off during the day.

Between two and four in the morning, the body returns to its most inner self.

It is precisely between two and four in the morning, during sleep, that secretion of serotonin by the pineal gland stops and gives way to the secretion of melatonin, which is good for the immune system, increases the quality of sleep, and has a positive effect on enthusiasm, good disposition, and good humour. This moment in our sleep is very important because it is a very *yin*, very calm, and very *zen* time of regeneration of the person. Insomnia often happens during this time period, between two and four in the morning.

Sometimes headaches and migraines happen during periods of insomnia.

See *Headache* and *Migraine*

See also *Dreams* and *Pineal gland*

Intervertebral discs

See *Vertebrae*

Intestines

The word intestine is a synonym of the word bowel. If you are looking for problems in the intestines, you may find the answers you need in *Bowel – large bowel, Bowel – large bowel – amoebic dysentery, Bowel – large bowel – anus, Bowel – large bowel – ascending colon, Bowel – large bowel – bacillary dysentery, Bowel – large bowel – colic, Bowel – large bowel – colon, Bowel – large bowel – Crohn's disease, Bowel – large bowel – descending colon, Bowel – large bowel – descending colon – sigmoid, Bowel – large bowel – lower rectum (incontinence), Bowel – large bowel – transverse colon, Bowel – large bowel – ulcerative colitis, Bowel – large bowel – upper rectum, Bowel – small bowel – Crohn's disease, Bowel – small bowel – duodenum* and *Bowel – small bowel (diarrhoea and cancer)*.

Also see *Aerophagia, Tapeworm, Worms* and *Threadworms*

Ischaemia

See *Ischemia*

Ischæmia

See *Ischemia*

Ischemia

It may also be spelled **ischaemia** or **ischæmia**.

From the Greek, *isch* that means restriction and *hema* or *haema* that means <u>blood</u>. It is a restriction in blood supply, generally due to factors in the arteries, with resultant damage or dysfunction of tissues. It is the result of a masculine, stubborn, very *yang* behaviour.

Please see *Circulatory system – arterial system*

Isolation

When we talk about isolation, it is

imperative to talk about family, group, and clan. We all come from a family or clan. It is difficult to uproot the values of the clan. Usually we either act in complete accordance with the family or clan, or we act in total opposition. Either way we act because of the clan. The clan always calls back the person who got away.

The clan is very powerful. It is possible to change groups. Every time that you are between two groups, life becomes a crisis. "I am lost; I would like to find another group/herd/clan". It does not have to be the same group or the same clan, the same herd. Human beings are gregarious and do not like to live in isolation.

When a person feels lost from the group, he should thank the group (although this may be tuff) for this separation, this loss of references, and then, he needs to centre himself, that is, to let intuition be his guide and put an end to the daily grind that makes no sense. He must be attentive and listen for the sonar that will direct him to a clan, a group, a herd, a group that he can relate to. Independence is not experienced in isolation. Independence means having the ability to choose your clan.

The safety of finding a clan reenergizes the person. The individual is important to the species and that is why the species has a project for the individual. We must not confuse solitude with isolation. The person in solitude is in solitude by his own choice and is able to join the group whenever he feels like it. He is not isolated.

But, on the contrary, the person who experiences isolation, when he is alone, he would rather be in someone's company. And he waits endlessly for someone to call him but does not take absolutely any initiative to pick up the phone and call somebody. And, furthermore, when he is in the company of others, he can not wait to get away because he can not relate well to the group. He never feels happy may it be with or without people around. In isolation, a person suffers from an obstruction of the communication canals.

One of the ways to live in isolation is to completely block all communication, the fastest approach being the return to dust through suicide (see *Brain – blocked brain*). This is a shortcut. It is the immediate arrival at the destination. It is the radical isolation. There is the quick escape to get to isolation, provided by suicide, but there are many slower and more painful ways, physically and emotionally, such as Alzheimer's, Multiple sclerosis, Memory loss, Nervous breakdown, Insanity, Cerebral paralysis, Dementia, Parkinson's, Senility and Coma.

Any of these conditions may be resolved so long as the patient is willing to take a conscientious stand. Awareness of the condition is enough to stop the blockage and establish balance, so long as the person is willing to shed some tears and confront the causes of obstruction.

If you are used to working with charkas, it is common to say that the person in isolation has a problem with the 'crown charka'. He has a problem with the sense of humility.

People who suffer from the above mentioned symptoms, each one separately addressed in this site, are very mentally oriented people, very Cartesian, very *yang*, very controlling, people who want to be right and control others or, at least, their ideas. People who suffer from isolation have a problem with authority.

See *Authority*

Itchiness

See *Rash*

Itching rash

See *Herpes*, *Eczema* and/or *Rash*

Jaundice

See *Liver – jaundice*

Jaws

Jaws are the bones that allow teeth to chew food. They are the bones that support teeth.

The digestive system starts at the mouth. The mouth is the place where feeding starts.

The person with a broken jaw cannot chew. He can only take in liquids. He is prevented from using his teeth, making decisions, asserting himself and deciding what he needs to do in order to develop in his own life. On top of this, the mouth needs to be immobilized, which makes breathing quite difficult and prevents a person

from moving too fast, otherwise he would feel asphyxiating. The jaw hinders decision-making on the person's part, and also rapid movement.

This bone only fractures when accidents, fighting or practicing very violent, masculine sports occur.

The fracture of any bone denotes strong undervaluation in a person, but, equally, it produces a feeling of relief, because the person can be quiet at last.

Jaw-related problems indicate undervaluation and difficulty in asking for support when certain decisions need to be made.

They happen to people who are at a crossroads in their lives. The person is lost and with no sense of direction. However, he continues to have an excessively masculine behaviour, he faces up to others and acts like a warrior, instead of staying put and releasing the tension in his life.

Joints

Joints give people mobility.

Joint problems denote great undervaluation in the identity of movement (it often occurs in the practice of sports. The person did not like the performance of his movement) and/or inflexibility. The keywords for any joint problems are undervaluation and inflexibility. Stiffness, inflammations, distensions, muscle pulls, muscle strains, tendonitis, torn ligaments, all suggest that the person lacks flexibility in his thinking and mental pattern and feels undervalued.

And, of course, joint inflammation

hinders movement. It forces the person to stop.

The undervaluation can be felt as frenzy, anger, or rage. When it happens in the shin, the tension differs from that felt if the injury is in the shoulder. It is necessary to treat each case individually.

The joint lubricant is called synovial fluid. It is found in the mucus capsules of joints. When the liquid is released due to a tension in the joint, it means that the tension of undervaluation is very strong. A muscle strain is more severe when the release of this fluid occurs. **Bursitis** is the inflammation of a bursa, which is a small sac of fluid in the joints, whose job is to avoid friction between the tendon and the bone or the tendon and the muscle, as well as to protect bone protuberances. Bursitis is the inflammation of a serum sac. It reflects impotence and passiveness, undervaluation, one's desire to hit somebody without being able or allowing himself to do it.

See *Hips, Elbow, Fingers, Knee, Shoulder, Wrist* and *Legs (knee to foot)* for problems of tendonitis, ligaments, joint cartilages (menisci) or fracture of joint bones.

Arthrosis, polyarthritis, arthritis, pain in the hips, hip osteoarthritis are typical tensions in the joints.

See *Arthrosis,* Hip osteoarthritis, *Polyarthritis, Chronic evolving polyarthritis, Rheumatism, Acute articular rheumatism (children)*

Kahler's disease

This occurs when the person suffers from multiple mieloma.

See *Myeloma* and *Bone marrow*

Kidney stones

They result from the precipitation and crystallization of substances in the urine, such as uric acid, calcium phosphates and oxalates.

Too little liquid intake may also interfere in that crystallization process. The body's attempts to expel them provoke intense pain, which, according to some people, compares to pains during child birth. These calculus or stones are formed by substances which should have been eliminated. This means the person is clinging to a certain number of themes in his life that he should have put aside a long time ago, as they do not represent advancement for himself. The person chooses to remain stuck to old beliefs regarding social relations and relations as a couple, But in fact, these beliefs do not work for him And it must not be forgotten that this stubbornness causes the person intense pain. This is a form of self-inflicted violence.

Kidney stones are more in line with a very *yang* behaviour.

The gallbladder stones (see *Gallbladder*) are more typical of a feminine, passive, powerless, more *yin* behaviour than a masculine behaviour.

The *yin/yang* polarity matters when talking about symptoms associated to cysts, cancers, kidney stones, but it is not obvious. In this case, it is advisable to consider that the right kidney is the *yang* (masculine) kidney and that the left is the *yin* (feminine) kidney, for both right and left-handed people. However, there are no certainties about this. Problems in the *yang* kidney denote relational problems with the partner, because the person has an excessively *yang*, obsessed attitude, which probably comes from the man model (the biological Father?) that he has adopted and which does not work, and, still, the person does not let go. Problems in the *yin* kidney denote relational problems with the partner, because the person has an excessively *yang*, obsessed attitude, which probably comes from the woman model (the biological Mother?) that he has adopted and which does not work, and, still, the person does not let go.

See *Kidneys*, *Kidneys – cancer and cysts* and *Kidneys – renal insufficiency*

Kidneys

All substances entering the human body do so through the blood. Kidneys act like a filter. They need to be able to distinguish toxic from non-toxic substances and what needs to be retained from what needs to be eliminated. An initial filtering operation of the kidneys (like a mechanical sieve) retains albumin. Albumin will not pass through the holes of this initial sieve, so it stays behind, which is good for the body. The second filtering operation aims to retain the body's vital salts, on which the balance between acids (*yang*) and

alkaline (*yin*) substances depends on (the blood's PH), and to push urine towards the bladder. The kidneys' purpose is to filter the blood, and to remove variable amounts of waters and organic and inorganic substances from it. This way, it maintains the balance of the composition and volume of liquids in the body.

The kidney is the organ associated to the essential structures of the human body. In fact, the kidneys produce the erythropoietin hormone, which stimulates bone marrow to produce red cells.

The balance between vital needs and the need to explore the world is located in the kidneys, as well as the need to structure and balance out constraints.

The urinary system gets rid of residual waters and the large bowel empties organic matter.

The subterranean waters of the body are deeply connected to ancestral memories. Fecundity, childbirth, memory of the clan. In other words, they are linked to the effect that the clan and its descendants have on the person. Kidneys are closely related to the mission and life path of the person on earth. Kidneys regulate sleep and the person's dreams.

Kidney patients absolutely need to know the thinking pattern of their families, parents, great grandparents and the latter's parents (in short, the clan), namely in what regards life as a couple. Special attention should be paid to the life of the parental Grandfather on Earth, as well as to his ideas, paranoia, rigor, quest for perfection. The kidney patient needs to allow himself to reject the ideals and dogmatic paranoias that come to him through lineage and that have been disseminated by the children of a possessive clan, from generation to generation.

In this type of clan, the bringing of a child into the world is experienced as an epiphany and that person's birth is loaded with meaning, particularly in what respects the relation between the biological Father and Mother. It is important that the kidney patient knows about his own birth and consequences.

The kidney patient hates the feeling of being trapped, with no way out, and the feeling that his beliefs and life are crumbling down. He is deeply afraid of profound changes.

In kidney cysts and cancer, like in kidney stones, sides are important, but not obvious. Both for left and right-handed people, the right kidney is the *yang* (masculine) kidney, and the left kidney is *yin* (feminine). However, there is no certainty about this.

In case of renal insufficiency, there is no *yin/yang* polarity.

See *Kidney stones, Kidneys – cancer and cysts* and *Kidneys – renal insufficiency*

Kidneys – cancer and cysts

On this occasion, the central tension of the person who suffers from kidney cancer is linked to two keywords: crumbling (collapse) and huge fear.

From a biological perspective, the body is made of seventy per cent water. The person with cancer is someone who has a major conflict with liquids and who does not verbalize the major fear he felt, whether it originated in water-related problems (risk of drowning), snow (avalanche), petrol, milk, perfusions or money (the latter is often called liquidity).

The person's fear is so intense that it is as if he was afraid of losing his vital waters. And so, the person blocks out the exit of waters from his body (**liquid retention**).

When he sorts out the tension and the immense fear has gone, a huge cyst forms in the kidney. This consists of a strengthening of the kidney tissue that the body develops to fortify the role of the kidney, as it lost efficacy during the retention. The objective is that its functionality, interrupted during the tension, can be put back in the form of a flow of urine that is much higher than before the emotional shock. The body wants to recover its balance regarding the elimination of the retained waters, and thus produces a higher flow of urine. This is how cysts and cancers are formed.

The keyword for kidney **cancer** is huge fear, gigantic fear, associated to non-verbalized liquid issues.

As with any cancer, the affected organ becomes more productive. Therefore, as opposed to what occurs to the kidney of the patient affected by renal insufficiency, the cancer-ridden kidney produces high levels of the erythropoietin hormone, and encourages bone marrow to produce higher amounts of red blood cells, reaching abnormally high levels. Such as with the patient suffering from renal insufficiency, the person with a kidney cancer also has heamaturia (blood in the urine). Kidney cancer causes back pain and fever. Renal insufficiency, on the contrary, does not cause pain.

The essential tension associated to kidney cancer is the huge fear it provokes, as well as the feeling that the person's life is crumbling down. The bigger the conflict, the higher the chance that the cysts will be malignant and turn into cancer. In any case, for it to become cancer, it is necessary that the person has kept this huge fear tension for himself, within, and hidden it away.

In the animal world, there are examples of animals that suffer from retention of liquids. It is the case of salmons that return to the nascent of the river to spawn, around September. The route is tough and the bears are waiting and having a feast. Salmons' jumps are huge. One of them manages to go over the rock but falls on the side of the river, on the bank. Dry land! It is outside the water. Its life is at great risk. Fish need water to survive. This is when it will retain liquids. It blocks out all of the waters contained in the kidneys so that he stores as much water as possible, waiting for a wave to land near where he is. It will also block out the suprarenal glands (which are associated to the kidneys) in order to prevent the production of cortisone and enter a state of asthenia (major tiredness) so not to move and catch the bear's attention. This is its only chance of survival.

In kidney cysts and cancer, as well as with stones, sides are important, but not obvious. The right kidney is the *yang* (masculine) kidney and the left kidney is *yin* (feminine), both for right and left-handed people. Still, there are no certainties.

Problems in the *yang* kidney denote huge fear in the relation with liquids. This is associated to beliefs linked to the man model (the biological Father?) that he has adopted, which do not work, and still, the person does not let go. Problems in the *yin* kidney denote huge fear in the relation with liquids. This is associated to beliefs linked to the woman model (the biological Mother?) that he has adopted, which do not work, and still, the person does not let go.

See *Kidneys*, *Kidney stones* and *Kidneys – renal insufficiency*

Kidneys – renal insufficiency

The Berger disease and the glomerulonephritis are renal insufficiency diseases. Diseased kidneys retain poisonous substances and waste inside the body and get rid of proteins and of what is good for the body, through urine. They work in the opposite way. These wastes end up decaying inside the person. It is easily understood that when a person is filled with waste, he starts smelling putrid. And as a matter of fact, the typical smell of someone who has kidney problems is his putrid smell.

In the case of the patient suffering from renal insufficiency, we return to the issues of fear and crumbling. However, in this case, the person has a huge fear that his relationship with the other person crumbles down.

If the patient is a **child** or **adolescent**, who is not living a relationship with someone, the problem in the kidneys is associated to huge fear that his parents' relationship crumbles down. Should this happen, this child feels that his life will crumble down. This renal insufficiency problem that children have is associated to their strong dependence on the Mother.

On the topic of the feeling of crumbling that the child experiences, we may equally add that he may feel his life crumbling down due to the competition he has to undergo at school or in the sports he plays.

Sport is good, but competition is not, as it contributes towards the child's undervaluation (see *Acute articular rheumatism (children)*).

When the child realizes that his set of beliefs has crumbled down, he may have a cruel and bitter disappointment and develop glomerulonephritis (protein in urine).

Reciprocal tensions (kidney glomerulus) are managed right here. These are about conflicts associated to individuality and self-esteem, to the sense of individual value and integrity in the relationship between the two.

The pair of kidneys signifies coexistence. Renal insufficiency related problems are problems of coexistence and of relationship. Not so much regarding sexual relations, but the capacity to relate to his peers in general, how the person faces up to others, and particularly the couple's relationship.

The person who is complete is able to totally amalgamate his masculine and feminine sides. He is one, despite the fact that his body maintains his gender, be it a woman or a man. The person who is complete actually stops paying attention to what he is, man or woman, as being a man or a woman ceases to be important. The person becomes bisexual or asexual. As it is, we, in our society, humans, run away from the *yin/yang*, masculine/feminine balance. Men tend to hide their *yin*, feminine side (their shadow side) and women tend to do the same regarding their *yang*, masculine side.

It is necessary that each of us is aware of our hidden side (the shadow side) and make contact with it, experience it. When we embark on a two-person relationship, this is because we look in the other person, the partner, for the representation of the opposing pole, which, after all, is already inside us. Attraction for the opposite sex is normal, because it is something we lack.

Hence, a woman becomes aware of her masculine side when she projects it on a man, and the man becomes aware of his feminine side when he projects it on a woman.

When I come across someone who shows qualities that live on the surface of my shadow side (if I am a man, this will be my feminine side, my *yin* side), I fall in love with that person. However, I not only fall in love with her, I also fall in love with my shadow side (in this case, with my *yin* side). What we love or hate in others is inside us.

We hate the other person when he

shows us a side of our shadow that is no longer superficial, that is <u>so deep</u> that we do not wish to see it. For this reason, all the difficulties we experience with our partner are difficulties we experience with ourselves.

And we all know that in our relationship with our partner, we love certain things in him and there are things in him that irritate us. This is because we are always going in circles around our shadow. We like the superficial side of our shadow, but not the deep part of it.

A relationship between two people who are very different has a lot more growth potential, because we grow with the shadow side that the other person shows us about ourselves. People who are very much alike have a gentler, more comfortable and pacific relationship, but the growth is not as marked. It turns monotonous. In the latter case, the two find each other wonderful, they project their common shadow over those who surround them and try to avoid them.

The projection of my shadow over the other person and the shadow of the other person over me is something mysterious and fabulous. But it also undergoes difficult moments.

The couple becomes complete when none of them needs the other. When this happens, the relationship will be pure forever. There is total acceptance of the other person. Nothing repels or attracts us in the other person any more.

When none of the two becomes independent, the relationship is doomed, and the dependence is sickening, making any form of separation painful. When one of the two becomes independent from the other, the heart of the other person gets broken. He feels as if a part of him was taken away from him, because he continues to project his shadow on the other person. He feels that his life is totally <u>crumbling</u> down. The person feels he has everything to lose, and that he no longer has anyone. He feels he is in a void, and that everything linked to the family context has fallen over him, in a real and figurative sense. "Life is too hard! Too much is simply too much! I have ruined the best years of my life!" The person feels that he cannot face up to his life any longer.

Men who suffer from kidney problems (glomerulonephritis, renal insufficiency, Berger's disease), besides feeling major crumbling in their lives, will also blame their wives for the bad relationship. If a man blames his wife for the bad relationship, surely he will not be able to look at his shadow side (feminine). He will continue to project and will not accept his wife's feminine side, as she, after all, is showing him his own feminine side that he is not aware of. He should take advantage of the fact and grow with that other person's feminine side. For example, a man who finds his wife too *yang*, too masculine, should realize that he attracted her in order to understand that his own feminine part is equally too *yang*, too hard, not sensitive.

Women who suffer from kidney problems (glomerulonephritis, renal insufficiency, Berger's disease), besides feeling major <u>crumbling</u> in their lives, will also blame their husbands for the bad relationship. If a woman blames her husband for the bad relationship, surely she will not be able to look at her shadow side (masculine). She will continue to project and will not accept her husband's masculine side, as he, after all, is showing her own masculine side that she is not aware of. She should take advantage of the fact and grow with that other person's masculine side. For example, a woman who finds her husband too *yin*, too feminine, should realize that she attracted him in order to understand that her own masculine part is equally too *yin*, not sensitive and not very firm.

By being unable to <u>discern</u> what to accept in the relation with the other person, this man or this woman alter the filtering process of their kidneys and end up getting rid of vital substances and storing toxic substances. The person loses discernment and, instead of acknowledging the relational problems, puts the blame on the partner. Here, the person's inability to accept, and the need to blame the partner show the person's lack of discernment. The body will expose this through the bad functioning of the kidney.

As a matter of fact, the kidney patient has chronic problems with the other person (husband or wife, girlfriend or boyfriend), whom he/she always blames for the poor two-person relationship they have. Moreover, the person suffering from renal insufficiency tends to make judgements on the other person and, at the same time, is incapable of speaking to him in a clear and firm voice, in the right place and time, with tenderness. The person suffering from renal insufficiency has great difficulty facing up to people, although he is convinced of the contrary (that is his big illusion, which ends up destroying him). He will not confront the other with assertiveness, in a clear and firm voice, in the right place and time, with tenderness, love and respect. Instead, he digests what the other person has done to him, blaming the other person, becoming furious and ending up, when the real confrontation takes place, reacting violently, with anger and rage, which is not a synonym of a clear and firm voice, and only leads to fighting.

This difficulty to confront in a firm and simple way, which are attributes of our daily lives, is experienced mostly by people with renal insufficiency, who find it extremely difficult to say the word <u>No</u>.

The person suffering from renal insufficiency is the perfect example of the person who is afraid of saying No. However, he is convinced he is brave and that he can perfectly say No.

This patient chickens out when he assesses the consequences of saying No. For this reason, he will not say it and leaves it up in the air. Then he will charge for it.

The patient with renal insufficiency had a parental model, probably passed on to him by his Mother, of need to be loved by others. He needs others to find him a nice person, pleasant, altruistic, a butter-heart.

He needs to learn how to say No more often, with assertiveness. He needs to do it gently, clearly, immediately. Then his high blood pressure (potential volcano – the fire of water) will reach the state of equilibrium (the volcano will turn into a volcanic vent).

He should practice saying a firm No, that must be gentle, clear and timely, immediate. He must not wish to please others.

The person suffering from renal insufficiency should attempt to find out if his Mother did not wish to madly please his Father during pregnancy. This is probably the case, but the guilt cannot be attributed to the mother or to the father, or to himself. No one is to blame. But the responsibility (not the guilt!) is solely his. If he fails to assume his responsibility, he will not be able to solve his renal insufficiency.

The person suffering from renal insufficiency may have several tensions associated to money. In fact, the body waters are liquids, and money is also considered a form of liquidity. This patient will have money problems if he cannot say No to those who ask him for money.

The patient with renal insufficiency is normally the dumb charitable one. He will bend himself backwards in order to save others and be approved by them. What is the point of seeking approval if one is decomposing inside?

In short: we may say that the patient with renal insufficiency has chronic problems with the partner, whom he blames and does not accept the way he or she is because he/she does not accept him/herself as he/she is. For this reason, he/she loses discernment. He/she has major fears that he/she will not be able to follow the beliefs of the clan and he/she is afraid that the relationship he/she maintains with other person will crumble down. He/she is also afraid of saying No, almost always, namely when asked for money, which can bring him/her major financial troubles and a crumbling of his/her own finances. He/she needs others to find him/her a nice person, pleasant, altruistic, a butter-heart. For this reason, he/she runs away from conflict. This patient is incapable of being flexible and firm at the same time. He will not assertively confront others in a firm and clear voice at the right place and time, with tenderness and love. For this reason, he ends up fighting. He is profoundly imbued by the ancient memories of the clan that have been passed on to him by his parents or grandparents, and has lost the notion of what is good for him and what is not, in the process. In other words, the lack of discernment pattern comes to the fore again. His conception, and particularly his birth, must be analysed in detail and with transparency. The patient suffering from renal insufficiency has difficulty choosing what is best for him. He always thinks of others first. Not out of altruism, but out of the need of approval. If we had to choose a single keyword for kidney problems, it would be crumbling. When talking about the feeling of crumbling, it is the same as talking of deep fear, in other words, fear associated to a feeling of danger with extremely serious consequences.

It is this unique, individual sensation that the patient with renal insufficiency feels and that characterises his thinking pattern as a patient of this kind. In fact, there are people who undergo extremely hard episodes in their lives and who have never felt the type of crumbling that a patient with renal insufficiency feels and, accordingly, they did not experience renal insufficiency problems.

The kidneys of the patient with renal insufficiency stop producing the erythropoietin hormone, whose role is to stimulate bone marrow to produce red blood cells. In fact, from a physical perspective, the crumbling is, in this case, visible on the body. The person becomes anaemic and has no strength.

There is a category of people who show tendency to renal insufficiency. It is the case of deported people, exiled people, asylum seekers and emigrants. They may feel that their lives, roots, have completely crumbled. Emigrants are often found in dialysis rooms.

The degeneration of the kidney reaches its peak when all the functions cease and a dialysis machine must guarantee the vital task of blood purification. The machine is the perfect partner. In the absence of good relations, the machine has become the perfect partner, since the patient with renal insufficiency feels all relationships were bad. "At last, the ideal partner!" Nevertheless, as is well known, he becomes totally reliant. This is a violent way the body chooses to show the person what he never wanted to face up.

The patient with renal insufficiency finds it easier to communicate with the help of alcohol, coffee or tea, as these are diuretics that stimulate the kidneys. Thus, given that the kidney is an organ of communication in relationships, the person improves his relationships. Cigarettes stimulate the lungs and bronchi, which are organs for contact and communication with others. For this reason, in some gatherings with friends, there is drinking and smoking as a means to create contact and to stimulated the organs of contact, the bronchi, lungs and kidneys. Renal insufficiency patients normally enjoy these occasions and like to stand out. However, drinking and smoking do not solve the causes. They solve symptoms and effects. The core issues remain.

With renal insufficiency, it is not important to know which of the kidneys is *yang* and which is *yin*. In fact, both are caught in the renal insufficiency. This is because this is a two-person relationship.

The *yin/yang* polarity does matter when talking about symptoms such as cysts, cancers and stones.

Bladder problems are caused by stress. Kidney problems are provoked by obsessive fears.

See *Kidneys*, *Kidney stones* and *Kidneys – cancer and cysts*

Kink

See *Stiff neck*

Kissing disease

See *Mononucleosis*

Knee

The knee is a joint. Joints lend mobility to the body. The bones of the joints are kept in place by ligaments and tendons that only allow normal movement. Muscles also help determine joint stability. The joint is enclosed in a fibrous capsule filled with a thin membrane that constantly produces a small amount of fluid; this fluid, called synovial fluid acts as a nutrient and a lubricant to the cartilage. In a joint, like the knee joint, the top of the bones that make it up are covered by a cap of off-white elastic matter, the cartilage (meniscus), which allows the smooth movement of bones and acts like a cushion that absorbs the impact of bone movement and, particularly, weight. **Arthrosis** results from the progressive wear and tear of the joint tissue, particularly of the cartilage, that leads to increasing pain, deformity, and difficulty of movements. The onset of arthrosis starts with the deterioration of the cartilage, which loses its elasticity and becomes less effective. In the absence of part or all of this cushioning effect of the cartilage, the bones rub one another and cause friction, inflammation, pain, and difficulty in moving.

In very advanced stages of this condition, pieces of cartilage and bone may get loose and lodge themselves in the joint, seriously limiting or blocking movement altogether.

The hips, knees, shoulders, feet, and fingers are the body parts most frequently affected by this condition.

As we saw, the joint cartilage is located in the middle of the joints, where the bones come together. In the knee, for instance, it is where the femur and tibia come together and that cartilage is called meniscus.

Problems in the joints expose great undervaluation in movement identity, it happens frequently while playing sports (the person did not like the performance of his gesture).

The knees play an essential flexibility role in a person's life. They denote his internal flexibility. The keywords here, as in all joints, are inflexibility and undervaluation.

Stiffness, inflammations, torsions, distensions, and torn ligaments in joint areas reflect lack of flexibility regarding the person's mental pattern, inflexibility that ends up clearly abusing the person. This person is inflexible with ideas that do not work for him but which he insists on keeping. By not respecting himself, he is actually undervaluing himself. It is as if he were unhappy with his performance and forced himself to come up with another, totally disrespecting himself, punishing his own body. Of course, joint inflammation blocks movement. It forces him to stop.

Joint lesions may take place in ligaments, tendons, or bones. The knee is a likely area for joint problems.

In soccer and other sports that cause much wear on joints, the knees of players are frequently affected. However, knee problems do not necessarily occur as the result of unusual physical effort. It may happen as you cross a street. In fact, what really matters is the tension in your conscience and any movement may produce the symptom. It may be a conflict with the Father, the Mother, with a teacher, with spirituality, or with authority. It happens frequently to adolescents.

Besides flexibility, the knee shows humility, the acceptance of parental authority. When you bow before someone, you place a knee on the ground as a gesture of humility. When people pray, they place both knees on the ground as a gesture of humility and respect.

Many oriental practices, such as yoga, aikido, judo, and many others begin with the practitioners with their knees on the ground, as a gesture of humility.

The right knee is *yang* (masculine) and the left knee is *yin* (feminine). This is the same for left-handed and right-handed people. We should not forget that we are in the realm of the locomotor system and that, in this system, polarity is not always clear. Problems in the *yang* knee reflect inflexibility and undervaluation, due to the influence of a third party (a man, perhaps) or obsessive beliefs on the part of the patient. It shows a lack of firmness, because the person is too dependent on the Father or a male figure and, at the same time, it shows a lack of humility towards a man. The person does not feel confident, but prefers to ignore that feeling and strains the body. The person may be experiencing a conflict with his Father or with another man.

Problems in the *yin* knee reflect inflexibility and undervaluation due to the influence of a third party (a woman, perhaps) or obsessive beliefs on the part of the patient. It shows a lack of firmness, because the person is too dependent on the Mother or a female figure and, at the same time, it shows a lack of humility towards a woman. The person violates his sensibility and does not understand that he does not feel confidence in himself regarding a problem with the house, home, or money and the family budget. And he becomes ill!

The mental pattern of the person who becomes inflexible or lacking in humility may be connected with the fact that the person lets himself be influenced by someone who shakes his foundation, making him live a life that is not suitable to him.

We must look for a man or a woman connected with the person's roots (work, home, family, place where the person lives).

The mountain climber is an idealist who rises from Mother to Father, from Earth to Sky. When he feels undervalued, the symptoms affect his knees.

Kyphosis

See *Spine*

Larynx (larynx, aphonia, hoarseness)

The larynx is part of the breathing system. The previous segment, the pharynx, splits into the larynx, which carries air towards the lungs through the trachea (respiratory function), and the oesophagus, which carries food to the stomach (digestive function). The larynx is, therefore, the first organ of the respiratory system that is not shared with the digestive system. It is in the larynx that the vocal chords' sound is produced. The larynx is connected with the female brain, *yin*. **Laryngitis** is a female conflict. The respiratory system is associated with relationships.

Through the larynx, the body exposes a person's great fears. The vocal chords are located in the larynx and they can produce very high-pitch sounds. The role of females in nature is to alert the babies and call for protection, by producing loud sounds. Men, in general, do not suffer from laryngitis; they go directly on the offensive. Men materialize this conflict in the bronchi and their voice becomes stronger. When a baby cries, he produces high-pitch sounds. This touches men primarily, unless their brain is blocked.

In the case of **aphonia** (voice loss), the fear is so great that the best thing to do is stay very quiet to avoid calling the predator's attention.

Hoarseness is a less serious phenomenon than aphonia. Hoarseness deals with regret over something said, or regret over not voicing something.

The person who is hoarse following a night of partying, of singing and drinking, must not consider hoarseness as a symptom. The body needs to find harmony following the previous ex-cesses. This is nothing to cause alarm. However, if the person goes out night after night and then is hoarse every morning, hoarseness must be considered a symptom. In this case, it is a dependency associated with the need to go out and scream to establish some balance.

Lazy bowels

See *Bowel – large bowel – colon*

Lazy bowels is a synonym of constipation.

Left-handed and right-handed people

See *Brain, Brain – left-handed men, Brain – left-handed women, Brain – right-handed men* and *Brain – right-handed women*

Legs (knee to foot)

This is the area in the lower limbs from the knee to the foot.

The sense of accomplishment extends from the knee to the foot (from the least to the most concrete). For this reason, the leg shows that, following our integration and acceptance of something we have, we need to implement it and make it part of the living style and way of living as far as work, the home, the geographical place we are, money, matter and contact with others is concerned.

Elephant legs (extremely fat) are characteristic of people who are afraid of the future. They would rather stay inactive. The mothers of these people kept telling them to be extremely careful.

Problems in the legs can take place in the muscles (shin), the bones (tibia or fibula) or on the skin. Skin problems denote a tension related to separation or communication difficulties. Muscle problems indicate lack of mental flexibility and undervaluation. Bone related problems show strong undervaluation. "I am not good at this. I am not worth much when it comes to this." It indicates lack of assertiveness.

There is no absolute *yin/yang* polarity in the locomotor system according to the affected sides. The tension that is felt is related to undervaluation and inflexibility, independently of the side of the body that is affected. Nevertheless, it can be said, *a priori*, that in relational matters, the right side is *yang*, masculine and the left side is *yin*, feminine. This applies both to right and left-handed people. There are no certainties, though. Depending on the time of lesion, it is advisable to read *Bone*, *Muscles* and *Skin*.

See *Legs as lower limbs*

See equally *Amputation*, *Paralysis* and *Partial paralysis*, if appropriate.

Legs as lower limbs

Legs ensure mobility, flexibility, activity and firmness.

The lower limbs play a vital role in the locomotor system. They allow us to walk, run, jump, change direction and take roots on Earth.

They are the foundations of our body and the extension of the hips.

The hip is the main joint of the lower limbs. The legs start at the hip, and they are part of the *yin* axis, the feminine axis, the axis of femininity, symbolized by the Mother. The person's verticality starts at the hip and legs. This is where one goes from being quadruped to biped.

The legs reveal the relationship with autonomy and the capacity for internal and external mobility. They show the person's determination as the one responsible for his own life project. A project that has foundations!

The sense of accomplishment flows from the hip to the foot (from the least to the most concrete).

Tensions in the lower limbs are tensions in the relationship with the world or with other people. Lower limbs allow us to walk in the direction of others. They have a very obvious social meaning. They are also a good tool when we need to escape. They allow us to run. This is where the problems related to our roots are located. These problems are connected to the biological Mother, work, material accomplishment, money, home, the partner, and the place where we live, in short, to the roots. Actually, the legs are what connects us to the earth. This is where the quality of practical accomplishments is measured. What I think of myself and what I am doing in the world.

Our relationship with what we have is placed in the legs.

Look out for the area of the lower limb that has been affected.

See equally *Amputation*, *Paralysis* and *Partial paralysis*, if appropriate.

Leprosy

In cases of leprosy, the skin develops holes and the nerves of the dermis hide away. The person loses sensibility. This hole in the skin symbolizes separation between people. More than actual separation, it symbolizes fear of separation.

It reaches the dermis, which indicates that there is also a conflict regarding something dirty, something that disgusts the person. It hurts.

Leprosy represents the fear of permanent separation. Leprosy must be understood in the historic context where church wanted to unite human and divine. Church imposed itself as the mandatory passageway. This became unacceptable to people who possessed medium or paranormal qualities. The risk of being burnt at the stake was high. That was a great fear. There was great anxiety regarding the possible deep separation from God and the community (since priests claimed they represented God and were part of the mandatory passageway) through death.

Leprosy almost always ended in amputation (actual separation).

Leucopoenia

This is a reduction in the number of white cells (leucocytes) in the blood. The person looses immunity. Please see *Immune system* to understand the type of conflict the person is experiencing. Also see *Blood*.

Leucorrhoea

White discharge expelled through the vagina.

It denotes feelings such as: "We, women, have no power over men. My partner makes me so angry!" It is as if the vagina is shedding tears of anger.

See *Vagina*

Leukaemia

Leukaemia often involves fever, weariness, and swelling of glands. The person who suffers from leukaemia is pale, thin, diminished, and without defenses.

Leukaemia originates in the bone marrow and lymphatic system. The marrow is the part of the body where maturation of red blood cells, white blood cells, and platelets takes place. Platelets and blood cells are directly related to blood, that is, to the person's identity. This identity is constantly developing, it is in permanent movement. It is possible to change who we are. In fact, these cells and platelets change every one hundred and twenty days.

Blood shows the unique identity of the person that incarnated in earthly duality, but it also shows the person's connection to a lineage, a family, and a clan.

Therefore, what is at stake here is a person's connection with a group of ancestors (through contact with the family), while maintaining an individual identity.

Here, in the marrow, we witness an extreme conflict of undervaluation. "In the eyes of my people, I'm not worth anything!"

When the individual feels this immense undervaluing, the number of the three types of blood components, red blood cells, white blood cells and platelets is reduced (this bears no resemblance to anaemia), to give way, shortly afterwards, to an explosion of growth, of normalness, an exaggerated tendency to go back to the balance the person failed to find. This is when leukaemia occurs. The individual gets more white cells and fewer red cells. The person feels increased aggression and less oxygen, less life within him. The person destroys himself and wishes to kill a part of himself. This is a non-conscious process and the immense undervaluing feeling is never verbalized. Due to the fact that this has its origins in the bone marrow and in the lymphatic system, it can be said the person's deepest structures have been profoundly shaken. They were indeed shaken, as the tension concerns lineage, the family, the clan (it is advisable to read *Family*). Leukaemia is a type of **blood cancer**. Leukaemia is, thus, deeply associated to lack of self-esteem.

A person who undervalues himself wants to be helped. He wishes to be taken care of, as if he was a child.

However, we should not spoil him, otherwise he will never assume responsibility for his own actions. We need to help him look after himself. If we deal with the person suffering from leukaemia as if he was a baby, we will be proving him right and reinforcing the undervaluing feeling he has about himself. It is vital that the person suffering from leukaemia is authorized to express his tensions regarding his family. He urgently needs to verbalize his feelings of being prevented from being himself. However, when a person suffers from leukaemia, it is precisely the family who wants to assist him. And the family spoils the person, through loving, protection and feelings of deep sorrow. This is understandable, but will not help the person in question. The family has great difficulty understanding that the problem lies precisely in the way of thinking of the family itself. Therefore, the family will not help the sick person to verbalize what he feels regarding the family and its thinking pattern. This family, feeling impotent, ends up giving this person away to an extremely aggressive treatment, chemotherapy, which seldom has good results and only increases the person's lack of responsibility, given that it makes the person even more dependent on others than before, instead of assuming responsibility. In fact, the person continues to receive the message, from the doctors, not just from relatives, that he is in good hands and that they will look after him. He then concludes that, actually, he does not need to look after himself.

The leukaemia patient has a tremendous need to be aware of the tension he lives in and to verbalize it to anyone involved in it, particularly those who are part of the family and of the lineage.

Only on rare occasions is it possible to make the individual aware of this, because the person is too deeply rooted in family, religious or old beliefs of his clan.

Lice

These are parasites that live in hair.

The person who has parasites is handing out power to others. He is accepting that others control his life. He allows himself to be sucked by others and is not centered. He lacks self-esteem. He is incapable of saying **No** with assertiveness. His inner and outer beings are not aligned. "Who has been taking advantage of me and sucking me dry?"

The word parasite is essential in this context. If the person lets himself to be affected by parasites, this means he is not centred and does not know how to be assertive with the people around him. It means that there is someone in his life that is a parasite and lives off him, whether at home, work, one of his friends. It could also be his Mother. The person is clinging to the past and to his old beliefs, and this is the reason why he cannot stand up to the parasite with the degree of assertiveness he ought to have. He feels frustration because he is convinced he will no longer be accepted by that person, should he change his attitude towards him. The person feels unable to progress in a tranquil way.

Hair is a type of skin excretion. Its role is to protect and communicate. But it also acts as an antenna, and as a reflex of health, fidelity to the clan, as a symbol of strength and it even has a social role, particularly when moving in the direction of the other person and in communication.

Young people's hair depends a lot on the management of emotions through communication.

Lice are often found in the hair of school-aged children. These are children who do not feel well at school and feel vampirised by teachers or simply by the school or parents' attitude.

Ligaments

Ligaments are the bandages of the joints.

We are referring here to the connection between two bones (the bone and the joint bone), not between the bone and the muscle, as in the case of tendon. When ligament problems occur, this indicates that the person is looking for the best position for his gesture and that, suddenly, the ligament blocks out. This is when **torsion** or ligament **tearing** arises.

We can also refer to torsion in a figurative way, when we bend rules, when we make a transgression regarding the group or the family, or "twist" our marriage.

Ligament tearing indicates lack of elasticity and it represents a rupture in one's life. It is advisable to see in which part of the body the tearing took place. Underlying tension is associated to two keywords: inflexibility and undervaluation.

When a person has **Loose ligaments**, it means they were already present from birth. It means an anxious quest to be extremely efficient in the future. It has nothing to do with muscles. In this case, it is advisable to examine the relationship between the parents, and of each parent with the child. And also look at pregnancy (see *Babies*, *Child delivery*, *Pregnancy – problems* and *Family*).

Ligament problems occur more frequently in the knees and ankles. See these two joints.

Lipoma

This is a benign tumour of the adipose system (fat).

The adipose tissue (the fat) is present all over the skin. It has an isolating role and keeps the body's heat in. It is an important energy reserve that protects several organs. This adipose tissue stores triglycerides, the so-called neutral fats. The presence of lipoma indicates that a person has a small undervaluation conflict regarding his figure. "I am not sufficiently attractive". Lipoma can show up in several places in the body. When the person becomes aware of the tension he is experiencing, the lipoma stops growing.

Lips

The mouth shows good predisposition for receiving.

There is great parallelism between the lips of the mouth and the labia of the vagina. The lips have a sexual function as well as a sexual representation. It is in a woman's lips that we are able to detect her femininity, her flow of estrogens, and her sexual fire. From

a relationship perspective, the main function of the lips is to kiss. Tensions in the lips result from the desire associated with relationships.

See *Mouth sores (thrush)* and *Herpes*

Liquid retention

People keep hold of secretions and excretions that they should get rid of, and which remain in the different holes of the body. Oedema related to liquid retention may occur due to renal insufficiency (see *Kidneys – renal insufficiency*), lymphatic or vascular related problems (see *Circulatory system – venal system*) (and see *Lymphatic system*) or hormonal related issues (see *Thyroid*). It also happens to women who suffer from pre-menstrual tension (see *Menstruation*).

Liver

The liver belongs to the tree (or wood) element of the five elements of eastern philosophy. It is the largest internal organ of the human body and it has many uses. The liver is the laboratory of the human being. It disintoxicates the organism. It deactivates and hydrolyses the toxins we ingest and those already present in our body that are later eliminated through the kidneys and gallbladder. In other words, it works as a blood filter. So, the first keyword in understanding tensions in the liver is '**discernment**'. The liver, as a filter, needs to be able to distinguish toxic from non-toxic substances.

The liver is also the factory of the

body and a reserve for amino acids. It metabolizes albumin (a protein made up of amino acids). It produces human albumin from animal and plant albumin in food, thus changing the order of amino acids, breaking them down or synthesizing them. In other words, the liver accomplishes a qualitative jump from the animal and plant kingdom into the human dominion, but without ever compromising the identity of the components. For this reason, it is said that the liver makes possible the union of the human being with its origins. The liver represents unity on Earth. It operates a unique process, a process of reconnection. Here the concept of **discernment** doubles in strength, as the human being must realize that "all are one".

In addition, the liver stores energy. It produces and stores glycogen (energy and strength). It also converts ingested carbohydrates into fat, which is stored in different parts of the body. It produces glucose (energy) from ingested amino acids and fat, and emits bile, which is stored in the gallbladder.

Consequently, the liver is a true energy factory and we know that any person, anybody, with lack of protein or energy has a problem. For this reason, the body must have all it requires so that the person may feel energetic, vitalized, and healthy.

We now arrive at the second keyword associated with liver: **scarcity**, or, more precisely, the sense or **fear of scarcity**. Therefore, we have two keywords: **discernment** and **fear of scarcity**.

After the pancreas, the liver is the most *yang* organ of the body. Chinese philosophy refers to it as the General of Armed Forces. It is a hard-working organ. Thus, when a person experiences liver problems, the first thing to check is the relationship with the biological Father, the husband, or the male model imposed by society. People with liver problems are megalomaniacs and have a great desire for expansion, to the point of losing any sense of discernment of what they truly need. This extends to what they eat and drink. Since the beginning of time that megalomania is a masculine characteristic. The great territorial conquests, conquests of power, and love conquests, were perpetrated by men.

The person with hepatic problems is a person with an overly masculine behaviour, excessively *yang*, lacking discernment, and with a great fear of not having enough. This person fears having no energy, energy which he needs to make sure that his children, mainly if they are minor, want for nothing. That fear of scarcity may be associated with affection, support, safety, nutrition, or even comfort, depending on the person and his perception of what is superfluous.

Hepatic problems show a need for moderation, rest, continence, abstinence, freedom, and concentration. The lack of discernment and the sense of scarcity may derive from the clan, from a family with weak livers. It may result from the way of thinking of the clan, the same old way of thinking that does not change at all because what is important is to be loyal to the clan. Here we find ourselves in the middle of a family inheritance in the way of thinking. "On se bouffe le foie en famille depuis toujours"; This French saying means: "We have always chopped liver in the family". It is a family that is blocked and controlling.

The members of these families will insist on explaining that this is a lineage with weak liver and that nothing can be done, that it is in the blood. In this case, the presence of family members when the person is sick is harmful to the person, because it does not help change patterns.

The lack of discernment and the feeling of scarcity may also originate in a family with limited financial resources ("We won't have enough to eat…!"). In this case, like in the previous, the mental pattern of scarcity settles in.

Lack of discernment and the fear of scarcity may also derive from lack of affection, of love in general, particularly as a child. The liver associates love to food.

Finally, the lack of discernment and the sensation of scarcity may come from a person who is afraid of dying from bowel cancer (Discernment is also a keyword for the bowel, as the bowel must know what to assimilate and what to get rid of).

The skin is often connected with the liver and kidneys since it acts as the last filter following those two organs. Thus, liver problems are often apparent on the skin. However, they are not skin problems, they are liver problems. Skin problems are associated with tensions related to separation and difficulty in communication. Liver problems are primarily associated with lack of discernment, megalomania, and a sense of scarcity.

It is true that, sometimes, we have trouble distinguishing separation (skin) from scarcity (liver). They are different, though.

See *Liver – cancer and liver disease, Liver – cirrhosis, Liver – hepatitis* and *Liver – jaundice*

Liver – cancer and liver disease

Liver disease shows a small conflict of discernment and fear of scarcity. Liver cancer reveals a tremendous conflict of discernment and fear of scarcity which is not at the conscious level and is not verbalized. It is more likely to appear in a person who suffers from megalomania and excess levels high above average.

See *Liver, Liver – cirrhosis, Liver – hepatitis* and *Liver – jaundice*

Liver – cirrhosis

Cirrhosis is also associated with issues of discernment and scarcity, mainly when it is caused by alcohol. The person feels a great emptiness inside (a great sense of scarcity) and loses all discernment of what he may drink.

See *Alcoholism* and *Liver*

Liver – hepatitis

Hepatitis is a condition that includes liver and gallbladder problems.

The biliary canals start in the liver.

Hepatitis illustrates a lack of discernment and sense of scarcity combined with great anger and rage. Anger and rage are associated with the gallbladder, not the liver. See *Gallbladder*.

Hepatitis A is of nutritious nature. It does not involve anger and rage. It is a conflict of food shortage, of nutritious nature. It may be a lack of nutrition in a literal sense (food) or figurative (affection) sense. It may be due to the fact that the person did not receive food alimony. It may also derive from lack of love which, in children, is a form of nourishment.

The infection is done through collective unconsciousness. It is the brain of the herd gone to work! It happens frequently to children who have very demanding parents and who are unable to truly love.

It is common for tension to be associated with the relationship with the biological Father or with a Mother if she displays very masculine behaviour.

Hepatitis B is a conflict of resentments due to a feeling of insufficiency. It may happen, for instance, when a person is disowned or rejected by the family or clan and feels great rage. It may also develop when a person loses his parents. Additionally, it may occur when a young person is kicked out of the house by the parents and feels resentment and rage. In this case, we have a situation that combines fear of insufficiency, lack of discernment, and also megalomania. The individual expected much more than what he got and, therefore, feels angered.

In this case, too, it is important to understand the relationship with the biologic Father.

Hepatitis C is a conflict of resentment associated with a feeling of scarcity and the fear of the unknown. It happened in the dark. Some information is kept hidden. It may be because the person left home, misses his children (scarcity, as we saw with the liver, may be affective as well as material) and is afraid of the unknown (it is a situation that the individual did not anticipate having to deal with). "I can't live like this. What will happen to the children? I don't deal well with the unknown." Moreover, sometimes something confusing is going on.

Another instance is when this illness happens to children of unknown fathers. Hepatitis C is common in drug addicts. In fact, drug addicts do not live in the real world; they live in the unknown, in a different dimension. Drugs take them to that different, unknown dimension. They catch hepatitis C out of rage for their inability to reach (feeling of scarcity) that unknown dimension, that mysterious and obscure world, without having to use drugs.

Hepatitis C can also develop, for example, when a young drug addicted is kicked out of the house. The fact that he is kicked out, ostracized by the clan, may cause him to feel like he is facing a totally unknown situation. And this does not happen exclusively to drug addicts; it may happen to anyone.

In the case of hepatitis C, it is also important to find the male role model that the patient knew: Father, husband, male members of the clan.

See *Liver*

Liver – jaundice

The liver is responsible for cleaning the blood bilirubin (bile pigment). Bilirubin is absorbed by the liver and excreted to the bile which, in turn, expels it to the small bowel.

When there is an excess of bilirubin in the body, the person contracts jaundice (yellow skin). It may result from malfunction of the liver or the gallbladder, which holds bilirubin and fails to release it to the duodenum.

We saw that liver malfunction is associated with lack of discernment and fear of insufficiency. **Gallbladder** malfunction is caused by the repressed rage that a person could not get rid of and was unable to verbalize.

People who suffer from hepatitis or cirrhosis are prone to jaundice.

See *Liver*

Locomotor system

It includes bones, joints, tendons, ligaments, and muscles.

This is the area where we find contradictions: problems of structure, ability to stand up, inflexibility and undervaluation.

Inflexibility has its roots in beliefs, in the pattern of thought. Undervaluation has its origins in the person's identity, based on what he does or what he accomplishes rather than on what he is. It is the case of the person who needs to do and/or to reach and/or to have, just to show he exists, whether at home or at work. In this system we find all the tensions of the type: "What I must accomplish as well as what I must do for my family."

Here lie the problems of the relationship with the world.

It is here that we measure the quality of practical accomplishments. The feeling of individuality and self-esteem is at stake. What I do with myself and what I do in this world, my flexibility and my steadfastness, all are concerns.

One can only exist in function of others. How does the outside world affect my structure and how do I influence the outside world?

Here are the conflicts associated with my self-worth. What part of my consciousness is hidden in my relationship with the world?

In this system of bones, joints, tendons, ligaments and muscles, there is no common denominator relative to the *yin/yang* polarity based on the side of the body.

Locomotor system symptoms are associated with mental inflexibility and undervaluation.

Inflexibility and undervaluation are usually associated with communication issues, but they may also be associated with the sensation of physical or verbal aggression, which gives rise to a different *yin/yang* polarity that differs with each case.

In fact, communication questions are associated with the cerebral hemispheres of the cortex which have a cross effect in the body, as the right hemisphere controls the left side, and the left hemisphere controls the right side.

Therefore, in this case, a symptom on the right side of the body reflects excessive *yang* (masculine) behaviour, and a symptom on the left side of the body reflects excessive *yin* (feminine) behaviour. This is the same for left-handed and right-handed people. It is so because the cerebral hemispheres are identical for both left-handed and right-handed people.

However, issues related to aggression are not tied to communication. The person reacts to aggression and the tension trigger is associated with the medulla, in the brain. Thus, in the case of aggression, symptoms in bones, joints, tendons, ligaments, and muscles that happen on the right side show *yin* (feminine) behaviours, while those on the left side show *yang* (masculine) behaviours. This is the same for left-handed and right-handed people. In fact, the effect of the brain medulla on the body is not crossed: the right side of the medulla affects the right side of the body and the left side of the medulla affects the left side of the body. For these reasons, the diagnostic *yin* and *yang* relative to symptoms in the locomotor system solely based on side polarity must be extremely careful. Nowadays, communication issues are much more common than aggression. It is likely that the symptoms are almost all caused by relationship or communication issues. For this matter, in terms of diagnostic, we may assume that the right side of the locomotor system involves very *yang* behaviours, while the left side involves very *yin* behaviours, but we must allow some flexibility.

Lordosis

See *Spine*

The lordosis is a prominent abdomen and inward curvature of a portion of the lumbar spine.

Lou Gehrig's disease

It owes its named to Lou Gehrig, a north american baseball player.

Please see *Amyotrophic Lateral Sclerosis (ALS)*

Lower rectum

See *Bowel – large bowel – lower rectum (incontinence)*

Lumbago

The person is overloaded. Lumbago affects the lumbar area, just like sciatica, although the origin of sciatica is the compression of the sciatic nerve, which runs down the lower limbs.

However, from the perspective of a tension in the conscience, the cause for both is the same. Lumbago happens so that a person can stop to look at his own life.

It affects mostly intervertebral discs between L4-L5 or L5-S1. The person wants to present an image of greatness and diligence. The lumbar area is the place for tensions when it comes to the relationship with a partner, affection, family, work and money, material things, the house, space and mobility, the place where one lives. All things that represent a person's roots. See *Vertebrae – lumbar vertebrae.*

The compression in the discs that lumbago causes means, in the physical sense, that the person shrinks instead of growing, and ends up with a bent spine.

From a practical point of view, lumbago means a compressed nerve in the lumbar area. Since nerves represent communication, lumbago reflects difficulty in communicating with someone, at home or work. If legs are affected, it is important to check which one is affected, because, in principle, the right side is *yang*, masculine, and the left side is *yin*, feminine, both for left and right-handed people. The affected *yang* side denotes communication problems with a man who is close to the individual, either at work or home, and the affected *yin* side indicates communication problems with a woman from home or with the biological Mother.

Lumbar

See *Vertebrae – lumbar vertebrae*

Lung plague

It is similar to tuberculosis, the difference being that this is a collective disease. It is part of epidemics.

It shows that the community felt a collective intense fear of dying. It only strikes after an event, for instance, following a war.

See *Epidemics*

Lungs

The lungs form part of the metal element of the five oriental elements.

Breathing exemplifies the highest profile of duality. If we only inhale, we die. If we only exhale, we die. We need both. The act of inhaling is a contraction and the act of exhaling is an expansion. The act of breathing holds the polarity of welcoming (receiving) or of the refusal to receive (I will not take in what is not good for me); as well as the polarity of giving or not giving.

The main role of the lungs is to protect us from the outside. Lungs filter dust, get rid of carbon monoxide and respond, react to the aggressions caused by the environment.

The act of breathing, through its duality, connects us with the supernatural, the universe, the fountain of creation, and the metaphysical. Breathing allows our union with life. Breathing keeps human beings from isolation.

Consequently, breathing represents contact and relationship. This contact with the outside is carried out through the alveoli.

The contact we have with another person through the skin is voluntary. Either I want to touch or not. The contact through breathing, however, is not. It just happens, period!

The first blow gives life, the last releases it.

The first blow detaches us from the Mother. We become individual entities.

Here we use two keywords to describe the respiratory system's own duality: Freedom and grasp; Contact, liberation and communication.

People with respiratory problems have difficulty living life, protecting themselves from the exterior or even expressing themselves in the presence of people who assault them.

Lung-related tensions are thus connected to the feeling of being assaulted by someone, and, simultaneously, fear of death, whether physical death or the end of a cycle. It may just be the fear of losing a relationship. And it can be fear of dying, which is the fear of releasing the last breath. The person is very scared of asphyxiating. It must be stressed again that what we mean by attack is not something objective. We refer to what the person felt as being a form of attack.

Lungs are led by the cerebral hemispheres of the cortex. For this reason, the lung on the right side is *yang*, masculine, it represents the man, the Father, the husband. The lung on the left side is *yin*, feminine, and it represents the Mother, the woman. This applies both to left and right-handed people.

If the person feels a man assaulted him, this will affect the right side lung. If he felt assaulted by a woman, the lung on the left side will be affected.

Contrary to what happens with the **pleura**, when it comes to the lungs we are talking about all types of people, whether they are close or not. It could be a stranger, a schoolteacher, a sports teacher, a passer-by or even someone close. The pleura is connected only to very close people.

Another difference between the pleura and the lungs is that symptoms in the pleura, besides aggression being felt only when it involves people who are close, also indicate that something

disgusted the person. This does not happen in the case of the lungs.

The feeling of aggression affecting the lungs is mostly related to communication and aggressiveness issues.

In the case of **pneumonia**, an inflammation of the lungs by infectious germs, the tension is associated to a feeling provoked by serious external aggression, extremely painful, and it also shows that the person has no defenses of his own. "I need to be protected! Who will protect me? I have a serious communication problem. I cannot make myself understood. I am not understood. Who will protect me and understand my suffering?"

In the case of lung **cancer**, the body develops tumours in the alveoli, making the lung more efficient. In fact, a cancer-ridden lung works more efficiently than a healthy lung. The person needs more air in order to live and so the body grants the person a lung that is more efficient. In this case, the tension associated to aggression is enormous and, above all, the person does not verbalize it and keeps it within himself. The body always ends up uncovering it.

Tuberculosis follows a previous lung problem. It only shows up when the person no longer feels the aggression tension that lived in his conscience. Tuberculosis does manifest itself when the person is already recovering, no longer feels assaulted but still feels very fragile. The emotions that the person who suffers from tuberculosis feels are loneliness, melancholy, sorrow, and sadness. Loss of hope and confidence to go on living. It may be an unconscious manifestation of a repressed sadness from childhood.

See *Pulmonary embolism*, *Emphysema*, *Asphyxiation*, *Bronchi*, *Hyperventilation*, *Pneumonia* and *Pleurisy*

Lupus – discoid lupus erythematosus

This is considered to be an autoimmune disease. In this case, the immune system, which normally protects the body from germs, bacteria and viruses, looses discernment between what it should accept, like healthy tissues, and what it should reject. So, it produces antibodies that attack various healthy parts of the body, causing inflammation. Lupus comes from the Latin and means wolf. Erythematosus means red. Lupus erythematosus sores look like wolf bites.

Discoid lupus erythematosus only affects skin. It is skin tuberculosis, whose lesions are grouped in plaques and may infect. It happens mostly in the skin of the face and in the mucosal surfaces of the nose and mouth.

Therefore, in the case of lupus, the key tension is lack of discernment. Skin – epidermis problems are associated to incapacity to communicate issues and to a feeling of separation. The person feels separated from his clan, his family, and feels this separation as an aggression. And he tries to blame the other person for the aggression. As a result, he loses discernment. He feels enraged, attacked, and loses discernment regarding whom he should be with and

whom he should not.

Who does he see as a wolf in his life? This person he sees as a wolf is close to him, either at home, or is someone he has a relationship with.

The person's face becomes affected and this fact may constitute further tension, related to aesthetics, for the person: "I feel uglier". This aggravates self-esteem and, consequently, it further confuses the person's immune system.

Generally speaking, lupus is a symptom that affects women much more than men.

Please see *Lupus – systemic lupus erythematosus*

Lupus – systemic lupus erythematosus

This is considered to be an autoimmune disease. In this case, the immune system, which normally protects the body from germs, bacteria and viruses, loses discernment between what it should accept, like healthy tissues, and what it should reject. So, it produces antibodies that attack various healthy parts of the body, causing inflammation. Lupus comes from the Latin and means wolf. Erythematosus means red. Lupus erythematosus sores look like wolf bites.

Systemic or disseminated lupus erythematosus is much more serious than the discoid lupus erythematosus.

It affects organs, especially the kidneys (renal insufficiency), the skin (particularly the face and hands), the mucosal areas of the mouth, the pharynx and nose, and the locomotor system, causing rheumatoid poliarthritis.

Skin – epidermis problems are associated to incapacity to communicate and to a feeling of separation. The person feels separated from his clan, his family, and feels this separation as an aggression. And he tries to blame the other person for the aggression. As a result, he loses discernment. He feels enraged, attacked, and loses discernment regarding whom he should be with and whom he should not.

Who does he see as a wolf in his life? This person he sees as a wolf is close to him, he is either at home or is someone he has a relationship with.

The person's face becomes affected and this fact may bring aesthetics-related further tension to the person: "I feel uglier". This aggravates self-esteem and, consequently, it further confuses the person's immune system.

Kidneys (renal insufficiency) are linked to the relationship between two people, to lack of discernment and to the need to blame the other person for the bad relationship we have with him. The mucosal zones of the mouth (see *Mouth sores (thrush)*) are associated to the incapacity to communicate with someone and to give oneself to that person. The person wishes to have a good relationship with his partner, but that wish is stopped midstream. The pharynx is also associated to discernment regarding which food we should take (love is a form of nutrition), and which we should keep out. And poliarthritis is related to undervaluation. Therefore, the keywords for systemic

lupus are: lack of discernment and undervaluation.

Systemic lupus erythematosus occurs more often in women.

Please see *Lupus – discoid lupus erythematosus*

Lymph

See *Lymphatic system*

Lymphatic system

From a biological perspective, the human body contains mostly water, liquids. Those liquids need to circulate and they do so through the lymphatic vases.

The lymph occupies the spaces between cells and also circulates through the lymphatic vases. Lymphocytes are while cells produced by the lymphatic ganglia, in the bone marrow and in the spleen, which also play an important role in the immune system, by producing and transporting antibodies. Many lymphocytes mature in the thymus.

The lymphatic vases let the body liquids that do not belong to the blood stream and that are not inside the vascular system to get inside the veins. These liquids need to go back inside those vases and inside the blood stream before returning to the heart (through the veins). Lymphatic vases are thus the assistants of the veins in their draining capacity.

As they lack a heart to make them move forward, lymphatic vases depend on the muscles that are closer to them to perform their function.

Inflammation of the lymphatic ganglia (**adenitis**, **adenopathy**), as well as cysts in the so-called lymphatic ganglia (**lymphomas**, **Hodgkin's disease**) occur when the person feels tension associated to the feeling of needing to defend himself, to justify himself, in order not to feel undervalued.

Lymphoma is a tumour in the lymphatic ganglia. Although technically the problem is different from leukaemia, the tension the person feels in his conscience is the same as in leukaemia.

The lymphatic system works on immunity, just like the immune system.

See *Leukaemia*, *Thymus* and *Immune system*

Lymphoma

See *Lymphatic system*

Madness

See *Isolation*
Madness is a form of isolation.

Malaria

This is caused by the bite of a mosquito (a female mosquito, so it seems) that lives in tropical or subtropical areas. The bite is followed by the development of parasites in the blood and in the internal organs, which slowly destroys the erythrocytes (red cells). The person has intermittent fevers, anaemia, swollen spleen and sometimes the liver also swells. In the first place, it must be pointed out that urban people, used to being far from the countryside and from natural life, may feel some form of unbalance regarding life in the wild and nature. This information prompts authorities to make preventing treatment for this type of mosquito bites compulsory for all those going to tropical and subtropical areas of the planet. Not everybody gets malaria when bitten by these mosquitoes in tropical zones. But some people do get malaria. The words that must be stressed here are bite and parasite.

When the person is regularly bitten by isolated insects, the body is showing him that he is hard on himself, that he needs to punish himself and that he probably feels guilty regarding little things. Being bitten by a swarm of mosquitoes is not the issue here. When this happens, everybody gets bitten.

If the urban person decided to go to a subtropical area infested by mosquitoes, where all urban people are bitten, he must be asked why on earth he went there. Why did he agree to a situation whereby he would be bitten? What is going on in this person's life to make him need to be bitten?

When the person allows himself to be invaded by parasites, this reveals that the person is not centered, that there is no alignment between his inner and outer beings, and that, albeit in a non-conscious manner, he is handing out power to others. He is accepting that others control his life. He allows himself to be sucked by others. The person lacks self-esteem. He is incapable of saying **No** with assertiveness.

The person who catches malaria is, thus, the person who, for some reason, sought to go somewhere where he felt insecure. Above all, he did it out of little self-esteem. The person is not centered and is lacking assertiveness to say **No**, and has thus abdicated his personal power. Why? What is going on in this person's life to make him annul himself in such a way?

Mastoiditis

See *Ears about otitis.*

Mastoiditis is a problem that happens in ears. The inner conflict is the same as for otitis.

Measles

This causes an inflammation of the nose, throat and eyes, especially in children.

Eruptions indicate that something has been repressed. And they uncover something that had hitherto remained invisible.

As in all children's diseases, eruptions bring out something new in the child, and they contribute to the significant advancement in the child's development. Measles shows up in the holes that are related to the outside world (the respiratory system) and they indicate the child's capacity for reaction and defense. The appearance of red spots is a sign that the child is developing his immune system.

Besides, getting measles grants the child permanent immunity.

See *Babies*

Meninges

They are the membranes that cover and protect the brain and the spinal chord. They are part of the body's envelopes, the sacs that act as attack and defense mechanisms, particularly verbal attacks, from people who are close.

The meninges are the place where tensions with close relationships occur, with the people who are close, particularly with the Father or Mother figures.

See *Meningitis*

Meningioma

This is a tumour that starts in the meninges. It may be benign or malignant. Although, technically, a meningioma is not the same as meningitis, the tension at the level of conscience is the same.

See *Meningitis*

Meningitis

Meningitis can be of cerebral type, spinal type or cerebral-spinal type. Meningitis is an inflammation of the meninges (meninges are the membranes that cover and protect the brain and the spinal medulla. They are part of the body's envelopes, the sacs that act as attack and defense mechanisms, particularly verbal attacks, from people who are close).

Meningitis causes fever, headache, motor and psychic disturbances. It may occur just in the encephalon, just in the spinal medulla or in both. Meningitis indicates the person's fear of not being sufficiently able (performer), from a brain perspective. The degree of exigency on the Father's or Mother's part is too high. Someone is ruthless with the person's mistakes.

Meningeal problems also reveal that someone disgusted the person, that something filthy happened to him. "This person disgusts me!" It is possible that this person feels angry. This is a symptom whose causes are related to the relationship with his Father, or with the male model he had or has.

Problems in the meninges show that the person felt assailed, attacked, not physically, but intellectually, by someone very close to him. One should first look at his relation with the Father. If not the Father, it will be someone who plays his role. It could be a very masculine Mother, or a Mother who is under the influence of her own father (the person's maternal Grandfather).

The body takes upon itself to show what the person is feeling in his tension with the Father, or someone who plays the role of the father, and which he does not dare to think about or verbalize in a conscious manner. When I say the person has a problem with the Father, this could be because he does not see him as often as he would like, due someone forbidding it. It could also be the case of a child who is told horrible things about his Father and who, for this reason, feels harassed every time he is with him.

Meniscus

See *Knee*
The meniscus is the joint cartilage between two bones.

Menopause

Menopause means profound hormonal change.

Menopause is a stage of reassessment of a woman's life project. To reach the age of 50, in Hebrew, means jubilee, happiness.

Menopause tells a woman that she can no longer have children. Consequently, this means the loss of an exclusively feminine capacity. However, it also marks the passage to a wiser stage in her life.

A woman's sexual past and the form she lived her sexuality are important in the way the woman will deal with the changes that will take place in her body. The body change is as dramatic as the one she went through when she reached puberty.

It is common for women to become anxious, unstable, and to lose energy. This is part of adapting to this new stage in life. It is also usual for women to experience heat flushes and to have their last menstrual haemorrhages. These are part of the woman's last body and conscience upheavals before accepting this new stage in life.

Heat flushes also denote the still existing body's sexual drive, that continues, and which must be accepted and experienced, since there is no reason for it to disappear.

Menopause is part of a process of losing part of femininity and, for this reason, is a *yang* process. In other words, the woman becomes more masculine.

In fact, what the contraceptive pill,

which many women take, actually does is to block out their feminine brain (by blocking estrogens) and act like a sort of small menopause.

It is important that a woman undergoing menopause makes up for this loss of femininity by adopting a more feminine and delicate attitude to life. Above all, it is important that she realizes that her sexual drive has not been reduced at all. The menopausal woman should live her sexuality in full.

The osteoporosis process that menopausal women experience has nothing to do with menopause itself, rather with the person's own undervaluation. Some women who reach menopause believe they are no longer worthy and, consequently, undervalue themselves. These are women whose past rested more on their motherhood role than on their role as women, and who threw their feminine female function to the background. This may also happen to women whose sexuality has always been repressed as, in their view, sexuality was only used to procreate.

African women who stop being fertile cease to have a reproductive function and may join the council of the sage. The clan interests them again. They may start using their two brains and not just the feminine side of it. A woman such as this will not develop osteoporosis, because she does not feel undervalued. As it is, she feels valued.

Certain health professionals deal with menopause as if it was a disease. But it is not. It is an extremely natural process and should not manifest itself through symptoms in women.

This moment of badly experiencing menopause may also be an open door to breast cancer.

See *Breasts*

Menstruation

Menstruation goes together with the moon cycle. When ovulation occurs during full moon, menstruation will take place during the new moon. Births occur more frequently during full moon.

The ovulation process takes place from the outside to the inside. It is a *yang* process. It concentrates things. The menstruation process goes from the inside to the outside. It is a *yin* process. It releases things. It is more natural to have a period during the new moon (the more *yin* moment) and ovulation during full moon (a more *yang* moment). However, the opposite may take place. Nowadays, women tend to have their periods during full moon, because they are becoming more *yang*, more masculine.

The menstrual flow is a true feminine expression of fertility and receptivity. A woman is subject to this continuous rhythm. She has no option other than shape herself to this rhythm and accept it. This acceptance and surrender to this rhythm constitute a very *yin*, feminine attitude. Surrender is very much a *yin* process.

Menstruation shows the woman that her role is *yin*, not *yang*. The more *yang* her life style is, the worst will be the woman's relationship with her menstrual period.

Amenorrhoea (absence of menstruation) happens to very *yang* women, who feel aversion for themselves, or for their woman pattern. A woman such as this does not wish to be a woman, to be feminine. The female model that her biological Mother represents is very important in this context. This woman has not ceased being a daughter. She cannot become an adult woman. It is important to examine the feeling this woman had or has with her biological Mother's behaviour towards her.

Menstruation is part of the body's liquids, discharges and waters. Water itself has no shape, it shapes itself to things. This is the role of feminine women, to shape themselves to things and to others.

With her blood, women sacrifice, that is, offer a part of their vitality. Periods are a small pregnancy (ovulation) and a small birth delivery (menstruation). In the case of **dysmenorrhoea**, which is a difficult and painful menstruation, there is pain in the lower abdomen, in the head, breasts, the lumbar area and on the legs. At times, some anxiety may also be felt.

This happens to women who are very rigorous and demanding of themselves and of other people. These are women who find it difficult to be feminine and to live their femininity. They have a non-conscious blockage regarding themselves as women or with the feminine female side of their clan. They are hard women.

They may be women who belong to a family that has a marked pain pattern amidst its women, either due to social or religious beliefs, very old beliefs or collective thinking patterns in the family.

They belong to families that punish femininity and female power, and that have prejudices regarding the purity of the cleansing capacity of women, and regarding their capacity for regeneration. It is equally true that, for many centuries and in many cultures, the woman has been subject to submission or cancellation, abuse, punishment, prohibition, and genital mutilation. This historical past weighs down in the collective unconsciousness of humanity and on the woman's capacity to shake off and rise above this femininity's violent and castrating inheritance.

A woman who sails through the sexual act, without inhibitions, particularly when it comes to having an orgasm, will have fewer disturbances when having periods.

Very *yang* women, whose lives are a struggle, whose minds take over their sensibility, whose egos play a predominant role, will try to fight off the "troubles" of menstruation. However, this is a fight they will always lose.

See *Menopause*

Migraine

There is a tendency to distinguish migraines from headaches, in that migraines come with visual or digestive disturbances (vomit and diarrhoea).

A migraine will vanish with orgasm. It is an emotional/sexual tension that was displaced to the head. The blockage that the person suffering from headache feels is connected with his inability to loosen up, to let his emotions surface, to live his impulses. Orgasm is a very strong emotional display. This person needs to learn how to loosen himself up in his daily life without it always being in bed, with a sexual partner.

The person who vomits also brings relief to the migraine. In this case, vomit is a relief for the person and the pain is alleviated too.

The migraine sufferer should pay more attention to emotions and stop being mind oriented and led by his Cartesian thinking, always weighting up the consequences.

See also *Headache*

Milk intolerance

Intolerance to mother's milk must be considered in the same manner we consider intolerance to cow's milk. Intolerance to cow's milk is much more common.

It is natural and desirable that all children be breastfed by their mothers. It is through breastfeeding by the Mother that the child experiences with greater harmony the passage from the world of unity, from where he came, into the world of duality he entered upon earthly incarnation. The child spent nine months sheltered in the Mother's womb, completely fed and loved in a totally darkened environment, sheltered from outside interventions. The child was literally part of the Mother. Delivery is a violent moment of descent into the world of duality.

It is a moment of difficult adaptation for the child. To be deprived from the physical contact of regular breastfeeding with the Mother is a violent event for the child.

When this happens, the passage between the two worlds is done without transition, without gradual adaptation. Besides, as stated above, the mother's milk is a great source of immunization and, in this case, the child is deprived of it.

The child who is lactose intolerant is a child who, whenever in the presence of milk, is reminded that his Mother left him precisely at the very moment he most needed her to breastfeed him. Then, at that moment, the child develops a skin problem. Skin problems always indicate separation. And, after all, that is what happened. The child felt the separation from the Mother. The lactose intolerance is no more than a reminder of the separation from the Mother.

In the whole animal world, milk symbolizes the Mother and the relation with the Mother.

Let us now consider the opposite case, the case of the adolescent, the teenager or even the adult who drinks milk every chance he gets. This also shows a problem with the biological Mother but, in this case, it shows the inability to cut the umbilical cord. This is the person who continues to need his mummy. In the case of females, they will have a difficult time assuming the role of mothers if they bear children, since they still consider themselves simply as daughters.

In the case of men, they will have the tendency to select women who resemble their Mothers. They anticipate problems with their spouses, whom they will treat as if they were their Mothers, and not their wives.

Miscarriage

See *Abortion* and *Child delivery*

Mononucleosis

This disease shows the same symptoms as leukaemia, but it is much less intense and not cancer-related.

It only affects the lymphatic system, not the bone marrow, which means that the affected structures are not as basic. It can sometimes lead to hepatic conditions.

It is often called the kissing disease. It occurs more frequently amongst teenagers, although it may affect adults. It is the result of temporary reduction of self-esteem, due to a guilt feeling about something that has taken place. It shows itself when the young person feels remorse about jumping from relationship to relationship and feels an immense guilt tension. The youth is punishing himself.

He has put the other person first and stopped caring about himself.

When it affects adults, it could be because he feels angry for not receiving love or recognition. In any case, in adults, his partner and the relationship between the couple are at stake here.

The adult suffering from mononucleosis wants to hide his tension, the anger he is experiencing for not being recognized, and so the body exposes this to him. The adult has the illusion of being able to hide his feelings from his body.

Young people accept the causes for mononucleosis much more easily than adults. Adults stick to their guilt pattern much more deeply.

Mouth

Food is moistened and chewed inside the mouth, with the aid of teeth, tongue and salivary glands. This allows the alimentary bolus to be swallowed. This is the first stage of digestion.

The mouth, with its digestive role, is an entryway for food (nutrition) and also an exit for food (vomit). In its communication function, it is an exit for sounds and words, communication and expression of affection. In its breathing function, it allows us to inhale and exhale air. The mouth also has a sexual function. In fact, there is a great similarity between the lips of the mouth and the labia of the vagina.

Mouth infections reveal the things we do not wish to intake, in any form, or which we do not wish to try out in our lives.

When the mouth is at rest, it should be closed and relaxed. In short, the mouth indicates good receptivity to receive something.

See *Candidiasis (thrush)*, *Palate*, *Herpes*, *Gums*, *Mouth sores (thrush)*, *Lips* and *Teeth*

Mouth sores (thrush)

The mouth, with its digestive role, is an entryway for food (nutrition) and also an exit for food (vomit). In its communication function, it is an exit for sounds and words, communication and expression of affection. In its respiratory function, it allows to inhale and exhale air. The mouth also has a sexual function. In fact, there is a great similarity between the lips of the mouth and the labia of the vagina.

In conclusion, the mouth is a welcoming environment for taking in.

Mouth infections show the things we do not want to take in, whatever the circumstance, or the things we do not want to experiment in our lives.

Mouth sores develop in the mucus membrane surfaces inside the mouth. They are related to digestion, but primarily with the digestion of communication problems. For example, a person had a communication problem with a friend, a conflict, and the friend started avoiding him/her. However, the person still desires to see the friend and speak to him/her to repair the friendship. The friend, nevertheless, continues to avoid the person. When the person finally gives up, a mouth sore appears in the mucus membrane surface of the mouth. This does not imply that the person should contact the friend. It simply means that the hurt he/she felt and the desire to see the friend took a toll on the person and the body expresses that with the mouth sore. The tension is related to the desire to communicate with someone close, some-one who is part of the person's roots. It can be a friend, a colleague, a boss… The mucus membranes in the mouth are controlled by the cerebral hemispheres. Thus, for both left-handed and right-handed people, the inside of your mouth is *yang* (masculine) on the right side and *yin* (feminine) on the left side.

So, a mouth sore on the *yang* side shows tension with a man, and one on the *yin* side shows tension with a woman.

Multiple myeloma

See *Leukaemia*

Myeloma is a tumour, almost always malignant, which develops at the expense of the bone marrow. But the inner conflict is very close to the one of Leukaemia.

Multiple sclerosis

Multiple sclerosis is a form of paralysis. Paralyzing illnesses always affect the locomotor system and, namely, the muscles and/or the nerves. They are connected with a great feeling of undervaluation and a communication problem. The person experiences opposing ideas and impulses.

The individual is faced with two contradictory movement orders. The person who suffers from multiple sclerosis (or plaque sclerosis) is usually a young adult who experiences destruction of myelin, a protective envelope of the central nervous system. The muscles fail to respond due to a lack of nerve conductivity and the person suffers paralysis, *nystagmus* (constant trembling of the pupils – see *Eyes*), trembling, disorders of the senses, incontinence, and psychic disorders (see *Isolation*). It develops slowly and with irregular outbreaks. It evolves by plaques.

It is important to look at this person's relationship with his biological Father. It is likely that the individual displays mental rigidity, insensibility, an iron will, inflexibility, and an unconscious fear of his Father. It has much to do with the person's relationship with the Father or male figure. In the case of a woman, it could be associated with the relationship with her husband.

In the case of plaque sclerosis, we are faced with three related issues: a problem of movement – the person gradually loses the ability to move around; a problem of undervaluation as the person feels strongly undervalued by the group, and primarily by the Father; and a problem of verticality – the person has trouble maintaining verticality in several ways, including posture and, in the case of men, the ability to have an erection (see *Impotence*). So, the body keeps the person from moving around. The person would like to feel some recognition and be able to relax. This individual does not feel recognized and feels undervalued. As a result, he fears socialization and seeks isolation. It must be noticed that the person is afraid, which means that nothing has yet happened to prove the lack of recognition but, based on past beliefs, he anticipates what may

happen to him. That results in the development of multiple sclerosis. In this case, we are dealing with a mental projection. This individual's beliefs do not work for him. Besides, he pays excessive attention to the ideas and attitudes of his Father, either to follow or to resist them.

Mumps

See *Salivary glands*

Mumps is a condition that happens in the salivary glands.

Muscle contraction

See *Muscles*

Muscles

Muscles are part of the locomotor system, which includes bones, joints, ligaments, tendons and muscles.

It is in the locomotor system that contradictions are found; Structural problems and being able to stand on your feet. The locomotor system is the connection between the animal and the rational being.

This is where problems in our relationship with the world rest. What seems indispensable to me and also what I need to do for my family. This is where the quality of practical actions is evaluated. The feeling of individuality and of self-esteem is at stake here.

What do I think of myself and what is my role in the world? This has to do with my assertiveness and my stability and with conflicts of a personal nature. What part of my conscience is in the dark regarding my relationship with the world? One can only exist through others. How does the outside world influence my structure and how do I influence the outside world?

Muscles represent the capacity for movement in life, flexibility and activity, dynamics.

In all cases, muscle-related problems denote a sense of undervaluation on the person's part. It indicates that he is allowing himself to be undervalued because his life does not flow naturally. And his life does not flow naturally because the person pays excessive attention to what others say (and/or demand from him), thus ending up being influenced by thoughts that do not work for him.

Problems in muscles reveal undervaluation, but also resistance to new experiences. They indicate some degree of stubbornness, inflexibility.

There are muscles that are associated to the central nervous system, which are muscles of voluntary control that are connected to the skeleton and have the purpose of producing movements in the bones of the body, in the human skeleton. They are striated muscles and they are connected to the bones and therefore allow the skeleton to move.

There are also muscles that are connected to the autonomic nervous system, and they are involuntary control muscles that line the inner walls of blood vessels and internal organs. Their function is to produce automatic movement in internal organs. They are plane muscles. There are only two exceptions to this: bladder muscles are plane, although they are of voluntary mental movement, and the heart muscles are striated, although they are of involuntary control.

Muscular problems are always a sign that the body wishes to stop. It is an inner cry for non-action, at least in those conditions. Tensions experienced in the striated muscles are distinct from those experienced in the smooth muscles. In striated muscles, we find undervaluation tensions associated to movement. In smooth muscles, we find tensions connected to the corresponding organ, which may also mean undervaluation regarding the function of that particular organ. If this is the case, then we refer to the organs in question and not to the muscles of the locomotor system.

Muscles in the locomotor system reveal what happened before, during and after the action.

The **before the action** is characterized by everything related to projects to come.

Doubts and fears.

The **after the action** is related to regrets over the action that was taken.

The **during the action** is related to what the person is thinking at the time the action is taking place.

A **cramp** is an involuntary contraction. It is like a ball. The muscle contracts a lot, as if it had reached the highest point in the action. It may occur when resting, after the action. However, it may also happen when resting, before the action. In this case, the person is still at rest, but his brain is already throwing his deepest fears and uncertainties to his face. "You must go over the limits! You must not fail!"

Nevertheless, cramps can also happen during the action. When the person thinks he is not running fast enough, his brain impels him to run faster (the brain can only see the next instant, it does not weigh up the consequences, and simply wants to move faster), and of course the person ends up with a cramp during the action.

The person who suffers from cramps is someone who demands of himself a lot of effectiveness in the action. His behaviour is like that of a predator. Cramps show up because the body wants to show us that we are raising the stress levels. It shows us that we are not listening to our intuition and that we are trying to sort things out with our mind and leading a very *yang* behaviour.

All cramps are, therefore, the product of excessively *yang* behaviour that does not respect the body and its metabolism enough.

If a person makes an effort to prove something but realizes he does not like that sport after all, then he is acting like a predator, instead of accepting that the sport is not an attitude that he likes, and assuming a more *yin*, less masculine, less *yang*, more focused attitude.

For these people who, after all, are acting like predators due to their egos and to demonstrate something they are not, a meat free diet, to avoid cramps, may be a good option. And it works. Cramps will stop. It is true that predators are *yang*, hunters and determined beings. The impala, an herbivorous, is more feminine, more *yin*. The person who stops eating meat and carries on practicing sports, this time cramp free, should interpret that result as a clear sign of the type of behaviour he should start adopting in his everyday life. He should stop being a predator and become more *yin*, more sensitive, more of a prey (to give himself more). Not just in sports, but in everything.

Muscular distension occurs when action is in full play. It indicates that the person believes he is not being good enough, efficient, in his action. This normally happens when carrying out physical activity. His mind impels him to go further and it is obvious that the person ends up having muscular distension. The person is going through a very *yang* mental process and does not listen to his body. And the body manifests itself.

This is a person walking the wrong path of life. He is in search of approval and attempts to be a person he, in fact, is not.

The undervaluation that a person experiences in the locomotor system in general and in the muscles, in particular, is related to the fact that he is unable to do what he was persuaded to do. Could this be that this person is part of a group that he wishes to please so that the group totally accepts him? And this could be, independently of the community or of the group in question. It could be the family clan, the sports clan, the friends' clan etc.

In principle, but with caution, the muscles of the locomotor system that are on the right side of the body are *yang* (masculine) and those on the left side are *yin* (feminine). This applies to both left and right-handed people. See *Introduction page 11* about brain polarity.

Problems in the *yang* muscles denote inflexibility and undervaluation [due to the influence of a third person (a man?) or the person's own beliefs]. The person wants to go further than what is reasonable. He will insist, be stubborn, a fighter, somehow harsh. And he will stretch his body without paying attention to it.

The fact that the person wishes to affirm himself through what he does and reaches indicates he does not value what he is, which in itself is undervaluation. He just values what he does and achieves.

Problems in the *yin* muscles denote inflexibility and undervaluation [due to the influence of a third person (a woman?) or the person's own beliefs]. The person's sensitivity is hurt in the efforts it made. The person feels fragile. He feels he lacks the necessary value to do or to get there. It also denotes undervaluation.

Muscular distension

Muscles reveal what happens before, during and after the action.

The **before the action** is characterized by everything related to projects to come, doubts and fears. The "**after the action**" is related to regrets.

Muscular distension occurs **during the action**. When the person thinks he is not being good enough in the action he is taking.

This normally happens in the course of physical activity. The brain impels the person to go further (the brain only sees the next moment) and of course the person ends up with muscular distensions. This is always a demonstration of the undervaluing the person is experiencing.

The question we may ask is: Why does this person need to show increased performance? What makes him feel undervalued if he does not succeed in attaining the desired performance? What makes him harm a part of his body? What is happening to this person's life balance? The reason is that, in fact, all the problems affecting the locomotor system, and, in particular, the muscles have their root in the person's undervaluation

Muscle related problems may occur in the muscles of internal organs or in the muscles of the locomotor system.

The polarity of the locomotor system is not always obvious. However, it is important to consider that muscles that are part of the locomotor system on the right side of the body are *yang* (masculine) and those on the left side are *yin* (feminine). This applies both to left and right hand-sided people.

Problems in the *yang* muscles denote undervaluation and inflexibility [due to the influence of a third party (a man?) or too rigid beliefs on the person's part, inflexibility]. The person wants to go further than what is reasonable. He will insist, be stubborn, a fighter, somehow aggressive. And he will strain his body without looking after it.

The fact that the person defines himself by <u>what he does and attains</u> reveals that he does not value <u>who he is</u>, which in itself is undervaluing.

Problems in the *yin* muscles denote undervaluation and inflexibility [due to the influence of a third party (a man?) or too rigid beliefs on the person's part, inflexibility]. The person's sensitivity is hurt in the effort he makes. The person is afraid of straining the body and feels fragile. He feels he does not have the required value to do or to get there. It denotes undervaluing.

Muscular dystrophy

Although not all muscular dystrophies technically correspond to myopathy, the tensions in the conscience are the same. See *Myopathy* and *Growth (growth disorders)*

Myalgic encephalomyelitis (chronic fatigue syndrome)

See *Fibromyalgia (chronic fatigue syndrome)*

Mycosis

See *Fungi*
Mycosis is a parasitical condition provoked by a fungus.

Mycosis fungoides

This is a malignant cutaneous lymphoma. Plaques and lymphocyte nodes penetrate the skin.

A lymphoma is a malignant cyst in the lymphatic ganglions and it occurs when a person feels tension related to the feeling of needing to defend and justify himself in order not to feel undervalued.

Therefore, a lymphoma is a tumour in the lymphatic ganglions. Although, technically, this problem is different from leukaemia, the tension that the person experiences at conscience level is the same: lack of self-esteem, dependence on the family, inability to distinguish what is good for him from what is harmful. The person allows himself to be judged by others. And he lets others (relatives or close people) lead his life. Besides having great difficulty in discerning what is good for him from what is harmful, the person also finds it difficult to move away from things (mostly from people) that squeeze her dry, act as parasites and disgust her.

It is vital to help this person become aware of the family beliefs that are not good for him. Some of these beliefs disgust him.

This problem, like in the case of leukaemia, is a paradox that becomes a vicious circle and which the person has great difficulty to acknowledge, and, consequently, to free himself from.

Myelitis

This is an inflammation in the spinal chord. It affects muscles.

The processing of ascending and descending nervous impulses becomes completely blocked in one or more segments. When inflammation occurs, the person's body heats up and becomes numb from the feet upwards. What is going on between my Mother and a man (my Father?)? The person is not aware he is burning and that his structural foundations are unstable.

See *Poliomyelitis* and *Acute anterior poliomyelitis (child paralysis)*

Myeloma

See *Bone marrow*

Myeloma is a tumour, almost always malignant, which develops at the expense of the bone marrow.

Myopathy

Myopathy is a neuromuscular, paralyzing disease. This sort of illness always affects the locomotor system, namely the muscles and/or the nerves. They are associated to a big sense of undervaluation. This is the first key-tension. The second key-tension is that associated to feelings about ideas or impulses that are opposite.

The person imposes on himself two contradictory orders regarding movement. The person has opposing wishes. These tensions that provoke two opposing ideas may occur when, for instance, the person wanted very much to do something, did it, and then bitterly regretted it.

If this happens to a newly born baby, we are in the presence of a child who has incarnated but has doubts whether he should have done it (opposing feelings) because he feels neither balance nor harmony in his life to grow free-

ly. In cases like this, it is vital to look at what went on between the parents during pregnancy, birth or early childhood.

Myopathy is a degenerating disease in the muscle tissues and may manifest itself in several places. It denotes major undervaluation, as we have seen.

Duchenne myopathy (pseudo hypertrophic) starts in the lower limbs, proceeds to the upper limbs and reaches the muscles of the torso. It acts very rapidly and loss of movement happens very early in children. According to medical registers, it is transmitted through chromosome X. The child starts showing hypertrophy in the shin muscles (the muscle is replaced by adipose tissue) and it develops to muscular retraction, with the usual cardio-respiratory complications in the long run.

The **Becker type myopathy** is a late muscular dystrophy. It takes longer to develop than the Duchenne's (inability to walk only happens around 30 years of age), but its origins are also associated to the X chromosome.

The **Emery-Dreifuss myopathy** is a variant of Duchenne's myopathy, characterized by tendon contractures that appear during childhood and affect primarily the upper limbs, the shin muscles and the extensors of the nape of the neck (rigid spine).

These are all diseases that affect the locomotor system. It is precisely in the locomotor system that we find many contradictions, structural problems, issues related to the ability to stand on your feet.

Problems regarding relationships

with the world are located here.

Feelings such as individuality, self-esteem and undervaluation are at stake.

What do I think of my self and what is my role in the world? Where are my assertiveness and my stability? What part of my conscience is in the dark, regarding my relationship with the world? We are talking of conflicts of a personal nature. The diseases mentioned above and other muscle degenerating diseases occur mostly to children, even to very young children, and have their origin at conception. The X chromosome that was referred to earlier is related to fecundation, to the conception of a new being. The emergence of a new being is associated to the relationship between parents and the family, the lineage, the clan.

Therefore, myopathy and other muscle degenerating conditions expose a child who is born with a feeling of guilt and undervaluation (opposing feelings). The person's body shows that by starting to destroy the muscles responsible for certain functions. It affects the legs (connection to the biological Mother, feminine waist), it affects the arms (connection to the biological Father, masculine waist), affects all the muscles of the torso and even of the back of the neck. And, in the end, it destroys the heart and respiratory functions. The person punishes himself, as if he felt guilty.

The event has taken place. "I have been born!" "What am I doing here? Is there enough room for me?"

In this case, it is important to ac-
knowledge that we are dealing with a symptom that is associated to the clan and its representatives, the biological parents.

Conception, such as birth, is a three-person creation, which will only bear fruit if the three agree to it (the Father, the Mother and the future baby) and jointly create that epiphany which is the incarnation of a new being.

As soon as the baby is born, his memory of lineage becomes non-conscious. In fact, the baby forgets the entire luggage he brought with him, and he will need all his living experience and communication skills with the family to slowly understand the thinking pattern of his genealogical tree and also how it thinks and behaves.

Thus, it is crucial that the child is told about his family members, that he becomes fully aware of past events, not just the good and epic ones, but all events! Emotions, wars inside the family, hidden scandals, kept information.

One of the most serious problems affecting people nowadays is having to face up to a family pattern that keeps the past hidden, particularly emotions of the past, because this fact will force the body to unveil them as the person lives. As a matter of fact, the body does not lie, as pointed out in the introduction. And the body always exposes what has been kept hidden.

Myopia

See *Eyes – nearsightedness*
Myopia is commonly used as nearsightedness.

Nail biting

See *Nails*

Nail biting is a condition of nails.

Nails

Hair, body fine hair and nails are skin excretions produced by a protein called keratin. All of these excretions have a protective role. Nails, body hair and hair are annexes of the skin.

Nails are to humans what claws are to animals. Nails have the purpose of holding and defending oneself. They are instruments of aggression. They have the purpose of protecting and attacking.

In the case of human beings, nail-related problems indicate difficulty to communicate. **Nail biting** indicates a prohibition to defend oneself and, above all, to attack someone. Biting shows that the person does not allow himself the right to be the predator. The nail bitter is castrating his aggressiveness. The person is afraid of his own aggressiveness and is unaware of this fact. "I am afraid to stick my claws out." "Who is the person that the individual does not want to hurt?" The individual feels sorry for someone, but is unable to communicate with the person.

In the case of children and young people, they normally bite their nails because one of the parents strongly represses their behaviour. In other words, in their view, one of the parents is aggressive towards them, but they do not feel allowed to show the same aggressiveness to that parent through simple communication. Therefore, the body shows the youngster that he is not respecting his aggressiveness.

Basically, this child does not respect himself and is afraid of hurting one of his parents through communication. However, this does not work well for him. He needs to acknowledge he is holding back his aggressiveness, whether it is regarding his parents, or a third person, which is rare. This third person could be a teacher or any of the child's educators.

A parent who feels sorry about his child's aggressive behaviour is inviting him to bite his nails.

This nail biting issue may also apply to the person who forbids himself from taking the lead, even if he is the leader.

To **bite the ring finger nail** means one is biting union. In other words, the person does not want to be aggressive towards the partner, possibly because he pities him or her.

Long nails indicate the person knows how to defend herself.

Polished nails indicate the person wants to look pretty and attractive.

Ingrown nails denote worry and concern about the person's right to move forward. The person is violent with himself.

People who **chew** on their own skin are anxious about eventual separation; But not the Nail biters, because nails are connected to protection.

Nanism

See *Small stature syndrome*

Nape

The nape is the back and side of the neck, which is more masculine and more *yang* than the front side, which is *yin*.

Problems in this area of the neck are typical of people who have a controlling and fighting attitude. It denotes the person is obsessed about something, and that he is fighting in order to obtain something. The body indicates it is time to give yourself and to loosen up.

See *Stiff neck* and *Vertebrae – cervical vertebrae*

Narcolepsy

Tension in the narcolepsy related conscience is the same as that associated to fainting.

"Get me out of here! I cannot deal with this problem. I am afraid! I do not want to face up to this. I would rather disappear, I would rather die!" Fainting symbolizes a form of momentary death.

Nausea and vomiting

This is a typical occurrence in people who make their minds busy and then fail to digest their thoughts and their lives. They make their own lives difficult by using their minds so much. It makes it difficult to digest. It is as if we had a stone in our stomach. This is the manifestation of confusion and denial and of uncertainty (very common during pregnancy). Anxious people are more prone to nausea. "To think of it makes me sick", "it made me lose my appetite", "it turned my stomach inside out" are well known expressions that translate how difficult it can be to digest one's thoughts. Nausea often occurs when somebody makes other person sick. "This guy makes me sick!"

Nausea stops right here. It represents the sick feeling regarding something that is going on in someone's life. Vomit is an even more categorical demonstration of repudiation and defense. Vomiting simply means lack of acceptance. "I am not digesting this." It may occur during pregnancy also.

In any case, both nausea and vomiting are forms of letting control go loose. Consequently, the person feels relief after vomiting.

In the case of some migraine, the action of vomiting gets rid of the migraine, loosens up the person and brings intense relief.

Neck

The neck supports the head and is the link between the head and the torso. It corresponds to the passage of concepts, ideas, wishes and will (all coming from the brain) to practice (action, fulfilment, expression, relation). The neck is a passage. Not yet the action itself. The neck precedes the action and the mental formation of the action.

The neck represents flexibility and the capacity to look around and back, with respect for oneself.

The back of the neck, the nape, is the most *yang* part of the neck, and the one that is most affected by excessively *yang* behaviours. The front part, where the larynx, the trachea, the throat and the vocal cords are located, is affected by excessively *yin* behaviours.

People who store up anger have chronic tension on their shoulders, neck and arms. If you wish, see *Anger*.

Neck related problems can occur in the muscles (see *Stiff neck*), in the bones (see *Vertebrae – cervical vertebrae*) or in the skin (see *Skin*).

Nephritis

See *Kidneys*

Nephritis is an inflammation of kidneys.

Nerves

See *Nervous system*

The nerves represent communication.

Nervous breakdown

A nervous breakdown is typical of a person who has great mental rigidity, wants to do things his way, and would like for all others to do as he pleases. Obviously, that does not happen and the person wears himself out as a result of inglorious efforts. This person lacks humility and is extremely controlling, wants to take care of everything. His true desire is to let go of everything because he can no longer stand it, and to isolate himself. And, in fact, he ends up isolated, in depression, unable to see anyone, and in rest. If the person is a woman, it is likely that she does not get along with her husband. The fact that she does not get along with the male model she lives with probably extends itself to the relationship with her boss at work, whether that person is a man or woman. The boss function is a masculine function, *yang*. This type of breakdown occurs much more frequently in women. If it happens to a man, it is necessary to find out his idea of male role model. Perhaps it is his Father.

See *Isolation* and *Depression*

Nervous system

The nervous system is basically divided in two systems:

The Central Nervous System (CNS) and the Autonomic Nervous System (ANS), also called vegetative nervous system.

Nerves are like pieces of string connecting nervous centers to organs. Some nerves are connected to the central nervous system. They are called spinal nerves, and include the rachidian nerves (linked to the spinal cord). There are also the cranial nerves.

There are nerves that are linked to the autonomic system, vegetative parasympathetic and sympathetic nerves.

The nerves that form the peripheral nervous system are the cranial nerves, which connect the head and face directly to the brain, the nerves that connect the eyes and the nose to the brain, and all the nerves that connect the spinal marrow to the rest of the body.

The brain communicates with most of the body through the 31 pairs of spinal nerves that come out of the spinal marrow. Each pair of spinal nerves includes a nerve in the anterior side of the spinal marrow, which allows the transmission of information from the brain to the muscles, and a nerve in the posterior side of the marrow, which transmits sensitive information to the brain. The spinal nerves join together through plexuses on the neck, the shoulder and the pelvis and, subsequently, they divide again to innervate the most remote parts of the body.

The central nervous system is formed by the encephalon (brain) and the spinal marrow. It rules the voluntary movements of the body.

Conditions affecting this part of the nervous system will be dealt with separately in this book.

The autonomic nervous system controls the vegetative system, which is autonomous: circulatory system, digestive system, respiratory system, reproductive and urinary systems and endocrine system.

It rules the autonomous movements of the body.

It includes the parasympathetic system, which regulates the organs, and the sympathetic system, which stimulates.

The sympathetic system prepares one for fighting or fleeing. It reacts to sudden situations, and is activated by adrenalin. When this happens, the heart beats faster and the blood pressure increases, the trachea expands, breathing becomes heavier, the pupil dilates, there is perspiration, the blood flows to the voluntary muscles of the

skeleton (connected to the central nervous system) and the sexual and digestive systems become inactive.

The so-called sympathetic trunk, next to the spine, is formed by a group of nervous cells that do not form part of the CNS and which are called ganglia.

There are muscles that are linked to the central nervous system, which are the voluntary control muscles. They are linked to the skeleton. Their role is to produce movement in the bones of the body, in the skeleton. They are striated muscles. There are equally muscles that are connected to the autonomic nervous system and that are involuntary control muscles and line the walls of both blood vessels and internal organs. Their role is to produce automatic movement in the internal organs. They are smooth muscles.

There appears to be just two exceptions: Muscles in the bladder are smooth, although they are voluntary movement muscles. And the muscles in the heart are striated, although they are involuntary control muscles.

Of all the systems in the body, the nervous system is the slowest to react, because it is the deepest. It is the most *yang* of the systems. And since cure occurs from the outside inwards, it takes longer to come up.

Nervous tics

These are motor movement disturbances that affect people who like to show others that they are very much at ease, but are not. In fact, their nervous tics prove they are lying.

The person is afraid and has the feeling he is being observed. The person is afraid of his Father's scolding. He feels under observation and represses himself. Facial tics indicate that the person lost face in the presence of his Father or Mother (in case the Mother plays a Father role).

Neuralgia

The word neuralgia (nevralgia) is formed by the word *neuron*, meaning nerve, and the word *algo*, meaning pain.

Basically, these are nervous pains that can occur at different parts of the body. They are often pains that affect the peripheral nerves. They may manifest themselves in several parts of the body, such as the lumbar area, the ribs and the face. They denote difficulty in communicating with someone who is close. This could be someone at home (probably at home), or with other member of the family, or from work.

Neurofibromatosis

This is often called Recklinghausen's Neurofibromatosis.

Neuro comes from nerves, *fibro* comes from fiber and *matosis* means processed substance.

This is a condition that occurs at the nervous ends. The tension here is a wish to stop being touched or even a wish for separation. When the tension the person is experiencing is active, jelly type balls or spots are formed, which then turn to hard balls. They are hard nodes that sway under the skin. The person experiences a separation tension, and/or a great difficulty in communicating. This is a tension that the person feels regarding someone who is very close. His partner, for instance.

The balls prevent the person from feeling contact. In fact, caressing becomes painful.

See *Breasts – neurofibromatosis*

Newly-born

See *Babies*

Nightmare

A nightmare is a bad dream.
See *Dreams*

Nose

When there is a nose **fracture**, the body requests a break with a belief from the past and a change in behaviour. Fracture is normally the result of a physical or mental dynamic activity. It happens to hyperactive people. The body says: "Stop, take another route." The person who fractures his nose bone is a person who has become very rigid and inflexible in his activities. It is worth looking at the home or at the person's relationships. A nose fracture denotes root problems, problems at home, problems at school, sexual problems. The home has been severely shaken.

The nose assimilates the subtle side of things and exposes our relationship with breath, air, and heaven. The nose is closely associated to life through smell.

Smell adds volume and colour to taste, and is indissociable from it, in the same way the two eyes are indissociable from each other. Smell-related problems (chronic, not momentary) represent fear of allowing subtle things of life inside us, due to lack of self-esteem.

Loss of smell may also be caused by fear of acknowledging the animal that lives inside us. In fact, in the animal world, smell is a great tool for hormonal, hence sexual, recognition. The nose is associated to sexuality. The person who suffers from smell-related problems is also someone who contains his sexual impulses.

Blockage is another indication of this tension. The person whose nose is constantly blocked, or half-blocked, normally suffers from smell-related problems. It denotes the person has difficulty accepting intimate information that comes to him from the outside or the inside. He does not wish to acknowledge the symptoms. It is quite likely that the relationship at home is not flowing as he wishes. However, he does not want to examine the details. What is rotting in the relationship that the person refuses to smell? Absence of smell reveals pain, bitterness, or even a wish for revenge that we allowed to get rotten inside ourselves.

This type of symptom is often associated to a nasal **discharge** that runs down to the mouth, indicating the presence of an inner silent cry and impotence regarding changing things.

When the person has the nose **bleeding**, (spontaneously, not after being hit), this condition indicates a need for recognition. The person feels ignored and mistreated. This exposes a non-conscious loss of happiness, as well as an immense self-demand and a lack of confidence in oneself. There is no opportunity for mistakes to happen. The person loses his happiness. He suffers, and bleeds. He loses vitality, but is unaware of it. This is a natural process. It occurs mostly to children, in children who demand a lot of themselves and, as it happens, are quite successful. It may well be that this self-demanding imposition results from an extremely demanding Father or Mother.

Nystagmus

See *Eyes – nystagmus*

Obesity

Before we start, let's remember that obesity has nothing to do with cellulite.

Obesity is characterized by excessive fat in several parts of the body. Cellulite (or adiposity) is characterized by excessive subcutaneous cellular fat circumscribed to certain parts of the body. Cellulite occurs at the level of the dermis.

Fat is also a reserve and a means to protect sugar levels, the person's identity. Fat represents values and beliefs. Obesity is, above all, a mental issue, a question of beliefs.

What prevents the obese person

from losing weight is that he first looks at what he would like to be, instead of looking at what he is. First, we need to accept ourselves as we are. One needs to accept the image conflict, the conflict of appearance. It is necessary to love everything about oneself. To vibrate a genuine vibration.

For example, a fat person whose competence is acknowledged starts to lose weight. Why not start with oneself?

There are several causes for obesity:

First cause: Feeling of abandonment. The person has to make himself seen in order to be noticed.

This may happen after a separation that the person has felt as abandonment. "He (she) left me, I feel abandoned." It should be pointed out that the separation was provoked by just one of the parts, and, for this reason, it qualifies as abandonment, as the separation was not caused by both. "I was not important to him (her)"! This makes the person put on weight (it may have nothing to do with bulimia). These people are the spherical obese, very quick and speedy, who run very fast. They want to be seen!

Watch out, separation has nothing to do with obesity. Separation shows on the epidermis, whereas obesity is associated to the feeling of abandonment.

Second cause: Fear of loss (this is when the liver comes in). Here we have **Bulimia** (an anxious need to build up reserves). This may be due to lack of love. The person fills himself up to fulfil a need. The person has the illusion of filling in the void in his love through intake of food.

If these people are women, they put on weight mostly on the female parts and on the legs. If they are men, they put on weight especially on the shoulders and on the scapular waist (shoulders, neck). This is symptomatic of men who fear losing their force, their territory. They are afraid of losing their resources. This could be from a sexual perspective. See *Addiction*.

Third cause: To impress the opponent. The day I get to be like the elephant, no one will bother me anymore. I swell up so much that I finally get respected. To earn other person's respect. Cats do this.

Body builders are amongst these people. This is not necessarily about fat, but it could be. This is more the muscles that are absolutely filled with water. They end up getting covered by fat. Here we are talking about the ultimate need to defend oneself from the enemy.

Curiously, these people's shoulder blades (the area of the heart and of emotions) are very delicate. As a matter of fact, this type of obesity is typical of people who need to demonstrate a lot of outer force because they feel major vulnerability inside and because they have some difficulty dealing with relationships and emotions.

Fourth cause: Material success (cultural). People with large stomachs and hanging bellies exemplify this. Suspenders sustain and ensure the image of success. It is a cultural thing.

People who are afraid of the future

typically have **elephant legs** (extremely fat legs). They prefer to stand still. Their mothers always told them to be very careful.

Oedemas

Oedemas are swellings produced by liquid retention. See *Liquid retention* and *Kidneys*

For brain oedemas, see *Heart – heart attack*

Oesophagus

The oesophagus makes up the third segment of the digestive system. The pharynx, the previous segment, splits into the larynx, which extends towards the bronchi (respiratory function), and the oesophagus, which carries food to the stomach.

The first third of the oesophagus is associated with the communication domain. It has more to do with what someone else said or did than with the digestive domain. The remaining two-thirds have more to do with the digestive domain. Oesophagus related problems tend to be in the first segment. Here we are entirely in the realm of social conflict and communication with the outside.

When a problem with the first third occurs, people do not even want to digest the problem. So, the person does not allow the problem to come in. "What she told me stays here, it doesn't go down. I refuse to swallow it". In this case, the tension comes out like: "You bastard, I don't even want to digest that!"

In the case of **cancer** of the oesophagus, the person feels tremendous violence over what people did to him and that tension literally translates into a blockage of the oesophagus. The body expresses what he feels. Nothing goes down. The oesophagus is blocked. The individual is unable to verbalize the intensity of how he feels about what was done to him and literally refuses to feed himself, because, if he did, he would be forced to digest the impossible. Oesophagus cancer is extremely hard. In fact, the person is not able to eat, loses much weight, starves, and ends up dying after much suffering.

Nutrition is associated with the biological Mother. So, the tension related with cancer of this first third of the oesophagus has to do with the relationship of the patient with his mother, or the female role model in his family.

For any problem in the last two-thirds of the oesophagus, see stomach, since the tension is the same that causes stomach problems. In this case, the person allows things to come in but is unable to digest.

Old people

See *Elderly people*

Osteomyelitis

The word comes from the Greek *osteos*, which means bone, and *myelos*, which means marrow.

Osteomyelitis is an infection of bone marrow, usually caused by bacteria or a fungus, that can stay localized or spread out, compromising the bone marrow, the cortical part of the bone and the periosteum.

According to some doctors, this designation is incorrect, because this symptom corresponds to an inflammation not of the bone marrow but just of the cortical part of the bone (the cone itself).

It denotes emotional pain, anger and frustration regarding life. "I feel I have no support". It means undervaluation and that a person has annulled himself.

See *Bone marrow*

Osteoporosis

This means a person has pores (holes) in the bones. Osteoporosis is caused by a strong feeling of undervaluation. It is often found in elderly people, who have been bedridden for a long time (stayed in bed for a long time), and in menopausal women.

All of these categories of people is suffering, in their own way, from an undervaluation tension, thus creating the necessary conditions for osteoporosis to develop. "I am not worth anything. I am getting old and disposable."

On top of it all, this person believes he deserves no support in his useless life.

Many doctors deal with menopause as if it was a disease. Menopause means a major hormonal change, but it is a natural process (see *Menopause*).

African women who stop being fertile cease to have a reproductive function and therefore may join the council of the sage. The clan interests them again. They may start using their two brains and not just the feminine. A woman such as this will not develop osteoporosis because she does not feel undervalued.

Menopause is a stage of reassessment of a woman's life project. To reach the age of 50, in Hebrew, means jubilee, happiness.

A woman who sails through her menopause does not develop osteoporosis. A woman who lives through her old age well does not get it either.

Otitis

See *Ears*

Otitis is one of the most common problems in baby ears nowadays.

Outbreaks

See *Epidemics*

Ovaries

The ovaries are the female gonads.

They are the reservoir of the power of Earth, *yin* and feminine. They are the essence of femininity. Men do not have ovaries. Ovaries are to women what testicles are to men. Removing a woman's ovaries has the same energetic effect as removing testicles from a man.

The hormones produced by these glands control sexual characteristics, such as hair and breast growth, etc. Both men and women have male hormones (testosterone) and female hormones (estrogens), only in distinct proportions.

Ovary-related problems indicate the loss, or the feeling of loss, of a loved one. It may have been a boyfriend, a son, etc.

The ovaries polarity is not obvious. However, for diagnosis purposes, it should be assumed that the right ovary is *yang* and the left ovary is *yin*, for all women, right and left-handed. But this is not certain. Problems in the *yang* ovary indicate the loss of a male loved one, and in the *yin* ovary, of a female loved one.

So, the *yang* ovary denotes the loss of a major male friend, of a boyfriend, son, or any male the person was very fond of. The *yin* ovary indicates the loss of a major female friend, a girlfriend, a daughter or any female the person was very fond of.

In any case, this ovary polarity is not terribly important, because the person is able to quickly identify which loved one caused the feeling of loss.

Ovary **cancer** makes the ovaries become more productive. It is as if the body is showing how anxious the person is to create, to generate, a new loved one to replace the one that was lost. This is a typical example of wishing to protect the species before protecting the individual. Because, in fact, the person is offering a part of her body in order to be able, in a virtual manner (here lies the illusion) to recover someone who is gone from her life. When the tension the person is experiencing is huge and not verbalized, exteriorized, the person develops cancer. When the situation is not serious, the person develops a **cyst**.

It seems ovarian cysts take about nine months to develop. It must be pointed out that the fact it takes nine months is curious, because this is the normal gestation period before birth.

Palate

The palate is the upper part of the mouth, separating it from the nasal cavities. It is also called the roof of the mouth. Matter, which comes from Earth, gets digested in the mouth, in the form of food. It is the palate that prevents matter, which was at the lower level, from being taken up (to the brain), to Heaven, to a higher level. The power of the Earth is represented, in the family, by the Mother, and the power of Heaven is represented by the Father. Problems in the palate show the person's confrontation with the memory of what took place within the family. "I cannot swallow this! I need a much bigger mouth!"

A child born without a palate shows that there is a conflict between the two parents. What the body is showing is that the child's palate is far too small. It shows the person has to swallow a much bigger chunk in order to be able to survive. It shows that the person needs a lot of space to be able to digest what he needs to digest.

Palpitations

See *Arrhythmias*

Paludism

See *Malaria*

Pancarditis

This is an inflammation of the pericardium (a sac covering the heart and the roots of the major blood vessels), of the myocardium (muscle responsible for pumping the heart) and of the endocardium (inner layer of the heart). *Pan* means total.

In this case, we are in the presence of someone who is totally unable to deal with his emotions and who feels profoundly wounded by somebody close, either the partner or the family.

Emotions provoke changes in the heart.

Anything that involves passion, emotion in the relationship, takes place in the heart. It is the symptom of love, of passing flirts. "He broke my heart! I feel as if he torn my heart out. My heart is jumping up and down."

However, when the individual controls his natural emotions like fears, joys, passions, sadness, envies (in other words, when he allows his mental process, his brain, to stop the flow of natural emotions), then problems arise. The mind starts taking control over these natural emotions, thanks to beliefs or any other type of rules that the person imposes on himself, either in a conscious or unconscious form. In fact, when Cartesian thinking intervenes, the heart gets unregulated (and other organs too).

The person who suffers from a heart condition does not accept nor live with his emotions. He is a very *yang* person, has a very masculine behaviour, he is a fighter.

He has long-term emotional problems that he does not face up to, he lacks happiness, and believes in the need for effort and stress. All of these constitute good ingredients that lead to heart problems.

Pancreas

The pancreas is a gland that has a double purpose.

It has an exocrine function, through the external secretion of pancreatic fluid that is sent to the duodenum. It is a digestive function. It digests fat.

It also has an endocrine function, through the internal production of insulin, which is involved in the absorption of sugar by the cells in the body and in the regulation of sugar levels in the blood. Therefore, in its blood regulating capacity, the pancreas is an endocrine gland and forms part of the endocrine system.

The exocrine side does not necessarily have to influence the endocrine side.

The pancreas is a busy, hard-working organ. Of all the internal organs, it is the most *yang*, masculine organ of the body. It teams up with the spleen, which is a more feminine organ. In fact, Chinese medicine calls them the spleen-pancreas. They both form part of the earth element of the five eastern elements.

Pancreas literally means "made of flesh". Yes, because *Pan* means the whole, the universe, the god of creation and *Crea* means flesh.

Everything connected to the value of the soul takes place here. The flesh rots, but the soul is everlasting. The relationship with the might of Heaven, that is, the biological Father, husband or the male model the person has/had in her life is expressed here.

Any person with escalating physical symptoms that have nothing to do with pancreas, usually end up with symptoms in the pancreas. In this case, the analysis of the pancreas symptoms is not very important.

The person who suffers from hyperglycaemia and the person who has diabetes feel they have not received love, that they were not loved enough. The person who has hypoglycaemia feels he does not deserve the love of others. The person who has cancer is a very serious, boring and rule bound person, who is convinced he was the recipient of the utmost ignominy and who does not allow the word love to enter his vocabulary.

You will see all the details in *Pancreas – endocrine gland (diabetes)*, *Pancreas – endocrine gland (hyperglycaemia)*, *Pancreas – endocrine gland (hypoglycaemia)* and *Pancreas – exocrine gland (cancer of the pancreas and pancreatitis)*

Pancreas – endocrine gland (diabetes)

When diabetes symptoms exist, it is because the person felt he was not able to keep sugar reserves. In diabetic people, sugar escapes through urine. Diabetic people are unable to assimilate and store sugar in their own cells.

Previously, in certain countries, diabetes was known as "sugar diarrhoea", which actually means "diarrhoea of love".

The body of the diabetic person is showing him that he deprives himself of love. The word diabetes comes from the Greek, which means *to throw* or *to pass* through something.

The pancreas produces a type of sugar that is very alkaline. For this reason, diabetes causes the hyper-acidulation of the body. The person becomes sour, acid, and aggressive.

The body is showing the person that the one who does not love becomes sour, that the one who moves away from sugar, sweetness and love becomes sour.

In other words, the person who does not know how to enjoy himself becomes unbearable. The diabetic person longs for love, but does not dare searching for it. He is waiting everlastingly. He has not learnt what love is. The key word here is love. Being able to receive love or moving away from love.

Let's take an example from the animal world.

When an animal dies, the smell is terrible. The animal that stayed behind understands that the stench, this very bad smell, is very unpleasant, so it does not stay around. It goes away. It is a revolting smell. It is disgusting. This is what nature does. By making the animal follow its instincts, it makes it move away from death in order to survive. The ghastly smell does it.

The image in diabetes is that of the animal that stays close to what is filthy and does not move away. Why should an animal stay close to another who dies and stinks? This actually only happens in cases when an offspring stays behind when its mother dies. In fact, the baby animal does not know where to go. Then he stays close to the stinky, filthy corpse. And then it develops diabetes.

In the case of diabetes, the person's tension translates as: "I cannot oppose fate. And I am not receiving my correct share of sugar (love, affection). I would like to get out of this because it disgusts me, but I can't." Therefore, from the key word love, we get to another key word: **revulsion** (repugnance).

In this case, the tension is due to: "It is my duty to stay close to someone who smells like a corpse." The person remains close to someone who revolts him. And he stays. And he tries to resist.

Please see *Pancreas* and you will see it derives from *Pan* (which means the whole, the universe, the god of creation) and from *Crea* (which means flesh).

The person suffering from diabetes rebels against the god of creation. And the representative of the relationship with the divine force, the force of heaven, is precisely the biological Father. The person who causes revulsion to the diabetic patient is his Father, or her husband, or her male model.

It is paramount to find out what happened in the relationship with the Father, who revolted the person and caused him revulsion and who, still in this person's understanding, never gave the love, the sugar he needed.

In this case, it is important to work with the person in his acceptance of love for himself and for the other person.

The pancreas temporizes our glycaemia. It stores our sugar for when we need it later. The internal insulin secretion plays a role in the absorption of sugar by the cells of the body. It is the insulin that stores the sugar.

When there is absence of insulin, the cells do not absorb the blood's sugar properly and it gets stored in an irregular manner. This storage characterizes **diabetes**. The medical treatment for diabetes consists precisely in injecting insulin into the body.

We have seen earlier that, in a diabetic person, sugar escapes through urine, which prevents the patient from maintaining adequate sugar levels in his blood.

For this reason, diabetics drink and eat a lot. Nevertheless, they still lose weight.

So, this person may have both hyperglycaemia and hypoglycaemia crises.

"I must turn this page", he thinks. And so, the person resists and becomes hyperglycaemic and starts eating many sweets and sugary things. Then, his brain will reply: "lower down your resistance." Then he becomes hypoglycaemic.

The brain will do these two things in alternating form. For this reason, the patient will alternate between hyperglycaemia and hypoglycaemia crises. He is unable to balance the sugars of his life, the sugars in his blood.

The diabetic person spends his life resisting a lot (hyper) and then ends up letting go (hypo) in the face of everything that revolts him and causes him revulsion.

The diabetic person has cerebral dysfunctions and major losses of contact with reality.

When the glycaemia levels are balanced, the diabetic person functions perfectly.

See *Pancreas*, *Pancreas – endocrine gland (hyperglycaemia)*, *Pancreas – endocrine gland (hypoglycaemia)* and *Pancreas – exocrine gland (cancer of the pancreas and pancreatitis)*

Pancreas – endocrine gland (hyperglycaemia)

The person who suffers from hyperglycaemia has too much sugar in his blood. In his life, and probably in his education, the person has felt, and still does feel, shortage of sweetness. Whether in a conscious or unconscious manner, the person is progressively destroying his affective beliefs. And he attempts to make up for the loss of love, loss of sweetness, loss of sugar. For this reason, he looks for support in his Mother, who is represented by food. He will eat sweets, eat a lot, grow fatter and put on weight.

See *Obesity* (second cause). See *Pancreas*, *Pancreas – endocrine gland (diabetes)*, *Pancreas – endocrine gland (hypoglycaemia)* and *Pancreas – exocrine*

gland (cancer of the pancreas and pancreatitis)

Pancreas – endocrine gland (hypoglycaemia)

The person who suffers from hypoglycaemia has too little sugar in his blood. This is the opposite of hyperglycaemia. This is a person who has feelings that oppose those of diabetic sufferers.

In this case, it is the person who does not believe he deserves sweetness, tenderness, and love. He is in constant search for norms, regulations he never actually had. In this case, the Father was basically non-existent in his functions as a Father. The Father was a softie. This may be connected to the family and/or with the pattern of men in the clan. These are people with a very dry type of body, with too many sharp ends, not rounded, not sweat. These are arid people. Fat acts as a reserve and also as a protecting agent of sugar and of the person's identity. Fat represents values and beliefs. This person does not have any fat at all. See *Pancreas*, *Pancreas – endocrine gland (diabetes)*, *Pancreas – endocrine gland (hyperglycaemia)* and *Pancreas – exocrine gland (cancer of the pancreas and pancreatitis)*

Pancreas – exocrine gland (cancer of the pancreas and pancreatitis)

Cancer of the pancreas is associated to the exocrine function.

People who have problems associated to the digestive function of the pancreas are people who allow little time for fun and pleasure. Duty and the professional activity are more important. Life lacks joy. The influence of the biological Father is felt, like in all the other cases (see links down below), mostly regarding the beliefs and values that must be followed. These are regimented, serious and boring people.

This sort of people goes to lengths to keep the past alive. However, they do it because they do not know how to deal with the present.

Cancer in the pancreas indicates that the person needs to fully digest everything that has happened. He feels the injury was very strong. The conflict in his conscience is the feeling that tremendous injustice was made. What was done to him was profoundly unfair. It was particularly unfair because rules were broken. Those rules the person is such a devotee of.

The person digests himself with the digestive enzymes he produces, because he feels very angry and has decided to repress that anger. He feels doubt, confusion, and a great inability to be happy. However, he will not verbalize any of this. He bottles up. And he carries on grinding and being eaten by his own enzymes.

In this type of cancer, we are dealing with utmost ignomiy. However, the person only experiences this feeling due to his own beliefs, not because of what was done to him. This is an extremely fast cancer. The person peels off like an onion.

Pancreatitis is an inflammation of the pancreas in its digestive capacity. On occasions, it happens to HIV patients due to the anti-HIV medicine they have taken. Pancreatitis is also common in people who drink too much alcohol. Symptoms include a feeling of sickness and pain. The digestive capacity of the pancreas is affected, as the pancreas stops working properly. Food is not properly digested, and this can lead to weight loss, the presence of non-digested fat and diarrhoea.

We are dealing with someone who hates his life, who finds it boring and who attempts to solve his problems by drinking alcohol.

In this case, see *Alcoholism*

Also see *Pancreas, Pancreas – endocrine gland (diabetes), Pancreas – endocrine gland (hyperglycaemia)* and *Pancreas – endocrine gland (hypoglycaemia)*

Pancreatitis

See *Pancreas – exocrine gland (cancer of the pancreas and pancreatitis)*

Pancreatitis is an inflammation of the pancreas in its digestive (exocrine) capacity.

Panic

Panic attacks are usually anxiety attacks. But they can also be fear attacks. When we talk about anxiety attacks, we talk about someone who is very much afraid of the future: "Something could happen to me!" I don't feel safe when I am alone." "Someone should protect me in case something may happen!". Hypochondriac attacks are in fact anxiety attacks. It shows a lack of trust; A lack of faith. This person needs to develop his or her spiritual life. I do not mean religious; Just spiritual. Faith and spirituality have to do with Heaven, with the *yang* model, the father, with a failure in my sense of direction.

When we talk about fear attacks, here we talk about failure to acknowledge fears. This is a person who does not face up to himself. This means that fears have not been acknowledged for a long time. It indicates a problem with roots. What is going on with the life pattern of the women of the clan? The family hides information. We are dealing with a person who belongs to a clan who hides information from his descendants, information that would be very useful to the person, to enable him to face up to himself. Hidden information is the key, in this case. Things related to the birth, pregnancy and conception. The Mother has not told him everything. This person needs to talk to his biological Mother. If the Mother is dead already, this person needs to focus and get centered to be able to connect to his intuition. This way, he will be in a position to catch all the signs that will allow him to uncover everything that has happened to the women of the clan. Alternatively, he will need to ask members of the family and of the clan about his lineage and that of the women of his lineage.

See *Family*

Paralysing diseases

See *Paralysis*

Paralysis

Paralysis affects the locomotor system, namely the muscles and/or the nerves. They are linked to a huge feeling of undervaluation. This is the first keyword. The second keyword concerns two feelings, ideas or impulses that are contradictory.

The person imposes on himself two contradictory orders regarding movement. The person has wishes that contradict each other. These two contradictory ideas that provoke tension may occur when, for example, the person wished very much to do something, did it and then regretted having done it. I pushed someone off the cliff, she was badly hurt as a result and I felt very guilty about it, unable to forgive myself. In this case, the muscles are affected. Remorse is an undervaluation feeling that affects muscles.

If this happens to a newly born, here we have a child who has incarnated but who doubts whether he should have done it, because he feels neither balance nor harmony in his life to allow him to grow freely. In situations like this, it is paramount to examine what went on between the parents during pregnancy, at the time of birth or during the early childhood of the individual in question.

Paralysing diseases are characteristic of the locomotor system and of the nervous system, as we have just seen.

The feeling of individuality and of self-esteem is the issue here. This is about what I think of myself and what am I doing in this world. This is about my assertiveness and my flexibility and conflicts related to my personal worth are kept here. What part of my conscience is in the dark in my relationship with the world?

In a condition such as paralysis, the person's thoughts tie him down. He stopped being able to move, whether partially or totally. In case of partial paralysis, it is important to check which part of the locomotor system is affected.

See *Multiple sclerosis, Myopathy, Stammering, Brain paralysis, General paralysis, Acute anterior poliomyelitis (child paralysis), Partial paralysis, Bell's paralysis, Parkinson's disease, Poliomyelitis, Nervous tics, Stiff neck* and *Amyotrophic Lateral Sclerosis (ALS)*)

Parasites

The person who has parasites is someone that has surrendered power to others. He accepts that others take control of his life. He allows himself to be sucked dry by others. He is not centered and lacks self-esteem. He is incapable of saying **No** in an assertive manner. His inner and outer beings are not aligned. "Who has been taking advantage of me an sucking me dry?"

The word parasite is essential in this context. If the person lets himself to be affected by parasites, this means he is not centred and does not know how to be assertive with the people around him. It means that there is someone in his life that is a parasite and lives off him, whether at home, work, or amongst friends. It could also be his

Mother. The person is clinging to the past and to his beliefs, and this is the reason why he cannot stand up to the parasite with the degree of assertiveness he ought to have. He feels frustration because he is convinced he will no longer be accepted by that person if he changes his attitude towards that person. The person feels unable to progress in a tranquil way.

Parasympathetic nervous system

See *Nervous system*

The parasympathetic nervous system is a part of the Nervous system.

Parathyroid glands

These are endocrine glands. These are four parathyroid glands on the side of the thyroid. They secrete parathormone, which regulates calcium levels in the blood, and has an effect on the locomotor system and on the circulation system.

From the perspective of tension in the conscience, the parathyroid glands are identical to those of the thyroid.

See *Thyroid*

Parkinson's disease

Parkinson's disease affects the dopaminergic cells. The person has shortage of dopamine. Dopaminergic cells are neurotransmitters that regulate adrenalin, which is responsible for the acceleration of heartbeat, the increase in blood pressure, dilation of bronchi and pupils and the rise in sugar levels in the blood.

Dopamine is connected to no-radrenalin, and the latter distributes the effects of adrenaline all over the body.

Therefore, Parkinson's disease reveals an inhibition of an agitation, of an anger process, and the inhibition of a reaction process. People who, for a long time, had to accept other people's control without being able to react, or who did not let themselves explode, may develop Parkinson's.

Parkinson's disease occurs to people who feel deeply upset about what they do, and mostly regarding the people or the community they deal with.

This type of tension is related to movement and is experienced in alternate ways, some stages being more active and others more passive. It is linked to the crown chakra. This was the case of Pope John Paul 2nd since he got to the Vatican, where he stayed for over twenty years. He probably did not deal well with the community he lived in.

The person who suffers from Parkinson's disease is afraid of isolation but will not admit it. This happens to aging husbands who are afraid of losing their wives, or to aging wives who fear losing their husbands.

Partial paralysis

This is where tensions with the immediate surroundings, with close ones, are located. This is mostly with the Father figure, or the male model, or with the Mother, or the female model.

Partial paralysis shows to the person that there is a deep tension in the side of the body that suffered the paralysis, and that he must not go on like this. This is massive self-inflicted violence. It reflects the person's tremendous difficulty in understanding what his emotions would tell him if he did not control them, and if he took the opportunity to acknowledge and examine them.

Partial paralysis is the result of major undervaluation and remorse, regret about something that was done in the past. The person cannot bear the contradiction in his life. And he is unable to verbalize this. It is advisable to examine which side of the body is affected. The person who suffers from paralysis is inflexible, static in the way he thinks, and he feels undervalued and afraid.

If paralysis affects the lower limbs, this indicates a great deal of fear regarding home, the relationship between the couple, with the family and a major absence (and/or separation) of the biological Mother. It may be an indication that the person has a thinking pattern that is identical to that of the biological Mother. "I cannot escape, I cannot find the way out, and I do not know what to do." In any case, the person feels a major crisis in his roots but he keeps it to himself without confronting the people with whom he has problems. It is important to find out what happened with this person at birth or during pregnancy. Any way, if it is a woman, it is possible that she may be experiencing the same inner conflict as her mother.

If paralysis affects the upper limbs,

this shows that the person feels under-valued and unworthy of others, of matter and, above all, that he is unable to put a stop to the aggression he feels in others. Aggression by the partner? The family?

The person who suffers from paralysis thinks in such a way that there is little room to let things flow, and lives his pain in silence. He has created a prison for himself, through his extremely rigid life. The person sticks to beliefs that mean nothing to him.

This is the result of repetition of the thinking pattern that runs in the family, which does not work for him. This is the result of the person feeling attacked on his ideas.

Check the parts of the body that have been affected by paralysis.

Also see *Paralysis* for other types of paralysis.

Patchy hair loss

See *Hair*

Patchy hair loss is a condition of hair.

Pelvis

The pelvic zone is formed by the bones of the pelvic waist. They are the two iliac bones, on the right and left sides, respectively, also called hips, and the sacral bone lies behind.

It is normally called the sacroiliac area. *Sacral* means sacred. The sacral bone holds the tensions which bear witness of who I am. When talking about fractures in this area, it refers to

fractures of one of the two iliac bones or of the sacral bone.

Here lies what people consider to be fair or unfair. Tensions are very much like those produced at the cervical vertebrae, the only difference being that here they are restricted to the family side and to things belonging to the family.

Here we are dealing with bones, which are part of the locomotor system. The common denominator here is, as with other vertebrae, undervaluation.

When I have problems with my pelvis, it is when I feel that those at home are judging me. Sacra vertebrae are directly connected to the individual's *yin* axis, to the female axis, the axis of femininity, symbolized by the Mother.

Pelvis-related problems reveal the sense of injustice the person feels regarding the way his family and his clan look at him, disapprovingly, and at the way he leads his life.

Penis

In animals, the penis denotes power and usefulness. Not in the social sense of the word, but as a means to procreate and ensure the preservation and survival of the species. Functional problems in the penis represent lack of capacity to stress masculinity.

Nowadays, the penis is increasingly given a social meaning that does not make any sense. It is often said that the size of the penis denotes more power. The penis shows masculine power, but not more power than that held by somebody else. Actually, when it comes to sexual intercourse, the size of the penis only matters to those who have a sexual dependency, and who are under the illusion that sex will fill the void in their lives. For this reason, in their view, the bigger the penis, the greater their power to dominate is (see *Sex – addiction*). Problems in the **glans** are associated to tensions allied to a feeling of uselessness, sexual frustration or problems communicating with his partner. Above all, they indicate a connection with the biological Mother (the umbilical cord has not yet been cut and the person is still dependent on the biological Mother).

Problems in the **frenulum** often cause pain. Problems on the **fold** strangulate the head of the erected penis, making the act somehow clumsy and often painful. They unveil a guilt complex. These are issues that come from birth. They are related to the person's build. For this reason, the person should be asked why he was born with a guilt complex regarding sexual intercourse. Who in his family, Father, Grandfather, had beliefs that punished sex? This person must be aware of this issue. In any case, this problem is easily solved with surgery.

In fact, **circumcision**, either in young men or adults, indicates the definite cut with the umbilical cord, something the person had been unable to do earlier. It indicates the person is taking a new route in his life.

Glans **herpes** may be painful. This is a disease provoked by contact with tenderness. It is charactcristic of couples that adore each other but are permanently quarrelling. The person wants to contact intensely, the nerve is very much alive, but then, as the relationship does not work properly and the person spends a lot of time quarrelling, the body shows that fighting through herpes, which is painful and hampers sexual intercourse. Herpes reveals that the contact relationship with the other person is painful. People who are prone to having herpes are people who have difficulty being on their own and being tender with themselves. They are depend on love. Herpes shows there is self-inflicted violence in the relationship. If the person is violent to himself in the relationship, this means he feels guilty about something.

See *Impotence* and *Sex – addiction*

Pericarditis

Pericarditis is an inflammation of the pericardium, which is the sac covering the heart. It happens when someone close threatens the heart, whether physically or symbolically. It often occurs following a heart attack or chest angina, when the tension becomes: "I need to protect my heart." This happens when the person is afraid that his heart might be hurt.

The pericardium is part of the membranes covering the body, of the sacs whose purpose is to defend from attacks that can be verbal or physical. Given that the heart is the center of our emotions and feelings, it can be said that the person felt his emotions threatened by someone. Someone has threatened this person's feelings. As if the person was not allowed to feel what he feels. This person is close, and most probably is part of the family. Maybe even be at home. Could it be the partner?

Periodontitis

See *Gums*

Periodontitis is a progressive regressing of the gums.

Periosteum

When referring to bones, it is important to distinguish three levels: the actual bone, the bone marrow and the periosteum (the membrane that covers the bone).

The periosteum is the membrane or "skin" covering the bone.

When fracturing a bone, the pain we feel is in the periosteum. This is where the bone connects with the conscience, through pain. This has to do with communication.

This is where contact is made. "What I did wrong or what did I simply fail to do?"

A pain in the bones calls for immobility. I must stop and rethink my actions. A non-stopping pain leads to inactivity.

Pain is ninety per cent periosteal and may, accordingly, be worked on from a psychic perspective. Ten per cent of pain is, nevertheless, truly physical, which makes it much more difficult to deal with and means that pain killers need to be used.

See *Bone*

Peritonitis

The peritoneum forms part of the group of membranes covering the body, of the sacs whose purpose is to attack or to defend. Conflicts with closed ones take place here. The attacks can be verbal or physical. The peritoneum is irrigated by many vessels and has many nerves. It is extremely sensitive.

Peritonitis is an extremely hard condition. The pain is very intense, and it means the peritoneum is inflamed. The peritoneum involves the bowels, so, we have no bones here, and the condition gets there straightaway. This is a very vulnerable part of the body.

Intestinal perforation is an extremely dangerous condition. The bowel that is oppressed reacts immediately. The abdomen is in danger. The abdomen contains the triple heating system that Chinese medicine refers to. The transmutation of things, that is, the assimilation of knowledge, takes place in the abdomen.

Children always complain a lot of bellyache when it is time to go to school (assimilation of knowledge).

Problems in the peritoneum indicate that the person felt under attack, assailed, by someone close to him. It reveals that something disgusted the person, that something filthy has taken place. It could be physical dirt or something disgusting that someone has done. "This person disgusts me".

Peritonitis sometimes occurs after appendicitis. In this case, see *Appendix*

Peritonitis may also affect patients undergoing dialysis and who are using the peritoneal dialysis method.

In the case of the latter, see *Kidneys – renal insufficiency*

Peroneum

The fracture of the peroneum shows strong undervaluation.

See *Legs (knee to foot)*

Perspiration

Perspiration takes place in the skin and is related to communication problems. Sweat has a smell, is sticky and gluey.

In the animal world, these are characteristic of frogs and fish.

To grab a frog or fish is a difficult thing to do. They are slippery.

The person who sweats without having done any physical activity is someone who does not want to get caught. He is a bar of soap, an eel (very slippery fish). Children who want to escape from their Fathers or Mothers, or from any adult, sweat more. Perspiration is very diluted urine. It changes from person to person. In the old times, doctors tasted their patients' urine or sweat: "Tell me what your odour tastes like and I will tell you about your emotions (fear, resentment, rage…)". Dogs are able to detect odour immediately, which may make them very nervous quite fast.

Feet perspiration shows the child wants to escape the control of his Mother.

Sweaty hands indicate people who want to escape social control.

Sweaty shoulders indicate a desire to escape the Father.

Sweaty head shows a desire to escape certain ideas.

When a baby sweats through the head, this means he does not want to get caught in his parents' ideas, as they do not make sense to him.

Sweaty armpits show the person is aware he is not allowed the right to use his imagination. This person would like to fly away, like Pegasus.

In the same way, people who have a strong smell are showing their emotional state, women and men who use a lot of perfume do so to mark their territory.

Pharynx

The pharynx makes up the second segment of the digestive tube and of the respiratory system. It is a common access route for food and air. It carries food to the stomach and air to the larynx. The split takes place when the epiglottis (small valve) closes as we swallow, keeping the food from going into the larynx. Thus, the pharynx is a crossroads between the air that goes in and comes out, and the food that goes in and, occasionally, comes out, too.

The pharynx has a vital connotation with survival. It is the so-called "primitive mouth" (between the mouth and the oesophagus). It is a funnel and a precipice. The person who experiences a problem in the pharynx, namely **pharyngitis**, is someone who feels tension associated with greed. "I'd better swallow before someone takes my food; it's not enough for all." This condition is characteristic of someone with a sense of shortage. In the pharynx, the body shows that the person desires to 'take property', both in a material and in a more abstract sense. The greedy need to 'take property' reveals a feeling of scarcity and also a lack of discernment to discriminate what must go into the body from what should not, as well as what goes into the body from what comes out of it.

If you have any problem with the Pharyngeal tonsils, or the also called Nasopharyngeal tonsils, please see *Adenoids*

Phlebitis

Phlebitis (or thrombophlebitis) may occur in any surface vein of the body, but it happens more frequently in veins in the legs. Phlebitis, venal strokes like thrombosis, varicose veins, and haemorrhoids happen in veins.

The venal system is the *yin* portion of the circulatory system. It carries used blood to the liver and kidneys to be filtered, and to the lungs to replace carbon dioxide with oxygen. Vein problems indicate an excessively passive life with little happiness, a life that lets happiness go by at a distance.

Phlebitis develops in people with varicose veins. A varicose is a venal swelling that almost always takes place in the lower limbs. Varicose veins result from an accumulation of blood in the surface veins of the legs, blood that should have returned to the heart but did not.

A varicose vein keeps venal blood from circulating and is the perfect ingredient for phlebitis. Phlebitis and deep venal strokes (thrombosis) are the way the body expresses that the person is fed up with his lifestyle, that he is angered but passive, too *yin*.

Phlebitis denotes rage and frustration. The individual blames others for his limitations and lack of happiness. We are in the presence of someone with strong opinions, strong ideas, and inflexible judgments.

The fact that phlebitis happens in the legs suggests that the person has trouble following his path in life with gentleness, harmony, and fluency. The legs are associated with questions related to roots, home, spouse, and the model of biological Mother the person has.

Pimples

Pimples indicate an infection of the hair and sebaceous follicles, particularly on shoulders, face, back and chest.

They represent eruption, the expulsion of a tension related with communication difficulties.

For pimples on the face, see *Acne*.

Pimples that erupt on the body may be one-offs or recurrent. They always indicate that there is tension in the process of communication.

For pimples on the back, see *Back*.

For pimples on the shoulders, see *Shoulder*.

Pineal body

See *Pineal gland*

Pineal gland

The pineal gland (or pineal body) is also called Epiphysis.

This is a relatively unknown endocrine gland placed between the two cerebral hemispheres. It is tucked right in the middle of the cranium. For those who work with chakras, it is directly connected to the crown chakra, the seventh chakra, purple chakra. This gland is in the conduit connecting the seventh chakra to the first. It is directly connected to the day's solar cycle. It secretes serotonin and melatonin. Serotonin gives life to the body; it gives it dynamics and vibrancy. This hormone is responsible for the *yanging* process of the person (it reinforces the person's structure). It makes the person energetic. It is between two and four in the morning, during sleep, that secretion of serotonin by the pineal gland stops and gives way to the secretion of melatonin. Melatonin is good for the immune system, increases the quality of sleep, and has a positive effect on enthusiasm, good disposition, and good humour. This moment in our sleep is very important because it is a very *yin*, very calm, and very *zen* time of regeneration of the person.

People who suffer from depression often have shortage of serotonin. Insomnia often occurs between two and four in the morning.

When the person does not allow the *zen* moment enter his life, either due to an excessively *yang* or regimented behaviour, then the natural production of melatonin will be much weaker, the person becoming then much weaker, and this, in turn, weakens the production of serotonin. Then the person has poor serotonin and feels tired and depressed.

People who suffer from depression often have a shortage of serotonin and suffer from insomnia between two and four in the morning.

The pineal gland also appears to play a role in the form the person reacts to exposure to sunlight and, above all, to the way he metabolizes melanin. In fact, the pineal gland is linked to the so-called force of Heaven, to the energy that comes from Heaven, namely to the energy that comes from the Sun. The person who has pineal-related problems is someone who has severe disturbances in his sense of direction, in the route he needs to take in his life, in issues related to humbleness and authority. This person has a major problem in his relationship with his biological Father or with the male model (could be the person's husband). He is a very mentally oriented person, very rational, who wants to sort everything out by himself. He believes he knows all the answers and that he needs to be in command. He leaves no space for intuition.

See *Authority*

Pinealoma

This is a tumor in the pineal gland. It denotes major repressed tension. If the person is a woman, look for the causes in the relationship with men in general, with her biological Father or, particularly, with her husband. If the person is a man, look for the causes in the relationship with men in general and/or with his biological Father.

See *Pineal gland*

Pituitary gland

The pituitary gland is also called Hypophysis.

The pituitary/hypophysis is the conductor of the whole orchestra of endocrine glands.

For those who work with chakras, the pituitary is directly linked to the indigo chakra, the chakra of the third eye, the sixth chakra. It has multiple functions. It stimulates other glands (suprarenal, thyroid and gonads) to produce their respective substances. Therefore, it has a role in the reproduction system and in growth.

Growth disorders are very much associated to the endocrine system. There are three glands that participate in the balanced growing up process of individuals: the pituitary, the thyroid and the thymus. See *Growth (growth disorders)*.

The hide and seek game that the person is doing is played at the pituitary gland. This happens when the person's behaviour towards others is not straightforward, and he pretends to be someone else he is not. This occurs when the person refuses to respect his intuition.

At the level of the pituitary, the tension lies in the misalignment between the inner being (the person's interior voice, his intuition) and the outer world (his everyday life and what the person pretends to be).

One of the hormones the pituitary produces is the growth hormone, which influences the person's growth and maturing.

We shall not talk about people who are very small and do not grow up. We will talk about very tall people, with very long extremities. In these cases, the person's tension is: "I need to be as tall as possible so that I can reach…" Then the person grows a lot (we are referring to tall people who come from smaller families).

This tendency comes from the parents. Once more, this is connected to the parents' behaviour. Probably with the Father or the male model in the family, who always wanted to go further and higher. The child grew up to collect the reward. This is a body build-related type of issue and is associated to the genetic inheritance that the child brings with him since conception.

If a child thinks he needs to grow very tall to be worth something, his body will take him high up.

There is an anterior hypophysis and a posterior hypophysis.

The **anterior hypophysis** secretes the hormones that will provoke the functioning of other endocrine glands.

The **posterior hypophysis** is called the neurohypophysis. Its purpose is to balance the kidney and the pancreas.

When its functioning is disturbed,

the person may develop insipid diabetes. He drinks and pees a lot. He recycles his own liquids. This is a person who washes using a lot of water. "There is black money here". "There is liquid to be washed" (money = liquid).

Tumours in the pituitary (**adenomas** and **fibromas**) are normally benign. They call the person's attention so that he realizes that he misses himself and that he is carving a path for himself that will take him further than what is advisable. The person is obsessed with something related to matter, and which is acutely abusing him. The person is not respecting his deep essence.

Plague

Rats transmit this disease. It still exists in many countries. It strikes when human beings lose the concept of effective management of natural resources. There is a correlation between rats and human behaviour. In the middle ages, plague followed famine. When humans lose their fear of starving to death, when the event has taken place, plague follows, like a sort of hangover.

Human beings are capable of killing for the management of natural resources. Plague follows subsequently.

These days, in the USA, rats have begun to show up in great quantities. The same applies to supermarkets worldwide, where a lot of food (and money) is wasted. Rats work in a symbiosis with human beings. They are a clear indicator of mismanagement of natural resources. Rats are the typical image of the selfishness of human beings. This is the reason we hate them so much.

See *Epidemics*

Pleura

It belongs to the group of membranes covering the body, of sacs that protect the organs. In this particular case, the pleura protects the lungs. It has the purpose of preventing attacks and ensuring defense. These could be verbal or physical attacks. In this case, we are only referring to attacks perpetrated by people close to us. When talking of the lungs, all types of attack are possible, whether by people close to us or not.

It must be stressed again that what we mean by attack is not something objective. We refer to what the person felt as being a form of attack.

See *Pleurisy*

Pleurisy

This is an infection of the pleura. The person feels a threat in his life. Pleurisy reveals the existence of negative emotions. Above all, the person is afraid about what lies inside the pleura (the lungs). This is not a conscious fear. The person just feels a great need to protect himself from aggression.

Pleural problems denote that the person felt attacked, assaulted. The big difference between the pleura and the lungs is that symptoms in the pleura, besides aggression, also indicate that something disgusted the person, and that something filthy has taken place. This could be physical dirt or something disgusting that someone has done to this person. "This person disgusts me!" The fact that pleurisy is painful is merely a metaphor of the pain that the person feels at the level of disgust. It prevents the person from doing almost anything, even breathing. In short, the person protects himself from aggressions and things that disgust him.

In this case, it does not matter if the protection refers to the left or right lung. The metaphor for the pleura-related defense mechanism is to stick the hands in front of the body for protection. There is no time to think which side the person uses to defend himself.

See *Pleura*

Pneumonia

Inflammation of the lungs by infectious germs. It is characterized by high fever, cough, pain in the chest, general unwellness, difficulty in breathing, mental confusion and changes in blood pressure.

It denotes a feeling provoked by serious external aggression, extremely painful. Pneumonia shows that the person has no defenses of her own. "I need to be protected! Who will protect me? I have a serious communication problem. I cannot make myself understood. I am not understood. Who will protect me and understand my suffering?"

This situation may occur when the person feels that the person who would be ideal to protect her from aggressions

he is experiencing is absent.

The right lung reveals the *yang* side, masculine, and the left lung shows the *yin* side, feminine. This applies to left and right-handed people.

Pneumonia in the *yang* side shows the feeling of being assaulted by a man or incapacity of being protected by a man. Pneumonia in the *yin* side denotes the feeling of being assaulted by a woman or incapacity of being protected by a woman.

See *Lungs*

Pneumothorax

See *Pleurisy*

Poisoning

See *Food poisoning*

Polarity of the body

See *Introduction page 11* about brain polarity.

Poliomyelitis

Poliomyelitis is an inflammation in the spinal marrow, which is the part of the central nervous system inside the rachidian canal, running from the occipital hole (in the cranium) down to the second lumbar vertebra (L2), where several pairs of nerves start.

Symptoms in this area denote difficulty to take action and to get close to other people.

Paralyzing diseases always affect the locomotor system, namely the muscles and/or the nerves. They are linked to a huge feeling of undervaluation. This is the first keyword. The second keyword concerns the feeling of opposite ideas.

The person imposes on himself two contradictory orders regarding movement. The person has wishes that contradict each another. These two contradictory ideas that provoke tension may occur if, for example, the person wished to do something very much, did it and then regretted having done it. Remorse is an undervaluation feeling that affects muscles.

If this happens to a newly born, we have a child who has incarnated but who doubts whether he should have done it, because he feels neither balance nor harmony in his life to be able to grow freely. In situations like this, it is paramount to examine what went on between the parents during pregnancy, at the time of birth or during the early childhood of the individual in question (see *Acute anterior poliomyelitis (child paralysis)*). Also see *Partial paralysis*, *Pregnancy – problems*, *Babies* and *Family*.

Paralysing diseases are characteristic of the locomotor system and of the nervous system, as we have just seen.

The feeling of individuality and of self-esteem is the issue here. This is about what I think of myself and what am I doing in this world. This is about my assertiveness and my flexibility and where conflicts related to my personal worth are kept. What part of my conscience is in the dark in my relationship with the world?

In a condition such as paralysis, the person's thoughts tie him down. He stopped being able to move, whether partially or totally. In case of partial paralysis, it is important to check which part of the locomotor system is affected.

See *Partial paralysis* and check the parts of the body that have been affected. Also see *Acute anterior poliomyelitis (child paralysis)*

Polyarthritis

This means arthritis in several areas of the body. This causes a painful alteration of the joints and muscle tissues, better known as rheumatism. The keyword here for the origin of symptoms is contained aggressiveness.

Where there is polyarthritis, there is an inflammation. A flame is burning. The person is on fire. The tissues and muscles become swollen and the joints get deformed. The pain is so intense that the person needs to restrict his movements as much as possible. However, he is unable to stop because the pain is most acutely felt when resting. The body is telling this person that he had/has excessive movement and so it slows him down, making the person realise that his activity, even hyperactivity, had been hiding a rigidity in his way of thinking that he refused to acknowledge. The body now shows it to the person. As a matter of fact, the person who suffers from polyarthritis is usually rigorous, stubborn, inflexible, meticulous and perfectionist. It may also be a person with a great self-sacrificing behaviour, almost masochist, melancholic and extremely moralistic.

As it is, these are people driven by a very masculine, *yang*, bossy behaviour.

People with this type of symptoms were very active in the past, very dynamic, and probably played sports. Muscular hyperactivity, such as it happens in sports competitions, may be the form the person found to channel his aggressive behaviour. This person did things, many things. But he was never prepared to acknowledge, recognize, examine or accept his aggressiveness. Since he never admitted his aggressiveness, he was never able to live it through, and, so, he kept the aggressive energy within himself. He always solved the effect but not the cause. Therefore, the aggressiveness even increased, and accumulated in the joints, causing polyarthritis.

The person who has rheumatism feels a non-conscious guilt regarding this everlasting contained aggressiveness. For this reason, he dedicates himself to carrying out benevolent acts, abnegation, as if he wanted to expiate the guilt.

Polyarthritis affects women much more than men. This is because, in our society, women have much less capacity to assume their aggressive impulses.

Polyarthritis often comes with stomach or **bowel** pain, frigidity, impotence, anxiety, depression and even heart problems.

See *Anger*

Also see *Chronic evolving polyarthritis* and *Rheumatism*

Posture

See *Spine*

The posture is very much linked to the spine.

Precocious ejaculation

See *Premature ejaculation*

Pregnancy – ectopic pregnancy

The fertilized egg moves exceedingly slow down the fallopian tube causing the embryo to develop outside the uterus and creating several problems that may pose a risk of death to the pregnant mother.

See *Pregnancy – problems*

Pregnancy – imaginary pregnancy

This condition is also known as spurious pregnancy and feigned pregnancy. It happens when a woman feels all the symptoms of pregnancy without actually being pregnant. These symptoms include food cravings, nausea, vomit, feeling bloated, swelling of breasts, darkening of the nipples, and milk secretion. On occasion, some women even feel what seems like a foetus moving in their bellies. This denotes a great desire to have children. It may be the case of a woman who desires to have children but, for whatever reason, does not allow herself to get pregnant. It may be the case of a woman who wants to be a mother without having to engage in the dirty deed of sex. However, it may also occur in the very opposite case, when you have a woman who loves having sex but does not necessarily want to get pregnant by the men she has sex with. Her sexual desires and experiences constitute a sexual addiction but are not consummated with the partner by whom she would like to get pregnant. We are in the presence of a woman who is imbalanced and out of sink with her femininity. In this case, see *Sex – addiction*.

There are women who get pregnant even when using birth control. The body shows the woman's great desire to be a mother.

Pregnancy – problems

Pregnancy problems always expose some degree of rejection, conscious or unconscious, of the baby who is on the way. A miscarriage is an unconscious abortion. The woman gets rid of the baby because she does not get along with the husband or his invading and controlling family, or perhaps because she has new plans for her life.

In very *yang* women, very masculine, bouts of nausea and vomit expose their fear of pregnancy and rejection of femininity and higher oestrogen production levels. This does not keep the woman from being happy and rejoicing over the arrival of her baby. Nausea is associated with pregnancy process, not with the child. In any case, pregnancy problems always involve the risk of losing the baby. Consequently, see *Abortion*. Also see *Pregnancy – ectopic pregnancy* and *Pregnancy – imaginary pregnancy*

Premature ejaculation

Ejaculation is the attribute of a masculine, *yang* force. It carries with it a group of spermatozoids, which are the seed that origins life. Ejaculation is also a moment of the man's external orgasm. It is the moment when a man gives himself totally and looses himself up. It is also a moment when he loses all of his energy. Precocious ejaculation is typical of adults who turn *yin*, passive, too early in the sexual act. He turns feminine too early. In fact, this is because the man who ejaculates gets a more feminine, passive, more giving energy.

Precocious ejaculation may happen for a variety of reasons. For instance, it occurs when the person wants to finish the sexual act as quickly as possible, either in a conscious or unconscious way, because it is in his external orgasm that he attains pleasure, and not in the contact with the partner he is with at that moment. In this particular case, the person just wants to finish the whole thing off.

It may also be because the person is in search of tremendous relief; he attempts to get rid of a tension he is experiencing, through the expulsion of energy that an external orgasm produces. And he is attempting to obtain relief as soon as possible.

Premature ejaculation is an attribute of adults who have little sexual experience or little self esteem and fear not being able to satisfy their partner. It is provoked by shyness or insecurity. In this case, this is a totally natural occurrence and it is, besides, a good test of the love the partner feels for the individual, of her capacity to accept the early eagerness of the partner and his subsequent need to pause to recover energy for the next intercourse.

In adolescents and young men full of testosterone and tremendous vitality, multiple ejaculations during the same sexual act are common. It is normal. It should not be seen as a problem, merely huge eagerness. In this case, we are not talking about precocious ejaculation. In fact, frequent ejaculation enables the man to satisfy his partner, which also boosts his confidence and allows him to gain expertise and dispel the fear and shyness felt before.

Due to the fact that adults have less vitality than young men, those who have precocious ejaculation experience increased difficulty in boosting up their testosterone levels. It takes them a lot longer to feel aroused, and this is if they get aroused again in the same sexual relation. For this reason, adults are a lot more prone to blaming themselves for premature ejaculation. This is the reason why so many adults blame precocious ejaculation.

Many adults, as well as many youngsters, blame themselves for precocious ejaculation because they start seeing themselves as ineffective males.

When guilt sets in, so does the vicious circle of rising premature ejaculation. Effectively, the body shows the person what he thinks of him when he ejaculates immediately: a male who turns into a female excessively quickly. This person needs to work up his self-esteem and to accept himself as he is, without attempting to be something else.

Preoccupation

See *Anxiety* and *Panic*

Presbytis

See *Eyes – presbyopia*

Presbytism

See *Eyes – presbyopia*

Priapism

Priapism is a permanent and painful erection of the penis that occurs without sexual stimulation and lasts over 4-6 hours. It occurs without sexual desire or pleasure. The self-injecting programmes for treatment of impotence turned this formerly rare condition into a relatively common occurrence.

In the beginning, this problem affected only people suffering from rare blood diseases, such as certain types of anaemia. It is almost always provoked by medication. In this case, priapism shows the body is suffering from exaggerated medication against impotence.

Prostate

The prostate is a gland annexed to the male genital system. Its secretion contributes to the production of sperm and mixes with the spermatozoids that come from the testicles. It secretes an alkaline substance that stimulates the movement of spermatozoids. From an energy perspective, the prostate is a sexual catalyst. The key tension associated to prostate-related problems is to feel useless.

It is important to remember that, in the case of animals, territorial questions are associated to reproduction. For them, the survival of the species is more important than the individual. Hence, the territory is linked to the species, reproduction and offspring. This is what we call our roots. The animal concept of territory includes the males' conflicts of a sexual nature and corresponding undervaluation feeling when they lose their territory. The animal that contributes to the survival of the species feels useful. Actually, his usefulness is indispensable. This ancient animal feeling makes us, humans, feel territorial conflicts in the cervix (also called neck of the womb or cervical canal of the uterus) in the case of women, and in the prostate, in the case of men. Therefore, from an animal perspective, men feel their territorial conflicts in the prostate. Prostate related problems are characteristic of people who lost a sexual partner or are afraid of losing him or her. These people feel undervalued, useless and without a chance of marking their territory, from an animal standpoint. But this is not all. In our society, male usefulness is also judged by the capacity to accomplish things, by the capacity to do useful things. Retired men often have prostate problems. Not out of sexual frustration or because they are unable to procreate, but because they are men who used to centre their lives on their profession and believed that anything not related to the profession was unimportant. Upon their retirement, they began thinking they are useless and empty.

Therefore, the cause for prostate-related problems, such as prostate **cancer** is remarkably *yang*. It is typical of very masculine men, who are very regulated, very hard working, who lack sensitivity and who have blocked their feminine and sensitive side, which was the non-professional other side of their lives. They do not know how to live without their masculine, professional or active side.

All prostate-related problems are connected to the same tension in the conscience: "I feel useless!" The bigger the tension and the more lived in silence it is, the more serious is the symptom.

Benign tumours in the prostate (**adenomas** and **fibromas**) are not cancer, they are a form of drawing attention, in a non-violent way, to something deep that is not working properly in the person regarding his feeling of usefulness.

Hypertrophy of the prostate (too large) hinders normal urinary release. The person has difficulty in letting go of the waters of his body, as he has deep fears about his power, his capacity to give life, that is, to be useless.

Psoriasis

This is a symptom whose origins lie in the feeling of separation that has actually been experienced. However, in the case of psoriasis, the person feels two conflicts and two separations.

Psoriasis causes raised and flattened areas in the skin. It creates lumps and holes in alternate form. Certain areas in the skin become inflamed and covered with silvery white scaly skin.

The person is living two distinct things at the same time. One is always missing. This is the conflict of double separation. In any case, the person is always suffering from tension given the fact that one thing is always missing.

It is very difficult to convince a psoriasis sufferer about the causes of his illness. The person does not understand.

It is as if the person is producing a shield in alternating ways. He wears an armed shield between himself and the others. The person is afraid of being hurt. He is extremely sensitive. The problem is that, once more, the vicious circle is present. The larger the shield is, the bigger the fear and sensitivity to aggression. This is actually because the shield does not allow anything to go through, not even love. The person becomes even more vulnerable and has only one solution: To give himself and let go. This person's acceptance of the wound(s) that separation(s) provoked on him must be worked on.

Psoriasis may cause skin ulcers and infections, which is a vicious circle taken to the limit. The person injures himself not to be injured by others.

Pubic bone

This is a transversal bone located in the lower part of the abdomen. It is one of the protections of the pelvis, where our non-conscious relational mechanism is placed. In the front, it protects the bladder, the lower part of the large bowel and the genitals, which are organs located in the pelvic waist and also elimination and reproduction organs. Fractures in the pubic bone indicate that the person experienced intense undervaluation. The bones that protect the bladder, the colon and the genitals felt this undervaluation. The bladder is connected to territorial conflicts. The colon is associated to family troubles, problems at home, to a feeling that what was done to us was filthy, wicked. The genitals (vagina, penis, testicles, ovaries) are associated to the capacity to experience sexual impulses and to procreate. This person's home is crumbling down. What is going on with this person's private life?

Pulmonary embolism

Here, we are talking of a thrombus, a blood clot that obstructs a vein and moves into a pulmonary artery.

See *Thrombosis*

Punctuality

Chronic lack of punctuality can be understood as a symptom. Be it because the person is always late, or because the person rushes everybody around not to be late, being always in a hurry when it comes to timings. Usually, these people cause people close to them to stress out about time.

This sort of people has a problem. In fact, they rarely are at the right time, with the right people, in the right place. These are very mentally oriented people that leave little room for intuition. They think they can sort everything out in their own way, think a lot, rationalize things a lot and end up being quite impractical people. Apart from this, they bring the nerves of people close to them to the brim, which indicates that, for them, their own mental reasoning is more important than having a good tranquil relationship with the other person. They have a problem with authority.

See *Authority*

Pyorrhea (periodontitis)

Pyorrhea is a condition of gums (regressing gums, just like periodontitis).
See *Gums*

Radius

It is the external bone of the forearm. A fractured radius denotes strong undervaluation. "I am not worth much."
See *Forearm*

Rash

Here we also include pruritus and itching.

Rash can appear together with hives or on its own.

Itchiness, with the burning feeling, pins and needles and stinging that come with it, is associated to sex, which is aggressive and loving.

Pruritus comes from the Latin *prurigo*, meaning itching, joy, and *prurire*, which means to sting, to irritate. This means that excitement always precedes rash. It can be pleasant or unpleasant.

The body reveals, through the itching, that excitement has passed the person by. The person did not pay attention to it, but it was there, independently of the fact that it was good or bad. Scratching has a symbolic meaning. The person picks and digs, and this means he is looking for something.

The person keeps scratching until he realizes the tension in his conscience.

Scabies is part of the tensions associated to rash. The most peculiar characteristic of scabies is intense itching that worsens at night. Burrows appear more frequently and itching is more intense in the webs of fingers, flexing surfaces of the wrists and armpits, the areolae of the breasts in females and on genitals of males (penis and scrotum), along the belt line, and on the lower buttocks. The face usually does not become affected, except in children, where lesions show up as water-filled blisters. With the passage of time, borrows may be difficult to spot as they are hidden by the inflammation caused by scratching. Scabies is provoked by acarids and is considered to be a parasite disease. The person has stagnated over beliefs that do not work for him. The past controls his everyday life. He is clinging to the past. Infections caused by mites are parasite infections.

The word parasite is essential in this context. If the person lets himself be affected by parasites, this means he is not centered and does not know how to be assertive with the people around him. It means that there is someone in his life who is a parasite and lives off him, whether at home, work, or amongst friends. It could also be his Mother. The person is clinging to the past and to his beliefs, and this is the reason why he cannot stand up to the parasite with the degree of assertiveness he ought to have.

Red spots

They are broken capillary veins, small-localized haemorrhages. Eruptions indicate that something has been repressed. In this case, the tension is very small. It may not necessarily be considered a symptom. Eruptions uncover something that has hitherto remained invisible.

Any loss of blood denotes a disturbance and lack of respect for oneself. Perhaps demanding too much of oneself or of others. In any case, it represents something somehow *yang*, warrior, masculine, but unconscious. Haemorrhages may occur in many parts of the body.

Renal insufficiency

See *Kidneys – renal insufficiency*

Reproductive system

Along with the urinary system, the reproductive system belongs to the water element of the five elements of the human body. Our association with our deepest beliefs lies in the waters. The waters are associated with the beginning of life. The reproductive system includes the ovaries, fallopian tubes, uterus, vagina and breast, in women; in men, it includes testicles, prostate, and penis.

Problems with this system reflect the difficulty of women to accept their femininity and problems in men to accept their masculinity. They also reflect the difficulty in finding one's opposite within himself.

Just like the breathing and digestive systems, this system belongs to the group of the most primitive functions. Here we deal with everything which is absolutely necessary to preserve the species: the passage of genetic material from one generation to the next. In nature, priority is given to the species; the species comes always before the individual.

Problems in the reproductive system are only connected with *yin* and *yang* polarity based on the specific side of the body when dealing with pairs of organs (ovaries, breasts, fallopian tubes, and testicles) but there is not a constant common denominator. They are treated on an individual basis.

Problems on the *yang* side may indicate the influence of a man or a very masculine behaviour, very hard, on the patient's part. Problems on the *yin* side may indicate the influence of a woman or a very feminine behaviour, excessively passive, of self-denial from the patient. Each case must be considered individually.

Retinal detachment

See *Eyes – retinal detachment*

Retinitis pigmentosa

See *Eyes – retinitis pigmentosa*

Rheumatism

This is a painful inflammation of the tissues in joints and muscles. It occurs in the joints cartilage, where bones come together. For instance, where the femur meets the tibia (kneecap). In this case, we are dealing with gesture. If our gesture is not appropriate, we develop a joint condition.

The quality of the gesture is the issue here. A person may be undervalued through gesture. Sports activity is a very good example of this, as well as manual work. This is the case of surgeons, dentists, pianists, and secretaries. This occurs in sports or in any other form of gesture. It may take place in any of our lives' actions that implies a change in direction and/or flexibility. In fact, all symptoms reflect our consciousness. A nice gesture, or a protocol-related gesture, or a courteous gesture, or one that shows violence or kindness, may be considered gestures that imply a change in direction or in flexibility in someone's life, such as it happens in sports or in manual activities.

Joint-related diseases are related to undervaluation tensions. They strike when, for instance, the person thinks: "I am no longer good at this as I used

to be. I am no longer good at this gesture."

There is a flame burning inside the person. The person is burning. Rheumatism causes tissues and joint muscles to swell up. For this reason, they get deformed. The pain is so intense the person has to restrict movement as much as possible, but he cannot stop. The pain becomes more acute when the person attempts to rest. This is what happens in the case of poliarthritis.

See *Polyarthritis*

Rheumatoid polyarthritis

See *Chronic evolving polyarthritis*
Also see *Acute articular rheumatism (children)*

Rhinitis

Rhinitis is an inflammation of the mucosal membrane of the nose, and is characterized by continuous discharge and nasal congestion.

Rhinitis may be acute (short-lived) or chronic (long term). The nose forms part of the breathing system and is associated to the relationship with the exterior. The nose assimilates the subtle side of things and shows the relationship with gasp, air, and the sky. The nose is in straight connection with life, though smell.

It is important to understand if the person feels attacked by something or, above all, by someone. A cold is an indicator of small sorrows and some mental disorder. It is likely that there is a problem with a person close to the individual in question. This could be related to the home, husband, wife, girlfriend or boyfriend, teacher, work, biological Mother.

Smell adds volume and colour to taste, and is indissociable from it, in the same way the two eyes are indissociable from each other. Smell-related problems (chronic, not momentary) represent fear of allowing subtle things of life get inside us, due to lack of self-esteem.

Loss of smell may also be caused by fear of acknowledging the animal that lives inside us. In fact, in the animal world, smell is a great tool for hormonal, hence sexual, recognition. The nose is associated to sexuality. The person who suffers from smell-related problems is also someone who contains his sexual impulses.

Blockage is another indication of this tension. The person whose nose is constantly blocked, or half blocked, normally suffers from smell-related problems. It denotes the person has difficulty accepting intimate information that comes to him from the outside or the inside. He does not wish to acknowledge the symptoms. It is quite likely that the relationship at home is not flowing as he wishes. However, he does not want to examine the details.

What is rotting in the relationship that the person refuses to smell? Absence of smell reveals pain, bitterness, or even a wish for revenge that we let rot inside ourselves.

This type of symptoms is often associated to a **nasal discharge** that runs down to the mouth, indicating the presence of an inner silent cry and impotence regarding changing things.

Ribs

The ribs are the long curved bones that surround the chest (thorax) and whose upper extremities are attached to the vertebrae. Their function, like that of the stern and shoulder blades, is to protect the area around the heart and lungs.

The heart region stands for emotions and the lungs area represents the relationship with the outside. Fractures on the ribs, which are bones, indicate that the person has experienced undervaluing but that, by breaking them, also felt a sense of relief in the immense tension he was going through. This undervaluing feeling was felt in the bones that protect the thoracic cavity. This means that in this particular case, the person felt attacked by someone on his emotions. Somebody attacked the person on his feelings. And the person feels that someone is not allowing him to feel what he feels. Normally, the person or thing, against whom or which the physical shock that led to the fracturing of the ribs took place, has little to do with the life of that individual. That person, a third party, is a mere vehicle that makes perceptible the tension the person was feeling. This is the reason why it becomes necessary to ascertain if that third person has anything in common with someone who is part of the life of the injured person, or if he matches any model of a person who forms part of the nucleus the injured person belongs to.

In principle, ribs on the right side are *yang*, masculine, and those on the left side are *yin*, feminine. This applies both to left and right-hand sided people. This polarity, however, is not at all obvious, for which reason it must be handled with care.

A lesion in the *yang* ribs denotes a feeling of being attacked (or aggression) by a man, and if it happens on the *yin* side, by a woman.

Rickets

Contrary to what happens with Small stature syndrome (nanism), the rickets symptom is not felt at birth, and it only manifests itself during childhood or adolescence. This is a problem related to emotional sub-nutrition. This is lack of love and safety. It is important to look at the family atmosphere the child grew up in.

Sufferers often have problems with exposure to sunlight. The problems the child faces are connected to his biological Father and Mother. Growth-related problems are very much linked to the endocrine system. Two glands are involved in the person's balanced growth: the thyroid and the thymus.

If a child is convinced that there is no point in growing up, the body will show him his tension from a physical perspective. And he will not grow up. Why should a child be convinced there is no point growing up? There could be various reasons, but they all point to the parents.

The **thymus** plays a very important role in the child's development, up to adolescence. It is involved in growth and in metabolism, as well as in the child's immunity. The memory of human beings is located in the thymus, and this memory is impregnated with the experiences the child has had in his life and with his parents (mostly with his parents), as well as with the man and woman models that he has met throughout his life. The child comes to the conclusion that: "If adults are like this, then I do not want to grow up." The conflict is silent and profound. This is the form the child has found to immunize himself from his parents.

The **thyroid** is an essentially feminine gland. It regulates the entire metabolism of the body, growth, weight, and the body's full harmony.

It reveals the person's capacity to express himself and to make himself understood. It is in the thyroid that the body shows the person's calculating attitude, as he learnt when to speak up and when to shut up. And the child who is not allowed to speak up, or who has realized that no one has made (or will make) any effort to understand him, gives up on himself, gives up on accelerating his own metabolism and stops it. Consequently, growth does not take place. The tension the body exposes is: "I cannot create my own space in this adult world. It is not worth growing up. I do not want to be like them."

Right-handed and left-handed people

See *Brain*

Ringing noise

See *Tinnitus*

Roof of the mouth

See *Palate*

Rubella

Eruptions indicate that something has been repressed. Eruptions uncover something that had until then remained invisible.

As in all children's diseases, eruptions bring out something new for the child, and they contribute to a significant advancement in the development of the child. The more virulent the eruption is, the quicker the child will develop.

All skin related problems denote aggression and communication difficulty. Being born into this world, and growing up, are not easy processes for children, because of the very strong identification of society and of the families with the ego, religious beliefs, ancient beliefs of the clan and the unstoppable absurd need to obey rules that go against nature.

The child is beginning to develop his own defenses against society and his family. Rubella is connected to the breathing system, in other words, with the exchange with the outside and the child's defenses. The child is develop-

ing his immune system.

As a matter of fact, catching rubella makes the child immune to it forever.

Besides, rubella is contagious, which means the child wants to keep people at bay.

See *Babies*

Sacrum

Sacrum means sacred. This is where the tensions associated to the witness of who I am are located. The sacrum consists of five fused vertebrae. The sacrum is linked to the hipbones, the iliac bones and, together, they form the pelvic bone.

See *Vertebrae – sacral vertebrae*

Sacrum-iliac

See *Vertebrae – sacral vertebrae*

The two iliac bones, on the side, join the sacrum and together form the pelvic bone.

Salivary glands

Saliva, which is fluid, diluted, and plentiful, keeps the mouth moist. A dry mouth is characteristic of someone who is experiencing fear or tension. More concentrated saliva is used for digesting food.

When the salivary glands become infected it is as if the person were saying: "I had all I needed to feed myself and, at the last minute, they took my food away."

The person with **stones** in the salivary glands is an individual who forces himself to be super efficient so that no one will take the food out of his mouth. Mumps play a role here and translate a child's fear: "Will the ones in charge allow me to continue doing what I was doing?" Mumps is just one of many child illnesses. Again, it is important to remember that children do not deal well with the type of repression that society and families impose on them recurrently. It is good to look into family dynamics, particularly where the freedom of children is concerned. Are the rules too strict, excessively harsh?

Scabies

See *Rash*

Scabies is a symptom that is included in Rash.

Scarlet Fever

Scarlet fever is an infectious disease, which affects primarily children.

Any outbreak is as sign that something was repressed.

Children do not live well in face of the type of continuous and recurrent repression imposed on them by a large part of our society and families.

An outbreak shows the child something that, up till then, was invisible. The child's desire to control and hide what he feels was betrayed by his body.

Usually, along with any child illness, there tends to be a significant leap forward in his development. Something new comes of it.

The worst the outbreak, the faster the child will develop. See other child illnesses such as *Mumps* and *Chicken-*

pox.

Also see *Skin*

Schüller's disease

Osteoporosis only in the skull. See *Skull* and *Osteoporosis*

Sciatic nerve pain

The person is overburden. Sciatic pain occurs in the lumbar area, like lumbago. This may be due to the fact that the person is attempting to portray an image of grandeur and diligence or because the person is proud, does not like to ask for help and believes he can take care of himself and does not need anyone else. Sciatic pain happens for the person to stop and examine his life.

The need to demonstrate grandeur results from a hidden feeling of inferiority. In fact, the person finds it extremely difficult to move away from old beliefs and habits. The need to be self-sufficient and not asking for help indicates pride, which also denotes difficulty in backing off from old beliefs and habits. Sciatic pain occurs mostly in the intervertebral disc, between L4 and L5, or between L5 and S1.

It is precisely in the lumbar area that tensions in the relationship with the partner are located, the same applying to affection, family, work and money, material things, the home, space and mobility, the place where one lives. Everything that represents the person's roots.

The compression of the disks that sciatic pain represents, instead of leading to a person's increased grandeur, rather leads to a literal physical shrinkage. The person often ends up with a bent back.

In Eastern medicine, sciatic is related to a problem in the gallbladder meridian. The gallbladder is an organ that facilitates digestion. It is a form of psychological assistance to digestion. The tension that the person feels at this stage is that of anger, resentment, and a taste of something that left a bitter tang.

Gallbladder related conditions indicate difficulty in managing problems, in getting situations clear. What is my place? Am I being given the right recognition? The person undergoes major anger fits, feels helpless, but will not express his feelings. For this reason, he will not expel the bile, keeping it in instead.

There is bitterness, disapproval, pride, hard, rigid thoughts, and self-inflicted violence. The person is excessively controlled and does not allow his life to flow.

From a practical viewpoint, sciatic pain is a trapped nerve in the lumbar area. Since nerves represent communication, sciatic pain denotes difficulty to communicate with someone at home or at work. It is important to start by examining which of the legs is affected.

See *Legs as lower limbs*

Scleroderma (systemic sclerosis)

This is separation truly experienced.

It is eczema taken to the tenth degree. The person who suffers from scleroderma experienced a separation anxiety that lasted all life long. The epidermis kept disappearing all along; and it did disappear until it exposed the dermis. The person becomes totally wrinkled. It is as if the skin has shrunk. This is a person who never truly lived life, a person who was never able to let go of the person from whom he separated. This is an individual who always sheltered himself from life and from his own person. It is someone who lacks self-esteem and confidence, a person who did not take care of himself. It is a human being who was not present, someone who cancelled himself out. This person must change the way he thinks. Absolutely!

Scoliosis

Scoliosis happens during puberty. This condition is a curvature of the child' spine and is connected with the relationship between the models of Father (shoulders' axis) and Mother (hips' axis). The child does not want to grow, does not want to raise his shoulders and forces the spine to bend somewhere between the two axis. The spine continues to grow but the child does not grow in height. "I don't want to be an adult if this is the way it is". This phenomenon only happens during puberty and stops after puberty.

Seborrhoea

Eruptions indicate that something has been repressed. And they uncover something that had hitherto remained invisible.

Seborrhea is a type of eczema that affects babies due to tension related to separation.

The Mother has little contact with the child or does not look after him from an emotional viewpoint. The child then tries to pull down the invisible wall that stands between him and the Mother, and develops seborrhoea.

As it happens, these mothers normally justify their separation from the baby due to the seborrhoea. However, what happened was precisely the opposite, they were the cause for seborrhoea to appear in the baby.

Self-immunity

See *Immune system*

Senility

This indicates refusal to deal with the world as it is: Despair and abandonment. Isolation. There is a going back to the so-called childhood. Tenderness and a lot of attention are required.

The people who want to change the way their relatives behave and think, anxious to control them, are very mentally oriented, very Cartesian and not open to sensitive issues. They are people who run away from reality to avoid looking inwards.

See *Isolation*

Septicaemia

From the Greek *septikos*, which means something that causes putrefac-

tion, and *haima*, which means blood.

This is a general infection in the blood. It can occur as a sequence of any serious infection in the body.

See the organ where the infection started and see also *Infections*.

Sex – addiction

All forms of addiction represent an escape. It is an escape that started as a quest. What actually happens is that the person literally projects the objective of his search on something he found along the way and decided his quest was over. He is pleased with what he has found. He remains trapped in fear and convenience. Anything can cause addiction: alcohol, drugs, sex, tobacco, gambling, food (bulimia, anorexia), but also, and even to a larger extent, money, power, rules, fame, influence, knowledge, entertainment, isolation, asceticism, cult, tradition, ancestral beliefs, religion…

The addicted person is the one who stops halfway through his quest. For this reason, he feels empty. And because he feels empty, he needs to fill the void with external substances that confer him the illusion of being balanced.

Basically, we could say that in all humanity, we all depend on something. The difference between the sick addicted and the healthy dependent lays in the quality of self-observation, that is, in the awareness of one self, of one's feelings and path. Dependence is a type of attachment. The non-addict, non-sick consumer is the one who is aware of his attachments.

The practice of sex results from natural impulses, hormonal impulses of the human body. It starts during adolescence, when the child ceases to be in a hormonal standstill. Sexual energy is the one that gives life. It is sexual energy that confers vitality to human beings. It is sexual energy that ensures the preservation of animals. Sexual energy stimulates our pleasure nervous centers. Learning how to give in to sexual energy is learning how to give in to emotions, is living the emotion (*ex-movere – moving out*), in other words, it is allowing the body to come untied.

Most physical problems in our body are due to control and attachment-related tensions, because we refuse to let go. Experiencing emotions is utterly natural and necessary. The extremely regulated society in which we live punishes sexual impulse and teenagers are taught to think that sexual behaviour is not a socially accepted behaviour. However, the fact that sexual behaviour is not considered to be an acceptable behaviour does not obviously stop the hormonal process. On the contrary, it hurries it up.

Any individual who looks for another person through a sexual act is looking for his opposite side inside himself. To punish sexuality is to punish integrity, authenticity, and the honesty of the human being. The person who controls his sexual impulses will surely have problems in several parts of his body. Women who behave just like mothers, and not as women with full rights to having sexual pleasure, tend to severely castigate their female

organs.

The person who does not engage in sex due to control and a prohibition is losing vitality, balance and harmony, the same way the person who defines himself through sex and believes that everything in his life must include continuous sexual activity is also losing vitality, balance and harmony.

Both excessive control (which restrains the practice of sex) and behaviour of sexual addiction share the same tension as a background. They are both dependent. The very controlled person depends on religious, family, cultural and ethnic beliefs and, as such, is not authentic. He is addicted. This person is addicted to regulations and merely repeats other people's ideas. The sexual addicted person depends on sexual pleasure and cannot live without it. He is also addicted, but to sex.

Shin bone

See *Tibia*

Shingles

This condition is like chickenpox in adults. It affects a particular area, aggravated by the fact that it is quite painful. It affects mostly the area around the eyes, the cheeks and the middle of the back. It is associated to communication problems.

Initially, the person feels pain (nerves). He feels quite hot and that part of the body appears to be burning.

The second stage is characterized by the eruption of water-filled bubbles, which means the body is protecting itself.

Sometimes, the second stage never comes and the person remains on state one.

Shingles can be cured via communication. Communication operates miracles in this case.

It is necessary to find out what is going on between this person and the partner, or between that person and someone living very close to him. He has a major lack of communication problem with that person and the relationship and communication lack transparency.

Shoulder

This is the key joint of the upper limbs.

It is the *yang* axis, masculine axis, the axis of will, symbolized by the Father.

A person who has large shoulders is a more masculine being, with a higher number of masculine hormones. Nowadays, with the masculinization of women, women have much wider shoulders, in some specific cases.

People with lowered shoulders are, in general, innocuous, with little aggressiveness, although sometimes their behaviour seems to indicate the opposite, albeit unsuccessfully.

Changes in the rhythm of action are located on the shoulder. For instance, in the case of tennis, when serving; in golf, when swinging; in handball, when aiming at the goal post. In all cases, it is the whipping movement that shoulder

makes that accelerates rhythm.

The person needs to speed up something that needs to be done. He does this with his shoulder, either when playing a sport or in his daily life. When the person cannot make this accelerating movement, he feels undervalued and then the problem in the shoulder strikes. Problems in the joints are always associated to undervaluation.

The person suffering from shoulder-related problems feels that the future is not arriving sufficiently fast, or that his own goals are too distant. Shoulders represent what comes from the past and is to be projected in the future.

Will my arm be long enough to get there?

Shoulder-related problems denote undervaluation because the person has little flexibility with in his mental pattern. Lesions indicate that the person's mental pattern is not working.

In almost all cases, the right shoulder is *yang* (masculine) and the left is *yin* (feminine). This applies both to left and right-handed people. Problems in the *yang* shoulder show inflexibility and also undervaluation [due to the influence of a third person (a man?) or to the person's obsessive beliefs]. The person wants to go further than what is reasonable. He will insist, be stubborn, a fighter, somehow harsh, and he only wants to pursue his goal. Goals blind him. He may be following the Father model (in case the person is a Father) far too closely. However, as the person is trying to attain the unattainable, his deepest beliefs regarding his capacity to make his will and goals achievable are questioned or shaken. And so, the person feels undervalued.

Problems in the *yin* shoulder show inflexibility and also undervaluation [due to the influence of a third person (a woman?) or to the person's obsessive beliefs]. The person's sensibility is hurt in his way to attain the goal. It denotes a type of behaviour that goes against the person's sensibility and fragility in what concerns goals. The person may be following the Mother model (in case the person is a Mother) far too closely.

Shoulder-related problems are linked to the fact that the person wishes to intervene in issues that are none of his business, either by speeding them up or by changing them. In other words, the person stretches so that he can reach where he cannot reach. In these cases, problems in the **shoulder tendon** are common, and they are extremely painful, forcing the person to be still.

Inability to move the shoulder means that the person sees no future for his action. It means he will remain inflexible in his way of thinking and in stipulating his objectives, trapped in his stubbornness that things must happen in the exact way he wanted. **Shoulder fractures** represent a shock at the level of deep beliefs regarding the difficulty in taking action, and, simultaneously, a major relief from the pressure the person was feeling.

People who accumulate anger have chronic tension on their shoulders, neck and arms.

Pimples on the shoulders denote tension associated to separation and, above all, difficulty in communicating with the Father or with the man, or with someone who plays a typically masculine role.

See also *Collar bone.*

To find out more about lowered shoulders, kyphosis, hump, see *Vertebrae – dorsal vertebrae.*

The shoulder is a joint. Joint bones are kept in place by ligaments and tendons that only allow normal movement. Muscles also help determine joint stability. The joint is enclosed in a fibrous capsule filled with a thin membrane that constantly produces a small amount of fluid; this fluid, called synovial fluid, acts as a nutrient and a lubricant to the cartilage. In a normal joint, the top of the bones that make it up are covered by a cap of off-white elastic matter, the cartilage, which allows the smooth movement of bones and acts like a cushion that absorbs the impact of bone movement and, particularly, weight. **Arthrosis** results from the progressive wear and tear of the joint tissue, particularly of the cartilage, that leads to increasing pain, deformity, and difficulty of movement. The onset of arthrosis starts with the deterioration of the cartilage, which loses its elasticity and becomes less effective. In the absence of part or all of this cushioning effect of the cartilage, the bones rub one another and cause friction, inflammation, pain, and difficulty in moving.

In very advanced stages of this condition, pieces of cartilage and bone may get loose and lodge themselves in the joint, seriously limiting or blocking movement altogether.

The hips, knees, shoulders, feet, and fingers are the body parts most frequently affected by this condition.

Shoulder blade

The shoulder blade is called *Omoplate* in Latin languages.

Omo derives from Latin and means shoulder, scapula. *Plate* also comes from Latin and means flat, even. The shoulder blade is, therefore, the flat bone of the shoulder. That is why it is called shoulder blade in English. It is a large and flat bone located in the upper part of the thorax. On the back, it protects the heart and the lungs, which are organs kept in the chest cavity and organs of communication, of feelings and of quite delicate emotions. The area of the heart represents emotions and the area of the lungs represents a relationship with the outside. Fractured shoulder blades, which are bones, shows that the person felt extremely undervalued, but also that, by breaking them, he felt enormous relief in the tension he was experiencing.

This undervaluation was experienced in the bones that protect the back of the chest. This means that, in this particular case, the person felt attacked on his emotions by someone. Someone has attacked this person's feelings. As if the person was not allowed to feel what he is feeling. The particular aspect here is that the attack was on the person's back, therefore, it was betrayal.

In almost all cases, the right shoulder blade is *yang* (masculine) and the left is *yin* (feminine). This applies both to left and right-handed people. Problems in the *yang* shoulder blade indicate that the person felt attacked in his emotions, betrayed, by a man, and in the *yin* shoulder blade, show that the person felt attacked in his emotions, betrayed, by a woman.

Sickness

See *Nausea and vomiting*

Sigmoid

See *Bowel – large bowel – descending colon – sigmoid*

Silhouette – image conflicts

There are many silhouette conflicts. Please see *Obesity, Cellulite, Slimness, Bulimia* and *Anorexia*.

Sinusitis

This is an inflammation of the mucosal membrane covering the cheeks and the forehead.

The person is extremely irritated regarding a particular person close to him, but is unaware of that irritation. When the person is told this, he becomes aware and immediately identifies whom he feels irritated with. This is clearly a symptom associated to family or relational issues. For this reason, it is ruled by the cerebral hemispheres. Accordingly, the right side of sinuses is *yang*, masculine, and the left side is *yin*, feminine. This applies both to right and left-handed people. Problems in the *yang* sinus denote problems in the relationship with a man, and in the *yin* sinus denote problems with a woman.

Skeletal system

See *Bone*

The skeletal system is covered in Bone.

Skin

All internal organs are reflected on the kin. And what happens in the skin is reflected in the internal organs. Think of shiatsu, reflexology, acupuncture, massage, etc.

The skin's main function is to ensure the person's protection. Skin sets the limits and protects. It also allows cutaneous breathing, and, for this reason, forms part of the breathing system, because it assists the lungs in their relationship with air. It contains thousands of reserves that allow us to capture signs from the outside through emotions, touch and temperature. It sweats out and regulates temperature. Skin is responsible for making contact, it is the door to gesture, it is a sexual stimulus. The skin is multidisciplinary. It is the largest organ in the human body.

When the kidneys, liver, and also the large bowel and the lungs are trapped, skin takes over and starts releasing toxins that the organism cannot otherwise get rid off, through perspiration, smells and dermatoses. Finally, it is useful to know that the skin covering the muscles (Aponeurosis) and the skin covering the organs (Pericardium, Pleura, Peritoneum, Meninges, Epidermis) memorises experiences and emotions. For this reason, massages of the shiatsu type have such a strong effect at psychosomatic and emotional levels.

The skin may break from the inside out (**abscess, furuncle** (boils), **infections**, eruptions such as **acne, seborrhea, psoriasis, eczema, hives, rash** (pruritus), **itching, measles, rubella, scarlet fever, scabies** (rash), **chickenpox, leprosy, warts, vitiligo, herpes** and **perspiration**) and from the outside inwards (**wound, cuts, surgery**). It is always the result of an aggression.

Eruptions indicate that something has been repressed, and show us something that had been invisible up to then. Skin also has a social role.

You may want to check on *Mycosis fungoides*. Although it is a lymphoma, it has effects on the skin.

The Dermis (see *Skin – dermis*) and the Epidermis (see *Skin – epidermis*) form the skin.

Skin – dermis

Here, at the dermis, we will also be talking about skin **cancer**.

The dermis is the deep layer of vertebrates skin. This is the layer where the roots of the animal's hair (and the scales of fish) can be found, besides the sebaceous and the sweat glands and the nails. The blood and lymphatic vessels that irrigate the epidermis and the sensorial organs and nerves associated to them are also located in the dermis. Tensions on the skin are always related to aggression and protection.

However, the tensions that cause symptoms on the dermis are different from those that provoke symptoms on the epidermis.

The tensions that cause symptoms on the dermis are linked to protection and aggression in the most primary sense. They are representative of people who feel their territory has been invaded and who feel attacked in the most primary sense of the word, and who feel a major tension regarding uncleanness. This could be basic material uncleanness or something filthy carried out by someone. It could be of a sexual nature, a con, etc.

In short, the most basic protection-related conflicts occur at the level of the dermis.

The dermis has nothing to do with separation, it has more to do with the idea "other person dominates me, and I feel my territory has been invaded".

Relationship, communication and separation-related conflicts occur at the level of the epidermis. Like with the dermis, here we will find aggression and need for protection, but these are of a more social and relational nature, more to do with communication.

Protections have the purpose of attacking and defending from verbal or physical aggression. Someone who has profoundly felt aggression and disgust regarding something, such as "he makes me sick", or "that makes me sick", and is unable to verbalize the tremendous feeling of disgust he is experi-

encing, may develop skin **cancer**. Skin cancer occurs at the level of the dermis.

The person needs to move away from that person or thing that revolts him. The person who has skin cancer tends to say that he has solved things, that he is not being assaulted any more. He says it is ok, that he has sorted it out, that he has moved away or forgotten about the issue and pretends it does not matter any more. So he keeps it all to himself, and will not verbalize it. However, it is here that his illusion lies. He will not move away from the other person, precisely because his beliefs do not allow it or because he is physically unable to do so. As he fails to move away from the other person, the body shows him the distancing from a physical perspective and it grows a mass, a volume that "keeps" the person away from the aggressor. The person with skin cancer lives through this tension silently, unable to verbalize it. This person absolutely needs to verbalize what he feels.

People who are cleanliness freaks, extremely particular about hygiene issues, are more prone to developing skin cancer. They feel assaulted by things that, after all, are inoffensive.

See *Skin* and *Skin – epidermis*

Skin – epidermis

The epidermis is the protection of the dermis. The skin's skin. The dermis is under the epidermis. The epidermis is like an envelope, a sac, a protection covering the dermis. However, the dermis itself is a sac, a protection, acting as the envelope of the body. Tensions on the skin are always related to aggression and protection.

Yet, the tensions that cause symptoms on the epidermis are different from those that provoke symptoms on the dermis.

Symptoms connected to actually experienced tensions of separation are felt on the epidermis, the same applying to tensions about fear of separation and communication-related tensions.

These are relational and social tensions connected to communication.

The dermis has nothing to do with separation, rather more with the idea that the other person controls me, and that I feel my territory has been invaded.

Relational and separation conflicts take place at the level of the epidermis. Like in the case of the dermis, here we will find aggression and need for protection, but now they are more of a social and relational nature, and connected with communication issues.

It is through the skin that we maintain contact with someone.

At conscience level, separation manifests itself through the skin. Contact with a baby is always made through the skin.

People who live in a state of separation often become absentminded. These are people who do not focus well.

A possessive person is a person who is afraid of being separated. This could be physical fear of being physically separated from someone, from a place, from an animal or even from a group, a family, a herd, a clan.

There are three major causes for epidermis related problems:

Eczema, **Psoriasis**, **Scleroderma (systemic sclerosis)**, **Wart** and **Vitiligo** belong to the group of symptoms of an actually experienced separation feeling (See each of these symptoms separately).

Leprosy belongs to the group of symptoms caused by **fear of separation**. This separation fear feeds on itself and causes simultaneously varicose ulcer and memory loss, which is what characterizes leprosy.

Shingles, **Chickenpox**, **Recking Hauser Neurofibromatosis** (RHF), **Herpes**, **Acne**, **Hives**, **Perspiration**, **Hair** and **Nail** problems (see each of these symptoms separately) belong to the group of symptoms caused by communication problems; Separation through communication.

These people would like to open up and communicate, but this hurts them.

"I need to protect myself! He/They may hurt me."

People who **chew** on their own skin are anxious about eventual separation; But not the Nail biters, because nails are connected to protection.

See *Skin* and *Skin – dermis*

Skin infections

See *Skin*

Skin tuberculosis

Although skin tuberculosis is not the same as discoid lupus erythematosus or systemic lupus erythematosus, the tensions people experience are also related to the immune system and the inner conflicts are very much alike.

Please see both *Lupus – discoid lupus erythematosus* and *Lupus – systemic lupus erythematosus*

Skull

The skull, or the cranium, is the hardest bone of the body. Problems in the skull reveal a major undervaluing in the relationship the person has with his biological Father or with the male model he has had. It denotes obstinacy and stubbornness. The bigger the cranial lesion, the more intense will be the tension the person experiences in his life with regard his incapacity to take his Cartesian thoughts and his controlling obstinacy further.

It is sometimes said that the person has deeper or more superficial cuts in the cranium, particularly in the case of children, when the person has broken his head. This extremely common saying is not exact, because, in most cases, there is no bone lesion. These cranial problems must be understood as originating in small tensions with the biological Father. The Father is likely to be extremely controlling and demanding.

Slackness

The person who chooses to be slack needs someone to look after him. He cannot look after himself. He is not self-sufficient. He has difficulty keeping the house tidy, in organizing his

ideas, in setting up priorities. The person's unkemptness, be it regarding his car, his home, his papers, his clothes, in other words, anything connected to matter, mirrors what goes on inside the person's head.

Slimness

The person who is very slim believes that, to be happy, it is necessary to hide, to fade away. We are talking about an excessively thin person, whose parents are too demanding, or who needs to break free from the claws of his/her family or wife/husband, which takes up too much space. Due to the fact that he/she is unable to express his/her feelings and has low self-esteem, probably because of the way his/her parents or family treat him/her, and with whom he/she is unable to deal, the only solution is to disappear. His/her body shows the person what he/she is feeling.

See *Anorexia*

Small stature syndrome

Nanism is also called small stature syndrome.

Growth problems are very much related to the endocrine system. If a child believes it is not worth growing up, the body will show him that tension from a physical perspective. And the child will not grow.

And why should a child believe it is not worth growing up? It could be due to several reasons, but all pointing to his parents.

humbleness? Which path is my own? Where shall I go?

In the case of **cancer**, the body is showing the person that he has a major tension regarding the male figure (Father, husband…), which he is unable to verbalize.

In the case of inflammation, **myelitis**, the person's body is showing him he is boiling. He starts going numb from the feet up, and the numbness progresses upwards. What is going on between my Mother and a man (my Father?)? The person is unaware he is boiling and that his structural foundations are unstable.

Spinal marrow

See *Spinal chord (spinal medulla)*

Spinal medulla

See *Spinal chord (spinal medulla)*

Spine

The outer posture of a person reflects his inner posture.

When human beings became erected and started to be biped instead of quadruped, the most fragile parts of the body became unprotected. This means human beings have a larger capacity than animals to give themselves out, to open up and to receive.

The hard vertebrae/soft disks polarity is what confers flexibility to the spine.

Telling a child "stand up right" will not solve that child's posture. She is prostrated because she feels the world collapsing upon her. She is carrying a heavy load on her back. Understanding why the child curves down and is prostrated and talking to her about life is more important than making her walk upright.

The spine allows us to maintain an upright and firm posture. It confers verticality, balance and flexibility to human beings.

If we look carefully, we notice that the spine has a double *S* shape. It works in accordance with the principles of amortization. The *S* has two inward facing curvatures (cervical and lumbar) called the lordosis and an outward facing curvature (dorsal) called kyphosis.

The excessive bending of the lordosis curvature on the lumbar vertebrae is called **lordosis**. People suffering from lordosis have an extremely forward pushing belly. The weight of the family, clan, beliefs and society are all concentrated here. The taking on of the responsibility: "I am the mainstay of a clan. Others depend on me." Lordosis reveals that this person's home is not working properly.

The excessive outwards bending of the curvature in the dorsal area is called **kyphosis**. It forms a small hump and the person ends up with curved shoulders. Kyphosis reveals that the person feels the weight of the world upon his shoulders. Life is not easy for him. And then he bends down, instead of realizing that he is taking upon himself what was not meant for him. This often occurs to excessively mental oriented people who would like to change their own world at any cost but cannot do it.

In the army, where soldiers are required to have a vertical, extremely upright posture, the paradox between inner and outer posture is almost permanent. Because, at the end of the day, they are taught to be stiff and simultaneously bend down, to take orders without questioning them, in a submissive manner. It is easy to understand the confusing feelings inside their heads and bodies... Cultivating just the outer firmness is self deceiving, because the body will end up showing the person, through symptoms, the parts where he is not that righteous. Soldiers have stiff and blocked joints.

What we should cultivate is inner firmness. The spine will show it naturally.

Sick people adopt postures they would never take up on a volunteer basis. The person who goes about with a very upright head more often reveals haughtiness, pride, inaccessibility and intransigence than balance.

A **too stiff spine** that takes a bamboo shape (Bechterew's disease) denotes a non-conscious huge ego and a tremendous lack of flexibility which the person will not acknowledge. With time, the spine solidifies from top down and the head leans forward. The sinuosity (the S) disappears or gets inverted. This is the body showing the person what he never wanted to see.

The **hump** denotes a problem similar to the excessively stiff spine. This is a non-accepted humbleness that is forced on the body.

Spina bifida can be of two types:

The first is spina bifida *occulta*, in which half of the vertebral arches do not develop, resulting in a split vertebra, normally occurring in one single vertebra, the fifth lumbar vertebra (L5) or in the first of the sacral vertebrae (S1). Many people are unaware they suffer from it. It is only revealed by a small depression on the area, or by an accumulation of hair in that part of the body.

The second type is cystic spina bifida, characterized by a defect in the upper part of the neural tube (where nerves pass through). In any form of spina bifida, the spinal medulla is left unprotected, although the second type (cystic) is more dangerous from a medical viewpoint than the first type (*occulta*).

In any case, spina bifida reveals a separation between Father and Mother, either at conception stage or during pregnancy.

Spleen

The spleen, like the pancreas, belongs to the earth element, one of the five Eastern elements.

Like the pancreas, the spleen is a busy, hardworking organ. It regulates the blood and it teams up with the pancreas. It is a lymphatic organ which filters the blood, collaborates with the liver in the production of bile and produces white cells (it has an immunological role). The pancreas, its cousin, is a much more *yang* type of organ, much more masculine, more intense than the spleen, which is more *yin*, more feminine. The spleen regulates women's menstrual cycles and contributes towards the good functioning of the female genital organs. Spleen **cancer** occurs more often in women than in men, although men also suffer from it. Spleen cancer is more feminine, whereas pancreas cancer is more a male thing.

See *Pancreas*

Spleen problems indicate that the sufferer allows little time for fun and pleasure. Duty and the profession (even if that profession is being a housewife) represent what is really important. Life lacks joy. The person annuls himself; his attitude is too feminine, too passive. That person will go to lengths to hang on to the past, he excessively cultivates the past, just for fear of not being able to deal with the present. That person will be too regulated, normative, rigid, radical, obsessed about duty, just because of fear of annulling himself. He will not pay attention to himself or to his self-esteem. Women who experience difficulty in taking part in the celebration of life are more prone to having spleen cancer.

Women who suffer from spleen cancer find it more difficult to live out their femininity and to celebrate life because they focus, just like a man would do, on the daily rules that present themselves to them. Moreover, when these women are married, they often attract husbands who enjoy celebrations and parties and will participate in them, whether the wife is present or not. And they will do it in several ways, even in sexual terms. And these women just observe, passively, and focus on the only purpose of their lives, the rules, the home, domestic work, and, paradoxically, they do it very much in a *yang* and controlled way.

Spots in the eyes

See *Eyes – eye spots*

Sprains

These are provoked by problems in the ligaments. Ligaments are the bandages of joints.

Here, we have the connection between two bones, not between the bone and the muscle, which is the case of tendons.

A ligament's strain occurs when the person is looking for the best position for gesture. The person is looking for it and, suddenly, the ligament blocks out. Then sprain happens. It also happens when the person twists regulations, transgresses the clan or prevaricates in his marriage.

In any case, this symptom denotes inflexibility and undervaluing.

It is important to see which joint was sprained, in order to understand the tension it is connected with.

Stammering

Stammering is a condition of paralysis which affects speech. This paralyzing illness is associated with a great sense of undervaluation. Undervaluation is the first keyword associated with stammering. The second keyword associated with this condition is the sense of opposing ideas and impulses.

The person gives himself two contradictory orders for movement. The stammerer has opposing wills. For example, the individual may have the will to express himself but, at the same time, he may feel the desire to please his Father (who does not like what the son has to say when he expresses his emotions) and this conflict of wills causes stammering.

Stammering happens in the vocal chords located in the larynx, which is part of the throat. The throat is located in the neck, which is the channel between head and shoulders. When a person stammers, the words do not flow, they do not come out easily.

The person who stammers transfers his emotional and sexual problems to the head. He feels undervalued due to the inability to communicate with the parents and, specially, the Father. The stammerer is a reserved person who does not like to open himself to the instincts and demands of the body. He is someone who was trained to repress instincts, particularly those of sexual nature. Most likely he was not free to express his emotions or cry as a child.

It is not stammering that makes children act shy. It is shyness, the fear to express and communicate emotions that makes children stammer. The person who stammers assesses the consequences (here we find again the conflict of wills I mentioned above). When a stammerer is able to express himself, he usually has very strong spells of sexuality, aggressiveness, and logorrhoea (excessive flow of words).

We must find out about this person's childhood relationship with his Father and, only then, with his Mother. We must find out about the model of sexuality he was exposed to, as well as the model of control he experienced. Many people develop stammering because they are surrounded by people who strangle them, in a figurative sense.

Sterility

See *Infertility*

Sternum

The sternum is a thick and flattened bone located in the front wall of the thorax and it articulates with the clavicle (collar bone) and the first seven ribs.

It protects the heart and lungs. The area of the heart represents emotions and the area of the lungs represents a relationship with the outside. A fracture of the sternum, which is a bone, shows that the person felt extremely undervalued. This undervaluation was felt in the bone that protects the thorax area. It means that, in this case, the person felt attacked on his emotions by someone else. Someone has attacked the individual because of what he feels, as if he were not allowed to experience his emotions. As if the person was not allowed to feel what he feels. The sternum, the hip, as well as the large bones of the body, are the areas where the maturation of red blood cells, white blood cells, and platelets occurs. The cells and the platelets are directly associated with blood, that is, with the person's identity. Whenever there is a problem in the sternum, the person feels (though not consciously) that his identity is at stake. It is important to know who he feels in conflict with and verbalize it. First look at the couple, then the home, and finally, the work environment.

See *Bone*

Stiff neck

The neck supports the head and is the link between the head and the torso. It corresponds to the passage of concepts, ideas, wishes and will (all coming from the brain) to practical action (action, fulfilment, expression, relation). The neck is a passage. Not yet the action itself. The neck precedes the action. The neck represents flexibility and the capacity to look around and back.

Problems affecting the neck may occur in the muscle (kink), in the bone (see *Vertebrae – cervical vertebrae*) or in the skin.

The back of the neck is the nape, and it is its most *yang* side. This is the area where kinks normally occur. They could be muscular contractions or problems in the cervical vertebrae.

A kink indicates that the person is too *yang*, very confrontational, too much of a fighter, even stubborn. A kink shows that the person is feeling undervalued about himself, from an intellectual perspective. He feels challenged by someone. He feels angry or discomfort (People who store up anger

have chronic tension on their shoulders, neck and arms).

Kinks force people to become more *yin*. They force people to be passive. The person wishes to turn his head to face up to the other person, but cannot do it because it is painful. The person was forced to repress his aggressiveness. The person is prevented from looking to the other person in the eyes. His own body will not allow him to go to war.

Stomach

The stomach makes up the fourth segment of the digestive tube. It stores recently eaten food and takes it down to the duodenum.

It belongs to the earth element of the five elements of eastern philosophy.

The stomach's first function is to serve as a recipient, so we may say that it represents the capacity for hospitality towards another person. To receive implies abnegation, passivity, and surrender. In this perspective, the stomach is a *yin* pole, feminine.

The stomach's second function, this one more masculine, more *yang*, is to produce acids that attack, corrode, and decompose the food, since the stomach is the organ in charge of digesting matter in the first instance. So, the stomach digests the person's feelings and emotions.

So stomach problems represent, first of all, a difficulty in allowing oneself to experience feelings and emotions, and, secondly, a great difficulty to digest them.

In the stomach resides the conflict of not being able to digest the chunk (digest what happened to me), whether real or virtual.

When the emotional conflict is very active, the stomach needs more gastric fluid to digest better. The person remains mulling over what others did to him. Here the emotional tension is of the type: "You bastard, I can't even digest it!" The stomach patient does not like confrontations. His stomach calls for baby food.

The stomach patient cannot deal with his anger, his emotional wear, either to turn it into a verbal aggression or simply to verbalize the emotion he feels. Emotion comes from *ex-movere*, which means to move out. The stomach patient finds himself forced to swallow his temper, his rage. Literally, he swallows bile and then feels the stomach acids in the form of **heartburn** because, to digest all this, the stomach must produce much more gastric acid. Gastric secretion is directly associated to the mind.

These suppressed emotions that the stomach patient deals poorly with are associated to material problems, professional problems, money issues, legal and educational matters. Stomach problems are very much down to earth. They have much to do with a person's roots and essence (work, home, Mother, place where he lives, and money). A **burp** (see *Aerogastria*) is a release of air, of stomach tension, and it gives relief. An **ulcer** is also associated to roots, but exclusively with the relationship aspect. It is associated to the couple and

the home.

The person who does not get along with one of the people he lives with, constantly feels that he cannot digest the tensions he feels towards that person. Yet, for whatever reason, he continues to live with that person (either because his beliefs do not allow him to leave or because he does not have the material possibility, or maturity, to leave that environment) and is continuously forced to face that person. He may well develop an ulcer as a result. In the beginning, when the tension is active, the person feels a stinging pain in the stomach and later he bleeds.

The ulcer results from the continuous aggression that the person creates against himself by fearing to effectively confront others or to allow himself to get out or to leave. The ulcer is directly associated to relationships. It is as if the body was saying that it needs more space to digest and then proceeds to make a hole (the ulcer).

Strabismus

See *Eyes – strabismus*

Stretch marks

Stretch marks are cutaneous scars of the skin that result from small fractures of the dermis due to distensions incidents. The tensions that provoke symptoms on the dermis result from protection and aggression in a more primary sense. They are characteristic of people who feel their space invaded, who feel victimized, in a primary sense of the word, and who feel a strong tension regarding dirt, whether it is material dirt or a dirty behaviour on somebody's part. It may be sexual "dirt", fraudulent behaviour, etc.

In conclusion, more primary protection conflicts happen in the dermis. The dermis is not associated with separation, it has more to do with the sense that someone has control over me and invades my space.

Check and see in what part of the body you find stretch marks.

Sty

See *Eyes – sty*

Sudden death

Sudden death in newly born babies has its origins in the prolonged apnoeas that some babies experience.

When this symptom occurs in newborn babies, it is normally when they are asleep, and can lead to sudden death. In this case, apnoea indicates that the baby is not doing well in the relationship involving his parents. The baby has an unconscious desire to disincarnate. It is paramount that, in this case, parents assume responsibility.

See *Babies*

Suicide

See *Brain – blocked brain*
Suicide happens easily when the person has a blocked brain.

Suprarenal glands

They are endocrine glands located over the kidneys.

They secrete adrenalin, which has an effect on the body on how it consumes energy for immediate consumption. Adrenaline raises the cardiac and respiratory rhythms. The suprarenal glands also secrete hormones that are essential to the body, and also sexual hormones.

These glands are directly linked to the person's energy. Those who have problems linked to **hypoactivity** of the suprarenal glands feel tired, lack of energy and loss of libido. The **Addsion' disease** is one of these examples.

It is the case of a person who is completely lost, disoriented and far away from other people. This person is afraid of many things, and will not give himself away. He is excessively controlling and has a very *yang* behaviour. If you check under *Family*, you will see that each human being needs to be part of a group, a herd, in order to live. But the herd does not have to be the same all the time. When one ceases to belong to a community, a group, family or clan, it is possible to join another group we have found, in the meantime. If the person finds another clan, he will stop having problems in his suprarenal glands.

Two examples in the animal world illustrate the problem of hypoactivity of the suprarenal glands very well.

Let us start with sheep.

Contrary to what happens with wolves, where each individual wolf, when part of a pack, is not essential (one wolf leaving the group does not impact on the pack), in the case of sheep, and, more precisely, a sheep herd, any reduction in the number of heads originates a situation of danger. Sheep depend on the group, reason for which they bet on it. The herd cannot attack the wolf, nor run away from it, only gather together. Predators do not attack a herd. What they see when looking at the herd is a huge sheep. The sheep led astray is the one that becomes the prey.

For the lost sheep, the only valid direction is the course that will take it back to the herd. For this reason, the lost sheep stays still. The lost sheep has to focus on itself, and, for this reason, its brain needs to generate a mechanism that calms it down. What the body does then is to act over the suprarenal glands, calming them down and literally draining them. The sheep becomes exhausted as a result. It gets worn out, and then lies down, still. When we see a sheep looking like this, it means it is lost. It is trying not to move any further away from the herd. It waits for it to show up, and, when it happens, then its suprarenal glands come back into force and the sheep runs fast to the herd, to be part of it and feel safe again. An animal under stress is a very active animal, and the suprarenal glands of an animal under stress are very active. The keywords for problems related to suprarenal hypoactivity are: <u>lost from the group</u>, from the family, from the herd, from the clan or <u>very scared</u>. Key symptoms: extreme tiredness, lack of vitality.

And now the example of salmons that return to the nascent of the river to spawn, around September. The route is tough and the bears are waiting and having a feast. Salmons' jumps are huge. One of them manages to go over the rock but falls on the side of the river, on the bank, on dry land. It is outside the water. Its life is at great risk. Then it blocks out all the waters kept in the kidneys (see *Kidneys – cancer and cysts*), in order to store as much water as possible, waiting for a wave to land near where it is. It will also block out the suprarenal glands (which are associated to the kidneys) in order to prevent the production of cortisone and enter into a state of asthenia (major tiredness) so not to move and catch the bear's attention. This is its only chance of survival away from the clan and in a danger situation.

Problems related to **Hyperactivity** of the suprarenal glands (**Cushing's disease** or **Conn's disease**) are also provoked by fears. Excessive fear of things that have not yet happened, but which the person is afraid may happen.

Sweat

See *Perspiration*

Swelling

If swelling results from trauma, see *Haematomas*.

If it is caused by fluid retention, see *Liquid retention, Kidneys* or *Heart*.

Swollen glands

See *Lymphatic system*

Sympathetic nervous system

See *Nervous system*

The sympathetic nervous system is a part of the Nervous system.

Synovial fluid

Joint bones are kept in place by ligaments and tendons that only allow normal movement. Muscles also help determine joint stability. The joint is enclosed in a fibrous capsule filled with a thin membrane that constantly produces a small amount of fluid; this fluid, called synovial fluid, acts as a nutrient and as a lubricant to the cartilage.

Therefore, synovial fluid is the lubricant of joints. When someone feels major undervaluation in the identity of his gesture, that is, when he feels his gesture is clumsy and this fact makes him feel bad, joints get a cold and the synovial fluid flows out. Just like in the nose. A torsion becomes more severe when this fluid flows out.

Syphilis

See *Gonorrhoea*

Tabagism

All forms of dependence represent an escape. It is an escape that started as a quest. What actually happens is that the person literally projects the objective of his search on something he found along the way, and decides his quest was over. He is pleased with what he has found. He remains trapped in fear and convenience. Anything can cause addiction: alcohol, drugs, sex, tobacco, gambling, food (bulimia, anorexia), but also, and even to a larger extent, money, power, rules, fame, influence, knowledge, entertainment, isolation, asceticism, cult, tradition, ancestral beliefs, religion…

The addicted person is the one who stops halfway through his quest. For this reason, he feels empty. And because he feels empty, he needs to fill the void with external substances that confer him the illusion of being balanced.

Basically, we could say that in all humanity, we are all dependents. The difference between the sick dependent and the healthy dependent rests in the quality of self-observation, that is, in the awareness of oneself, of one's feelings and path. Dependence is a type of attachment. The non-addict, non-sick consumer is the one who is aware of his attachments.

Tobacco stimulates the lungs and the bronchi, which are organs of contact and communication with others. The smoker who holds the smoke in is stimulating his bronchi. It is a masculine attitude and a form of marking the territory. Bronchi are, in fact, linked to territorial conflicts, which are male conflicts. This need for territorial marking is typical of the person who cannot express himself as he should, at home or at school or work. Ninety five per cent of people start to smoke during adolescence, which is when youngsters are dizzy over their hormonal and human development and fail to communicate well with parents and teachers. Then he hides behind tobacco. He is trying to stimulate communication and mark his territory through tobacco. It is a movement whose causes he is unaware of. Besides, exhaling smoke keeps people away. This is another way young people use to mark territory that they believe to be threatened. A woman who smokes is marking her own territory. Women smokers are more aggressive, more *yang*, more masculine.

Tobacco also stimulates communication, through the lungs. And alcohol, coffee and tea, that are diuretic, stimulate kidneys, organs that are also linked to communication. For this reason, at gatherings with friends, people drink and smoke, as a means to create contact and to stimulate the organs of contact, the lungs and kidneys. In these meetings, smokers communicate very well amongst themselves.

However, smoking and drinking do not resolve the causes. They merely resolve symptoms and effects.

Taenia

See *Worms*

Tapeworm

See *Worms*

Taste

Taste depends directly on the action of the tongue.

In animals, the tongue is the first thing that touches food. The tongue

savours liquids. The tongue is a conduit to transport liquid, such as water. The tongue allows us to identify food.

Taste-related problems are connected to the capacity to recognize what is bad from what is good, and to enjoy life with happiness, with flavour, with taste.

In the beginning, being able to distinguish sweet from sour was enough. Nowadays, everything has become more difficult. Artificial smells and flavours affect our taste.

Taste is very close to smell. Smell adds volume and colour to taste and is inseparable from it, just like the two eyes from each other. Often, the person with no sense of smell also suffers from poor taste.

Both taste and smell are connected to our capacity to let life's subtle things pervade us and to distinguish them from those that are not good for us. The person who has no taste is not interested in feeling the subtle signs.

See *Smell*

Teeth

Biting is an act of firmness, the expression of the capacity to grab, to subdue, to attack and feed. Poor teeth is an attribute of the person who has difficulty showing his assertiveness or even his aggressiveness and also of the person who finds it difficult to take decisions, since deciding is to provoke a rupture. It is to break.

We all know that one of the things that are most repressed by the society we live in is our assertiveness and, above all, aggressiveness, despite the fact that it is something deeply natural. The more we allow our aggressive emotions to come out, the less we will need to deal with our own aggressive behaviours or even with some symptoms which are not more than signs of a controlled and punished aggressiveness. **Cringing teeth** is a process that occurs mostly at night and which symbolizes repressed, not expressed aggressiveness. One needs to understand that aggressiveness only became aggressiveness because the firm and clear cut demonstration of an upsetting feeling was never allowed, neither by the person, nor by those surrounding him.

On the other hand, teeth are equally a demonstration of our own vitality. In fact, when we dream we lose a tooth, it means loss of energy and vitality.

One of the vital roles of teeth is nutrition. Teeth have the purpose of taking in food and keeping it in. Here we are referring to solid food, not emotional nutrition. We should take teeth into consideration before we turn vegetarian.

See *Teeth – buck teeth (rodent)*, *Teeth – canine (the 4)*, *Teeth – caries*, *Teeth – front teeth pushed back (carnivore)*, *Teeth – last left upper and lower molar*, *Teeth – last right upper and lower molar*, *Teeth – left lower molar teeth*, *Teeth – left lower premolar teeth*, *Teeth – left side incisive teeth (2 up and 2 down)*, *Teeth – left upper molar teeth*, *Teeth – left upper premolar teeth*, *Teeth – right lower molar teeth*, *Teeth – right lower premolar teeth*, *Teeth – right side incisive teeth (2 up and 2 down)*, *Teeth – right upper molar teeth*, *Teeth – right upper premolar teeth*, *Teeth – space between molars* and *Teeth – straight and aligned front teeth*

Teeth – buck teeth (rodent)

These teeth are not good for retaining food. As a result, the rodent needs to keep trying, biting, going at it, to achieve its goal, which is to be able to eat.

For this reason, these are very determined people, very strong-minded. These are people who will go to the end of things. They leave nothing halfway. They are stubborn and resolute people.

Teeth – canine (the 4)

If a person has an infection in the canine teeth (which may require removal), the body is telling the person that he is suffering from tension associated to discernment and the feeling of shortage: "Food will not be enough, I need more!" This food may be affection, considered to be emotional food. Infections also denote anger, resentment, incapacity to be who one wants to be.

Teeth – caries

People who have enamel related problems believe they do not have the right to bite. Those people's bones are harder than enamel. The jaw is stronger than enamel.

"I am not strong enough to bite!" This causes caries to appear.

Ambitious youngsters in companies are often wiped out. And they have caries: "My bite is not as strong as I thought it was."

Caries related problems are but related to psychological problems, the inability to bite. To bite is a decision, both in the literal and figurative sense.

Teeth devitalisation is an extreme case of inability to bite. It shows the person's inability to stand up and be assertive.

If the child likes to bite, he should be given an apple. This means the child feels endangered. Eating apples is very good for children.

Yin/yang polarity in teeth only occurs when it concerns enamel, that is to say, when caries occur. Enamel reveals communication problems and is ruled by the two cerebral hemispheres. Therefore, right hand teeth enamel is *yang* (masculine) and those on the left hand side are *yin* (feminine), whether we are dealing with right or left-handed people.

Caries in the *yang* side teeth are a symptom of the person's undervaluing and denote the person's powerlessness regarding a man. On the *yin* side, they are a symptom of the person's undervaluing and denote the person's powerlessness regarding a woman.

Teeth – front teeth pushed back (carnivore)

This type of teeth is a characteristic of carnivores, predators. Unlike rodents, carnivores need to grab and hold on to the prey. Teeth like these are distinctive of people who behave like predators. They do not let go. "I got

you and I am not letting you go!"

One needs to be very fast when dealing with this type of people. It is necessary to surprise them. It is the only way to make them release tension.

Teeth – last left upper and lower molar

Infections or problems in these last molar teeth (which may require removal) denote tensions connected with the emotional experience of the person regarding his acceptance of his own emotions, his feminine sensitivity, in the case of a woman, or, if it is a man, his feminine side. They also indicate that the person feels that everything is going too fast: "Am I on the right rhythm? I am not sure that I am assimilating properly". It is a question of rhythm. The person cannot assimilate emotions nor accept them. The outside world is too vast and compact for the person to be able to take it in.

Thus, in the case of this molar tooth, we are in the presence of a pattern of non-experiencing emotions. Problems affecting this tooth reveal a huge control of emotions and also denial to accept or be aware that something is wrong at home. The person merely shoots the ball forward. He will not analyse. He will not confirm things. He hides fragilities.

Teeth – last right upper and lower molar

Infections or problems in these last molar teeth (which may require removal) denote tensions connected with the emotional experience of the person regarding his acceptance of his own emotions, his feminine sensitivity, in the case of a woman, or, if it is a man, his feminine side. They also indicate that the person feels that everything is going too fast: "Am I on the right rhythm? I am not sure that I am assimilating properly". It is a question of rhythm. The person cannot assimilate emotions nor accept them. The outside world is too vast and compact for the person to be able to take it in.

The person is unable to find his identity in this world, particularly in his own home.

Teeth – left lower molar teeth

Infections or problems in these molar teeth (which may require removal) denote family disturbances, problems at home, a feeling that what has been done to the person is disgusting, sordid.

Teeth – left lower premolar teeth

Infections or problems in these premolar teeth (which may require removal) denote tensions connected with the digestion of emotions and also indicate that the person allows little time for fun and pleasure. Duty and the profession (even if that profession is being a housewife) represent what is really important. Life lacks joy.

Teeth – left side incisive teeth (2 up and 2 down)

Infections or problems in these inci-sive teeth (which may require removal) denote tensions regarding ancestors, deep rooted social beliefs, beliefs within the clan, regarding birth and the relationship the person maintains with his parents as well as the relationship between his parents. This applies both to children and adults.

They also reveal difficulty in accepting femininity, in the case of a woman, and masculinity, in the case of a man. They disclose equally the passage of genetic material from one generation to the next.

Teeth – left upper molar teeth

Infections or problems in these molar teeth (which may require removal) denote tensions connected with the digestion of emotions and also indicate that the person allows little time for fun and pleasure. Duty and the profession (even if that profession is being a housewife) represent what is really important. Life lacks joy.

Teeth – left upper premolar teeth

Infections or problems in these premolar teeth (which may require removal) denote tensions connected with external aggression and, simultaneously, with fear of dying. This could be physical death or the end of a cycle. Could just be fear of losing a relationship, a loved one. Fear of dying is fear to exhale the last breath. The person dreads asphyxiating.

Teeth – right lower molar teeth

Infections or problems in these molar teeth (which may require removal) denote family disturbances, problems at home, a feeling that what has been done to the person is disgusting, sordid.

Teeth – right lower premolar teeth

Infections or problems in these premolar teeth (which may require removal) denote tensions connected with the digestion of emotions with the feeling of having been victim of unfairness.

Teeth – right side incisive teeth (2 up and 2 down)

Infections or problems in these incisive teeth (which may require removal) denote tensions regarding ancestors, deep rooted social beliefs, beliefs within the clan, regarding birth and the relationship the person maintains with his parents as well as the relationship between his parents.

This applies both to children and adults.

Teeth – right upper molar teeth

Infections or problems in these molar teeth (which may require removal) denote tensions connected with the digestion of emotions and to the feeling of having been victim of unfairness.

Teeth – right upper premolar teeth

Infections or problems in these premolar teeth (which may require removal) denote tensions connected with external aggression and, simultaneously, with fear of dying. This could be physical death or the end of a cycle. Could just be fear of losing a relationship, a loved one. Fear of dying is fear to exhale the last breath. The person dreads asphyxiating.

Teeth – space between molars

The bigger the space between teeth, the more carnivorous the person should be. Be active, a predator, *yang*, masculine. Teeth that are too close to each other are typical of ruminants.

Teeth – straight and aligned front teeth

These are a characteristic of ruminants. In this case, canines are almost like the molars. They exemplify people who lead quite balanced lives. They live well with their *yang* side, masculine, and with their *yin* side, feminine.

Tendon

This is where the bone starts being a muscle and where the muscle starts being a bone.

Two realities come together here.

Tendons are quite inextensible. They fix bones to the muscles. In this case, we talk about the undervaluation of gesture at the time it starts. It is the stopping of image.

This means the undervaluation of action in the present. "He is better than me." "I cannot beat him." I am not powerful enough". I cannot get there". This may happen when practicing a sport or merely by crossing a street, or even walking. In other words, this happens to the person who thinks he is not worth much.

A problem in tendons is called **tendonitis**.

There are differences between tendons and ligaments. If appropriate, see *Ligaments*.

It is usual to find tendon problems on shoulders, elbows, ankles, wrists and fingers. Check each one individually, because each unveils distinct conscience tensions.

Testicles

Testicles are equivalent to the female gonads.

They are the reservoir of the force of Heaven, *yang* and masculine. Removing testicles from a man provokes the same energetic feeling as removing ovaries from a woman. Testicles are the essence of masculinity. Men do not have ovaries. Ovaries are to women what testicles are to men.

The hormones from these glands control sexual characteristics, such as hair and penis growth. Both men and women have masculine hormones (testosterone) and female hormones (estrogens), albeit in different proportions.

Problems in the gonads denote the feeling of true loss of a loved one. This could have been a girlfriend or boyfriend, a son, in short, someone very close to the person.

Cancer in the testicles makes them more productive. It is as if the body is showing the person's desire to procreate, to generate a new loved one. This case clearly indicates the typical need to protect the species before the individual. In fact, this is a person who is offering part of his life to virtually get back (and this is what makes this an illusion) someone who has gone from his life.

When the tension he feels is huge and not verbalized or brought out in the open, the person gets cancer. When it is not so serious, the person gets a **cyst**.

The testicle's polarity is not a determining factor, because the person is able to quickly identify which loved one caused the feeling of loss. The testicles' polarity is not obvious. However, for diagnosis purposes, we should start assuming that the right testicle is *yang* and the left testicle is *yin*, for all men, right and left-handed. But this is not certain. Problems in the *yang* testicle indicate the loss of a male loved one, and in the *yin* testicle, of a female loved one.

Accordingly, the *yang* testicle denotes the loss of a major male friend, son, or any male the person was very fond of. The *yin* testicle indicates the loss of a major female friend, a girlfriend, a daughter or any female the person was very fond of.

Thigh

Thighs are part of the body's lower limbs. The lower limbs play a vital role in the locomotor system. They allow us to walk, run, jump, push, change direction in the way we move. They allow us to stand up, as well as conferring mobility, flexibility and activity, but also firmness.

Tensions in the lower limbs mean tensions with the world or with people. As we progress down from the thigh to the foot, energy becomes more dense. The femur is the largest bone in the human body and is located in the thigh. The bone structure represents our deepest rooted beliefs.

Problems in the thigh may take place in the muscle, bone (femur) or in the skin. If it happens in the muscle, it denotes undervaluing and inflexibility. On the skin, it shows difficulty in communicating, or tension provoked by separation.

To fracture the femur is a serious impediment for anyone. The body is saying: "Stop, take a different route."

Problems in the thighs indicate undervaluing due to inflexibility in the person's way of thinking regarding his own life, his foundations, roots, deepest beliefs, work, home, family, money. The person's decisiveness has been totally shaken.

The right thigh, at the onset, is *yang*, masculine, and the left is *yin*, feminine, both in the case of left and right-handed people. We are talking about the locomotor system. But we must remember that the *yin/yang* polarity regarding the sides of the body is not obvious in this system.

Therefore, problems affecting the *yang* thigh unveil obstinacy concerning the way one leads his life and thinking, mostly regarding work and profession-

al projects, and the likely (harmful) influence of a man's way of thinking (perhaps the Father or the male model at home or in the couple). Problems in the *yin* thigh disclose obstinacy concerning the way one leads his life and thinking, mostly regarding home and the family, and the likely (harmful) influence of a woman's way of thinking (perhaps the Mother or the female model at home or in the couple). In both cases, the person's firmness has been questioned.

Threadworms

See *Worms*

Throat

The problems in the throat can be various. Therefore, please see *Tonsils, Larynx (larynx, aphonia, hoarseness)* and *Pharynx*.

Throat angina

It's stuck in my throat!
See *Tonsils*

Thrombophlebitis

See *Thrombosis*
Thrombophlebitis is a condition of Thrombosis.

Thrombosis

Thrombosis may occur in any blood vessel, whether it is an artery, vein or capillary vase, or even in a cardiac cavity. A thrombus is a blood clot. Thrombosis is the obstruction of a vase by a clot. The danger of thrombosis is when the thrombus gets loose and may reach the lungs or brain, causing **pulmonary** or **brain embolism**. Blood clots because it is too thick. It is not as thin as it should.

Thrombosis in arteries, namely in the **coronary**, denote a very *yang*, masculine and warrior behaviour. They occur more often in the upper parts of the body, in the chest, arms and head, which are the most *yang* and masculine parts of the circulatory system.

Thrombosis affecting the pelvic area or the lower limbs is normally of the deep venous type (affecting the veins).

Vein-related problems denote a life without joy, a cancelling off on the person's part, a life that is so passive that happiness just passes by without staying. Thrombosis, phlebitis, varicose veins and haemorrhoids are conditions that affect the veins.

Phlebitis is a thrombosis in a superficial vein. It normally occurs in varicose veins. It is also called **thrombophlebitis**. **Deep venous thrombosis**, phlebitis (thrombophlebitis) and **varicose veins** are occurrences of the venous system. The venous system is the *yin* part of the circulatory system. It carries the used blood to the liver and kidneys to filter it, and to the lungs to get rid of carbon dioxide and replace it by oxygen.

The person who has varicose veins prevents the blood from circulating.

The body shows the person he is fed up with the life he is leading by developing thrombophlebitis (it affects the most superficial veins) or deep venous thrombosis. The body shows the person he is enraged but passive, too *yin*. It denotes anger, frustration and impotence. The person blames others for his limitations and lack of energy but will not do anything about it. He just stays excessively passive. This indicates the person has typecast opinions, typecast ideas and says typecast sentences. People who are bedridden for some reason tend to develop thrombosis because they are immobilized.

Life should flow. If the person's life flows, his blood will flow too.

Thrush

See *Mouth sores (thrush)*

Thymus

The thymus is a gland located in the upper portion of the chest cavity, just above and in front of the heart. Its action slows down after reaching puberty, and its size decreases with age.

The thymus plays a major role during children's development, as it is an organ that is able to mature certain types of lymphocytes (a type of small leucocytes – white blood cells).

The thymus plays a major role in children until they become adolescents. It is involved in the process of growing up, metabolism and immune system. This is where the university of white cells can be found. It is connected to children's growth and metabolism (metabolism is the group of chemical reactions through which the body assimilates what it needs and gets rid of what it does not). The memory of human beings is located in the thymus, and that memory is impregnated of childhood experiences that the child recalls about himself and about his parents (mostly about the parents), as well as with the male and female models he has come across in his life.

Problems related to the Thymus are linked to the relationship the individual has with the world of adults, which is represented, in the first place, by the individual's parents. The tension that brings about problems in the thymus is silent and profound. This is a non-conscious process. The issue here is the person's belonging to the family, always attempting to respect his unique identity. (At this point it is advisable to read *Family*). It is paramount that the person who suffers from problems in his thymus is allowed to express the type of tension he is feeling in his life and with his family.

Growth disorders are very much associated to the endocrine system. There are three glands that participate in the balanced growing up process of individuals: the pituitary, the thyroid and the thymus.

If a child believes it is not worth growing up, the body will show him that tension from a physical perspective. And the child will not grow.

And why should a child believe it is not worth growing up? It could be due to several reasons, but all point to his parents.

Thyroid

The thyroid is located in the lower neck under the larynx (this is where the chakra of the throat is located, for those who work with chakras). It produces thyroxine, which has a stimulating effect on the body. Thyroxine helps the body tissues consume oxygen. The thyroid regulates the use of oxygen, the metabolism of cells and the development of human beings. It plays a relevant role in metabolising calcium, fats and carbohydrates (metabolism is the group of chemical reactions through which the body assimilates what it needs and gets rid of what it does not).

The thyroid accelerates all metabolisms. It is responsible for the body's entire internal performance. It acts as our accelerator.

The person who suffers from **hyperthyroidism** (**goiter**) is someone who cannot express himself with the right person at the right time. He cannot confront the other person. He cannot express himself when he should and is convinced that other people do not understand him. Accordingly, he turns into a person who is neither straightforward nor frank. As he was not firm nor upfront, he believes he is victim of impositions and keeps complaining and moaning with everybody. He feels frustrated with his life. He does not accomplish himself.

He is permanently running away from others, and, more precisely, escaping direct confrontation with other people. He is constantly deceiving himself.

He is always thinking of doing something. He is extremely busy and never stops. He does not necessarily have a feeling of loss, nor is he afraid he will feel a loss, and for this reason, he does not necessarily have problems with his **liver**.

He needs to be asked:" What are you so afraid of that makes you be always on the run at high speed?" He is a very fast forward type of person, and very restless. He feels he must get on with it very fast, and that he is always excessively busy. He needs to hurry up!

Since the thyroid is our body's accelerator, the body exposes that acceleration and accelerates the thyroid, creating **hyperthyroidism**. When the conflict is huge and fails to be verbalized, thyroid **cancer** develops.

Tumours in the thyroid (**adenomas** and **fibromas**) may be benign, that is when the tension in the conscience is lighter.

The person with this condition never lives the present moment, he never lives the "now" moment. Thyroid-related problems are a feminine symptom. It affects mostly women. It is advisable to look at the clan's female pattern.

When the thyroid slows down, **hypothyroidism** occurs. This is the opposite situation and here the body has come to the conclusion that running away serves no good. The person gets into the opposite situation, he becomes apathetic but not in a state of asthenia (asthenia means extreme tiredness). He feels indifferent towards the world. He is not tired, only feels indifference.

Growth-related problems (see *Growth (growth disorders)*) are very much associated to the endocrine system. There are three glands that participate in the balanced growing up process of individuals: the pituitary, the thyroid and the thymus.

As we have seen, the thyroid denotes the person's capacity to express himself and to make himself understood. It is in the thyroid the body shows the person's calculating attitude, as he learnt when to speak up and when to shut up.

The child who is not allowed to speak up, or who has realized that no one has made (or will make) any effort to understand him, gives up on himself, gives up on accelerating his own metabolism and stops it. Consequently, growth does not take place. The tension the body exposes is: "I cannot create my own space in this adult world. It is not worth my growing up. I do not want to be like them." When this tension occurs during pregnancy, the child is born with small stature syndrome (see *Small stature syndrome*).

Tibia

The tibia, or shinbone, is the larger and stronger of the two bones in the leg. A fractured tibia indicates difficulty to accept a painful life experience and is a sign of major undervaluation.

See *Legs (knee to foot)*

Tinea

See *Fungi*
Tinea is a fungal skin infection.

Tinnitus

Buzzing noise or ringing noise in one ear.

This condition indicates refusal to listen to the inner voice. It is a refusal to acknowledge the call of intuition. This is a sign of a very stubborn person, very mentally oriented, very Cartesian.

Tiredness

See *Asthenia*

Toes

It is difficult to dissociate toes from feet. Feet illustrate the quality of our contact with Mother-Earth. They reveal our awareness of being on Earth, our implantation, the way we feel gravity and counter gravity.

Feet must be dynamic. They are the place for dialogue between levitation and gravitation. People who have feet or toes related problems are people who are badly rooted on earth. They will experience problems wherever they live, whether with their biological Mother or even with their own incarnation. In the case of the latter, see *Child delivery*.

Toes are the accessories which allow the foot to stand and maintain its balance. A person without toes experiences more difficulty walking, and has a lot more trouble running when it is necessary to run away.

Toes are thus the feet's details, the final look of our positions.

There is not always a common denominator regarding the toes *yin/yang* polarity when it concerns the locomotor system (bones and muscles). However, it is appropriate to assume that, both in case of right and left-handed people, the right foot toes are *yang* (masculine) and the toes of the left foot are *yin* (feminine).

Lesions in the bone or muscle on a *yang* toe denote undervaluing regarding his assertiveness and self-esteem at home, between the individual and a close male person.

Lesions in the bone or muscle on a *yin* toe denote undervaluing regarding his capacity to communicate with a close female person, or one who plays a feminine role.

When amputations occur, this is because an actual separation has taken place, provoked by huge undervaluing. If it affects a *yang* toe, the tension was with a man, and if it occurs on a *yin* toe, it was with a woman.

See *Toes – joints* and *Toes – bones and muscles*

Toes – bones and muscles

Lesions in the bone or muscle in a *yang*, masculine toe denote undervaluing in the relationship with a man from home or work. Lesions in the bone or muscle of a *yin*, feminine toe indicate undervaluing regarding a woman, home, couple or the biological Mother, or even financial issues related to the family budget. When amputations occur, this is because an actual separation has taken place, provoked by huge undervaluing.

Problems affecting the bone of the **big toe** denote undervaluing provoked by the person's lack of attentiveness, even megalomania. If the tension takes place in the *yang* big toe, tension is related to a man from home or work and, if it takes place in the big *yin* toe, the tension is related to a woman, or to home, or to the couple or the biological Mother, or even to financial issues related to the family budget. See *Toes* for *yin/yang* polarity.

Problems affecting the bone of the **second toe** indicate undervaluing that is basically connected to material issues, very much down to earth and which the person cannot digest, which makes him feel undervalued.

If the lesion affects the *yang* toe, material tension is connected to a man or work and, if it takes place in the *yin* toe, the tension is related to a woman, or to home, or to the couple or the biological Mother, or even to financial issues related to the family budget.

Problems affecting the bone of the **third toe** are basically linked to strong emotions due to a feeling of incoherence that the individual perceives on the other person, which makes him be extremely inflexible and undervalued.

If the lesion affects the third *yang* toe, the feeling of incoherence is related to a man from home or work and, if it takes place in the third *yin* toe, the tension is related to a woman, or to home, or to the couple or the biological Mother, or even to financial issues related to the family budget.

Problems affecting the bone of the **fourth toe** are basically linked to feelings of unfairness which makes the person enraged.

If the lesion affects the fourth *yang* toe, the feeling of unfairness is related to a man from home or work and, if it takes place in the fourth *yin* toe, the tension is related to a woman, or to home, or to the couple or the biological Mother, or even to financial issues related to the family budget.

Problems affecting the bone of the **little toe** denote undervaluing linked to issues connected with changes involving old beliefs, deep rooted habits, towards which the person feels undervalued.

If the lesion affects the little *yang* toe, the tension associated to change is related to a man from home or work and, if it takes place in the little *yin* toe, the tension is related to a woman, or to home, or to the couple or the biological Mother, or even to financial issues related to the family budget.

Toes – joints

Joints confer mobility to people.

Problems in the joints denote major undervaluing in the identity of the gesture (it happens a lot when playing sports – the individual did not like his gesture performance) and/or inflexibility. The key words for all joint related problems are, therefore, inflexibility and undervaluing.

Stiffness, inflammation, tearing, distensions, sprains, tendonitis or ligament ruptures in the joints of the fingers denote the person's lack of sensitivity regarding what he thinks, and his mental pattern. And, of course, an inflamed joint impedes movement. It makes one stop.

Problems in the **big toe** joint are basically linked to the presence of bunions, which result from inflammation and thickening of the sac around the joint (bursa) at the base of the big toe, causing the outcropping of the joint and the rotation of the toe inwards. It can become very painful when the joint's sac of liquid gets inflamed (bursitis). A bone expansion may also happen. It happens to women much more than men. In fact, the area of the toe where the bunion develops corresponds to the spleen's meridian, and symptoms in the spleen are the product of very *yin*, feminine behaviours, excessively passive. Spleen problems indicate that the sufferer allows little time for fun and pleasure. Duty and the profession (even if that profession is being a housewife) represent what is really important. Life lacks joy. That person will go to lengths to hang on to the past; she cultivates the past excessively, just for fear of not being able to deal with the present. That person will be too regulated, normative, rigid, radical, obsessed about duty.

Moreover, when these women are married or live with someone, their husbands or partners enjoy celebrating and will participate in celebrations, as the women just stay there watching, passively, focusing on their only interest in life, rules.

If tension affects the big *yang* toe, it will be with a man, and, if it affects the *yin* big toe, the tension will be with a woman or with the biological Mother. See toes for *yin/yang* polarity.

Problems affecting the joint of the **second toe** are basically connected with material issues, very much down to earth and which the person cannot digest, which makes him feel undervalued.

If the lesion affects the second *yang* toe, material tension is connected with a man (from home?) or to work and, if it takes place in the second *yin* toe, the tension is related to a woman, or to home, or to the couple or the biological Mother, or even to financial issues related to the family budget.

Problems affecting the joint of the **third toe** are basically linked to strong emotions due to a feeling of incoherence that the individual perceives in the other person, which makes him be extremely inflexible and undervalued.

If the lesion affects the third *yang* toe, the feeling of incoherence is related to a man from home or to work and, if it takes place in the third *yin* toe, the tension is related to a woman, or to home, or to the couple or the biological Mother, or even to financial issues related to the family budget.

Problems affecting the joint of the **fourth toe** are basically linked to feelings of unfairness which makes the person enraged. The person becomes very inflexible and feels undervalued by infamy.

If the lesion affects the fourth *yang* toe, the feeling of unfairness is related to a man from home or to work and, if it takes place in the fourth *yin* toe, the tension is related to a woman, or to home, or to the couple or the biological Mother, or even to financial issues related to the family budget.

Problems affecting the joint of the **little toe** are basically linked to issues connected with changes involving old beliefs, deep rooted habits, towards which the person shows a large degree of inflexibility and a feeling of under-valuing.

If the lesion affects the little *yang* toe, the tension associated to change is related to a man from home or to work and, if it takes place in the little *yin* toe, the tension is related to a woman, or to home, or to the couple or the biological Mother, or even to financial issues related to the family budget.

Tongue

In the animal world, the tongue is the first thing that touches food. The tongue tastes food and it acts as a conduit to take liquids in, such as water. The tongue recognizes food. Tongue related problems are associated to the capacity to differentiate good from bad, and to enjoy life, living it taste-fully.

In the beginning, it was enough to distinguish between sweetness and bitterness. Nowadays, things are much more complicated. Flavours are no longer natural. Differentiating has become more difficult, in all aspects.

The tongue also captures the spoken word. And, socially speaking, the tongue plays an increasingly major role as a kissing tool. The so-called *French kiss* represents the capacity to taste life's flavours with joy.

Tonsils

The tonsils are more connected to the breathing system than to the digestive system, although they participate in both.

The tonsils are the first defence, the first sentinels, and the first filters of the human body. They represent the first discernment of what we can swallow. They are areas of lymphoid tissue that is also found in other mucus membranes, such as the pharynx, the palate, and the tongue, and whose job is to block the passage of swallowed or inhaled objects that are not welcome.

An inflammation of the tonsils, called **tonsillitis**, makes swallowing painful. The body tells the person that he is having trouble swallowing what someone did or said to him. The tonsils are controlled by the cerebral hemispheres. Thus, the right tonsil is *yang* (masculine) and the left tonsil is *yin* (feminine). This is true for right-handed and left-handed people.

An inflammation of the *yang* tonsil shows that the person felt victimized by a man, and an inflammation of the *yin* tonsil shows that the person felt victimized by a woman. It is true that, in most cases, people experience inflammation of both tonsils, but usually symptoms start only in one.

Inflamed tonsils also occur in a very concrete situation when a person was to receive something and, at the last minute, it was taken away from him and given to someone else. It is tough to swallow. "At least they could have warned me!"

Swollen tonsils show that a person is guarded; he does not want that to happen again. They also show that the person can not speak for himself, ask for what he needs, and show disagreement.

When we remove someone's tonsils, we are saying to him "Swallow everything, my darling!" It is an act of aggression that violates the integrity of the person. Again, it takes care of the effect but does not address the causes and, very often, problems simply move down to the area of the bronchi.

Also see *Adenoids*

Torticollis

See *Stiff neck*

Touch

Of all the senses, touch is the one that gets more punished by society. Touching is dangerous because it may mean sex. But touching has nothing to do with sex. It has to do with sensitivity and the capacity to accept one's emotions. The quality of our touch is directly linked to the quality of our self-esteem and to our capacity of giving ourselves to other people. Touching is done through the skin and is a form of communication.

If a person has lost the sense of touch, it means he is a person who wants to distance himself from others. He is a person whose life rules stand higher than his capacity to give in. The person who loses the sense of touch is someone with an excessively *yang* and masculine behaviour, too controlling.

Trachea

The trachea is the long pipe that starts at the larynx (breathing system), opposite the oesophagus, and ends in the chest cavity, at the vertebral level of C5 (see *Vertebrae – cervical vertebrae*) and of the sternum, where it bifurcates into the bronchi. The trachea transports the air from the upper airway routes down to the bronchi and lungs.

Tracheitis is an infection of the trachea. The person felt attacked by someone. This infection does not come alone. If the trachea is infected, this means there is some other infection in the respiratory system.

See *Larynx (larynx, aphonia, hoarseness)* and *Bronchi*

Tremors

Tremors, particularly in the head, indicate inhibition of an agitation, of anger, of a reaction process. People who had to accept other people's control for a long time without being allowed to react or who did not allow themselves to explode may end up with tremors.

These are typical of a person who feels deeply opposed regarding what he does and, mostly, regarding the people or community he lives with or within, mostly regarding a man (husband or biological Father) or the male model.

This tension is associated to the crown chakra. Parkinson's disease is an example of this type of symptom.

Tuberculosis

See *Lungs*

Tuberculosis is a condition of lungs.

Tumours

See *Cancer*

Malign tumours are called cancer.

Ulcerative colitis

See *Bowel – large bowel – ulcerative colitis*

Upper rectum

See *Bowel – large bowel – upper rectum*

Uraemia

Uraemia is a condition that indicates excess urea in the blood. Urea is a substance that kidneys have to dispose of. If it is found in the blood, it indicates the kidneys are not working properly as they did not get rid of what they should. This condition shows the person is experiencing difficulty filtering correctly.

See *Kidneys – renal insufficiency* and *Kidneys – cancer and cysts*

Uretheritis

This is an inflammation of one ureter, or of both of them, and this is associated to the same tensions found in the kidneys. Problems in the ureters are linked to problems in the kidneys.

See *Kidneys*

Urethritis

This is an inflammation of the urethra and is associated to the same tensions found in the bladder. Problems in the urethra are linked to problems in the bladder.

See *Bladder*

Urinary system

Along with the reproductive system, the urinary system belongs to the water element of the five elements of the human body. Our association with our deepest beliefs lies in the waters. The waters are associated with the beginning of life. The urinary system is made up of the kidneys, the ureters, which connect each of the kidneys to the bladder, the bladder and the urethra, which expels the urine from the bladder to the outside. The main function of this system is to maintain the homeostasis in the organism by adjusting the composition, volume, and pressure of the blood. This way, it eliminates and keeps specific amounts of water and liquid solutions. The renal tissue includes the nephrons, which are functional units of the kidney that filter, separate, and absorb body fluids. Problems in the urinary system may be several, and must be analysed on an individual basis. They are all associated with ancestors, deep social beliefs, clan, society, birth, the relationship with parents, and the parents' relationship. This applies to both children and adults. In this system, there is polarity between the right and left sides, but only regarding the kidneys and ureters, and not for all symptoms. So, when there is polarity, the right side is *yang* (masculine) and the left side is *yin* (feminine) for left-handed and right-handed people alike. Problems in the *yang* kidney or ureter indicate difficulties in the relationship with the male model or in the relationship with liquids, due to a masculine influence, and problems in the *yin* kidney or ureter show problems with the female model or in the relationship with liquids, due to a feminine influence. In the case of renal insufficiency, this polarity is not applicable.

Urinary tract infections

See *Cystitis*

Urticaria

See *Hives*

Uterus

See *Womb*

Vagina

In animals, the vagina symbolizes the capacity to give itself, not in a social sense, but in terms of being capable of receiving semen and to embark on the production of offspring. Vagina-related problems denote lack of capacity to give herself to another person, inability to live one's own femininity, one's *yin* side, and they also expose sexual frustration or communication problems.

The mucus is the intimate part of me. The mucosal membrane in the vagina is the place in the body where the woman abolishes her frontiers and gives herself completely to the other person.

Vaginal **cancer** is not frequent. It happens more frequently to post-menopausal women. Vaginal cancer denotes a woman's huge frustration that she has to live her femininity, mostly in its sexual aspect. It is true that when a woman gets older, she becomes more *yang*, more masculine. The proof is the natural loss of fertility. However, this masculinization process should be smoothened by the woman's capacity to live her feminine sexual side in full. A woman who has entered Menopause is a woman who should live her feminine side, her sensual side. Vaginal cancer precisely indicates that the woman has punished her sexual side.

Vaginal **herpes** is associated to nervous issues and to the skin.

It takes place in the mucus junctions of the skin, at the junction between the skin and the mucosal membrane, more frequently in the labia of the vagina, which is the place where contact is made with higher level of tenderness.

It denotes a tension regarding communication with the partner, husband or boyfriend.

Herpes may be painful. This is a symptom provoked by contact with tenderness. It is characteristic of couples who adore each other but are always fighting. The person wants to contact intensely, the nerve is very much alive, but then, as the relationship does not work properly and the person spends a lot of time quarrelling, the body shows that fighting through herpes, which is painful and hampers sexual intercourse. Herpes reveals that the contact relationship with the other person is painful. People who are prone to herpes are people who have difficulty being on their own and being tender with themselves. They depend on love. Herpes shows there is self-inflicted violence in the relationship. If the person is violent to herself in the relationship, this means she feels guilty about something. And guilt is something that does not exist. It is an emotion totally fabricated in the mind of the person.

Leucorrhoea (white discharge expelled through the vagina) denotes feelings such as: "We, women, have no power over men. My partner makes me so angry!" It is as if the vagina is shedding tears of anger.

Candidiasis (thrush) is a fungal infection caused by a fungus called Candida, which affects the mouth and vaginal mucosal membranes.

Fungal infections are of a parasitic type. The word parasite is essential, in this context. If the person lets herself be affected by parasites, this is because she is not centred, does not show firmness to the people who live around her, and it means that there is someone in her life who is a parasite and lives off her. The person is clinging to the past and to her beliefs, and this is the reason why she cannot stand up to this person who is sucking her out like a vampire with the degree of assertiveness she ought to have.

The fact that it develops both in the mouth and in the vagina is deeply meaningful. Actually, both the mouth and the vagina are places that symbolize giving one self and reception regarding the other person.

See *Gonorrhoea*

Varicose veins

A varicose vein is a venous growth almost always in the lower part of the body and mainly in the lower limbs. Varicose veins result from accumulation of blood in the veins of the surface of the body, blood that should have returned to the heart and did not.

Therefore, there is a predominance of circulation in the lower part of the body. Like in the case of high blood pressure (see *Blood pressure – high*) and anaemia, we are dealing with people who are incapable of facing up to those who upset them. These people become apathetic (indifferent), cowards and sometimes lazy. They are people who are upset, but who do not know how to express their emotions to the right person, at the right time, in the right place, and end up having an excessively passive and impotent behaviour. Haemorrhoids are varicose veins in the anus.

Variola

See *Smallpox (variola)*

Vegetations

See *Adenoids*

Veins

You can find vein problems in *Circulatory system – venal system*, *Thrombosis*, *Phlebitis*, *Varicose veins* and *Bowel – large bowel – anus*.

Venereal diseases

The person feels he was bad, feels guilty, feels he needs to be punished. The person needs to move away from any sexual contact. It shows some violence and, above all, guilt. This may occur when, for example, the person feels the tremendous responsibility to carry out a demanding role in the sexual relationship with the partner. The person is unable to perform up to the standard expected by the partner and, consequently, develops a guilt tension regarding the demanding attitude of the partner. The body, as a result, takes him away from sexual contact by creating the venereal disease.

This may also happen to the person who has prevaricated (who had extra-matrimonial sexual intercourse), felt remorse and thus developed a feeling of guilt. In the process, he also blames the third party who contributed to that extra matrimonial sexual relation.

It may also be that the person rejects the partner totally, at a non-conscious level. The body takes it on to itself to make that feeling a conscious one, through symptoms. And the couple can no longer touch each other.

The conscience tensions referred to are valid for any venereal disease, whether it was acquired through phys-ical contact with someone or transmitted in an occasional public toilet. The tension is there. Accidents do not happen by chance.

See *Gonorrhoea*

Venous system

See *Circulatory system*

The venous system is a part of the Circulatory system.

Verruca

See *Wart*

Vertebrae

You can find many things in vertebrae.

Please see *Vertebrae – cervical vertebrae*, *Vertebrae – discs*, *Vertebrae – dorsal vertebrae*, *Vertebrae – lumbar vertebrae*, *Vertebrae – sacral vertebrae*, *Vertebrae – terminal vertebrae – coccyx*, *Lumbago* and/or *Sciatic nerve pain*.

Vertebrae – cervical vertebrae

This is composed by seven vertebrae located in the neck. The neck supports the head and is the link between the head and the torso. It corresponds to the passage of concepts, ideas, wishes and will (all coming from the brain) to practice (action, fulfilment, expression, relation). The neck is a passage. Not yet the action itself. The neck precedes the action and the mental formation of the action.

People who store up anger have chronic tension on their shoulders, neck and arms.

Neck-related problems can occur in the muscles, the bones or in the skin. However, here we are dealing with the bones of the neck. And bones form part of the locomotor system. The common denominator here is undervaluation.

This area is associated to <u>what the person is</u>. The cervical vertebrae show **who I am**.

I have problems in those vertebrae when I feel judged. The conflict I have has to do with unfairness. "I was only loved for what I had or did, not for who I was." For those who work with chakras, the neck, like the collarbone and shoulders, is in the blue chakra area, the chakra that connects to the metaphysical world, the chakra through which the entrance of energy into the body takes place.

One needs to look after the cervical vertebrae with love.

C1 supports the cranium. It is like a ring. C2 is the bony protuberance that goes through the ring of C1. C1 and C2 correspond to the so-called Buddha shape. If they break, we could die. They show what the person thinks of the quality of his being, at the highest level.

Problems in C3-C7 indicate what the person perceives as being the abominable side of his life (the guillotine fell on the C3). This is where most cervical lesions regarding the feeling of injustice take place: "It is not fair! This is abominable! How could they do this to me?"

Between C7 and D1, there is a curvature, which is the first curvature, the first "S" of the spine. This area represents the border between **what I am** and **what I have**.

Undervaluation and intellectual and moral humiliation are stored in the cervical vertebrae. The person was not worth as much as he thought he was, and he was forced to lower his head.

Please see *Vertebrae – discs, Vertebrae – dorsal vertebrae, Vertebrae – lumbar vertebrae, Vertebrae – sacral vertebrae, Vertebrae – terminal vertebrae – coccyx, Lumbago* and/or *Sciatic nerve pain*.

See also *Spine*

Vertebrae – discs

Discs constitute the mobile part of the spine. They have a corrective role in the spine. Discal spinal hernia may be intermittent or permanent. Check in which vertebral disc the hernia is, in order to understand which tension in this person's life the problem is related to. In any case, it can be said that the person's structural basis has been severely shaken by an event in his life and that he lost mobility in the affected part of the column.

Please see *Vertebrae – cervical vertebrae, Vertebrae – dorsal vertebrae, Vertebrae – lumbar vertebrae, Vertebrae – sacral vertebrae, Vertebrae – terminal vertebrae – coccyx, Lumbago* and/or *Sciatic nerve pain*.

See also *Spine*

Vertebrae – dorsal vertebrae

They are twelve in total and are located immediately after the cervical vertebrae. They go from the D1 to the D12 and indicate the relationship I maintain between **what I have** and **what I attain**.

They are linked to the organs of rhythm: Heart, lungs, diaphragm and duodenum. They are vertebrae that start at the first "S" of the spine.

In this case, we are talking, once more, of bones. Bones are part of the locomotor system, and the common denominator is undervaluation.

When a person has problems in these vertebrae, this means he is attached to something or someone. Attachment is a non-conscious undervaluation. The person defines himself by what he has and not by whom he is.

I have, but I definitely need to let go. I give and I receive. This is about giving to and receiving from Earth. This is a difficult thing to do. Dorsal vertebrae become stiff rapidly, when the person has a problem with this giving-receiving duality.

In the army, where soldiers are required to have a vertical, extremely upright posture, the paradox between inner and outer posture is almost permanent. The reason is that, at the end of the day, they are taught to be stiff and simultaneously bend down, to take orders without questioning them, in a submissive manner. It is easy to understand the confusing feeling inside their heads and bodies... Cultivating just the outer firmness is self-deceiving, because the body will end up showing the person, through symptoms, the parts where he is not that righteous.

What we should cultivate is inner firmness. The spine will show it naturally.

Sick people adopt postures they would never take up on a volunteer basis. The excessive outward bending of the curvature in the dorsal area is called **kyphosis**. It forms a small hump and the person ends up with curved shoulders. Kyphosis reveals that the person feels the weight of the world upon his shoulders. Life is not easy for him. And then he bends down, instead of realizing that he is taking upon himself what was not meant for him to carry. This often occurs to excessively mentally oriented people who would like to change their own world at any cost, but cannot do it.

On the contrary, the person who goes about with a very upright head often reveals haughtiness, pride, inaccessibility and intransigence, and not so much balance. A **too stiff spine** that takes a bamboo shape (**Bechterew's disease**) denotes a non-conscious huge ego and a tremendous lack of flexibility that the person will not acknowledge. The ego is represented by what the person has and not by what the person really is. With time, the spine solidifies from top down and the head leans forward. The sinuosity (the *S*) disappears or gets inverted. This is the body showing the person what he never wanted to see, and that he defined himself rather more by what he had than by what he was.

People who feel the weight of the Earth, the density of the earth and that the world is falling upon them, have half-hearted hump and bulges. The hunchback is a prostrated person, who has lost his ideal in life but who will not give up his stubborn ideas. The **hump** exposes a problem that is similar to that of the excessively stiff spine. This is un-assumed humbleness forced upon the person by his own body.

The size of the dorsal vertebrae indicates the person's generosity.

Animals cannot move their dorsal vertebrae, only humans can.

Please see *Vertebrae – cervical vertebrae, Vertebrae – discs, Vertebrae – lumbar vertebrae, Vertebrae – sacral vertebrae, Vertebrae – terminal vertebrae – coccyx, Lumbago* and/or *Sciatic nerve pain.*

See also *Spine*

Vertebrae – lumbar vertebrae

This is a group of five vertebrae. They are the extension of the dorsal vertebrae and go from the L1 to the L5. They indicate the relationship I have with **what I do**. They are directly linked to root-related problems *i.e.*, home, relationships, family, partner, affections, work and money, the place where I live, material issues, the home, space and mobility.

This takes us back to the bones. And bones form part of the locomotor system. The common denominator here is undervaluation. This is the undervaluation that the person feels, in the form of frustration, regarding everything that affects his roots. This is where the so-called pains on the back are. They are linked to our connection with the partner and what we do with matter.

This is where our individual evolution and our relation with the world are kept. L1 shows our capacity for individualization. The person begins to get autonomous. He is capable of individual action. The weight of the family, clan, beliefs and society is all here. This is the acknowledgement of responsibility. "I am the anchor of a clan. Others depend on me. Will I be able to withstand it?"

L4 and L5 are affected when the person feels he is outside the family or the clan's norms and feels worried about it.

The prominent inward curvature of a portion of the lumbar spine is called **lordosis**. This is when people have prominent abdomens. It indicates they have problems at home.

Please see *Vertebrae – cervical vertebrae, Vertebrae – discs, Vertebrae – dorsal vertebrae, Vertebrae – sacral vertebrae, Vertebrae – terminal vertebrae – coccyx, Lumbago* and/or *Sciatic nerve pain.*

See also *Spine*

Vertebrae – sacral vertebrae

The sacrum is formed by five vertebrae that are fused in the direct extension of the lumbar vertebrae. It articulates with the hipbones, the iliac bones and, together, they form the pelvis. This is called the **sacrum-iliac area**. Like in the cervical vertebrae, this area bears witness to **who I am**.

This is the area that shows what the person sees as being fair or unfair. The tensions are very similar to those felt in the **cervical vertebrae**, the difference being that, in this case, they are limited to the family side and to the feeling of belonging to a clan.

We are dealing with the bones, which form part of the locomotor system. The common denominator here is undervaluation. Whenever I feel problems in those vertebrae, this is when I feel judged in my own home.

The sacral vertebrae are directly connected to the *yin* axis of the person, to the feminine axis, the axis of femininity, symbolised by the Mother.

The person's verticality starts here. This is where one goes from being quadruped to biped and this is where our relationship with autonomy and our capacity for internal and external mobility are located. "I agree to have my own life project".

Problems in the sacral vertebrae indicate the person has a feeling of unfairness regarding the way his family and clan criticize the way he leads his life.

Please see *Vertebrae – cervical vertebrae*, *Vertebrae – discs*, *Vertebrae – dorsal vertebrae*, *Vertebrae – lumbar vertebrae*, *Vertebrae – terminal vertebrae – coccyx*, *Lumbago* and/or *Sciatic nerve pain*.

See also *Spine*

Vertebrae – terminal vertebrae – coccyx

This is a group of fused vertebrae, normally four, and the extension of the sacral vertebrae. It is the "tail" of the human body, the appendage that no longer exists. Coccyx-related problems are normally linked to the person's *yin*

axis, the feminine axis, the femininity axis, symbolized by the Mother.

We are dealing with the bones of the back. And bones form part of the locomotor system. The common denominator here, like in the case of other vertebrae, is undervaluation. The person feels affected and loses his self-esteem. Problems in the coccyx represent a fear of imposed sexuality, fear of the imposition of an excessively feminine behaviour or even compulsory submission (in the animal world, this is the case of the non-dominating wolf with his tail down, denoting submission).

It is important to understand what is going on in the relationship this person has with his partner, with his model of Mother or with her female model. If the coccyx problem is affecting a man, he is no doubt having a relationship problem with the person (woman or man) he is living with and feeling a huge tension about it. If the coccyx problem is affecting a woman, she will need to understand why she is so afraid of her husband or any other man (or someone who plays the role of a man), and look out for the woman pattern in her clan.

Please see *Vertebrae – cervical vertebrae*, *Vertebrae – discs*, *Vertebrae – dorsal vertebrae*, *Vertebrae – lumbar vertebrae*, *Vertebrae – sacral vertebrae*, *Lumbago* and/or *Sciatic nerve pain*.

See also *Spine*

Vertigo

Vertigo happens when the person is high up somewhere, but still connected to the earth. When travelling on a plane, the person does not suffer from vertigo. The person who has vertigo cannot look down. Many people have vertigo when they are up on a skyscraper, and this is quite normal. In our case, we are referring to the problem experienced by people who have vertigo when they are two meters above ground. The feelings associated to vertigo are the feelings of rotation and loss of balance.

What in fact is going on is that the person is losing his roots, despite being tied down to the ground. The person is unsure about things in his life, about his roots, in other words, about matters related to his home, work, place where he lives or his biological Mother. People who have kidneys conditions tend to lose their balance more and are prone to suffering from vertigo.

Vice

See *Addiction*

Vision

See *Eyes*

Vitiligo

Vitiligo is a condition caused by loss of pigment in the skin in several parts of the body. The issue here is tension linked to a separation that was actually experienced.

This is a conflict of separation and uncleanness. Something happened that made this person feel the need to wash, whiten. "It is necessary to wash!" And the skin becomes whiter.

For instance, when the person wishes to wash off what others are saying, he has vitiligo around his mouth. When the person needs to clean up appearances, he has vitiligo on his face. When he needs to wash off what happened with the Father, he develops vitiligo on his arms and/or torso. When he needs to wash off what someone (the Father?, the Mother?) did, like taking what did not belong to them, he develops vitiligo on the hands. When the person needs to wash off what happened with his Mother (perhaps in her relationship with the Father?), he develops vitiligo on the legs and feet.

Vitiligo can show up on the legs, hands, any part of the body. Whitening indicates a desire for purification, and, for this reason, it takes melanin away. And, indeed, the body shows a white skin in the part of the body with vitiligo.

This may also be related to issues connected with money laundering (washing out).

The relationship with the sun is associated to the relationship with the Father. Some of these people are never on good terms with the Father.

If this condition happens to a newly born, it is important to understand what happened during conception and pregnancy between the Mother and the Father and also what is happening with this family's mental pattern (see *Family*).

Also see *Babies*

Vocal cords

See *Larynx (larynx, aphonia, hoarseness)*

Vomit and nausea

This phenomenon is typical of people whose minds are really busy and then they cannot digest neither thoughts nor their lives. They have complicated their own lives by using their minds so much.

It is difficult to digest. It is as if they had a stone inside their stomachs.

This is the expression of confusion, denial and uncertainty (very common in pregnancy). Anxious people feel nausea more often. "Just to think of it makes me sick", "It made me lose my appetite", "It turned my stomach" are well-known sentences that translate the difficulty in digesting what one is thinking about.

This is what nausea is. It represents the sick feeling about something that is going on in a person's life. Someone or something is making this person sick.

Vomit is an even more categorical expression of revolt and defense. Vomiting simply means refusal to accept. "I am not digesting this." It sometimes happens during pregnancy.

In any case, both nausea and vomit are forms of letting go of control. Therefore, after vomiting, the person feels relieved.

In the case of some migraines, vomiting gets rid of the migraine. It relaxes the person and brings him intense relief.

Wart

A wart (verruca) is a hardening on a particular spot of the body. This is a symptom of frustration and a feeling of undervaluation. It is associated to the skin and to the nervous system.

The person feels undervalued and frustrated because he needs to please others and also because he needs to hold on to the image he has of himself. For this reason, he is a person who compares himself to others and who becomes very competitive. This person lacks self-esteem and allows himself to be influenced by others in issues related to his image.

The child who looks for perfection to keep others satisfied and to run away from the negative assessment he fears others will make of him, is actually undervaluing himself. Accordingly, he is setting the ground for the appearance of a wart. This is a non-conscious phenomenon. It is important to talk to the child and make him verbalize his undervaluation, namely by having him talking to the third person involved.

It is important that the person with a wart is helped, as he is not aware of his undervaluation tension, nor of his inability to communicate. He will probably say that he did not feel anything important.

At school, the teacher criticizes a pupil's writing. The child concludes that his **fingers** write badly. "I am aware that my fingers cannot write properly." Consequently, the child develops a wart on his fingers.

When warts show up on the **back**

of the hand, the person believes he is not sufficiently good at what he does. His undervaluation is perceptible to all. Everybody can see a verruca on the back of his hand. The body reveals his frustration through his guilt and belief in ugliness (severe undervaluation).

When warts show up on the **palm of the hand**, this happens only to those who work with their hands; either manual workers or those involved in sports activities that require use of the hands. It indicates slight undervaluation.

When they show up on the **soles of feet**, it happens only to manual workers or sports persons. This indicates slight undervaluation, particularly connected to gesture. I do not feel good enough regarding what I see others do. My lack of performance keeps me away from the group. This is a typical example of a running competition, in which the runner only sees the soles of other people's feet, precisely because he is running after them.

Apart from anything else, warts are ugly. In other words: "I do not feel I am good enough regarding what I should be and, on top of all, this is ugly.

This is yet another example of undervaluation provoked by a comparing attitude and a desire to have an image that everybody likes and approves.

Look for any parts of the body where warts may have appeared.

Weight

Here we talk about gaining or losing weight.

See *Obesity, Slimness, Bulimia* and *Anorexia*

Windpipe

See *Trachea*

Womb

The womb (uterus) is an organ that expresses the woman's femininity as a Mother. The womb is the protective shelter of the baby. Womb-related problems indicate that the feminine side of the woman, with regard to her Mother side, is being punished. Problems in the **neck of the womb**, also called cervical canal of uterus or cervix are not related to the same tensions at conscience level and are dealt with separately (see *Cervix (neck of the womb – cervical canal of the uterus)*)

In this case, the Mother's tension is the potential loss of a child. Potential loss! In other words, the feeling of loss is the issue here, not the actual loss. The feeling of actual loss affects the ovary (see ovaries) not the womb.

We shall look at three womb-related problems: **fibromas**, thickening of the **endometrium** and **cancer**. In any case, the feeling of potential loss of the child remains, but there are subtleties. However, it is always a Mother's issue, not a woman's issue.

A **fibroma** (benign tumour) is a well-known condition that affects muscular and fibrous tissues in the womb, such as in the case of cancer in this area, to which we shall refer later. The tension is connected to undervaluation. It starts with a hole in the muscles of the womb, due to undervaluation, and it only becomes a fibroma after it cicatrizes.

This could occur when the person feels a huge tension associated to incapacity to have children. In this case, the frustration and undervaluation may be huge.

The woman who feels she has lost the person who was going to be the father of her future kids may also develop fibromas.

It may also occur when the woman who had been told she was unable to conceive becomes pregnant for the first time. "I was told I was unable to have children, but I can, after all. I must take good care of this child who is on the way." The person literally holds on to the child she finally managed to conceive and tries to give him as much space as possible. The body develops a hole (to increase the available space), which will turn into a fibroma following cicatrisation.

It also occurs quite frequently when the woman gets pregnant again after miscarriage or abortion. When the person had the miscarriage or the abortion, she was frustrated she was not having that baby she wanted, that had already been conceived and disappeared. When she becomes pregnant again, she holds on to him and gives him as much space as possible. The body develops a hole and the fibroma appears.

Basically, there is a simple explanation. The Mother felt a feeling of undervaluation and her body is trying to sort out the tension by creating more room for the child (by creating a hole and excavating the muscle).

Cancer in the muscle of the womb, which is much more rare than cervical cancer or cancer of the endometrium, must be analyzed, from the perspective of the tension experienced, as a malignant fibroma. In other words, it shows the same tension as a fibroma, but in a much more intense way that is never verbalized.

The **endometrium** is the internal mucosal membrane of the womb.

When the woman is ovulating, the mucosal membrane swells in order to host the egg that is ready to be fecundated. After ovulation, if the egg is not fecundated, the thickening of the wall of the womb goes back to its normal size in the form of haemorrhage (menstruation). The **thickening of the endometrium** in a Mother shows that she feels that her daughter, son, daughter or son in law, or someone she feels as her own child, has moved away. That person has not disappeared but went away, and the mother has major communication problems with that person. She feels a potential loss of that person. She is going through a major frustration of not being able to get close to that son or daughter, whether of her own flesh or by affinity. The fact that the endometrium does not go back to its original size indicates that the person would like, in a non-conscious manner, to be pregnant again, to create a new person. This happens despite the fact that her son or daughter never actually disappeared. This woman needs help to let her ego break free, to let go of the warrior side that is destroying her femininity. She is a very possessive woman who feels deeply hurt.

Endometrial cancer and cervical cancer (see *Cervix (neck of the womb – cervical canal of the uterus)*) are the most common. Endometrial cancer indicates the tension was very big and that it involved ignominy in a family drama, whether with a true son or daughter or someone the person felt as a son or daughter, and that the tension was not verbalized. The drama may have been related to the sexuality of that true or virtual son or daughter. That person may have had a dishonorable sexual problem. For instance, she could have been raped. In this case, the tension is: "How shameful! This is not something one does!" The "not something one does!" is very important here. It is an inner cry (not verbalized) that expresses the feeling of ignominy. If the person does not verbalize and brings what she felt out in the open, and, instead, keeps it to herself, the tension she feels projects itself in the womb, the protecting sanctuary of babies, like a cancer.

This ignominy tension in a family drama may also relate to the rape, in a figurative sense, of that son or daughter. For example, the person may have felt that the freedom that son or daughter had to be what he or she wants to be was castrated. The fact that the Mother was unable to avoid it happening and had to watch as an impotent witness causes enormous tension in her.

It is important to help the person verbalize the tension she felt. When she starts doing it and talks about her pain to someone, she will normally haemorrhage.

For problems related to the neck of the womb, see *Cervix (neck of the womb – cervical canal of the uterus)*.

Worms

Worms are parasites that live in a person's bowel but which may end up infesting the whole body. The person who has worms feels unprotected regarding others around him whom he believes are infesting him. The person allows himself to be invaded by other people's attitudes that are not good for him. And these are people who are close to him. The fact that the worm finds a host in the bowel denotes lack of discernment in the person's life and unwillingness to look at hidden information that he does not want to face up to. This is a person who chooses to seal up his sub-world, his hidden side. In short, this is a person who does not face up to his own life.

See *Bowel – large bowel*

Wounds

See *Skin*

Wrist

This is the joint with more mobility in the entire body. The wrists allow the connection between the forearm (that means the capacity to start and complete something that has already been accepted following the difficulty in choosing how to act) and the hand (that represents understanding, gentleness, capacity to hold on to what one has achieved, give and receive tenderness).

Therefore, the wrist is the joint that allows action to be transmitted to the hand. The wrist supports the gesture and decides on the fine-tuning of that gesture before the decision to carry out the action as well as possible is made, and thus obtain the best result for the person.

Thus, the wrist is a joint that allows the hands' dexterity to show with increased tuning and better support. As in the case of other joints, the keywords are inflexibility and undervaluation. If the support for the gesture is not good, the person feels undervalued. This may happen if the person hears his gesture is being criticized, which makes him feel humiliated and undervalued. If the person is inflexible regarding his own person and the quality of the support he managed to fine-tune for the gesture, be it in its delicate dexterity, be it in a sport, be it in the delicate gesture he needs to make to someone, then he may develop a problem in his wrist.

Problems in the wrist may affect the bones, tendons or the skin. Problems in the skin denote a tension associated to separation or difficulty communicating with someone. Problems in the bones indicate strong undervaluation: "I am no good at this. I am not worth much at this." Problems in the tendons also reveal undervaluation and inflexibility. At the onset, although it may not always be like this, when we refer to the *yin/yang* polarity of the joints of the locomotor system, the right side is *yang* (masculine) and the left side is *yin* (feminine). This applies to everyone, both left and right-handed people. In any case, we are in the presence of a tension that is associated to undervaluation and inflexibility, independently of the side of the body that is affected.

Problems in the *yang* wrist denote problems with a man (or lack of his own flexibility as a man, in case the person is a man). Problems in the *yin* wrist denote problems with a woman (or lack of her own flexibility as a woman, in case the person is a woman).

CATEGORY INDEX

Addictions

Addiction 26
Alcoholism 30
Dependence 106
Drugs 110
Sex – addiction 266
Smoking 275
Tabagism 285
Vice 309

Breathing system

Adenoids 27
Alveoli 32
Aphonia 40
Apnea 40
Asphyxiation 46
Asthma – bronchial asthma 48
Breathing system 83
Bronchi 84
Bronchopneumonia 85
Cough 103
Emphysema 116
Hoarseness 172
Hyperventilation 175
Larynx (larynx, aphonia, hoarseness) 194
Lung plague 206
Lungs 206
Nose 229
Pharynx 246
Pleura 250
Pleurisy 250
Pneumonia 251
Pneumothorax 251
Pulmonary embolism 257
Smoking 275
Snoring 275
Sore throat 276
Sudden death 283
Tabagism 285

Throat 292
Throat angina 292
Tonsils 299
Trachea 300
Tuberculosis 301
Vegetations 303
Vocal cords 310
Windpipe 311

Circulatory system

AIDS 29
Anaemia 35
Aneurysm 35
Arrhythmias 43
Arterial tension 43
Arteries 43
Arteriosclerosis 43
Auricles 49
Blood 55
Blood pressure 55
Blood pressure – high 55
Blood pressure – low 56
Bone marrow 58
Brain embolism 76
Brain stroke 77
Chest angina 93
Cholesterol – high cholesterol levels 96
Cholesterol – low cholesterol levels 97
Circulatory system 98
Circulatory system – arterial system 98
Circulatory system – venal system 99
Coronaries 102
Coronary thrombosis 103
Gangrene 149
Haematomas 154
Haemophilia 154
Haemorrhages – capillary or vascular 155
Haemorrhoids 155
Heart 159
Heart – angina 161

Heart – arrhythmias 162
Heart attack 167
Heart – communication between auriculae....165
Heart – heart attack......................................165
Hematuria 168
Henoch-Schonlein Purpura disease..............168
Hypertension 174
Hypotension 175
Ischaemia 181
Ischæmia 181
Ischemia..181
Leukaemia 197
Nose..229
Palpitations 234
Pancarditis...235
Pericarditis..244
Phlebitis 247
Pulmonary embolism 257
Red spots...259
Thrombophlebitis...292
Thrombosis 292
Varicose veins 303
Veins 304
Venous system 304

Digestive system

Aerogastria 27
Aerophagia 28
Amebiasis 33
Amebic dysentery (amebiasis).........................33
Anal fistula 35
Anorexia...39
Anus...39
Aphtas..40
Appendix...41
Appetite 41
Bacillary dysentery 51
Bad breath 51
Bile...53
Bilirubin...53
Bowel – large bowel..59
Bowel – large bowel – amoebic dysentery........59
Bowel – large bowel – anus..............................59

Bowel – large bowel – ascending colon 60
Bowel – large bowel – bacillary dysentery........61
Bowel – large bowel – colic 61
Bowel – large bowel – colon 61
Bowel – large bowel – Crohn's disease 62
Bowel – large bowel – descending colon...........63
Bowel – large bowel – descending colon –
    sigmoid 63
Bowel – large bowel – lower rectum
    (incontinence)...64
Bowel – large bowel – transverse colon 65
Bowel – large bowel – ulcerative colitis............65
Bowel – large bowel – upper rectum................65
Bowel – small bowel – Crohn's disease.............66
Bowel – small bowel (diarrhoea and cancer) 67
Bowel – small bowel – duodenum...................67
Bulimia 85
Burping..87
Candidiasis (thrush) 90
Caries...90
Colic 101
Colon..101
Constipation 102
Crohn's disease 104
Diabetes 107
Diarrhoea..107
Difficult digestions 107
Digestive system 107
Diverticulosis 109
Duodenum..112
Dyspepsia..112
Enamel..117
Flatulence..143
Food poisoning 144
Gallbladder 147
Gallbladder – gallbladder stones 148
Gallbladder – hepatitis 148
Gallstones..149
Gas..150
Gastroduodenal ulcer 150
Gastroenteritis...150
Goitre..152
Gums 154
Haemorrhoids..155
Heartburn 167

Hepatitis 169
Hyperglycaemia.....................................174
Hypoglycaemia.......................................175
Incontinence 177
Indigestion 179
Inner bites...180
Intestines..181
Jaundice 183
Jaws...183
Lazy bowels 195
Lips..200
Liver...200
Liver – cancer and liver disease 202
Liver – cirrhosis.....................................202
Liver – hepatitis.....................................202
Liver – jaundice......................................204
Lower rectum 205
Milk intolerance 215
Mouth..216
Mouth sores (thrush).............................217
Mumps...218
Nausea and vomiting..............................226
Oesophagus...232
Palate 234
Pancreas – exocrine gland (cancer of the
    pancreas and pancreatitis) 238
Pancreatitis..239
Periodontitis..245
Peritonitis..245
Pharynx..246
Poisoning 251
Pyorrhea (periodontitis) 258
Roof of the mouth..................................263
Salivary glands...263
Sickness..270
Sigmoid..270
Sore throat 276
Stomach 281
Taenia 286
Tapeworm 286
Taste..286
Teeth...286
Teeth – buck teeth (rodent)...................287
Teeth – canine (the 4) 287
Teeth – carics 287

Teeth – front teeth pushed back (carnivore)...288
Teeth – last left upper and lower molar..........288
Teeth – last right upper and lower molar 288
Teeth – left lower molar teeth 289
Teeth – left lower premolar teeth 289
Teeth – left side incisive teeth (2 up and
    2 down) 289
Teeth – left upper molar teeth 289
Teeth – left upper premolar teeth 289
Teeth – right lower molar teeth 290
Teeth – right lower premolar teeth 290
Teeth – right side incisive teeth (2 up and
    2 down) 290
Teeth – right upper molar teeth 290
Teeth – right upper premolar teeth 290
Teeth – space between molars..........................290
Teeth – straight and aligned front teeth 290
Threadworms 292
Throat 292
Thrush...293
Tongue 299
Tonsils 299
Ulcerative colitis..301
Upper rectum 301
Vomit and nausea 310
Worms 313

Epidemics

AIDS...29
Cholera...96
Epidemics..120
Outbreaks 233
Plague 250

Five senses

Hearing

Buzzing noise 87
Deafness..106
Ears..112
Eustachian Tube 121

Hearing 159
Otitis 233
Ringing noise 263
Tinnitus 296

Smell

Nose 229
Smell 275

Taste

Taste 286

Touch

Touch 300

Vision

Aging eyes 29
Astigmatism 49
Blepharitis 55
Blindness 55
Cataracts 90
Colour blindness (Daltonism) 101
Conjunctivitis 102
Convergent strabismus 102
Daltonism (colour blindness) 105
Divergent strabismus 109
Dyslexia 112
Eye infection 121
Eyes 121
Eyes – astigmatism 121
Eyes - blepharitis 122
Eyes – blindness 122
Eyes – cataracts 122
Eyes – conjunctivitis 123
Eyes – convergent strabismus 123
Eyes – Daltonism – colour-blindness ...123
Eyes – divergent strabismus 124
Eyes – dry eye 124
Eyes – dyslexia 124
Eyes – eye spots 124
Eyes – farsightedness 124
Eyes – glaucoma 125
Eyes – nearsightedness 126
Eyes – nystagmus 128

Eyes – opacity in the middle of the eye 128
Eye spots 121
Eyes – presbyopia 128
Eyes – retinal detachment 129
Eyes – retinitis pigmentosa 129
Eyes – stains in the eyes 130
Eyes – strabismus 130
Eyes – sty 130
Glaucoma 152
Hyperopia (far-sightedness) 174
Myopia 224
Nystagmus 230
Presbytis 255
Presbytism 255
Retinal detachment 260
Retinitis pigmentosa 260
Spots in the eyes 279
Strabismus 282
Sty 283
Vision 309

Glands

Addison's disease 27
Adenoma 27
Adrenal glands 27
Conn's disease 102
Cushing's disease 105
Endocrine system 117
Epiphysis 121
Glands 151
Goitre 152
Gonads 152
Growth (growth disorders) 153
Hyperthyroidism 174
Hypophysis 175
Hypothyroidism 175
Mumps 218
Ovaries 233
Pancreas 235
Pancreas – endocrine gland (diabetes) 236
Pancreas – endocrine gland (hyperglycaemia) ...238
Pancreas – endocrine gland (hypoglycaemia) .238

Pancreas – exocrine gland (cancer of the
   pancreas and pancreatitis) 238
Parathyroid glands 241
Pineal body 248
Pineal gland 248
Pinealoma 248
Pituitary gland 249
Prostate 255
Rickets 262
Salivary glands 263
Spleen 278
Suprarenal glands 283
Testicles 291
Thymus 293
Thyroid 294

Immune system

Allergies 31
Autoimmune diseases 50
Hay Fever 158
Immune system 175
Immunity 177
Infections 179
Kissing disease 193
Leucopoenia 197
Leukaemia 197
Lupus – discoid lupus erythematosus 208
Lupus – systemic lupus erythematosus 208
Mononucleosis 216
Self-immunity 266
Septicaemia 266
Spleen 278
Thymus 293

Isolated symptoms

ADD and ADHD 26
Animal bites 37
Anxiety 40
Apathy 40
Asthenia 46
Bad breath 51

Balance   lack of balance 52
Bipolarity 53
Cephaleas 91
Colds 100
Coma 101
Dizziness 110
Ears 112
Fainting 130
Fat 134
Fatigue 134
Fever 138
Fibromyalgia (chronic fatigue syndrome) 138
Flu 144
Fungal infections 146
Glandular fever 152
Haematomas 154
Headache 158
Hyperactivity 173
Infections 179
Inflammation 180
Influenza (flu) 180
Insect bites 180
Liquid retention 200
Malaria 210
Migraine 214
Nanism 225
Narcolepsy 226
Nervous tics 228
Nightmare 229
Oedemas 232
Paludism 235
Parasites 241
Rhinitis 260
Ringing noise 263
Sinusitis 270
Small stature syndrome 274
Snoring 275
Stammering 279
Suicide 283
Tiredness 296
Tremors 300
Vertigo 308

Locomotor system

Acute anterior poliomyelitis (child paralysis) ...25

Acute articular rheumatism (children) 26

ALS...32

Amputation...33

Amyotrophic Lateral Sclerosis (ALS) 34

Ankles 37

Ankylosing spondylitis 38

Aponeuroses...41

Arms (as upper limbs) 42

Arm (shoulder to elbow) 41

Arthritis..45

Arthrosis...45

Back 51

Back pain 51

Bechterew's disease 52

Bells's paralysis...52

Bone 57

Bone fracture...58

Bone marrow..58

Bone structure...59

Brain paralysis 77

Bunions..86

Bursitis...87

Buttocks...87

Cervical...91

Charcot's disease...92

Child paralysis..96

Chin...96

Chronic epicondylitis 97

Chronic evolving polyarthritis.......................98

Chronic polyarticular rheumatism..................98

Clavicle (collar bone).......................................99

Claw feet..100

Coccyx 100

Collar bone 101

Coxarthrosis..103

Cramps 103

Cranial trauma 104

Cranium..104

Cubit bone 105

Discal hernia 109

Dorsal 110

Duchenne's disease 112

Elbow..115

Feet 135

Feet – athlete's foot...135

Feet – flatfeet..136

Feet – pes cavus (hollow claw foot)..............136

Femoral head...136

Femur 137

Fibula...140

Fingers 141

Fingers – bones and muscles.........................141

Fingers – joints (arthrosis) 142

Forearm...145

Friedreich's disease..146

General paralysis 151

Hand..156

Heels 168

Hernia..169

Hips 170

Humerus 172

Hump 172

Iliac bone 175

Intervertebral discs 181

Jaws 183

Joints...183

Kahler's disease..184

Kink 192

Knee...193

Kyphosis...194

Legs as lower limbs 196

Legs (knee to foot) 195

Ligaments...199

Locomotor system...204

Lordosis...205

Lou Gehrig's disease 205

Lumbago 205

Lumbar 206

Mastoiditis 211

Meniscus 212

Multiple myeloma...217

Multiple sclerosis...217

Muscle contraction 218

Muscles 218

Muscular distension 221

Muscular dystrophy...222

Myelitis 222

Myeloma 223
Myopathy..223
Nape 226
Neck 226
Nose...229
Osteomyelitis 232
Osteoporosis...233
Paralysing diseases 240
Paralysis...240
Parkinson's disease 241
Partial paralysis...242
Pelvis 243
Periosteum 245
Peroneum 246
Poliomyelitis..251
Polyarthritis...252
Posture 253
Pubic bone 257
Radius 258
Rheumatism 260
Rheumatoid polyarthritis 260
Ribs...261
Sacrum 263
Sacrum-iliac 263
Schüller's disease...264
Sciatic nerve pain 264
Scoliosis 265
Shin bone..267
Shoulder..268
Shoulder blade 270
Skeletal system 271
Skull..274
Spasms 276
Spina bifida 276
Spinal chord (spinal medulla) 276
Spinal marrow 277
Spinal medulla...277
Spine...277
Sprains 279
Sternum 280
Stiff neck 281
Synovial fluid 285
Tendon..290
Thigh 291
Tibia 295

Toes...296
Toes – bones and muscles..............................296
Toes – joints 297
Torticollis...300
Vertebrae...304
Vertebrae – cervical vertebrae 304
Vertebrae – discs...305
Vertebrae – dorsal vertebrae..........................305
Vertebrae – lumbar vertebrae 307
Vertebrae – sacral vertebrae...........................307
Vertebrae – terminal vertebrae – coccyx........308
Wrist 313

Lymphatic system

Adenitis..27
Adenopatia..27
Hodgkin's disease..172
Lymph...209
Lymphatic system..209
Lymphoma 210
Myeloma 223
Spleen 278
Swollen glands...285
Thymus 293

Nervous system

Acute anterior poliomyelitis (child paralysis) ...25
ALS...32
Alzheimer's disease..32
Amnesia 33
Amyotrophic Lateral Sclerosis (ALS) 34
Aphasia 40
Autonomic nervous system.............................50
Bells's paralysis..52
Body lateralization...57
Brain 69
Brain – blocked brain 71
Brain – brain disorders 71
Brain – double brain 71
Brain embolism...76
Brain paralysis 77

Brain – tumour 75

Brain tumour 78

Central nervous system....................................90

Cerebral aneurysm 91

Cerebral haemorrhage 91

Charcot's disease...92

Child paralysis...96

Convulsions 102

Dementia 106

Depression 106

Encephalitis...117

Encephalomyelitis 117

Epilepsy..120

Friedreich's disease 146

General paralysis 151

Hydrocephaly..172

Insanity...180

Insomnia 180

Isolation 181

Lou Gehrig's disease 205

Madness 210

Meninges...211

Meningioma...211

Meningitis...211

Multiple sclerosis..217

Myalgic encephalomyelitis (chronic fatigue

   syndrome)...222

Myelitis 222

Nerves 227

Nervous breakdown 227

Nervous system 227

Neuralgia...229

Nystagmus 230

Paralysing diseases 240

Paralysis..240

Parasympathetic nervous system 241

Parkinson's disease 241

Partial paralysis...242

Polarity of the body.......................................251

Poliomyelitis..251

Senility..266

Spinal chord (spinal medulla) 276

Spinal marrow 277

Spinal medulla...277

Suicide 283

Sympathetic nervous system 285

Reproductive system

Abortion 23

Amenorrhea 33

Anorgasmia 39

Babies..50

Birth 53

Breastfeeding..78

Breasts 79

Breasts – cancer in the milk ducts....................79

Breasts – carcinoma (nipple cancer)..................80

Breasts – mastitis...82

Breasts – melanoma (skin cancer) 82

Breasts – neurofibromatosis 82

Candidiasis (thrush) 90

Cervical canal of the uterus 91

Cervix (neck of the womb – cervical canal

   of the uterus) 91

Child delivery...93

Dysmenorrhoea...112

Epidural 120

Erection – erectile dysfunction 121

Fallopian Tube...131

Frigidity 146

Glans (head of the penis)................................152

Gonads..152

Gonorrhoea...152

Herpes...169

Impotence 177

Infertility...179

Leucorrhoea 197

Lips...200

Menopause...212

Menstruation 213

Milk intolerance...215

Miscarriage..216

Newly-born..229

Ovaries..233

Penis..243

Precocious ejaculation 253

Pregnancy – ectopic pregnancy......................253

Pregnancy – imaginary pregnancy 253

Pregnancy – problems 254
Premature ejaculation 254
Priapism 255
Reproductive system......................................259
Sex – addiction..266
Sterility..280
Syphilis 285
Testicles 291
Uterus 302
Vagina 302
Venereal diseases...304
Womb 311

Silhouette

Anorexia...39
Bulimia 85
Cellulite 90
Lipoma...200
Obesity...230
Silhouette – image conflicts...........................270
Slimness 274
Weight 311

Skin

Abrasions, bruises..23
Abscess 23
Acne..24
Boils..57
Bruises (ecchymoses) 85
Burns 86
Chickenpox...93
Chilblains..93
Dark rings under the eyes..............................105
Dermis 107
Dry skin in the face 112
Eczema...114
Epidermis...120
Finger and toe calluses 140
Fingers – warts 143
Fungal infections 146
Fungi..146

Haematomas 154
Hard scar...158
Herpes..169
Hives..172
Itchiness 183
Itching rash 183
Leprosy...197
Lupus – discoid lupus erythematosus 208
Lupus – systemic lupus erythematosus 208
Measles...211
Mycosis 222
Mycosis fungoides 222
Neurofibromatosis..229
Perspiration 246
Pimples 247
Psoriasis..256
Rash 258
Red spots..259
Rubella..263
Scabies 264
Scarlet Fever 264
Scleroderma (systemic sclerosis)....................265
Seborrhoea 265
Shingles..267
Skin..271
Skin – dermis 271
Skin – epidermis...272
Skin infections..273
Skin tuberculosis 273
Smallpox (variola) 275
Smelly feet..275
Stretch marks 282
Sweat..284
Swelling..284
Tinea 295
Urticaria...302
Variola..303
Verruca...304
Vitiligo..309
Wart..310
Wounds...313

Skin excretions

Baldness 52
Body hair 56
Dandruff..105
Hair 155
Lice 199
Nail biting..225
Nails..225
Patchy hair loss..243

Urinary system

Addison's disease..27
Adrenal glands..27
Albumin..30
Balance – lack of balance 52
Berger's disease 53
Bladder..53
Bright's disease 84
Coli bacillus 101
Cystitis..105
Dark rings under the eyes..............................105
Enuresis..119
Glomerulus – glomerulonephritis..................152
Gout 153
Hematuria..168
Incontinence 177
Kidneys..185
Kidneys – cancer and cysts 186
Kidneys – renal insufficiency 187
Kidney stones..184
Liquid retention 200
Nephritis..227
Oedemas 232
Renal insufficiency 259
Suprarenal glands 283
Uraemia 301
Uretheritis..301
Urethritis..301
Urinary system 301
Urinary tract infections 302

Useful concepts

Accidents..24
Anger..36
Anxiety..40
Authority..49
Body lateralization..57
Brain..69
Brain – left-handed men................................72
Brain – left-handed women 73
Brain – right-handed men 74
Brain – right-handed women..........................75
Cancer..87
Cleanliness – cleanliness freaks 100
Cysts..105
Disease 109
Dreams..110
Elderly people 116
Emotional shock 116
Face..130
Family 131
Fear..134
Glands..151
Guilt 154
Left-handed and right-handed people..........195
Nervous system 227
Old people 232
Panic..239
Polarity of the body......................................251
Preoccupation 255
Punctuality..257
Right-handed and left-handed people..........263
Slackness 274
Suicide 283
Tumours..301

ALPHABETICAL INDEX

Abortion 23

Abrasions, bruises 23

Abscess 23

Accidents 24

Acne 24

Acute anterior poliomyelitis (child paralysis) ...25

Acute articular rheumatism (children) 26

ADD and ADHD 26

Addiction 26

Addison's disease 27

Adenitis 27

Adenoids 27

Adenoma 27

Adenopatia 27

Adrenal glands 27

Aerogastria 27

Aerophagia 28

Aging eyes 29

AIDS 29

Albumin 30

Alcoholism 30

Allergies 31

ALS 32

Alveoli 32

Alzheimer's disease 32

Amebiasis 33

Amebic dysentery (amebiasis) 33

Amenorrhea 33

Amnesia 33

Amputation 33

Amyotrophic Lateral Sclerosis (ALS) ...34

Anaemia 35

Anal fistula 35

Aneurysm 35

Anger 36

Animal bites 37

Ankles 37

Ankylosing spondylitis 38

Anorexia 39

Anorgasmia 39

Anus 39

Anxiety 40

Apathy 40

Aphasia 40

Aphonia 40

Aphtas 40

Apnea 40

Aponeuroses 41

Appendix 41

Appetite 41

Arm (shoulder to elbow) 41

Arms (as upper limbs) 42

Arrhythmias 43

Arterial tension 43

Arteries 43

Arteriosclerosis 43

Arthritis 45

Arthrosis 45

Asphyxiation 46

Asthenia 46

Asthma – bronchial asthma 48

Astigmatism 49

Auricles 49

Authority 49

Autoimmune diseases 50

Autonomic nervous system 50

Babies 50

Bacillary dysentery 51

Back 51

Back pain 51

Bad breath 51

Balance – lack of balance 52

Baldness 52

Bechterew's disease 52

Bells's paralysis 52

Berger's disease 53

Bile 53

Bilirubin 53

Bipolarity 53

Birth 53

Bladder 53

Blepharitis 55

Blindness 55

Blood 55
Blood pressure...55
Blood pressure – high 55
Blood pressure – low 56
Body hair 56
Body lateralization..57
Boils 57
Bone 57
Bone fracture..58
Bone marrow...58
Bone structure 59
Bowel – large bowel......................................59
Bowel – large bowel – amoebic dysentery 59
Bowel – large bowel – anus...........................59
Bowel – large bowel – ascending colon 60
Bowel – large bowel – bacillary dysentery........61
Bowel – large bowel – colic 61
Bowel – large bowel – colon 61
Bowel – large bowel – Crohn's disease 62
Bowel – large bowel – descending colon 63
Bowel – large bowel – descending colon –
    sigmoid 63
Bowel – large bowel – lower rectum
    (incontinence)...64
Bowel – large bowel – transverse colon 65
Bowel – large bowel – ulcerative colitis............65
Bowel – large bowel – upper rectum...............65
Bowel – small bowel – Crohn's disease............66
Bowel – small bowel – duodenum 67
Bowel – small bowel (diarrhoea and cancer) 67
Brain 69
Brain – blocked brain 71
Brain – brain disorders 71
Brain – double brain 71
Brain – left-handed men 72
Brain – left-handed women 73
Brain – right-handed men 74
Brain – right-handed women.........................75
Brain – tumour 75
Brain embolism 76
Brain paralysis...77
Brain stroke...77
Brain tumour 78
Breastfeeding...78
Breasts...79

Breasts – cancer in the milk ducts....................79
Breasts – carcinoma (nipple cancer)................80
Breasts – mastitis 82
Breasts – melanoma (skin cancer) 82
Breasts – neurofibromatosis 82
Breathing system 83
Bright's disease 84
Bronchi 84
Bronchopneumonia.......................................85
Bruises (ecchymoses) 85
Bulimia 85
Bunions...86
Burns 86
Burping 87
Bursitis 87
Buttocks 87
Buzzing noise 87

Cancer 87
Candidiasis (thrush) 90
Caries 90
Cataracts 90
Cellulite 90
Central nervous system.................................90
Cephaleas 91
Cerebral aneurysm 91
Cerebral haemorrhage 91
Cervical..91
Cervical canal of the uterus 91
Cervix (neck of the womb – cervical canal
    of the uterus) 91
Charcot's disease..92
Chest angina 93
Chickenpox..93
Chilblains...93
Child delivery...93
Child paralysis..96
Chin..96
Cholera 96
Cholesterol – high cholesterol levels 96
Cholesterol – low cholesterol levels..................97
Chronic epicondylitis 97
Chronic evolving polyarthritis 98
Chronic polyarticular rheumatism..................98
Circulatory system...98

Circulatory system – arterial system.................98
Circulatory system – venal system 99
Clavicle (collar bone)......................................99
Claw feet 100
Cleanliness – cleanliness freaks 100
Coccyx 100
Colds..100
Coli bacillus 101
Colic 101
Collar bone 101
Colon 101
Colour blindness (Daltonism) 101
Coma 101
Conjunctivitis 102
Conn's disease..102
Constipation 102
Convergent strabismus 102
Convulsions 102
Coronaries..102
Coronary thrombosis 103
Cough 103
Coxarthrosis 103
Cramps 103
Cranial trauma 104
Cranium...104
Crohn's disease 104
Cubit bone 105
Cushing's disease 105
Cystitis...105
Cysts 105

Daltonism (colour blindness) 105
Dandruff..105
Dark rings under the eyes 105
Deafness...106
Dementia 106
Dependence 106
Depression 106
Dermis 107
Diabetes 107
Diarrhoea...107
Difficult digestions 107
Digestive system...107
Discal hernia 109
Disease 109

Divergent strabismus.....................................109
Diverticulosis 109
Dizziness 110
Dorsal 110
Dreams...110
Drugs 110
Dry skin in the face 112
Duchenne's disease.......................................112
Duodenum..112
Dyslexia 112
Dysmenorrhoea..112
Dyspepsia...112

Ears 112
Eczema...114
Elbow...115
Elderly people 116
Emotional shock 116
Emphysema...116
Enamel 117
Encephalitis..117
Encephalomyelitis 117
Endocrine system 117
Enuresis..119
Epidemics...120
Epidermis...120
Epidural 120
Epilepsy..120
Epiphysis..121
Erection – erectile dysfunction 121
Eustachian Tube 121
Eye infection 121
Eye spots 121
Eyes..121
Eyes – astigmatism 121
Eyes - blepharitis 122
Eyes – blindness 122
Eyes – cataracts...122
Eyes – conjunctivitis.....................................123
Eyes – convergent strabismus........................123
Eyes – Daltonism – colour-blindness.............123
Eyes – divergent strabismus 124
Eyes – dry eye...124
Eyes – dyslexia..124
Eyes – eye spots 124

Eyes – farsightedness 124
Eyes – glaucoma 125
Eyes – nearsightedness 126
Eyes – nystagmus...128
Eyes – opacity in the middle of the eye.........128
Eyes – presbyopia 128
Eyes – retinal detachment..............................129
Eyes – retinitis pigmentosa 129
Eyes – stains in the eyes..................................130
Eyes – strabismus...130
Eyes – sty...130

Face 130
Fainting...130
Fallopian Tube...131
Family...131
Fat...134
Fatigue..134
Fear...134
Feet...135
Feet – athlete's foot...135
Feet – flatfeet...136
Feet – pes cavus (hollow claw foot)...............136
Femoral head..136
Femur 137
Fever...138
Fibromyalgia (chronic fatigue syndrome).......138
Fibula...140
Finger and toe calluses....................................140
Fingers 141
Fingers – bones and muscles...........................141
Fingers – joints (arthrosis) 142
Fingers – warts 143
Flatulence...143
Flu 144
Food poisoning 144
Forearm..145
Friedreich's disease 146
Frigidity 146
Fungal infections..146
Fungi...146

Gallbladder 147
Gallbladder – gallbladder stones 148
Gallbladder – hepatitis 148

Gallstones...149
Gangrene...149
Gas...150
Gastroduodenal ulcer 150
Gastroenteritis..150
General paralysis 151
Glands...151
Glandular fever...152
Glans (head of the penis).................................152
Glaucoma..152
Glomerulus – glomerulonephritis...................152
Goitre..152
Gonads..152
Gonorrhoea...152
Gout 153
Growth (growth disorders) 153
Guilt 154
Gums 154

Haematomas 154
Haemophilia 154
Haemorrhages – capillary or vascular.............155
Haemorrhoids...155
Hair 155
Hand...156
Hard scar..158
Hay Fever..158
Headache 158
Hearing...159
Heart...159
Heart – angina 161
Heart – arrhythmias 162
Heart – communication between auriculae....165
Heart – heart attack...165
Heart attack 167
Heartburn 167
Heels 168
Hematuria...168
Henoch-Schonlein Purpura disease................168
Hepatitis 169
Hernia...169
Herpes...169
Hips 170
Hives...172
Hoarseness 172

Hodgkin's disease..172
Humerus...172
Hump..172
Hydrocephaly...172
Hyperactivity..173
Hyperglycaemia...174
Hyperopia (far-sightedness)...........................174
Hypertension...174
Hyperthyroidism...174
Hyperventilation...175
Hypoglycaemia..175
Hypophysis..175
Hypotension..175
Hypothyroidism..175

Iliac bone...175
Immune system...175
Immunity...177
Impotence..177
Incontinence...177
Indigestion..179
Infections..179
Infertility...179
Inflammation..180
Influenza (flu)...180
Inner bites...180
Insanity...180
Insect bites..180
Insomnia...180
Intervertebral discs...181
Intestines...181
Ischaemia..181
Ischæmia...181
Ischemia..181
Isolation..181
Itchiness..183
Itching rash...183

Jaundice..183
Jaws...183
Joints...183

Kahler's disease...184
Kidney stones..184

Kidneys..185
Kidneys – cancer and cysts.............................186
Kidneys – renal insufficiency.........................187
Kink...192
Kissing disease..193
Knee...193
Kyphosis..194

Larynx (larynx, aphonia, hoarseness)...........194
Lazy bowels...195
Left-handed and right-handed people............195
Legs (knee to foot)..195
Legs as lower limbs...196
Leprosy..197
Leucopoenia..197
Leucorrhoea..197
Leukaemia...197
Lice..199
Ligaments..199
Lipoma..200
Lips..200
Liquid retention..200
Liver..200
Liver – cancer and liver disease......................202
Liver – cirrhosis..202
Liver – hepatitis..202
Liver – jaundice...204
Locomotor system..204
Lordosis...205
Lou Gehrig's disease.......................................205
Lower rectum..205
Lumbago...205
Lumbar..206
Lung plague...206
Lungs...206
Lupus – discoid lupus erythematosus............208
Lupus – systemic lupus erythematosus..........208
Lymph..209
Lymphatic system...209
Lymphoma..210

Madness...210
Malaria..210
Mastoiditis..211
Measles..211

Meninges..211
Meningioma...211
Meningitis...211
Meniscus 212
Menopause..212
Menstruation 213
Migraine 214
Milk intolerance..215
Miscarriage...216
Mononucleosis 216
Mouth...216
Mouth sores (thrush).....................................217
Multiple myeloma 217
Multiple sclerosis 217
Mumps..218
Muscle contraction 218
Muscles 218
Muscular distension 221
Muscular dystrophy......................................222
Myalgic encephalomyelitis (chronic fatigue
   syndrome)..222
Mycosis...222
Mycosis fungoides 222
Myelitis...222
Myeloma 223
Myopathy..223
Myopia..224

Nail biting...225
Nails..225
Nanism 225
Nape 226
Narcolepsy 226
Nausea and vomiting....................................226
Neck 226
Nephritis...227
Nerves 227
Nervous breakdown 227
Nervous system 227
Nervous tics 228
Neuralgia...229
Neurofibromatosis 229
Newly-born 229
Nightmare...229
Nose..229

Nystagmus 230

Obesity..230
Oedemas 232
Oesophagus...232
Old people 232
Osteomyelitis 232
Osteoporosis..233
Otitis...233
Outbreaks 233
Ovaries..233

Palate..234
Palpitations 234
Paludism 235
Pancarditis..235
Pancreas 235
Pancreas – endocrine gland (diabetes)............236
Pancreas – endocrine gland (hyperglycaemia) 238
Pancreas – endocrine gland (hypoglycaemia) .238
Pancreas – exocrine gland (cancer of the
   pancreas and pancreatitis) 238
Pancreatitis..239
Panic...239
Paralysing diseases 240
Paralysis...240
Parasites...241
Parasympathetic nervous system 241
Parathyroid glands..241
Parkinson's disease 241
Partial paralysis..242
Patchy hair loss..243
Pelvis...243
Penis..243
Pericarditis..244
Periodontitis..245
Periosteum...245
Peritonitis..245
Peroneum...246
Perspiration 246
Pharynx...246
Phlebitis..247
Pimples 247
Pineal body 248
Pineal gland...248

Pinealoma 248
Pituitary gland..249
Plague 250
Pleura...250
Pleurisy 250
Pneumonia..251
Pneumothorax...251
Poisoning 251
Polarity of the body 251
Poliomyelitis...251
Polyarthritis..252
Posture 253
Precocious ejaculation 253
Pregnancy – ectopic pregnancy.................253
Pregnancy – imaginary pregnancy 253
Pregnancy – problems 254
Premature ejaculation...............................254
Preoccupation 255
Presbytis 255
Presbytism..255
Priapism 255
Prostate 255
Psoriasis..256
Pubic bone 257
Pulmonary embolism 257
Punctuality..257
Pyorrhea (periodontitis) 258

Radius...258
Rash..258
Red spots...259
Renal insufficiency 259
Reproductive system..................................259
Retinal detachment 260
Retinitis pigmentosa..................................260
Rheumatism..260
Rheumatoid polyarthritis 260
Rhinitis 260
Ribs...261
Rickets 262
Right-handed and left-handed people...........263
Ringing noise 263
Roof of the mouth......................................263
Rubella..263

Sacrum..263
Sacrum-iliac 263
Salivary glands...263
Scabies 264
Scarlet Fever 264
Schüller's disease..264
Sciatic nerve pain 264
Scleroderma (systemic sclerosis).....................265
Scoliosis 265
Seborrhoea 265
Self-immunity 266
Senility..266
Septicaemia 266
Sex – addiction..266
Shin bone 267
Shingles...267
Shoulder..268
Shoulder blade 270
Sickness...270
Sigmoid...270
Silhouette – image conflicts.......................270
Sinusitis...270
Skeletal system 271
Skin...271
Skin – dermis 271
Skin – epidermis..272
Skin infections...273
Skin tuberculosis 273
Skull..274
Slackness 274
Slimness 274
Small stature syndrome...............................274
Smallpox (variola) 275
Smell 275
Smelly feet...275
Smoking...275
Snoring 275
Sore throat 276
Spasms...276
Spina bifida 276
Spinal chord (spinal medulla) 276
Spinal marrow 277
Spinal medulla...277
Spine...277
Spleen 278

Spots in the eyes 279
Sprains 279
Stammering...279
Sterility...280
Sternum 280
Stiff neck 281
Stomach 281
Strabismus..282
Stretch marks 282
Sty...283
Sudden death 283
Suicide 283
Suprarenal glands 283
Sweat..284
Swelling..284
Swollen glands..285
Sympathetic nervous system 285
Synovial fluid 285
Syphilis 285

Tabagism 285
Taenia 286
Tapeworm 286
Taste..286
Teeth 286
Teeth – buck teeth (rodent) 287
Teeth – canine (the 4) 287
Teeth – caries 287
Teeth – front teeth pushed back (carnivore)...288
Teeth – last left upper and lower molar..........288
Teeth – last right upper and lower molar 288
Teeth – left lower molar teeth 289
Teeth – left lower premolar teeth 289
Teeth – left side incisive teeth (2 up and
  2 down) 289
Teeth – left upper molar teeth 289
Teeth – left upper premolar teeth 289
Teeth – right lower molar teeth 290
Teeth – right lower premolar teeth 290
Teeth – right side incisive teeth (2 up and
  2 down) 290
Teeth – right upper molar teeth....................290
Teeth – right upper premolar teeth...............290
Teeth – space between molars......................290
Teeth – straight and aligned front teeth 290

Tendon..290
Testicles..291
Thigh 291
Threadworms 292
Throat 292
Throat angina 292
Thrombophlebitis....................................292
Thrombosis 292
Thrush...293
Thymus 293
Thyroid 294
Tibia 295
Tinea 295
Tinnitus 296
Tiredness 296
Toes...296
Toes – bones and muscles 296
Toes – joints 297
Tongue 299
Tonsils 299
Torticollis 300
Touch..300
Trachea 300
Tremors 300
Tuberculosis 301
Tumours..301

Ulcerative colitis.....................................301
Upper rectum..301
Uraemia 301
Uretheritis 301
Urethritis...301
Urinary system 301
Urinary tract infections 302
Urticaria..302
Uterus 302

Vagina...302
Varicose veins 303
Variola..303
Vegetations...303
Veins 304
Venereal diseases....................................304
Venous system 304
Verruca..304

Vertebrae 304
Vertebrae – cervical vertebrae 304
Vertebrae – discs..305
Vertebrae – dorsal vertebrae...........................305
Vertebrae – lumbar vertebrae..........................307
Vertebrae – sacral vertebrae............................307
Vertebrae – terminal vertebrae – coccyx.........308
Vertigo 308
Vice..309
Vision 309
Vitiligo...309
Vocal cords 310
Vomit and nausea 310

Wart 310
Weight 311
Windpipe..311
Womb...311
Worms 313
Wounds...313
Wrist 313

About the author

Luís Martins Simões often says that everything you do must be done with a soft will, little effort, work and a lot of fun, but most of all with the fantastic feeling of being driven by one's own intuition.

He believes that we cannot experience long lasting happiness without being connected to our intuition.

Luís is a dynamic and enthusiastic person who sees the world through eyes that are not restricted by any conformity, rule or regulation.

He believes that the evolution of mankind depends on the ability of people to be creators and not repeaters.

Many things on our planet work well, but many others simply do not work at all.

Those that work well are invariably the result of a new and creative paradigm, because when we feed our human mind with repetition problems occur.

Since 1987, he has been travelling the world teaching and coaching in leadership, communication, motivation and emotional intelligence in multinational corporations and local companies. He is widely recognized as a specialist in intrapersonal and interpersonal intelligence.

In 1994, life-changing events prompted him to focus on his own personal development. He started working with the intangible and the non-concrete. He explored the subtle energy in spirituality and the close relationship between the human conscience and the human body. Very quickly, he started to help people who came to him in search of some guidance for their lives and took them on a journey to the centre of their inner conscience.

So, since 1996, he has helped many people to develop their spiritual being and create a new life where repetition ceases to exist and where a love for oneself becomes the keyword.

As well as teaching classes, he speaks at conferences, in schools, universities and corporations around the world in English, Spanish, French and Portuguese.

Luís currently lives in Lisbon - Portugal, city where he was born.